Managing European Union Enlargement

CESifo Seminar Series
Edited by Hans-Werner Sinn

Inequality and Growth: Theory and Policy Implications
Theo S. Eicher and Stephen J. Turnovsky, editors

Public Finance and Public Policy in the New Century
Sijbren Cnossen and Hans-Werner Sinn, editors

Spectrum Auctions and Competition in Telecommunications
Gerhard Illing and Ulrich Kluh, editors

Managing European Union Enlargement
Helge Berger and Thomas Moutos, editors

Issues of Monetary Integration in Europe
Hans-Werner Sinn, Mika Widgrén, and Marko Köthenbürger, editors

Managing European Union Enlargement

Helge Berger and Thomas
Moutos, editors

CES

The MIT Press
Cambridge, Massachusetts
London, England

This book was set in Palatino on 3B2 by Asco Typesetters, Hong Kong and was printed and bound in the United States of America.

Library of Congress Cataloging-in-Publication Data

Managing European Union enlargement / Helge Berger and Thomas Moutos, editors.
    p.   cm. — (CESifo seminar series)
  Includes bibliographical references and index.
  ISBN 0-262-02561-2 (alk. paper)
  1. European Union countries—Economic policy. 2. European Union. I. Berger, Helge.
II. Moutos, Thomas. III. Series.
HC240.M226   2004
337.1′42—dc22   2003066514

10 9 8 7 6 5 4 3 2 1

Contents

Series Foreword   vii

1 **Introduction**   1
Helge Berger and Thomas Moutos

2 **Managing EU Enlargement**   11
Richard E. Baldwin

3 **Restructuring the ECB**   29
Helge Berger, Jakob de Haan, and Robert Inklaar

Comments   67
Alex Cukierman

4 **Who Needs an External Anchor?**   73
Daniel Gros

Comments   95
Margarita Katsimi

5 **Factor Mobility, Income Differentials, and Regional Economic Integration**   99
Michael C. Burda

Comments   125
Carlo Perroni

6 The Political Economy of Migration and EU Enlargement: Lessons
  from Switzerland   129
  Jaime de Melo, Florence Miguet, and Tobias Müller

  Comments   169
  Riccardo Faini

7 Eastern Enlargement of the EU: Jobs, Investment, and Welfare in
  Present Member Countries   173
  Ben J. Heijdra, Christian Keuschnigg, and Wilhelm Kohler

  Comments   211
  Sascha O. Becker

8 EU Enlargement: Economic Implications for Countries and
  Industries   217
  Arjan M. Lejour, Ruud A. de Mooij, and Richard Nahuis

  Comments   257
  Rajshri Jayaraman

9 The Political Economy of EU Enlargement: Or, Why Japan Is Not
  a Candidate Country   261
  Antonis Adam and Thomas Moutos

  Comments   297
  Ronald W. Jones

  Authors and Commentators   301
  Index   303

Series Foreword

This book is part of the CESifo Seminar Series in Economic Policy, which aims to cover topical policy issues in economics from a largely European perspective. The books in this series are the products of the papers presented and discussed at seminars hosted by CESifo, an international research network of renowned economists supported jointly by the Center for Economic Studies at Ludwig-Maximilians-Universität, Munich, and the Ifo Institute for Economic Research. All publications in this series have been carefully selected and refereed by members of the CESifo research network.

Hans-Werner Sinn

This volume is based on papers delivered at the first CESifo-Delphi Conferences (Munich, December 2001, and Delphi, September 2002), which are jointly organized by CESifo and the Department of International and European Economic Studies (DIEES), Athens University of Economics and Business (AUEB). The CESifo-Delphi Conferences are organized every two years and involve a two-stage process. Following an initial call for abstracts, a number of authors are selected and invited to present their papers at a workshop meeting in Munich. After further refereeing, some of the authors are invited to present (possibly revised) versions of their papers at the final conference meeting in Delphi. For more information regarding the CESifo-Delphi Conferences and the current call for abstracts, see ⟨www.cesifo.de⟩.

1 Introduction

Helge Berger and Thomas
Moutos

On 12–13 December 2002, at the European Council in Copenhagen, the
accession negotiations between the European Union (EU) and ten candidate countries (Cyprus, the Czech Republic, Estonia, Hungary, Latvia, Lithuania, Malta, Poland, Slovakia, and Slovenia) were officially
concluded. Subject to ratification of the accession treaty by member
states and the acceding countries, these ten countries will become
members of the EU on 1 May 2004. This is by far the largest expansion
the EU has witnessed in its almost fifty years of existence, both in
terms of the number of countries and languages involved and in terms
of their area and population as well.[1] Moreover the accession countries
are very diverse themselves, ranging from the small, services-oriented
Mediterranean islands of Cyprus and Malta to the much larger, but
still more agricultural, Poland. Last, but not least, the 2004 enlargement
will make the EU more diverse in another very important category: per
capita income. On average, the future members' GDP per capita is less
than half the GDP per capita of the existing members (in purchasing-
power terms). For comparison, when Spain and Portugal joined the EU
in 1986, their average GDP per capita was about 70 percent of that of
the existing EU countries (in purchasing-power terms).

For many observers (and, obviously, EU officials) the present enlargement is a reaffirmation of the underlying ideals, values, and objectives of the EU. Among the EU's stated objectives is the encouragement
of peace, stability, democracy, and prosperity throughout Europe. It
has been argued that enlargement will prove to be instrumental in the
achievement of these objectives by ending the artificial divide between
Western and Central and Eastern Europe through the promotion of
economic and political integration. Yet despite the many years of prep-
aration, and the considerable efforts made by officials of the EU and
member states in advertising the benefits of enlargement, the public's

uncertainty or even hostility, in both member and acceding countries, in regard to this European project remains strong.[2] It thus came as no surprise that the enlargement-related financing package remained a bone of contention between the candidates and the EU until the very end of the negotiations. Member and candidate country governments were worried that their parliaments and electorates could either delay or derail the enlargement process if they deemed the "costs" of enlargement to be excessive. The compromise reached in Copenhagen provides for financial aid to the accession countries under the current budget (which runs until the end of 2006) of a maximum of $40.85 billion for 2004–2006. This includes money for agricultural subsidies, infrastructure spending, regional aid, and funds to help improve nuclear safety, public administration, and border protection. The new members will also have to make contributions to the EU budget, however, amounting to about $15 billion for 2004–2006. Moreover, they may not be able to appropriate all the money that has been allocated to them in the budget by 2006. As a result, the commission estimates that the net budget-related cost of enlargement will amount to less than one-thousandth of EU GDP. This appears to be a small price to pay for European unity.

Nevertheless, enlargement may entail costs beyond its immediate budgetary implications by blocking reforms that are long overdue. An illustrative example of this is the so-called Franco-German compromise on the basis of which the Council in Brussels in October 2002 set the level of resources for the Common Agricultural Policy (CAP) up to 2013. The compromise shied away from expenditure cuts, all but ensured that the present beneficiaries of the CAP will continue to receive transfers at current levels, and made sure that CAP principles (including the controversial issue of direct payments) are fully extended to the new members. This decision paved the way for the acceptance of the overall financing package for enlargement within the EU. But it also implies that future reforms of the CAP will reflect the interests of both present and new members, with uncertain consequences for the likelihood of a fundamental overhaul of the EU's agricultural policies.

The example of the CAP invites the question of just how well the EU is prepared to manage enlargement—the question at the core of the chapters in this book. Richard E. Baldwin (chapter 2), in a thought-provoking overview surveying some of the most pressing issues of EU enlargement, discusses the CAP and a number of other key challenges brought about by the "big-bang" expansion of 2004. An important part of his analysis focuses on the reform of the policymaking mechanisms of the EU in the Treaty of Nice. Without much doubt, the EU's traditional, consensus-based approach needed streamlining, even before the dramatic increase in membership that enlargement will bring about. But Baldwin argues that the new procedures put in place by the Nice Treaty might be too complicated to deliver the decision-making efficiency needed to ensure that the EU can handle the vast task of managing enlargement.

1.1 Monetary Policy

Efficiency of decision-making is also a focal point in chapter 3 by Helge Berger, Jakob de Haan, and Robert Inklaar, who set their sights on the implications enlargement has for the European Central Bank (ECB). Within less than a decade, the number of member countries in the euro area could more than double, with the vast majority of accession countries being relatively small in economic terms, compared with current members. Absent reforms, such a significant but asymmetric expansion could impede the effectiveness of monetary policymaking. Moreover, the possible over-representation of small member countries on the ECB Council poses a risk that monetary policy could deviate from the targets specified in the Maastricht Treaty. The chapter illustrates these issues, describes the principles on which reforms of the ECB statute could build, and discusses specific institutional reform scenarios, including the recent ECB proposal. A key result is that, although centralization might be a "first-best" solution in many ways, it has possible disadvantages from a political-economy perspective, including a potential conflict with the established voting rights of current euro area member countries.

Alex Cukierman, in his comments on chapter 3, also sides with the idea put forward by Berger, de Haan, and Inklaar to aim at an overall Council size of about fifteen members (the ECB proposal suggests a Council of twenty) and to introduce an asymmetric rotation scheme to better reflect member countries' size and other economic characteristics. He cautions, however, that any such scheme must be flexible enough to accommodate changes, as enlargement itself would likely alter the fundamental behavior of many of the acceding economies. Cukierman concludes his discussion with a warning. As his research suggests that the link between central bank independence and disinflation in transition economies could be weak, too much emphasis on output stabilization after enlargement may raise the inflation bias in the euro area. He suggests that, rather than overburdening the ECB, other policy instruments should be charged with stabilizing real activity.

Continuing to focus on monetary policy, Daniel Gros (chapter 4) asks whether the accession countries would be well advised to fix their national currency to the euro prior to joining the currency union. It is well known that countries with high public debt—taken, in Gros's approach, to be synonymous with weak fiscal institutions—might benefit from such an external anchor. Chapter 4 argues, however, that the relationship between the strength of a country's domestic fiscal framework and its incentive to peg to the euro might be non-monotonic: Whereas countries with very high and very low debt levels will clearly profit from an external anchor, countries with moderate levels of public debt will generally have a stronger incentive to keep an independent national monetary policy, because countries with moderate debt levels require only some seigniorage revenue to supplement the government budget and might find the resulting equilibrium inflation still tolerable. In contrast, inflation would be too high in high-debt countries in the absence of a peg, and low-debt countries lack the incentive for raising seigniorage in the first place. Applied to the enlargement process, this implies that both countries with very strong and those with very weak fiscal institutions or debt levels might have an interest in joining the euro area quickly. For instance, the choices of Estonia (very strong) and Bulgaria (very weak) to adopt the euro/deutsche mark via currency boards could be interpreted as reflecting these considerations.

Margarita Katsimi's comments on chapter 4 take issue with two critical features of the Gros approach. On an institutional level, Katsimi argues that the setup of Gros's model neglects the time inconsistency problem related to seigniorage creation: Were money demand to depend negatively on inflation, the inability of the government to commit to not raising seigniorage would lead to a second inflationary bias. A second issue highlighted in Katsimi's comments is Gros's assumption in the chapter that weak fiscal institutions are not reflected in a country's budget constraint. Changing this assumption could leave countries with higher debt levels and weak fiscal institutions worse off after delegating monetary policy to the ECB because, although the fiscal inefficiency would continue to create a need for higher fiscal revenue, no more seigniorage income would be forthcoming.

1.2 Factor Mobility

The issue of the free movement of persons occupies center stage in the negotiations on EU enlargement—not least because of widespread public fear of a massive influx of Central and Eastern European labor into current member countries. The EU Commission and several studies have reviewed the pros and cons of alternative flexible transitional-arrangement proposals, ranging from the current bilateral guest worker arrangements used by some EU members to the establishment of fixed quotas during a limited period of time. But just how large is the potential for migration really? Chapter 5 by Michael C. Burda takes a fresh look at this issue, by adopting an efficiency perspective in the study of economic integration—that is, how would a social planner allocate capital and labor in two regions to maximize national output net of migration and investment costs? Burda stresses the importance of adjustment costs in determining the speed of efficient economic integration, as well as the interpretation of differences in factor returns across regions during the adjustment to the steady state. A significant implication of Burda's analysis is that if costs of adjustment are important, the fact that wages in some of the future members are far lower than in the EU provides no information about the extent of (efficient) economic integration. A corollary of this is that the currently observed large differences in factor rewards between the EU and the future members do not necessarily imply massive migration flows if the forthcoming changes in the institutional framework (e.g., adoption of the EU legal framework for capital ownership, elimination of capital controls, and the likely introduction of the euro in the acceding countries) make capital more mobile than labor.

Carlo Perroni, in his comments on chapter 5, initially draws attention to two issues that Burda's analysis abstracts from, namely, the importance of fixed factors of production and of agglomeration effects. Neither of these issues, however, would be expected to alter the chapter's conclusions with respect to long-run outcomes—they could even strengthen the model's main results. For example, Perroni notes that agglomeration effects might make long-run allocations more sensitive in the sense that very small changes in adjustment costs could lead to drastically different outcomes. All in all, Perroni concludes that economic policymakers may have every reason to take a close look at adjustment costs as one of the more important forces shaping factor migration in an enlarged EU. He also argues that, if the model were based on a set of somewhat more realistic assumptions, there might be more scope for policy intervention after enlargement than Burda seems to suggest.

Turning from emigration potential to immigration policy, chapter 6, by Jaime de Melo, Florence Miguet, and Tobias Müller, recounts the Swiss experience with immigration and draws on the unique direct-democracy setting Switzerland presents to bypass the problem of "hypothetical bias" plaguing the analysis of conventional survey data. The authors first draw out the political-economy implications of immigration policy within the context of the median-voter model. Under various assumptions about economic structure, they show that the evolution of immigration policy in the Swiss case can be explained as the outcome of majority voting by self-interested individuals who face different voting costs. In the empirical part of the chapter, the authors present an ingenious approach to analyzing the determinants of voters' attitudes toward immigration. To this purpose they use data drawn from an individual-level survey carried out two weeks after the Swiss referendum in September 2000 on a popular initiative asking for a limitation on the number of foreigners at less than their existing share of the Swiss population. The popular initiative was rejected by almost two-thirds of all voters even though survey data suggested that only a slim majority opposed it. The authors explain this startling result by appealing to differences in observed and unobserved characteristics between those who voted and those who did not. They conclude that opinion polls are likely to suffer from hypothetical bias and thus may be an unwise guide to policy regarding immigration.

In his comments on chapter 6, Riccardo Faini initially notes that the gap found by de Melo, Miguet, and Müller between Swiss voters' attitudes toward migration and the stance of Switzerland's migration policies has been a feature of migration policies since at least 1880: Migration policies have by and large been more liberal than warranted by voters' attitudes and interests. Faini also draws attention to what he considers to be a shortcoming shared by the chapter and the political-economy literature on migration policy, namely, the lack of a joint analysis of trade and migration policies. He argues that the fact that the Swiss data used by the authors refer only to migration and do not capture the effects of time-varying factors such as the evolution of the real exchange rate and trade policies may be responsible for the chapter's finding that observed characteristics, such as income and education, play only a minor role in determining voter attitudes.

1.3 The Motives (and Consequences) of Enlargement

Chapter 7 by Ben J. Heijdra, Christian Keuschnigg, and Wilhelm Kohler presents a thorough attempt at establishing the importance of different channels through which enlargement can affect the incumbent EU member countries. The main innovation of the chapter is that the authors combine a search-theoretic framework of job creation and destruction with an overlapping-generations model of household behavior and capital accumulation to address how commodity market integration, budgetary effects, and, notably, immigration can affect investment, unemployment, and welfare in the member states. The quantitative importance of their main theoretical results is then examined via a multisector dynamic applied general equilibrium model for the German economy, which they take as an example. An important finding is that if the economy faces some degree of wage rigidity, goods market integration yields further welfare gains beyond those traditionally assumed, because integration leads to lower capital and intermediate-goods prices, thus increasing the capital intensity of production and inducing firms to post more vacancies. The resulting decrease in unemployment yields a "fiscal dividend" that is larger than the increase in the net contributions to the EU budget that Germany has to face.

In his comments on chapter 7, Sascha O. Becker commends Heijdra, Keuschnigg, and Kohler for explicitly introducing unemployment into their model but questions whether the search model they employ explains a significant part of German unemployment. He notes that the institutional framework of powerful unions in Germany creates a situation of quasi–minimum wages, thereby making it less likely that unskilled workers in Germany will face a significant drop in their real wages as a result of migration induced by enlargement. Becker also points out that the authors assume that the budgetary costs of enlargement will be exclusively financed by a cut in the Regional and Structural Funds given to incumbent countries. Alternatively, one could assume increased contributions to the EU budget or cuts in the common agricultural policy funds, either of which might lead to smaller net benefits of enlargement for Germany.

Chapter 8 by Arjan M. Lejour, Ruud A. de Mooij, and Richard Nahuis provides an assessment of the economic costs and benefits of enlargement using WorldScan, a computable general equilibrium (CGE) model of the world economy. Unlike many previous studies that model accession to the internal market as a simple across-the-board reduction in trade costs, chapter 8 estimates gravity equations to derive more-precise estimates of the reduction in the barriers to trade for sixteen different industries. To calibrate the aggregate impact of enlargement, the chapter looks at three dimensions of enlargement: the move toward a customs union, the enlargement of the internal market, and the free movement of labor. The CGE simulations suggest that the aggregate impact of enlargement will involve large gains for the Central and Eastern European Countries (CEECs) and a modest welfare improvement for the EU. Their study also suggests that among the three dimensions of enlargement they examine, it is the accession to the internal market that yields the largest economic effects. Moreover, accession to the internal market has a positive impact for both the EU and the CEECs, although both the benefits and the changes in the allocation of production across sectors are much higher for the acceding countries than for the current members. In contrast, migration is found to produce adverse distributional effects for low-skilled workers in the EU; these effects tend to be more pronounced in the northern than in the southern EU countries.

In her comments on chapter 8, Rajshri Jayaraman commends Lejour, de Mooij, and Nahuis for providing a detailed sectoral analysis of the effects of EU enlargement, facilitated mainly by their attempt to estimate sectoral variations in the expected reduction of trade costs. She notes, however, that the chapter could have profited from additional sensitivity testing, even though such testing might have been difficult to square with the very detailed analysis undertaken by the chapter's authors. Concluding, Jayaraman points out that the finding that the CEECs will face small losses from labor migration may be due to the fact that the chapter does not capture the effects of remittances that the immigrants might be sending back to their country of origin.

In chapter 9, Antonis Adam and Thomas Moutos argue that strong political-economy forces could have been behind the big-bang approach to EU enlargement. They construct a simple model to show that, if trade involves the exchange of vertically differentiated products, the effects of enlargement on the EU's incumbent members can be asymmetric. One country may enjoy increased access to the joining country's market without having to face a displacement of domestic production by imports, whereas another may have to face increased import penetration. They demonstrate that producers in low-income (and technologically lagging) incumbent countries such as Greece would prefer that enlargement be directed toward technologically advanced countries (e.g., Japan), which have comparative advantage in producing high-quality varieties of differentiated products. By the same token, the opposite is true for high-income incumbent countries such as Germany. The authors then proceed to present evidence—based on the analysis of unit value data for about 1,500 products—supporting their assumptions regarding the relative position of individual EU countries, the CEECs, and Japan on the quality ladder. They also present econometric evidence showing that previous EU enlargements had asymmetric effects on incumbent members, in accordance with the predictions of their theoretical framework.

In his comments on chapter 9, Ronald W. Jones notes that the asymmetry identified in chapter 9 is a quite general underlying question in the theory of international trade: Is (beneficial) international trade encouraged more in a group of countries that are dissimilar in their factor endowments and technology or in a group of countries that are fairly similar in these characteristics? Jones also draws attention to the fact that the widely observed fragmentation of vertically integrated production processes implies that firms can reap gains by locating, say, the more labor-intensive segments of a production process in the low-wage CEECs, even if the final emerging consumer good (which is the focus of the chapter) is of high quality and would, without such fragmentation, be produced entirely in the high-income country in the EU. The extent to which EU enlargement facilitates further fragmentation of production activities implies that the asymmetry of effects identified in the theoretical part of the chapter may not survive in more detailed settings.

What have we learned? Although the chapters and comments presented in this volume point to a variety of issues deserving the attention of practitioners, policymakers, and academics alike, perhaps the most important lesson is that, this time around, EU enlargement is not just incremental, but really a big bang. The sheer scale of the 2004 enlargement effort has a number of significant consequences along many dimensions, ranging from the intercountry and intracountry distribution of benefits and costs, to issues of monetary management and migration flows, to the fundamental subject of decision making in an enlarged EU and euro area. By describing the more important challenges involved and pinpointing some possible strategies for meeting them, the volume provides useful guidance in shaping policies that will provide a secure underpinning to Europe's future.

Notes

The views expressed in this introduction are those of the authors and should not be interpreted as those of the International Monetary Fund or of the Athens University of Economics and Business.

1. Strictly speaking, the adjective "largest" pertains to the *absolute* increase. In *relative* terms, the increase in population (20 percent) and area (23 percent) resulting from the 2004 enlargement is somewhat less outstanding. The enlargement in 1973 (Britain, Denmark, Ireland) was proportionally larger in terms of population, whereas the enlargement in 1995 (Austria, Finland, Sweden) was proportionally larger in terms of land area involved.

2. Within current EU countries, on average, 66 percent of the respondents to polls are in favor of the enlargement of the EU, whereas 21 percent oppose it (European Commission 2002). The highest approval rates are registered in Italy, Ireland, and Spain (82, 79, and 73 percent, respectively), whereas the largest opposition to enlargement is found in Austria, Sweden, and Finland (32, 28, and 27 percent approval, respectively). Among the future member states, survey results (European Commission 2002) indicate that on average 52 percent of the respondents regard EU membership as "a good thing," and that 61 percent would vote "yes" in a referendum on EU membership. Hungary and Slovakia register the highest support for EU membership (77 and 69 percent, respectively, would vote "yes" in a referendum), whereas those surveyed in Estonia and Latvia seem least supportive (with rates of 39 and 45 percent, respectively). At the time of writing, the first referendum on EU membership had already taken place in Malta, with a result in favor of EU membership.

Reference

European Commission. 2002. "Candidate Countries Eurobarometer." November. Brussels.

2

Managing EU Enlargement

Richard E. Baldwin

2.1 Introduction

The looming EU enlargement is unprecedented in two ways: in its size, and in the newcomers' diversity. The 106 million people in the twelve nations negotiating for membership will expand the EU's population by 28 percent. The newcomers, however, are relatively poor (on average less than one-third as rich as EU15 citizens in real terms). In fact, adding their economies to the EU15 will expand the union's *nominal* GDP by only 5 percent (Eurostat 2002). In addition to being poor, the newcomers are about three times as agrarian as the incumbents. The fact that entrants are populous yet relatively poor and agrarian implies that enlargement will be difficult. This point, which I demonstrated a decade ago (Baldwin, 1992, 1994) still holds true. And understanding this point is the key to realizing that the great difficulties just cannot be papered over or wished away. Enlargement confronts the EU with a sequence of tough challenges that will require tough measures to overcome.[1]

To structure my comments on these challenges, I divide them into those that have arisen or will arise before enlargement and those that will arise after enlargement.

2.2 Pre-enlargement Tasks/Difficulties

The main pre-enlargement challenges are to complete the accession negotiations and the necessary reforms in the applicant and incumbent nations. I turn to these in order.

2.2.1 Finishing the Accession Negotations

According to political declarations made by EU leaders, the new members should join the Union in time for the European parliamentary elections in 2004. Since enlargement must be ratified by each of the fifteen incumbent member states—a process that typically takes eighteen months to two years—accession negotiations are supposed to concluded by the end of 2002. Halfway into 2002, the most difficult issues—agriculture, regional policy, and financial and budgetary provisions—have still not been settled (European Commission 2002). In particular, the EU's current negotiating position on agriculture is to grant a substandard status to farmers located in the new member states. For instance, farmers in newcomer countries would receive a lower level of direct payments from Brussels than those in incumbent countries, creating a rather unusual situation in which poor Polish farmers, to take an example, would receive significantly lower levels of support than the Queen of England (as the owner of substantial tracts of agricultural land, the Queen is a major recipient of Common Agricultural Policy subsidies). Naturally, the applicants oppose this position. I will have more to say on the CAP in the latter part of my comments.

The resistance of the applicants to uneven treatment may well delay enlargement of the Union somewhat, but my guess is that the applicants will want to be in the Union not much later than 2004, quite simply because the newcomers will want to be voting members when the Union's next five-year budget plan is drawn up. Judging from past budget rounds, discussions on that budget (for 2007–2013) will take place in 2004–2006.[2] Indeed, since any EU member can veto the whole five-year plan, the newcomers might very well, assuming they join the Union in time to vote, use their newfound power to reverse any sort of inferior financial treatment they agree to during the accession negotiations. An extra incentive to joining prior to 2004 is to be able to participate in the next Intergovernmental Conference (IGC), which is currently slated for 2004. Again, each EU member has veto power at IGCs, so this will provide the newcomer countries with another opportunity to right any wrongs they have agreed to in the accession talks.

This join-and-renege strategy may sound Machiavellian, but it is worth pointing out that there is no such thing as ironclad commitments in a democratic club that makes up its own rules. After the accession of the enlargement countries, citizens in the east may elect new leaders, and these leaders may decide that their predecessors caved in too easily to the bullying of rich EU members. The combination of a righteous cause (redressing what could be easily be characterized in the public debate as second-class treatment of the poor by the rich) and a great deal of voting power in EU decision making (more on this in what follows) could prove irresistible—something the current EU leaders should keep firmly in mind.

This is an important point, so allow me to underscore it with a little story. Three Finns go for a week's ice fishing, each carrying a bottle of vodka. As they are cutting the hole in the ice, the issue of what to do with the vodka arises. Being social-democratic Nordics, they decide to settle the issue democratically. A vote is held, and the outcome is two votes against one to share the first fisherman's bottle. After they have finished consuming the first fisherman's bottle, the question again arises of how to allocate the remaining vodka, and again they decide to resolve the issue democratically. Once again the outcome is two votes against one, but this time the decision is that each should drink his own bottle. The point of this anecdote should be clear: It is impossible to know what will happen in the future, if the rules are subject to voting.

To sum up, I guess that although much difficult negotiating remains before accession of the enlargement countries, the applicants' desire to be in sooner rather than later will lead them to agree to most of the EU's demands, even on the most sensitive issues. This means negotiations are likely to be closed in 2002 or 2003.

2.2.2 Completing CEEC Reforms

The applicant nations, most of which are so-called transition economies, have plenty of reforming to do before their economies, governments, and legal systems are ready for EU membership. The reform process, however, is well underway in most of the applicants, and although it will not be completed before they sign their accession treaties, this challenge is being met effectively via a close cooperation between the EU (especially the European Commission) and Central and Eastern European Countries themselves.[3]

A much greater problem lies on the EU side. The EU needs a great deal of reform to prepare for enlargement. The process of accomplishing this reform is not going well.

2.2.3   Severe Challenges to EU Institutional Structure

It has long been evident that enlargement of the European Union
would require reform of EU institutions. Institutions that were designed for six member countries are struggling to function with fifteen.
They will simply fail to work with twenty-seven members. EU leaders
recognized this, and to meet the challenge, they initiated the IGC that
led to the Amsterdam Treaty. The necessary reforms proved too bitter
a pill to swallow, however, so the Amsterdam Treaty skipped the most
difficult issues, creating the so-called Amsterdam leftovers. EU leaders
convened another IGC to deal with these leftovers. As the June 2000
Presidency Report on the IGC stated: "Faced with the challenge of virtually doubling membership of the Union, it seems indispensable that
the Conference adopt at an early date reforms which will, in the future,
ensure the efficiency of the institutions of the Union while preserving
its legitimacy as a Union of States and peoples and the fundamental
balances and originality of an enterprise that has shown its worth over
fifty years (EU President 2000, 7)." Some of these reforms were agreed
upon at the end of 2000 with the Treaty of Nice, which I have critiqued
elsewhere in detail (Baldwin et al. 2001a). Here I discuss the major
challenges facing the EU that the fruits of the IGC2000, the Treaty of
Nice, will not address.

2.2.3.1   Efficiency in Decision Making: The Council of Ministers

The EU is not a static concept. To take one important example, the
integrity of the Union's internal market requires continual action on
the part of its main decision-making body, the Council of Ministers, to
keep up with technological changes and the erosion induced by the
continuous introduction of subtly protectionist policies in individual
member states. The EU therefore needs to maintain its ability to act if
it is to continue to prosper.

Ensuring this ability to act was one of the main goals of the December 2000 Nice summit. Unfortunately, the changes proposed in the
Treaty of Nice will not accomplish the goal. Ignoring the careful prep-
aration and study that was undertaken during the year-long IGC, EU
heads of state and government adopted at the summit a massively
complex system for Council of Ministers decision making. This system,
which the presiding French brought to the table, had never been mentioned during the run-up the Nice Summit, which was supposed to
hash out the final details of the Nice Treaty.

The reasons for this negotiating "ambush" are obscure, but its consequences are clear. EU leaders had only a few hours to think through the implications of the decision-making system proposed. As it turns out, they did not do their sums well. The system adopted at the summit fails to maintain the Union's ability to act in the face of enlargement. Indeed, the Nice reforms made matters worse; the EU's ability to act post-enlargement would have been greater with no reform at all. Formal analysis elsewhere (see Baldwin et al. 2001a or Felsenthal and Machover 2001) has backed up this assertion, but it is easy to illustrate why the new system will make decision making substantially more difficult in an enlarged EU.

2.2.3.1.1 *The EU's Decision-Making Reforms* Under current rules, most EU decisions require approval of the Council of Ministers. Decisions on some of the most important issues (budget, treaty changes, etc.) require unanimous approval in the Council, but adoption of the most common measures, including legislation concerning the Union's internal market, involve a lower majority threshold in the council, known as a "qualified majority." A qualified majority requires 71 percent of council votes, but it is important to note that more-populous EU members have more votes than less-populous ones. Winning 71 percent of council votes thus does not require winning the approval of 71 percent of EU member states.

The Treaty of Nice significantly complicates the qualified-majority procedure. Specifically, it adds two new majority thresholds. Under the new decision-making procedure, to pass, a measure will need "yes" votes from nations that represent at least 62 percent of the total EU population and "yes" votes from at least half the EU members. Finally, instead of a measure's requiring 71 percent of the council votes to pass, the threshold for approval will rise to 74 percent. This means that under the new system, there will be more ways of blocking a decision in the Council of Ministers in the enlarged EU, when the goal was just the opposite: to prevent the decision-making paralysis that most observers believed would result from simply adding twelve new members under current rules.

Figure 2.1 illustrates the point. In the figure, the groups of three bars represent the three majority thresholds (members, population, and council votes) that each decision will have to surpass if the Treaty of Nice takes effect. The leftmost bar in each group shows the number of votes necessary to block a qualified-majority decision under the new

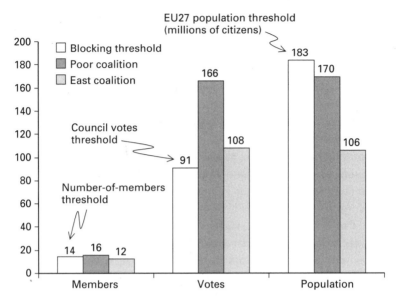

Figure 2.1
Treaty of Nice voting scheme in the EU27. *Source:* Baldwin et al. 2001a.

system. The middle bar in each group shows the size of a coalition of all poor nations (the four incumbent "cohesion" nations plus the twelve newcomers). The rightmost bar shows the size of the "east" coalition (the twelve newcomers). We see that the poor coalition will be able to block anything on either the members or the council votes criterion. The newcomer coalition will be able to block anything on the vote criterion. Given this power to block, it seems likely that the newcomers, or the newcomers in conjunction with the incumbent cohesion countries (Spain, Portugal, Ireland, and Greece) will attempt to re-orient the EU's priorities in their favor. Of course, these are just two examples of the possible coalitions among the twenty-seven nations of the expanded EU. The general point is that the Nice Treaty creates many, many more ways of blocking decisions in the Council, which will significantly reduce the EU's ability to act.

2.2.3.1.2 What's to Be Done? If enlargement happens on schedule, there will be no time to correct the Nice Treaty's shortcomings. Indeed, the EU leaders implicitly recognized their failure at instituting the necessary reforms by setting up the European Convention and agreeing at the Nice summit to pencil in a new IGC in 2004. Given this, I will address possible remedies below when I turn to post-enlargement challenges.

2.2.3.2 Efficiency in Decision Making: The European Central Bank's Numbers Problem

The near doubling of EU members resulting from enlargement will create problems in many other EU institutions, as representation in most of these is based on the principle of equal treatment of members. As the number of members rises, the number of decision makers also rises. Anyone who has been involved in committees knows that increasing numbers and paralysis go hand in hand. The Treaty of Nice eliminated most of these numbers problems, or at least provided a workable makeshift compromise, with one important exception. Although the treaty does touch on the subject, the ECB's numbers problem is still not solved. Nor does there seem to be any urgency in finding a solution. The ECB's numbers problem, however, is both serious and urgent.

There are already eighteen decision makers in the ECB interest rate–setting body: six Executive Board members and the central bank governor from each Economic and Monetary Union (EMU) member. Eighteen is already probably almost too large for efficient decision/making and is greater than what one see at other central banks, such as the U.S. Fed (twelve), the Bundesbank (fifteen), the Bank of England (nine), and the central banks of Canada (seven), Australia (nine), New Zealand (one), and Sweden (six). Under current Maastricht Treaty rules, however, each new EU member automatically gets a vote on the critical interest rate–setting committee when they join the EMU.

Without reform, enlargement would thus boost the committee size to something like thirty! This is too many voting members to enable decisions to be made on where to go for dinner, much less to run monetary policy for over 450 million people. Furthermore, the newcomers are more likely to be high-growth nations like Ireland with a substantially higher structural inflation than that of the incumbent nations, because of the so-called Balassa-Samuelson effect (as the newcomers get rich, they too become high-priced European nations, but accomplishing this requires them to have a positive inflation differential with respect to EMU core nations). This may make them more hawkish, but their national perspectives will systematically differ, as a result, from those of core nations. In one (hopefully improbable) case, the ECB could become divided into a dozen or more small, high-growth

"Irelands" and a handful of big core nations, with the Irelands having enough votes to set interest rates while accounting for only 20 percent of Euroland output.

The ECB's numbers problem is urgent. The key date for resolution of the problem is the close of enlargement negotiations, as any solution will require unanimous approval by the Council of Ministers and ratification by each EU member state. It is already too late to complete this procedure *before* enlargement; however, the Council of Ministers could and should approve a proposed solution and include it in the accession treaties. Ratification of the accession treaties by both incumbents and newcomers would thus solve the problem with little controversy. Accession treaties have always been used to adjust EU treaties to new members, so it would be natural to pack the solution to the ECB's enlargement-related problem into such treaties.

If the EU misses the 2002 train—if it does not have a proposed solution adopted by the council and included in the accession treaties—it will have to wait a long time for the next one. Worse still, the wait for a solution will create difficulties that could raise questions about the ECB's ability to manage its own affairs.

Here is the logic. The accession treaties specify exactly what the new members are joining; in particular, they specify the exact versions of the EU treaties that are binding on the new members. It is thus not possible—and certainly not fair—to change the EU treaties during the one or two years it will take to ratify the accession treaties in the fifteen incumbent nations and the ten or twelve acceding nations. After all, one cannot unilaterally change a contract during the interval between finalizing the text and the actual signature ceremony. This means that if the 2002 train is missed, the Union cannot begin to solve the ECB's numbers problem until the newcomers are full members (in 2004, according to the current plan).

Moreover, even if EU leaders managed to have the proposed solution ready in 2004, it would again take one or two years to get this ratified by all twenty-five or twenty-seven members states, delaying a solution until 2005 or 2006. This might cause two big problems.

First, the solution to the ECB's problem would likely get tangled in other reforms discussed in the 2004 intergovernmental conference (IGC2004). Horse trading is the modus operandi of IGCs, so haggling over, say, national positions on the Charter of Fundamental Rights or the autonomy of regions is quite likely to be mixed up with national positions on ECB reform. The result of this entanglement might nonetheless be sound, but given the sloppy outcome of the last IGC, ECB restructuring should be completely insulated from the IGC2004.

Second, the newcomers want to join the EMU as soon as possible, since the attendant reduction of the interest rate on their national debts will be a political bonanza. They will also have a veto once they join, so they might trade a lenient judgment on the Maastricht criteria by incumbent members for their vote in support of reform, a sort of "you can reform it, if we can join it" deal. The euro's status would not be bolstered by an exchange of EMU membership for an agreement on reform.

Plainly resolving the ECB's numbers problem is the most pressing challenge in the management of the upcoming EU enlargement. The exact nature of the solution is a tricky question. In a nutshell, there are three ways of reducing the number of ECB decision makers: representation (one country represents a group, as in the International Monetary Fund's board), rotation (the right to vote rotates among central bank governors, as in the U.S. Fed), or delegation (power is delegated to a small committee, as in the Bank of England). For a detailed discussion of the pros and cons of these potential solutions, see Baldwin et al. 2001b.

2.2.3.2.1 *How Did They Overlook ECB Reform?* It may seem incredible that EU leaders adopted reforms to fix the European Commission's numbers problem (each member gets a commissioner and each big member gets an extra, so an EU27 would imply a commission of thirty-two commissioners) but failed to reform of the all-important ECB. This seems, however, to have been a rather conscious plot to keep ECB reform out of the horse-trading atmosphere of IGC2000. Evidence of this plot can be found in the rather curious evolution of public statements made on the topic by ECB President Wim Duisenberg during the IGC. Here is an interchange between a questioner and Duisenberg at a 13 April 2000 ECB press conference in Frankfurt:

Question: "Have you also discussed any institutional changes that might be required with respect to the decision-making bodies of the ECB? For example: could you imagine a Governing Council consisting of about thirty members?"

Duisenberg: "We have not discussed it today, but we have discussed it many times before. And *we do not see the need for institutional changes in the organisation of the European System of Central Banks, including the ECB.*" (emphasis added)

Here is what he said on 12 September 2000 before the Committee on Economic and Monetary Affairs of the European Parliament: "There could be a problem with the Governing Council, currently consisting of 17 Members, if that number were to be greatly increased, but that is still a long way off.... [I]n our view, *the time is not yet right after a year and a half in existence to start thinking about or discussing changes in the composition or nature of the decision-making bodies of the ECB, and we have ample time to do that at a later stage"* (emphasis added).

Everything seemed to have changed, however, over the winter of 2000–2001. In response to a question about ECB reform proposals at a 21 June 2001 press conference in Dublin, he said: *"We will come with suggestions in that respect [solving the numbers problem], as soon as the Nice Treaty has been ratified by all the parliaments,* including of course the Irish Parliament, and we hope that at some time that will happen. At least that is my personal hope" (emphasis added).

2.3   Post-enlargement Tasks and Difficulties

Given the very narrow time window that is left before enlargement, most of the EU institutional reforms necessitated by the enlargement will have to be dealt with after the enlargement has happened. To keep my comments to a manageable length, I will mention only the three most pressing challenges facing the EU in regard to enlargement.

As I already mentioned, the twelve nations negotiating for EU accession are poor, populous, and agrarian. Because the Union spends 85 percent of its budget on poor regions and farmers, enlargement has important budgetary implications. There is a way to manage this enlargement problem, but it involves a fairly radical reform of EU spending priorities, starting with the two big-ticket items, structural spending (money to poor regions) and the CAP.

2.3.1   Structural Spending

Since the earliest reaches of recorded history mankind has struggled with the problem of giving away money. Two main models of money distribution have emerged; let me call them the charity and venture capital models. The charity model involves the well-to-do doling out money to the less well-to-do. The keystone of this model is a *means test* at the individual level. If a charity scheme is to work, it is absolutely essential to ensure that the citizens receiving the money are indeed badly off. The venture capital model is quite different. Paraphrasing one well-known parable, instead of giving fish to the poor, rich folks finance programs that teach the poor how to fish. The keystone of this model is *project evaluation*. If a venture capital approach is to work, the projects on which the money is to be spent must be shown to be feasible and viable and to have at least a good chance of attaining the desired goals.

The main problem with EU handout programs, such as the structural funds, is that they are an awkward mix of the charity model and the venture capital model. The main test for the largest program is based on income differences, but not on the incomes of those who receive the money. Under this program, which is poetically known as Objective 1 spending, the test is whether a *region's* income is less than 75 percent of the EU's average. How the money is spent within a region, once it is awarded, or even whether it stays within the regions to which it is given, is not considered, and the ultimate recipients are not subject to a means test. Anecdotal evidence suggests that much of the money ends up in the hands of rich owners of construction companies—some of them located in rich countries—rather than in the hands of poor citizens living in the region to which the money has ostensibly been awarded. This would not be a significant problem if the projects on which the money was spent could be shown to benefit the poor citizens of the region that received the money. This, however, cannot be determined, as the EU does absolutely no systematic economic project evaluation, either before or after the money is spent.

As long as the main criterion for handing out money under Objective 1 is regional per capita income, enlarging the Union to poor nations will be an expensive proposition. Moreover, the political fights over this money will certainly intensify with enlargement.

2.3.1.1 What to Do?
The solution to this problem is to radically overhaul structural spending. The EU should allocate all of its structural spending on the basis of economic and social evaluations of project proposals. This would automatically limit the cost of admitting new members to the Union, since the process of project evaluation would screen out many demands for structural spending. Indeed, history has shown that nations have a great deal of trouble in absorbing more than 3 to 5 percent of their GDP in project assistance. Thus, this solution would automatically (and justifiably) limit regional spending on the newcomers, and it might reduce the amount of wasted spending in the regions of the incumbent countries.

2.3.2   CAP Spending

The Central European countries are blessed with fertile land that is
well suited to the products most heavily protected by the CAP (e.g.,
dairy, beef, and wheat). Consequently, their accession is likely to cost
the EU dearly. Many calculations of the exact cost of accession of these
countries have been made, but the undeniable fact is that as long as
CAP subsidies are tied to output, costs will soar when eastern farm
productivities start to approach those of the west.

The solution here is even simpler than for the structural-spending
problem: nationalize CAP expenditures and delink them completely
from production following standard single-market rules. Although
there might have been some justification for making the CAP an EU-
wide program in the 1950s and 1960s, it has long since evaporated. EU
member states do, quite rightly in my opinion, intervene to support the
incomes of certain groups. Governments subsidize the old, the young,
and the sick. They also systematically support some industries, such
as the arts, airlines, and education. Each EU national government,
however, views the level of support to each of these groups as a national prerogative. Why should support for farmers be any different? If
France and Finland want to prop up their farmers' standards of living
more that than the Spanish and the British, why should EU policy stop
them? Where is the logic of imposing a single agriculture policy on a
land mass that reaches from the Adriatic Sea to the Arctic Circle? Of
course, the usual non-distortionary rules would have to apply to prevent unfair competition and beggar-thy-neighbor policies, but this is
not a barrier to the nationalization of CAP. The EU already has a well-
functioning system for surveillance and enforcement of members' support of their industries.

Note that both of these shifts (i.e., in structural and CAP spending)
would make enlargement much less of a threat to two of the most
powerful special-interest groups in the EU: farmers and poor regions.

2.3.3   Reduce the EU Budget

To me, the implication of all this is clear. Several decades ago, spending the EU's cash on farmers made good political sense. The CAP was
really just rich Western nations subsidizing their own farmers via the
EU budget, and doing so through the EU budget facilitated European
integration by providing some possibilities of side payments. Likewise,

when poor-region spending became significant in the late 1980s and early 1990s, it played an important role in facilitating European integration: In essence it was a side payment to Spain, Portugal, Ireland, and Greece for agreeing to economic and monetary integration that many felt would mainly benefit the EU's rich members.

Now, however, CAP and cohesion spending are getting in the way of European integration. Haggling over handouts to special-interest groups should not be allowed to paralyze the enlarged Union. One approach to preventing this would be to alter EU decision-making rules. The most direct approach, however, is much simpler and resembles the tactic used every day by mothers confronted with squabbling siblings: remove the object of dispute, that is, reduce the EU budget by 50 to 80 percent and national contributions by the same proportion. The EU is now held together by the internal market and the monetary union. Any significant increase in integration is surely going to take the form of enhanced cooperation arrangements (clubs within the club), and since these will be voluntary, the EU will not need to make large side payments to proceed with European integration.

Of course this solution is not likely to work, at least not before the enlarged Union struggles through a series of crises over the budget. My guess is that these crises will come, probably while the EU is working on its next five-year budget plan, called the "Financial Perspective" in EUese. If EU leaders come to believe that the budget is a major hindrance to European integration, solutions that sound radical today may in fact come to sound quite natural.

2.3.4   Decision-Making Reforms: Emergency Repairs of the Nice Treaty

If the truth be told, the Treaty of Nice is a treaty that only a mother could love. Despite its length and complexity, it falls short of its goals. The treaty has two aims: (1) locking in the EU's eastern enlargement and (2) adjusting EU decision-making procedures to the realities of a Union with twenty-seven or more members. The treaty partially accomplishes the first goal, since it removes the formal roadblocks imposed by the Amsterdam Treaty, but it fails to lock in a timetable for enlargement.

On the second aim, the treaty fails almost completely. In particular, the current decision-making rules in the EU's key policymaking body, the Council of Ministers, were widely touted as a recipe for deadlock in an enlarged Union. As discussed earlier, the quantitative tools from voting-game theory can be used to show that the treaty's new Byzantine decision-making system, set to go into effect in 2005, is no better than the current system, and in fact, it makes things worse; the Council's ability to act with twenty-seven members would have been better served by no reform at all.

Small EU members were told that a reduction in their power was necessary to allow the EU to operate after a near doubling of the membership. The final deal reached at the Treaty of Nice did reduce their power, yet it did not maintain efficiency. Moreover, the crippled decision-making process that resulted will weaken the European Parliament by greatly reducing the flow of legislation enacted. Further integration, if it occurs, is likely to rely more on member states' initiatives, perhaps channeled into new, enhanced cooperation arrangements. Given that this would naturally favor large countries, an observer more skeptical than myself might suggest that the French ambush at the Nice summit was deliberate.

This is not a positive assessment of the treaty, so should the treaty be rejected? It is not too late to do so, and indeed the outcome of the upcoming (fall 2002) Irish referendum on the issues is far from certain. My answer to the question is simple. The treaty should be ratified, since otherwise the Amsterdam Treaty roadblocks will hold up the historical imperative of enlargement. But the treaty should be repaired after ratification. The key emergency repair is to lower the majority thresholds: The 74 percent threshold on council votes should be lowered to two-thirds, and the population threshold should be lowered from 62 percent to one-half. This would restore efficiency without further weakening small members (for formal analysis, see Baldwin et al. 2001a). The IGC2004 would be an ideal time to effect these changes in the treaty, since the voting changes in the current version do not take effect until 2005.

Let me end my comments with some conjectures about the next wave of enlargement.

2.4   Where Is the End of the EU Rope?

Enlargement is a process, not an event. The looming EU enlargement is not the last. Indeed, I shall argue that the expansion of EU membership could accelerate in the coming decade. The basic logic behind this assertion is simple. The first pillar of the argument rests on the "domino theory of regionalism" (Baldwin 1995, 1997). The second is based on the EU institutional reforms that the current enlargement is likely to produce.

2.4.1 Domino Theory and Newcomers

The domino theory asserts that an idiosyncratic incident of regional economic integration tends to trigger a multiplier effect that knocks down international barriers to trade and investment like a row of dominos. The basic idea is that forming a preferential trade area or deepening an existing one produces trade and investment diversion. This diversion generates new political-economy forces in non-participating nations, a force that has been called "pressures for inclusion." These pressures increase with the size of the trade bloc, yet bloc size depends on how many nations join. Clearly, then, a single incidence of regionalism may trigger several rounds of membership requests from nations that were previously happy as nonmembers.[4] Applying the domino theory to the upcoming enlargement suggests that as Central European nations become EU members, European nations further east and south will redouble their efforts to join the EU.

2.4.2 Enlargements Will Get Easier

The upcoming enlargement will force reforms in EU institutions that will make it easier for the EU to enlarge. For instance, whatever solutions are adopted for CAP and cohesion spending will certainly lower the budgetary impact of further waves of enlargement. The same can be said of the reformed decision-making procedures that will eventually be adopted in all EU institutions ranging from the ECB and European Commission to the Court of Auditors.

Given both the push factor (domino theory) and the lubrication factor (institutional reform aimed at allowing many more member nations), it seems likely that the queue of EU applications will lengthen in the coming decade. Where is the end of this "EU rope"?

There are many implications of this, but I will focus on one. An EU of thirty or more members will be a very different beast from the EU we know today. There is really no way that so many nations can coordinate on anything but the most basic issues—unless either of two conditions is fulfilled: the decision-making procedures veer sharply toward simple majority voting, or the EU ceases to strive for uniformity.

Of the two, I suspect that the latter will triumph, at least as long as the current generation of leaders is in power. If my conjectures about these unknowables prove correct, enlargement will fundamentally transform the nature of the EU. It will be a union of nations that share a common base, mainly economic integration consisting of the single market and single money, but little more. Deeper and broader integration initiatives will be based on the clubs-within-clubs model put forth by the insightful study *Flexible Integration* (CEPR 1995).

Notes

1. Note that the final draft of this talk was delivered in September 2002, and as such it does not incorporate subsequent developments that occurred during the production phase of the book. I note, however, that some of the problems highlighted have been redressed. An ECB voting reform was adopted, and the draft Constitutional Treaty corrects many of the Nice Treaty's decision-making flaws.

2. The 2000–2006 financial perspective talks started with publication of Agenda 2000 in July 1997 and continued up to the official adoption at the General Affairs Council in June 1999.

3. Of course it is a bit strained to call Cyprus and Malta CEECs, but I will stick with the notation here.

4. The idea underlying the domino explanation is hardly new. A presentation can be discerned in Jacob Viner's (1950) account of how dozens of German principalities and city-states were cajoled and coerced into joining Prussia's Zollverien between 1819 and 1867. I imagine, however, that the notion is much older; Bismarck himself probably understood the political-economy dynamics of trade diversion.

References

Baldwin, R. 1992. "An Eastern Enlargement of EFTA: Why the East Should Join and the EFTAns Should Want Them." Occassional paper no. 10, Centre for Economic Policy Research, London.

Baldwin, R. 1994. *Towards an Integrated Europe*. London: Centre for Economic Policy Research.

Baldwin, R. 1995. "A Domino Theory of Regionalism." In *Expanding European Regionalism: The EU's New Members*, ed. R. Baldwin, P. Haaparanta, and J. Kiander. Cambridge, UK: Cambridge University Press. Republished in J. Bhagwati, P. Krishna, and A. Panagariya, eds., *Trading Blocs: Alternative Approaches to Analyzing Preferential Trade Agreements*. Cambridge: MIT Press, 1999.

Baldwin, R. 1997. "The Causes of Regionalism." The World Economy 20, no. 7: 865–888.

Baldwin, R., E. Berglof, F. Giavazzi, and M. Widgren. 2001a. *Nice Try: Should the Treaty of Nice Be Ratified?* Monitoring European Integration no. 11. London: Centre for Economic Policy Research.

Baldwin, R., E. Berglof, F. Giavazzi, and M. Widgren. 2001b. "Preparing the ECB for Enlargement." Policy paper no. 5, Centre for Economic Policy Research, London.

Centre for Economic Policy Research (CEPR). 1995. *Flexible Integration: Towards a More Effective and Democratic Europe*. Monitoring European Integration no. 6. London: Centre for Economic Policy Research.

EU President. 2000. "Presidency Report to the Feira European Council on Intergovernmental Conference on Institutional Reform." CONFER 4750/00, Brussels, 14 June 2000. Available at ⟨http://europa.eu.int/comm/archives/igc2000/geninfo/index_en.htm⟩.

European Commission. 2002. "State of Play, June 2002." Available at ⟨europa.eu.int/comm/enlargement/negotiations/chapters/⟩, accessed July 2002.

Eurostat. 2002. "Enlargement of the European Union." Available at ⟨europa.eu.int/comm/enlargement/docs/index.htm⟩, accessed July 2002.

Felsenthal, D., and M. Machover. 2001. "The Treaty of Nice and Qualified Majority Voting." Available at ⟨http://lse.ac.uk/votingpower⟩.

Viner, Jacob. 1950. *The Customs Unions Issue*. New York: Carnegie Peace Foundation.

3   Restructuring the ECB

Helge Berger, Jakob de Haan,
and Robert Inklaar

3.1   Introduction

On 1 January 1999, Europe entered a new era with the adoption of a single currency, the euro, by eleven of the European Union's fifteen member states. Greece joined the euro area in 2001. With the initiation of the EMU, the ECB is responsible for monetary policy in the euro area. The ECB's primary objective, as laid down in the Maastricht Treaty, is price stability, quantified by the ECB as inflation in the euro area below 2 percent in the medium run. The ECB Governing Council, which decides about interest rates, consists of the Executive Board of the ECB (made up of the president, the vice-president, and four other members) and the central bank governors of the twelve euro countries (see figure 3.1). When making monetary policy decisions, the members of the ECB Governing Council are expected to act not as national representatives, but in a fully independent personal capacity. This is reflected in the principle of "one person, one vote."

Even though the ECB is a very young institution, the need to reform it is already being debated in view of the upcoming enlargement of the EU. The European Council of Nice of December 2000 asked the ECB Governing Council to prepare suggestions for a reform of its statute by the end of 2002.

Reform of the ECB is on the political agenda for two basic reasons. First, ten Eastern European countries (Slovenia, Czech Republic, Hungary, Poland, Estonia, Slovak Republic, Latvia, Lithuania, Bulgaria, and Romania) and two Southern European countries (Malta and Cyprus) are expected to apply for euro area membership after accession to the EU.[1] Furthermore, three EU members that are currently not members of the euro area could adopt the euro in the near future (the United Kingdom, Sweden, and Denmark). So membership in

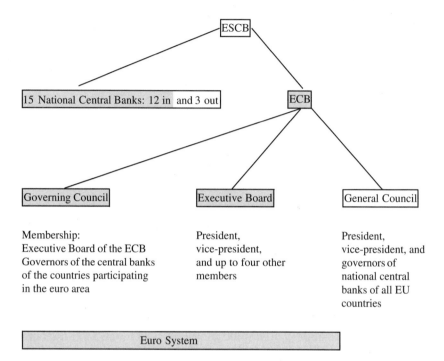

Figure 3.1
Structure of the European system of central banks. *Source:* Eijffinger and de Haan 2000.

the Eurosystem might increase from the current twelve to twenty-seven. In the absence of modification of the current ECB statute, this enlargement could have severe consequences for the efficiency of monetary policymaking in the euro area. A larger ECB Governing Council would experience greater *difficulties in decision making* than the smaller body governing monetary policy in the euro area today. Without reform of the current ECB statute, the size of the ECB Governing Council could increase from eighteen to thirty-three, making it by far the largest monetary policymaking institution among OECD countries. Because of this increase in membership, discussion and voting procedures would likely become more time-consuming and complicated. The central bank's tradition of consensus-based policymaking—said to play an important role in today's ECB decision-making process, too—could further amplify the ECB's "number problem" and increase decision-making costs.

Second, an increase in the number of euro area member states without ECB reform would affect the *wedge between the economic and political weights* of EMU member countries within the ECB. Since almost all accession countries are small in economic terms relative to current euro area members, enlargement within the given institutional setup would significantly increase the degree of over-representation of the area's smaller member countries in the council in terms of relative economic size. For instance, in a monetary union with twenty-seven members, the current ECB statute implies that the representatives of its smallest seventeen member states, representing only about 10 percent of the area's aggregated GDP, could determine monetary policy decisions in the euro area. Over-representation, although not necessarily a problem per se, has the potential to introduce an unwelcome bias into the ECB's decision making, if country representatives put at least some weight on national economic developments and these developments deviate notably from the behavior of euro area aggregates. Since the bulk of the accession countries are transition economies, they may be subject to idiosyncratic shocks and somewhat higher structural inflation than the core of the euro area. There is reason to believe that such asymmetries could have an impact on ECB policymaking.[2]

In this chapter we discuss various options for reforming the ECB. We argue that, although centralization might be a first-best solution to the problems potentially associated with enlargement in many ways, it might have disadvantages from a political-economy perspective, including a potential conflict with the established voting rights of current euro area member countries. An alternative solution to ensure the European perspective of decision making in the ECB Governing Council is to match economic size and voting power. When countries have voting power in proportion to their GDP shares, it matters less if they behave according to national instead of euro area–wide interests. One way to implement the principle of proportional voting power, even if imperfect in practice, is to introduce a rotation scheme for national central bank governors that takes economic differences between the member countries into account.

The remainder of the chapter is structured as follows. Section 3.2 discusses in somewhat more detail the two basic problems facing an enlarged EMU. Section 3.3 reviews options for reform, and section 3.4 focuses on one specific option: rotation. Various rotation schemes are discussed. Section 3.5 examines the reform proposal recently put forward by the ECB. The chapter's final section offers some concluding comments.

Table 3.1
Distribution of voting power in selected central bank models

	Federal central bank models			
	Board (1)	National central banks (2)	Council (1) + (2)	$\dfrac{(2)}{(1)+(2)}$%
Bundesbank pre-1957	1	9	10	90.0
Bundesbank pre-1992	7	11	18	61.1
Bundesbank[a]	8	9	17	52.9
Fed[b]	7	5	12	41.7
ECB 1999	6	11	17	64.7
ECB 2001	6	12	18	66.7
ECB with 27 EMU members	6	27	33	81.8

Sources: Central banks, authors' calculations.
[a] Since the 1992 Bundesbank reform, nine regional central banks cover all seventeen Länder. A further reform of the Bundesbank status is under discussion.
[b] At any given time, only five out of the twelve regional central banks hold Federal Open Market Committee (FOMC) voting rights. The New York Fed is allocated a permanent seat in the FOMC, and the remaining four seats rotate among the remaining eleven regional central banks.

3.2 The Main Problems

The upcoming enlargement of the euro area is likely to influence the effectiveness of the ECB's current policymaking framework through at least two channels: the increase in the number of decision makers and the growing heterogeneity of member countries in economic terms.[3] Turning first to the implied increase in the number of decision makers involved, table 3.1 reveals that the number of council members could increase from the currently eighteen to as many as thirty-three in the scenario that includes membership of the potential new EU countries as well as the United Kingdom, Sweden, and Denmark. An increase of this magnitude in the number of Council members could complicate the council's decision making. The table's fourth column shows that the ECB Governing Council, with its six board members and 12 national central bank governors, is already relatively large compared to the decision-making bodies of other federal central bank systems, like the Bundesbank's Zentralbankrat and the Fed's Federal Open Market Committee (FOMC). After enlargement, the number of voting members in the ECB Governing Council could be almost three times as high as the number of FOMC members and twice as high as the number of Zentralbankrat members.

Both the Bundesbank and the Fed have constrained the size of their decision-making bodies with a view to decision-making costs. For instance, Eichengreen (1992) argues that the organizational framework of today's Fed, which restricts the number of regional central banks voting in the FOMC to 5 out of the 12, was put in place, among other reasons, to reduce inefficiencies stemming from the involvement of too many decision makers. As far as the Bundesbank is concerned, it is interesting to note that the reform of 1992 prevented an increase in the number of Länder representatives on the Bundesbank Council after unification. Without a reform, the council could have increased to twenty-three or more members, which, according to the Bundesbank, "would have greatly complicated that body's decision-making processes" (Deutsche Bundesbank 1992, 50). This echoes concerns raised by Friedman and Schwartz (1963). In their seminal study of U.S. monetary policy, they attribute the severity of the depression of the 1930s to serious policy mistakes by the Federal Reserve resulting from its excessively decentralized decision-making structure:

There is more than a little element of truth in the jocular description of a committee as a group of people, no one of whom knows what should be done, who jointly decide that nothing can be done. And this is especially likely to be true of a group like the Open Market Policy Conference, consisting of independent persons from widely separated cities, who share none of that common outlook on detailed problems or responsibilities which evolves in the course of long-time daily collaboration. (415–416)

According to Friedman and Schwartz, the consequence of a weak center is that the decision-making process becomes too cumbersome and slow, possibly resulting in sub-optimal decisions. An ECB Governing Council with more than thirty members is likely to need significantly more time than today's council of eighteen to discuss and evaluate the state of the economy and to prepare monetary policy decisions. Even though a more extensive use of explicit voting procedures might help to limit decision-making costs, the prevalent culture of consensus-based decision making in the ECB Governing Council might limit the use of voting practices. Baldwin et al. (2001) argue that, in addition, the Executive Board's leadership ability will be seriously reduced as the number of countries in the euro area increases and the board's relative voting power within the Governing Council decreases.

A second insight provided by the fourth column of table 3.1 is that the political weight attached to national or regional central bank representatives within the ECB framework is comparatively large. In many industrial countries, monetary policy decisions are delegated to central banks with smaller decision-making bodies in which all members are centrally appointed. Both the German Bundesbank and the U.S. Fed have systematically reduced the political weight of regional representatives in their decision-making bodies (Eichengreen 1992; Berger and de Haan 1999). Whereas, at an earlier stage, both institutions resembled unions of national central banks, over time, the central element in both central banks was strengthened. Today, the vote share of regional representatives is about 53 percent of all votes in the case of the Bundesbank and about 42 percent in case of the Fed's FOMC. The political weight of national central bank governors in the ECB Governing Council, which currently stands at about 67 percent of all votes, is significantly higher, and this percentage could increase to as much as 82 percent after enlargement.

Under the current decision-making setup of the ECB, small member countries carry a larger political than economic weight (Berger and de Haan 2002). Figure 3.2a shows the economic weight (defined as the share of a country in the euro area's GDP) and political weight (the vote share of the country's central bank governor in the ECB Governing Council) of individual member countries in today's ECB.[4] On the one hand, countries like France or Germany produce about one-fifth and one-third, respectively, of the euro area's GDP but hold only one-eighteenth of the overall votes. On the other hand, the political weight allocated by the present ECB framework to smaller countries such as Ireland clearly exceeds their economic weight. In fact, according to figure 3.2a, political weight exceeds economic weight for more than half of all current euro area members.

Figure 3.2b shows that in a euro area of twenty-seven members without a reform of the ECB, nearly 80 percent of the countries will have a larger political than economic weight. If the one-person, one-vote principle were strictly applied, all newcomers but the United Kingdom would be allocated a political weight surpassing their economic weight, in most cases by a significant margin.[5] As already mentioned, a coalition of the smallest euro area members with enough votes to command the majority of overall ECB Governing Council seats after enlargement would represent merely about 10 percent of the euro area's total GDP. The equivalent figure in the current euro area is close to 50 percent.[6]

The over-representation of smaller member states could introduce an unwelcome bias into the ECB's decision making if (1) national central

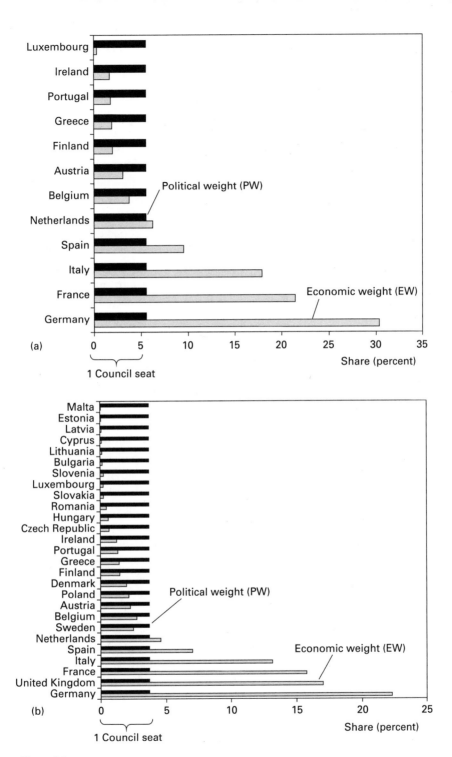

Figure 3.2
Economic and political weights of central banks before and after enlargement.

bank governors put at least some weight on national economic developments and (2) these developments deviate significantly from the behavior of euro area aggregates.[7] For instance, a decrease in euro area economic activity is probably more strongly felt in a country with relatively low per capita income than in better-off regions. Likewise, countries that already have a high level of inflation might be more sensitive to a euro area–wide increase in inflation than low-inflation countries.

Even though "members of the [council] do not act as national representatives, but in a fully independent personal capacity" (ECB 1999, 55), it is certainly possible that national economic welfare plays at least some role in the (voting) behavior of regional representatives on the ECB Governing Council. Indeed, if national background should not play any role in the ECB decision-making process, why have the European governments not delegated monetary policy fully to the ECB's Executive Board in the first place? In fact, the hypothesis that regional influences exist and exert themselves in a federal central bank system is supported by recent studies on U.S. and German monetary policy. Berger and de Haan (2002) present evidence that regional differences in growth and inflation had a significant influence on the voting behavior of Zentralbankrat members. Similarly, Meade and Sheets (2002) find that Fed policymakers do take developments in regional unemployment into account when deciding on monetary policy in the FOMC. They show that an increase in a region's unemployment rate (for a given national rate and evaluated at sample means) by 1 percentage point reduced the probability that an FOMC member dissented from the majority vote by about 2 percentage points over 1978–2000. Although no direct evidence of similar behavior exists for today's ECB, Meade and Sheets (2002) argue that recent interest rate decisions by the ECB Governing Council at least do not allow rejection of the hypothesis that national central bank governors vote with a regional bias in the euro area as well.[8]

As argued above, a too-strong representation of new national central bank representatives on the ECB Governing Council could introduce a bias into euro area policymaking after enlargement, if the behavior of their respective national economies deviates significantly from that of today's euro area. But just how different are economic developments, between candidate and incumbent countries and what consequences might follow for monetary policy?

Probably the most important distinguishing feature of the majority of candidate countries is their status as *transition economies*. Real per capita income in most accession countries is very low compared to current euro area levels, and the process of convergence is commonly thought to be slow. Fischer, Sahay, and Vegh (1998a, 1998b) estimate that it might take many Eastern European countries until the 2020s at a minimum to catch up even with the less well-off countries in the current euro area. Slowly diminishing income differences could make high growth rates an attractive policy target for some of the governors representing accession countries on the ECB Governing Council.

The data show that—as is to be expected during real conversion—the *average growth rate* of accession countries during 1996–2001, although falling short of the rates achieved in some faster-growing member countries such as Ireland and Finland, exceeded average growth in the euro area by about 1 percentage point (Berger 2002, figure 3.3). Recent empirical work suggests that this trend is likely to continue, contributing to a considerable increase in the dispersion of growth rates within the euro area compared to the status quo.[9] One likely consequence of higher-than-average growth in the accession countries in the years ahead is higher *inflation* than in the current euro area. Indeed, the average inflation differential between the euro area and accession countries was around 8 percentage points during 1996–2001, even with Bulgaria and Romania, two high-inflation countries, excluded (Berger 2002).

It is often argued that because of the Balassa-Samuelson effect, transition countries have experienced a real appreciation of their real exchange rates. When productivity growth in the traded-goods sector exceeds that in the nontraded-goods sector, prices of nontraded goods increase because of the wage equalization process between the two sectors. When productivity growth in the transition countries exceeds productivity growth in the countries in the euro area, the transition countries will have a higher inflation rate. According to Eurostat (2001), the average labor productivity level in manufacturing in transition countries was only about 40 percent of the EU average in 1998. A process of catch-up would imply high productivity growth in the future, and consequently, higher inflation rates relative to current euro area members.

There is, however, no clear consensus in the literature on the magnitude of the Balassa-Samuelson effect in the transition countries. Table 3.2 provides a summary of various recent studies. Various estimates conclude that it contributes about 2 to 4 percentage points to headline inflation.[10] Still, the estimates vary widely. Whereas Pelkmans, Gros,

Table 3.2
Estimates of the inflation differentials in the transition countries (in percent)

Study	Countries	Vis-à-vis (if relevant)	Size
Jakab and Kovacs 1999	Hungary		1.9
Pelkmans, Gros, and Ferrer 2000	CEE 10	29 OECD countries	3.8
Rother 2000	Slovenia		2.6 during 1993–1998
Sinn and Reutter 2001	Czech Republic Hungary Poland Slovenia Estonia	Germany	2.88 6.86 4.16 3.38 4.06
Halpern and Wyplosz 2001	Panel of 9 transition countries (including Russia)	Based on model for service-to-consumer goods price ratio	2.9–3.1 for the period 1991–1999
Coricelli and Jazbec 2001	Panel of 19 transition countries	Based on model for relative price of tradable goods	1 in the medium term (1990–1998)
De Broeck and Sløk 2001	Panel of transition countries		On average 1.5
Égert 2002a	Czech Republic Hungary Poland Slovakia Slovenia	Germany	0.648[a] 0.303 for 1991–2000 2.589 1.295 for 1991–2000 3.245 1.901 for 1991–2000 −0.154 −0.075 for 1993–2000 1.321 0.661 for 1993–2000
Égert 2002b	Panel of Czech Republic, Hungary, Poland, Slovakia, and Slovenia	Germany	With share of non-tradables as in GDP it ranges from 0.094 to 1.903 depending on time period and data. Estimates for 1996–2001 period range from 1.707 to 1.903. With share of non-tradables as in CPI the latter range from 0.810 to 1.059.
Backé et al. 2002	Czech Republic Hungary Poland Slovenia	Main trading partners[b]	0.35 1995–2000 3.84 1995–2000 9.76 1995–2000 3.88 1995–2000

[a] First column shows results using GDP deflator; second column shows results with CPI.
[b] Under the assumption that there are no productivity-inflation differentials between tradable and non-tradable goods in the main trading partners, which seems unrealistic.

Table 3.3
Business cycle correlation (with EU12) for 1990–2001

Current EU members		Future EU members	
Austria	0.49	Bulgaria	n.a.
Belgium	0.36	Cyprus	0.32
Finland	0.36	Czech Republic	0.11
France	0.76	Estonia	0.11
Germany	0.75	Hungary	0.20
Greece	0.18	Latvia	0.17
Ireland	0.26	Lithuania	−0.17
Italy	0.62	Malta	n.a.
Luxembourg	0.38	Poland	0.17
Netherlands	0.33	Romania	−0.04
Portugal	0.06	Slovakia	0.12
Spain	0.71	Slovenia	0.65
Denmark	0.52		
Sweden	0.36		
United Kingdom	0.31		

Note: See the appendix for sources and methods. n.a. = not available.

and Ferrer (2000), for instance, estimate that the Balassa-Samuelson effect is likely to imply almost four additional percentage points of annual inflation in the accession economies, Égert (2002a) finds little evidence of a higher inflation rate due to the Balassa-Samuelson effect in the Czech Republic and Slovakia.[11]

Part of these diverging outcomes is the result of differences in method from study to study. For instance, not all studies summarized in table 3.2 restrict themselves to estimates of the Balassa-Samuelson effect. The literature has pointed out various other channels that can give rise to inflation differentials, and some of the studies take these into account. For instance, Halpern and Wyplosz (2001), who estimate the Balassa-Samuelson effect for a panel of nine transition countries (including Russia), also include demand factors. The same is true for Coricelli and Jazbec (2001), who also add a variable capturing structural misalignments.[12]

Yet another distinguishing feature of the candidate countries might be the *business cycle*. Table 3.3 shows the correlation between the cyclical components of industrial production in the various (potential) member states and the cyclical part of industrial production in the euro area. Industrial production is decomposed into a trend and a

cyclical component, using a Hodrick-Prescott filter (see also Artis and
Zhang 1999 and Inklaar and De Haan 2001).[13] It follows that except
for Slovenia and, to a lesser extent, Cyprus, the accession countries
have business cycles that are hardly synchronized with the business
cycle in the euro area. Note, however, that this also holds true for
some euro area countries, notably Greece and Portugal.

Business cycles may differ across currency areas or regions within
a currency area for various reasons. First, currency areas and regions
may experience different shocks. Second, they may respond differently to common shocks. This may be caused by dissimilar reactions of
policymakers to a common shock, or because of differences in the currency area or regional composition of output. In addition, heterogeneity in financial and economic structure may lead to differences in the
monetary policy transmission mechanism.

Figure 3.3 sheds further light on the correlation of shocks. It displays
the correlation of demand shocks and supply shocks in quarterly real
GDP for individual euro area and accession countries with demand
and supply shocks in the euro area aggregate computed by Fidrmuc
and Korhonen (2001). The sample period is 1991–1992 through 2000

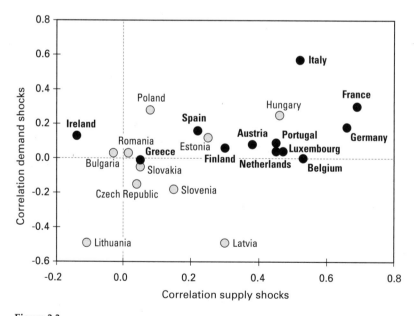

Figure 3.3
Demand and supply shocks in the euro area and in accession countries. *Source:* Fidrmuc
and Korhonen 2001, table 2.

for most countries. Shocks are identified using two-variable Vector Auto Regressions (VARs) for output and prices and the Blanchard and Quah (1989) assumptions. The results suggest that, on average, demand and supply shocks are more closely correlated to the respective euro area shocks for the euro area countries than for the accession countries. Most present euro area countries are located in the upper right of the figure, whereas the majority of accession countries can be found in the lower left, indicating non-significant or negative correlation.[14] Exceptions are two of the more advanced among the candidate countries, Estonia and Hungary. Greece, a latecomer to the euro area and still early in its real convergence process, and fast-growing Ireland look as loosely connected to the euro area as most accession countries.

The main message stemming from the analysis thus far is that most accession countries are subject to different macroeconomic shocks—and thus a different business cycle—than the current euro area. Although real convergence will probably work to reduce these idiosyncrasies in the long run, they will certainly remain in the short and medium term. In the absence of reform of the present ECB framework, this could have an impact on monetary policymaking in the euro area.

3.3   Reform Options

The discussion above suggests that potential reforms of the ECB should aim at keeping the number of decision makers on the ECB Governing Council within reasonable limits, strengthening the voting power of the Executive Board, and aligning the economic and political weights of countries on the Governing Council with one another.[15] A number of possible reform scenarios along these lines can be distinguished.

3.3.1   Centralization

A larger role for the Executive Board in ECB decision making would go a long way toward limiting *decision-making costs* and preventing possibly diverging economic developments within a larger euro area to have an undue impact on monetary policy in the euro area.[16]

A pragmatic application of the centralization scenario would be to put actual decisions on EU monetary policy into the hands of the existing ECB Executive Board. This would limit the role of the Governing Council to that of an informational forum in which the area's regional central banks would be informed of policy decisions and implementation issues would be discussed.[17] The EU Treaty states that the ECB's Executive Board (including the president of the ECB, the vice-president, and four additional members) is appointed by "the governments of the member states at the level of Heads of State or Government, on a recommendation from the Council, after it has consulted the European Parliament and the Governing Council of the ECB" (EU 1997, Article 112 2.(b)). A highly centralized political process like this on the European level should help support a *euro area–wide perspective* among those selected to serve on the board. There are, however, a number of arguments that suggest that national central banks should continue to play an important role in ECB decision making (Berger 2002):

• A first argument against allocating the ECB Governing Council's entire decision-making power to the Executive Board concerns *information*. Efficient monetary policy requires the timely provision, aggregation, and processing of information originating on the regional level, especially in the case of a currency union that encompasses a large number of heterogeneous countries and regions. It might therefore be helpful to ensure that ECB Governing Council members with a strong regional anchor, such as national central bank governors, are directly involved in actual monetary policy decision making.

• A second argument is that the absence of national central bank governors from the ECB Governing Council could have a negative effect on the ECB's political *independence*. The participation of all euro area member states in the selection of ECB Governing Council members (through the nomination of their respective national central bank governors) under the current ECB statute might help insulate the ECB from preference shocks at the government level, for instance, after elections.

• A third argument alludes to the *political feasibility* of centralization. As already mentioned, the statute governing the ECB clearly states, "Each member of the Governing Council, shall have one vote" (EU 1992, Article 10.2), which includes the national central bank governors. Thus, a reform of the ECB that fails to safeguard the established voting rights of current member countries' central banks might not be politically acceptable. After all, an equal right to participate in ECB policy decision making was an integral part of the Maastricht Treaty, which established the currency union. Governments of some member countries could experience opposition to their letting go of the countries' "last" bit of influence on ECB policymaking after having exchanged monetary sovereignty for a seat on the ECB Governing Council in 1999.

3.3.2 Matching Economic Size and Political Power

If centralization is not a feasible (or desirable) reform option, a reform of the statute governing the ECB should aim at an institutional design in which economic size is in line with political voting power are.[18] When countries have as much voting power as GDP share, it is less problematic if they behave according to national instead of euro area–wide interests. Decreasing the mismatch in the ECB between economic and political weights would bring actual stabilization policy closer to the outcome under the first-best solution. In fact, fully matching political and economic weights on the ECB Governing Board is likely to guarantee that actual monetary policy is perfectly in line with the ideal policy of stabilizing the euro area business cycle (and ultimately prices) based on a correctly weighted average of the underlying regional cycles. If the accession countries were to remain politically overrepresented (i.e., in the absence of the first-best solution, a reform of the current ECB decision-making framework as discussed in the previous subsection), this second-best solution would also be likely to reduce actual inflation, although inflation would probably remain higher than in the first-best solution (Berger 2002). The principal reform options for matching economic and political weights on the ECB Governing Council include vote weighting, representation, extending regional central banks across national borders, and rotation.

Under *vote weighting*, the votes of non–Executive Board members of the ECB Governing Council in regard to monetary policy decisions would be weighted, for instance, by using member countries' share in euro area GDP. By definition, a reform along these lines would better align the political and economic weights of the national council members. Vote weighting has a precedent in the qualified-voting schemes of the EU Council, which the Treaty of Nice has tentatively updated for the case of EU enlargement.[19] Another voting scheme that takes into account differences in economic size would be to require a "double majority" of votes and population for passage of proposed measures regarding monetary policy. Under such a system, there would still be an equal voting right for all Executive Board members. Every decision would require a majority of the votes on the board. In addition, however, double-majority voting would also require that the votes of board members in favor represent a majority of the population of the euro area as well. (An alternative would be to require that these votes represent a majority of the euro area's GDP.)

A problem with any vote-based reform scenario, however, is that such scenarios do not necessarily address the problem of decision-making costs. Decision-making costs in the narrow sense of voting on, say, interest rate changes need not be particularly problematic. In all likelihood, however, the council's decision-making process will involve more than the simple aggregation of votes, but also, for example, a more or less extensive discussion of the views of all members. In this case, weighting votes does not necessarily solve the ECB's number problem. Finally, similar to the argument made regarding the centralization solution, it should be noted that a weighted voting scheme might be viewed as interfering too much with the one-person, one-vote principle embedded in the ECB statute, although this criticism might apply somewhat less to a double-majority system.

An alternative reform scenario, *representation*, combines some of the characteristics of the centralization and the weighting approach. The principal idea would be to create groups of euro member countries with joint representation and joint voting rights on the ECB Governing Council, integrating the concept of a strong regional anchor with the necessity of restricting the size of the ECB's main decision-making body after the enlargement. The representation scenario would require a number of specific institutional decisions, in particular on group selection. The selection principle could be based on the idea of common economic regions (taking into account similarities in business cycles or economic structure), economic size, or both. Related issues would be the number of groups, the overall council size, and the delegation of voting power from group members to their representative on the council. Potential institutional designs include a restricted or "imperative" mandate (votes on the council are pre-determined at the group level) and an unrestricted mandate (group members delegate their full voting rights to their representatives).[20] Since the latter arrangement, however, could, in principle, deprive individual group members of their right to participate in the decision making, it potentially conflicts with the idea of national representation and the one-person, one-vote principle. This makes a solution entailing some form of explicit involvement of national central banks at the group level before a council decision (i.e., a restricted mandate for the group representatives on the council) a likely part of any representation scenario. Such a restriction would be likely to encompass contributions to council discussions as well as formal voting. In this sense, it would alleviate the decision-making costs problem at the level of the ECB Governing Council. However, these costs would substantially increase at the level of the group. If the mandate of group representatives in the Council were restricted, in the sense that their actions required the explicit consent of group members, the overall time and effort needed for a council decision would be of a similar magnitude to, if not higher than, that in the previously discussed scenario.

A variant of the representation idea is the *extension of central bank jurisdictions* across national borders. For instance, the regional central banks in the U.S. Federal Reserve System extend the borders of the states of the union, and some of the (post-1992) Landeszentralbanken in the Bundesbank Zentralbankrat represent more than one German Land. An application of this principle to the ECB after enlargement could help reduce the number of decision makers on the council. If the design of central bank areas aimed at establishing regional banks with approximately similar economic weight, it would also contribute significantly to avoiding mismatches between voting power and economic size. As with the previous reform scenarios, however, there could be issues regarding the political feasibility of a reform that included abolishing the existing voting rights of current euro area member states. Furthermore, extension of central bank jurisdictions would imply that one of the basic principles of the current ECB setup, that is, "representation" of countries, would be given up.

An alternative reform scenario that, in principle, might be able to address both the mismatch between political and economic weights and the decision-making problem associated with the enlargement of euro area membership (while avoiding some of the political constraints discussed above) could be (asymmetric) *rotation*. The basic idea is that national central bank governors would take turns sitting on the council, with the frequency of their participation scaled to match the relative economic weight of their countries. Rotation would thus work to weight implicitly the votes of national central bank governors. Arguably, therefore, rotation would pose less of a conflict with the one-person, one-vote principle than centralization, weighted voting, or the representation scenario. Although not all central bank governors would be participating in every council meeting, those who participated would be casting a full vote. Rotation could also serve to limit

Table 3.4
Various rotation groups according to economic criteria

	(1) Size 1	(2) Size 2	(3) Size 3	(4) Inflation	(5) Business cycle with other group members
Group1	GER	GER, FRA, ITA, UK, SPA	GER, FRA, ITA	FRA, GER, SWE	FRA, SPA, GER
Group2	FRA		UK, SPA, NET	AUT, FIN, LUX	POL, CZE, HUN
Group3	ITA		POL, BEL, SWE	BEL, DEN, UK	UK, FIN, SLN
Group4	UK		AUT, POR, GRE	ITA, NET, CYP	IRE, SLK, LAT
Group5	SPA	NET, POL, BEL, SWE	ROM, CZE, DEN	IRE, SPA, MAL	AUT, DEN, SWE
Group6	NET, POL		FIN, HUN, IRE	GRE, POR, CZE	ITA, LUX, EST
Group7	BEL, SWE, AUT	AUT, POR, GRE	SLK, BUL, SLN	LAT, LIT, SLK	CYP, BEL, GRE
Group8	POR, GRE, ROM, CZE	ROM, CZE, DEN, FIN	LIT, LAT, LUX	EST, POL, SLN	NET, LIT, ROM
Group9	DEN, FIN, HUN, IRE, SLK, BUL, SLN, LIT, LAT, LUX, CYP, EST, MAL	HUN, IRE, SLK, BUL, SLN, LIT, LAT, LUX, CYP, EST, MAL	CYP, EST, MAL	BUL, HUN, ROM	POR, BUL, MAL

Probability of occupying a council seat in any period (percent):

	(1) Size 1	(2) Size 2	(3) Size 3	(4) Inflation	(5) Business cycle with other group members
Austria (AUT)	30.36	38.70	33.3	33.3	33.3
Belgium (BEL)	38.61	44.50	33.3	33.3	33.3
Denmark (DEN)	21.27	25.40	33.3	33.3	33.3
Finland (FIN)	17.21	20.50	33.3	33.3	33.3
France (FRA)	100.00	80.00	33.3	33.3	33.3
Germany (GER)	100.00	80.00	33.3	33.3	33.3
Greece (GRE)	25.62	30.50	33.3	33.3	33.3
Ireland (IRE)	11.37	18.50	33.3	33.3	33.3
Italy (ITA)	100.00	80.00	33.3	33.3	33.3

Luxembourg (LUX)	2.52	4.10	33.3	33.3
Netherlands (NET)	55.11	66.00	33.3	33.3
Portugal (POR)	25.78	30.70	33.3	33.3
Spain (SPA)	100.00	80.00	33.3	33.3
Sweden (SWE)	31.03	35.80	33.3	33.3
UK (UK)	100.00	80.00	33.3	33.3
Bulgaria (BUL)	7.62	12.40	33.3	33.3
Cyprus (CYP)	1.79	2.90	33.3	33.3
Czech Republic (CZE)	23.26	25.90	33.3	33.3
Estonia (EST)	1.71	2.80	33.3	33.3
Hungary (HUN)	16.83	20.10	33.3	33.3
Latvia (LAT)	2.60	4.20	33.3	33.3
Lithuania (LIT)	3.85	6.30	33.3	33.3
Malta (MAL)	0.67	1.10	33.3	33.3
Poland (POL)	44.89	53.70	33.3	33.3
Romania (ROM)	25.34	28.20	33.3	33.3
Slovakia (SLK)	8.04	13.10	33.3	33.3
Slovenia (SLN)	4.53	7.40	33.3	33.3

the overall size of the ECB Governing Council by allowing only a fraction of central bank governors to participate in meetings. Rotation schemes' ability to address the potential problems posed by enlargement while avoiding, at least in part, the political-feasibility problems associated with some of the other reform ideas make rotation schemes a likely candidate for ECB reform. In the following section we will discuss a number of more specific options for an ECB reform scenario involving a rotation scheme.

3.4   Rotation Schemes

Reflecting the decision-making costs argument, we will discuss in this section a number of rotation schemes under the assumption of an ECB Governing Council with fifteen members, with six Executive Board members joining nine central bank governors drawn from the population of all euro area member countries. A characteristic that rotation scenarios share with representation schemes is the necessity to *pool countries*. We assume a situation in which all of the current twenty-seven potential EU countries have joined the euro area. Based on the discussion in section 3.2, we have constructed groups on the basis of three criteria:

• size, that is, constructing groups that are homogenous with respect to the share of euro area GDP represented by each member to ensure that the ECB Governing Council reflects, to the greatest extent possible, the euro area

• inflation, that is, minimizing the average within-group standard deviation of inflation

• correlation of each member's business cycles with those of other members in the group, that is, maximizing the within-group business cycle correlation

Table 3.4 shows the outcomes of various rotation groupings and the probability under those groupings that any country would occupy a seat in the ECB's Governing Council, and table 3.5 reports the characteristics of the various rotation schemes we examined. All calculations for correlation with EU12 averages exclude the country for which the correlation is being calculated.

A good starting point is rotation on the basis of *size*. The groupings under this heading aim at selecting countries of similar GDP share. The

Table 3.5
Characteristics of the Various Rotation Schemes

Grouping	(1) Size 1	(2) Size 2	(3) Size 3	(4) Inflation	(5) Within-group business cycle	(6) ECB proposal[d]
1. Average GDP share represented	80.65	68.48	33.33	33.33	33.33	73.21
2. Minimum/maximum GDP share represented	78.9/81.8	58.5/76.7	25.2/44.5	6.4/66.6	11.3/64.4	61.1/84.9
3. Mismatch between economic and political weight[a]	7.77	10.27	17.18	17.18	17.18	17.63
Within-group unweighted averages						
4. Average within-group standard deviation of inflation	3.31	6.86	7.94	2.80	7.64	9.69
5. Average standard deviation of correlation with EU12[b]	0.06	0.18	0.20	0.18	0.09	0.22
6. Average within-group business cycle correlation[c]	0.62	0.29	0.19	0.23	0.41	0.26

Note: See the appendix for sources and methods. GDP shares are calculated as an average for 1990–2001. Average correlation is calculated over 1999–2001. Average inflation is for 1995–2001 to exclude the first transition years.
[a] Measured as the sum of the squared differences between economic and political weights.
[b] Excludes Bulgaria and Malta.
[c] Excluding the country itself.
[d] As of December 2002.

reason for grouping countries with similar GDP shares is that otherwise a rotation scheme could (with some positive probability) acciden-
tally select only smaller countries to represent their respective groups,
which would run against the idea of ensuring that the central bank
governors present on the ECB Governing Council mirror the euro area
as a whole. In other words, group selection by size can help ensure a
high "minimum" representation of euro area GDP. A crucial issue here
is whether we can accept a group consisting of one country only. In
option size 1 we assume that the Big Five (France, Germany, Italy,
Spain, and the United Kingdom) have a permanent seat on the council.
The size of the other groups under this option ranges from two (the
Netherlands and Poland) to thirteen (see column 1 in table 3.4). Within
each of these groups, there is *unequal rotation*, depending on the size
of the countries concerned. For instance, in the group that includes
Poland and the Netherlands, the latter country has a higher chance of
occupying a council seat in each period (55.11 percent) than the former
(44.89 percent).[21] Obviously, permanent council membership for the
large countries has the advantage that the area represented in the decision making of the ECB is very high. So from the perspective of minimizing the risk of distorted policymaking, this is clearly an attractive
option, as—on average—almost 81 percent of the euro area GDP is
represented (see column 1 of table 3.5). Table 3.5 also shows the minimum and maximum of the area represented (row 2). The minimum is
the share of the euro area represented if the smallest countries in any
group would be on the council at the same time. Likewise, the maximum is the area represented if the biggest countries of the nine groups
were all on the council simultaneously. For our first rotation scheme
the maximum and minimum figures are fairly similar (78.9 and 81.8
percent, respectively).

How does the example fare with regard to the ratio of political and
economic weights of central bank governors?[22] As figure 3.4 reveals,
except for the largest four countries, all twenty-seven central bank
governors would, in this rotation scenario, still hold a political weight
(i.e., vote share) that exceeded the economic weight of their respective
country. The mismatch would be substantially lower, however, in
terms of magnitude (cf. figure 3.2b). Another way to show the mismatch is the sum of the squared differences between the economic and
political weights. In calculating this measure, we assume that the
board casts its votes based on a GDP-weighted average of the euro

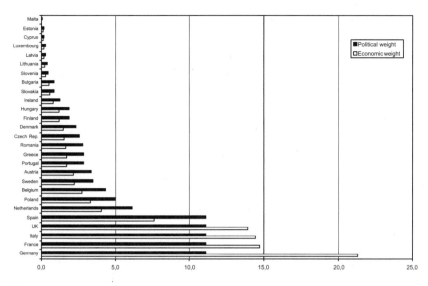

Figure 3.4
Economic and political weights with size-based grouping (option size 1).

area. This means that a country's political weight is determined by its own vote share as well as the board's vote share to the extent of the economic weight of that country in the euro area. The third row of table 3.5 shows the outcomes of this measure under the various rotation schemes that we discuss. It is clear that our first rotation scheme scores best (i.e., the mismatch between countries' economic and political weights is lowest under this scheme).

Group selection by size may, however, make groups heterogeneous along other dimensions. There is, for instance, reason to assume that business cycles are more closely correlated and *structural inflation* performance is more closely linked in some economic regions or within groups of countries of differing size. Indeed, the first column of table 3.5 shows that the average within-group standard deviation of inflation is 3.31, which is relatively high in comparison to that for other rotation schemes, despite the fact that five out of nine groups have a single member.

Furthermore, to maximize GDP representation in our rotation schemes, it is necessary to give a permanent seat to the Big Five. This would probably be politically unacceptable to a majority of the current EU member states. In *option size 2*, we therefore try to take political objections into account, while still securing sufficient representation of the euro area GDP on the council. In this scenario, all countries have to rotate, including the Big Five. We assume that the latter have to share four seats, and the four next-largest countries (Belgium, the Netherlands, Poland, and Sweden) have to share two seats. Each of the remaining three seats is shared among a group of countries: one group of three (Austria, Greece, and Portugal), another of four countries (Czech Republic, Denmark, Finland, and Romania) and a final group of the eleven remaining countries of the twenty-seven. Consequently, the GDP area represented on the council is somewhat lower (almost 69 percent) than in the previous option, and the minimum and maximum share represented are also lower: 58.5 and 76.7 percent, respectively (see column 2 of table 3.5). The mismatch between economic and political weights is somewhat higher than in the first scenario. Still, under this option the majority of the euro area, with respect to GDP, is represented on the Council at any time. As was to be expected, abolishing single-member groups yields a higher average within-group standard deviation of inflation (6.86). Likewise, the within-group standard deviation of business cycle correlation with EU12 is higher (0.18), and the average within-group business cycle correlation is lower (0.29), than in the first option.

Although this scenario takes as its starting point that all countries have to rotate, the rotation is still asymmetric, which may be hard for some EU members to accept. After all, the current ECB setup is based on equal treatment of all countries. In *option size 3*, we therefore assume equal rotation for all twenty-seven members. This leads to nine groups of equal size. Germany, France, and Italy are in one group, as are Spain, the Netherlands, and the United Kingdom. As a result, in this scenario, on average every central bank has a 33.3 percent probability of occupying a seat on the council. An obvious advantage of this approach is that all countries are treated in the same way with regard to council participation. By the same token, however, the average share of the euro area's GDP covered is, on average, only 33.33 percent, and the minimum and maximum shares represented are 25.2 and 44.5 percent, respectively. Thus, from the perspective of minimizing the risk of distorted policymaking, this is clearly not an attractive option. As figure 3.5 illustrates, under all groupings with equal rotation, the match between economic and political weights is less than under the grouping with unequal rotation based on size (option size 1). The sum of the squared differences between economic and political weights is substantially higher than under the previous rotation schemes.

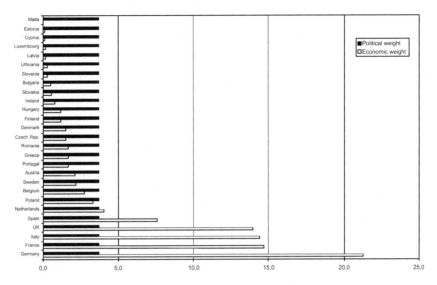

Figure 3.5
Economic and political weights in groupings with equal rotation.

In addition, the equal-rotation option based on size, although it ensures that groups are homogenous regarding the share of euro area GDP represented by each group member and thus secures a high minimum representation of euro area GDP, implies a rather high average within-group standard deviation of inflation and low business cycle correlation within the groups (see table 3.5). Heterogeneity along these lines could pose a number of problems for ECB decision making if country representatives paid at least some attention to national economic developments. The higher the within-group heterogeneity, the more likely it would be that the priorities of group representatives would change with each rotation of the group's voting right into new hands, possibly introducing unwelcome volatility into ECB decision making. Although this problem exists in size-based asymmetric rotation scenarios as well, it is amplified by the introduction of symmetric rotation into the scenario, because symmetric rotation increases the number of rotations and, thus, the number of national central bank governors that are involved in ECB decision making in any given period of time.

The final options we explore also take equal rotation as their starting points but try to improve the within-group characteristics. They are based in the first instance on minimization of the within-group standard deviation of inflation and in the second on the maximization of the within-group business cycle correlation. In other words, we group countries on the basis of similar inflation rates and business cycles. As before, because of the equal-rotation principle, rotation is based on nine groups of three countries. It is interesting to note that the first of these options, the *inflation* rotation scheme, results in groupings that (at first sight) could seem counter-intuitive to some. For instance, the Netherlands ends up in a group with Italy.[23] The average within-group business cycle correlation is somewhat higher in this scenario than under option size 3, but it is still rather low (0.23), which suggests that factors in addition to business cycle synchronization contribute to inflation differentials within our group of countries. On the other hand, the second of the two additional options we explore here, organizing groups on the basis of equal rotation with a view to maximization of the within-group *business cycle correlations*, yields a higher correlation (0.41) but results in a decidedly higher within-group heterogeneity with regard to inflation. As mentioned earlier, the first two reform options yield relatively high within-group business cycle correlations because they allow for asymmetric group sizes. Also note that the rotation scheme that takes business cycle correlations into account yields a relatively low standard deviation of business cycle correlation with the EU12, probably because under this scheme, countries that have a diverging business cycle vis-à-vis the EU12 are grouped together. The final two rotation options explored have very low minimum shares of the euro area represented (6.4 percent under the inflation rotation scheme and 11.3 percent under the business cycle correlation scheme).

To sum up, table 3.5 suggests that the assignment of countries to rotation groups involves a number of decisions and trade-offs. First, it is obvious that the representation of the euro area GDP suffers substantially if all countries are forced to rotate at an equal frequency. Equal rotation implies a higher degree of mismatch between economic and political weights than unequal rotation. Second, although it would seem that asymmetric rotation in combination with group selection by size goes a long way toward securing within-group homogeneity with regard to inflation and business cycle correlation, it has some costs as well. A comparison of the result for rotation schemes (3) to (5) shows that, holding rotation frequencies equal across countries and constant, group selection by size secures a relatively higher minimum representation of euro area GDP on the ECB Governing Council but also leads to a relatively higher within-group volatility for business cycle correlation and inflation. Third, there is an additional trade-off when group members are selected for rotation based on either of the last two schemes: Higher within-group business cycle coherence comes at the price of higher inflation dispersion and vice versa. Fourth, looking at average correlation with the EU12 business cycle across groups in rows (3) to (5), we find that selecting countries either by size or by inflation performance increases the similarity to the average business cycle.

The overall picture that emerges is broadly favorable for an asymmetric rotation scheme in the spirit of the first scenario explored. Although it does not aim at minimizing within-group inflation volatility or maximizing within-group business cycle correlation, an asymmetric rotation scenario that allows single-country groups fares almost as well on these criteria as rotation schemes (4) and (5). To the extent that political feasibility considerations would force all countries into rotation along the lines of scheme (2), however, or even into fully symmetric rotation as in schemes (3) to (5), the reform of the ECB decision-making framework faces a three-way trade-off among securing a sufficient representation of euro area GDP on the ECB Governing Council, homogeneity of inflation among group members, and comparable business cycle performance among members of the selected rotation groups.

3.5 The ECB Proposal

In late 2002, after the initial draft of this chapter was presented at the CESifo conference in Delphi, the ECB published its proposal for reform of the ECB after enlargement of the EMU, which will be considered by the EU Council in the spring of 2003. As in the rotation schemes discussed above, the ECB proposal limits the number of central bank governors who exercise a voting right. In contrast to reform options (1) to (3), however, the ECB puts this maximum at fifteen rather than nine. From a decision-making costs perspective, this may be considered a rather high number of voting members. It also reduces the voting weight of the Executive Board from 40 to less than 30 percent.

The ECB proposes that initially rotating voting rights will rotate among member states in two groups. Once the number of euro area member states reaches twenty-two, council seats will be assigned by rotation among countries in three groups. The ECB suggests that the assignment of central banks to the groups be based on a ranking of their share in the euro area according to a so-called composite indicator of representativeness. The principal component of this composite indicator would be the member state's GDP, with a weight of five-sixths, and the second would be the total assets of the aggregated balance sheet of monetary financial institutions (TABS-MFI) within the territory of the member state concerned, with a weight of one-sixth.[24]

In particular, the ECB proposes that the first group of countries will include the central bank governors from the five largest euro area member states according to the ranking of the representativeness indicator (the Big Five). This group will have four votes under the ECB proposal. The second group, with eight votes, will consist of half of all national central bank governors among the member states, selected from the corresponding number of subsequent positions in the ranking. The third group under the ECB proposal will be composed of the remaining national central bank governors. They will share three voting rights.

For purposes of comparing the proposal with our own schemes previously discussed, we will focus on the outcomes of the ECB proposal under the situation with twenty-seven members. Our calculations are based on a ranking of GDP only, as information on the second element of the representativeness indicator is not available yet. Based on these results, the membership of the first group (the Big Five) will remain the same as it has previously been conceived, and the second group will encompass the following countries: Austria, Belgium, Czech Republic, Denmark, Finland, Greece, Hungary, Ireland, the Netherlands, Poland, Portugal, Romania, Slovakia, and Sweden. The third group will then include the remaining eight countries of the twenty-seven.

The final column in table 3.5 compares the ECB proposal with the three size-based reform options (1) to (3) we examined in the previous section. Interestingly, the average share of GDP represented is quite high under the reform as proposed by the ECB, even somewhat higher (73 percent) than under reform option (2) (68 percent), which fared second best in the discussion in section 3.4 under the constraint that all council members rotate. In terms of within-group characteristics, however, reform option (2) outperforms the ECB proposal. The reason for the higher volatility of the ECB proposal is that there is a smaller number of groups in that proposal than in option (2), so the within-group variability will be higher. Furthermore, the mismatch between the economic and political weights of the countries is larger under the ECB proposal than in option (2). In part, the difference in the mismatch measures under the two reform options reflects the fact that the Executive Board has a smaller voting share in the ECP proposal than in our preferred option (40 versus less than 30 percent). As a result, the mismatch between economic and political weights under the ECB proposal is even bigger than under equal-rotation scenario (3).

In conclusion, the ECB proposal shows a remarkable resemblance to reform option (2), our preferred option for reform among those we examined in section 3.4. Both schemes are based on rotation, and the principle of one person, one vote applies to central banks with voting rights. In both proposals, the governors of the Big Five have a considerably larger chance of having the right to vote on council decisions than the other central bank governors. Under the ECB proposal for reform, the average share of GDP represented in the Governing Council of the ECB is slightly higher than in option (2). In terms of the mismatch between countries economic and political weight, however, our preferred reform scheme performs better than the ECB proposal, largely because of the larger number of groups and the stronger position of the Executive Board in the Governing Council suggested by reform option (2).

3.6 Concluding Comments

Enlargement will change the way monetary policy is made in the euro area. Within a few years, EU membership could more than double, with the majority of accession countries being small in economic terms compared to current members. In the absence of a reform of the ECB, such a significant but asymmetric expansion is likely to increase decision-making costs and to lead to a mismatch between the economic and political weights of national central banks on the ECB Governing Council. In this chapter we have discussed various options for reform, including the ECB proposal of late 2002. We have argued that, although centralization would be the first-best solution to the ECB's numbers problem in more than one way, a number of political and economic arguments speak against it. The second-best solution, we have argued, is to match countries' economic size with their voting power on the council. One way to implement this solution, even if an imperfect one in practice, would be to introduce a rotation scheme for national central bank governors that takes economic differences among the member countries into account. Alternative reform options to improve the match between member countries' economic and political power include forms of representation (including the possibility of introducing regional central banks encompassing multiple national

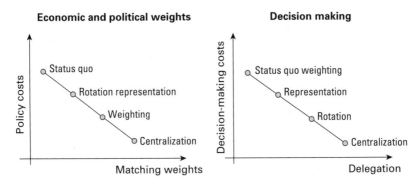

Figure 3.6
Costs of status quo and reform scenarios—a stylized view. *Policy costs* entail deviations from the first-best policy due to a mismatch between the political and economic weights of central bank governors on the ECB Governing Council, and *matching weights* involves the reduction of this mismatch. *Decision-making costs* are as defined in section 3.2; *delegation* describes the process of delegating voting power from central bank governors to (fewer) delegates through various institutional means. The assumed negative (but not necessarily linear) relations in both graphs have been explored in previous sections. The specific positioning of the various reform scenarios should be interpreted in qualitative terms. *Source:* Berger 2002, table 4.

central banks) and weighted voting. But although both vote weighting and representation could ensure that ECB Governing Council members carry a political weight roughly in proportion to their economic size, the large number of policymakers involved under these reform scenarios (directly or indirectly) raises concerns about their effectiveness at solving the problems they are designed to solve. Approaches that aim at the centralization of decision-making power or its reallocation by means of an asymmetric rotation scheme promise to address not only the possible wedge between the economic and political weights of council members, but also the issue of decision-making costs. Figure 3.6 illustrates these arguments by comparing the relative merits of the reform options discussed above with regard to decision-making costs and the possible problems stemming from the mismatch between political and economic power of euro area member countries.

To be sure, alternative reform scenarios to those examined in this chapter might be imagined, and many of the more detailed institutional design questions involved can be answered in more than one way. For instance, a crucial question is whether rotation should take place within a symmetric or an asymmetric (size-based) framework. In an equal-rotation scheme, countries present on the ECB Governing

Council represent, on average, just 50 percent of the euro area GDP; this is clearly not an attractive feature. We therefore prefer a system with asymmetric rotation, be it a system with a permanent seat for the five largest countries or a system in which all countries rotate, but large countries rotate with a lower frequency than the small countries.

The reform proposal presented by the ECB in late 2002 also comprises an asymmetric rotation scheme. Although the ECB proposal performs well with regard to many of the criteria discussed in the chapter, it is not without drawbacks. In particular, the proposal foresees an enlargement of the council, which is not attractive from a decision-making costs perspective. It also implies a reduction in the voting power of the ECB Executive Board. Notwithstanding these drawbacks, the ECB proposal goes a long way toward addressing the fundamental problems of euro area enlargement.

Appendix: Data Sources and Methods of Calculation

The data set we used in this chapter comes from a variety of sources, but the main source is the International Monetary Fund's International Financial Statistics (IFS) ⟨http://imfStatistics.org⟩. From the IFS, we took data on industrial production and inflation for most countries. Another important source is the Groningen Growth and Development Centre (GGDC) Total Economy Database ⟨www.eco.rug.nl/ggdc⟩.

For industrial production, we relied on monthly data for 1985–2001 for the current fifteen EU members and 1990–2001 for the twelve accession countries. For a number of accession countries, no data are available in IFS, or only for a subset of the 1990–2001 period. Also, a number of these countries do not report seasonally adjusted figures. First of all, no data are available in IFS for Bulgaria, Estonia, Latvia, Malta, and Slovakia; for Poland, the data stop at the end of 1995. The Central Statistical Bureau of Latvia reports (seasonally adjusted) industrial production on a monthly basis from 1995 onward. The Statistical Office of Estonia does not publish long time series for industrial production, but industrial sales are available on a monthly basis from 1994 onward. Using sales instead of production eliminates part of the cyclical behavior, since inventory adjustments are not taken into account in sales figures, so the figures for Estonia should be regarded with caution. Finally, data for Slovakia and a longer time series for Poland are available from the Vienna Institute for International Economic Studies (WIIW). The WIIW also reports data for Bulgaria, but our (visual) inspection of this series raised questions on its reliability. The very rapid inflation and the subsequent problems with deflating industrial production provide a further basis for doubting the reliability of the data in this series. We therefore dropped this series and do not report any business cycle correlations for Bulgaria, nor do we do so for Malta, since we could not find any data on industrial production for this country.

Next, we seasonally adjusted the industrial production figures for Cyprus, the Czech Republic, Estonia, Hungary, Lithuania, Poland, Romania, and Slovakia using the Census X12 procedure from the U.S. Census Bureau as reproduced in EViews 4.0. In the case of Ireland, the IFS data reveal a large structural break around 1995. To solve this problem, we took the monthly industrial production figures from the Irish Central Statistics Office, which run from 1995 onward, and applied the growth rates from IFS to all the months before January 1995. Finally, Portugal showed anomalous industrial production figures and a gap in the series between July 1994 and February 1995. We interpolated linearly to obtain data for these months. This eliminates cyclicality, but since the interpolated data are used only for a short period, our use of these data is unlikely to pose large problems. Table 3A.1 shows the beginning and end dates of our data series for industrial production in each of the twenty-seven member and accession countries.

We also formed a weighted euro area index in which we chose June 1995 as 100 and extrapolated forward and backward using the GDP-weighted growth rates of the twelve euro area countries. We chose to use this method for the whole period, since our method yields somewhat different results than the official series, which is published only from January 1999 onward. Possible reasons for the difference in results are our use of purchasing-power parities (PPPs) to weight the individual countries and of GDP weights instead of value added in manufacturing weights. However, the differences are not large, and this ensures comparability with the EU12 indices, which we also calculate excluding each country consecutively.

To decompose these series into a trend and a cyclical component, we filtered them using a Hodrick-Prescott filter with smoothing factor $\lambda = 14{,}400$ (the suggested value for monthly data). To minimize the endpoint problems present with all filters, we forecast the series for a full year assuming all series follow an AR(3) process. We used the trend series to calculate the cyclical component in each month as one

Table 3A.1
Starting and ending dates for monthly data on industrial production

EU15 members			Accession members		
Country	First month	Last month	Country	First month	Last month
Austria	Jan 85	Feb 01	Bulgaria	n.a.	n.a.
Belgium	Jan 85	Dec 00	Cyprus	Jan 90	Dec 01
Denmark	Jan 85	Dec 01	Czech Republic	Jan 90	Dec 01
Finland	Jan 85	Dec 01	Estonia[a]	Jan 94	Dec 01
France	Jan 85	Dec 01	Hungary	Jan 90	Dec 01
Germany	Jan 85	Dec 01	Latvia	Jan 95	Dec 01
Greece	Jan 85	Jan 02	Lithuania	Jan 93	Dec 01
Ireland	Jan 85	Dec 02	Malta	n.a.	n.a.
Italy	Jan 85	May 02	Poland	Jan 90	Jun 01
Luxembourg	Jan 85	Jul 00	Romania	May 90	Dec 01
Netherlands	Jan 85	Dec 02	Slovakia	Jan 93	Dec 01
Portugal	Jan 85	Nov 00	Slovenia	Dec 91	Dec 01
Spain	Jan 85	Dec 02			
Sweden	Jan 85	Jan 00			
United Kingdom	Jan 85	Dec 02			

[a] Data on industrial sales rather than industrial production. n.a. = not available.

plus the percentage deviation from trend in that month. Pairwise correlations for each country couple (including the euro area) were then calculated. We also calculated a set of correlations for the euro area countries, in which we excluded the country in question from the euro area index.

Inflation was derived as the annualized average monthly change in the Consumer Price Index (CPI). All data on the CPI are from the IFS. We followed a procedure similar to that used for industrial production to calculate euro area inflation before 1999 and EU15 and EU27 inflation for the whole period.

Our main source on GDP is the GGDC Total Economy Database, which includes data on (real) GDP for a large number of countries converted at PPPs to U.S. dollars. Since conversion to U.S. dollars using PPPs eliminates differences in the relative price level of countries, the resulting GDP levels can safely be compared. If we were to convert the GDP levels into a common currency using exchange rates, comparison of the GDP levels would generally not be possible. The GGDC database does not cover all countries in our sample, and in particular, a number of the accession countries (Luxembourg, Cyprus, Estonia, Latvia, Lithuania and Malta) are not covered. For those countries, we took GDP in current and constant prices from the IFS. We converted these from national currency to U.S. dollars using PPPs as published by the OECD (2002). Since these PPPs are for 1999, whereas the PPPs for the other countries are for 1996, we used the change in the country's price level relative to that in the U.S. to calculate 1996 PPPs. These were then used to calculate GDP in U.S. dollars. GDP levels for the euro area, the EU15, and the hypothetical EU27 were then calculated by summing the GDP levels of the relevant countries over each of the years. In constructing euro area, EU12, and EU15 industrial production and inflation, we used the GDP weight for a specific year for each month in that year.

Notes

The views expressed in this chapter are those of the authors and should not be interpreted as those of the institutions with which they are affiliated. We thank Daniel Gros and participants in the CESifo conference "Managing EU Enlargement" in Delphi 13–14 September 2002 and in the seminar at DG EcFin of the European Commission on 19 November 2002 for helpful comments and suggestions.

1. Since EMU membership is part of the *acquis communautaire* of the EU, accession countries will join EMU and the European System of Central Banks (ESCB) as they join the EU. EMU and ESCB membership do not, however, necessarily imply euro area membership, as countries wanting to adopt the euro must fulfill the Maastricht criteria.

2. Indeed, some critics of the ECB argued that its decentralized nature was a design flaw right from the beginning. For instance, *The Economist* ("Euro Towers or Fawlty Towers" 1998) stated that "[t]he Governing Council is supposed to set interest rates according to conditions in the euro area as a whole, but there is a risk that national governors will be unduly influenced by conditions in their home country. Small countries may also carry undue weight in the system.... A weak centre, combined with strong national interests, could create conflicts that undermine the whole system's credibility."

3. See Berger 2002 for a somewhat more extensive treatment of the issues covered in section 3.2.

4. We assume that the nationality of members of the Executive Board does not influence the political weight of a country.

5. See Berger 2002 for a more extensive analysis of the impact that enlargement will have on the mismatch between economic and political weights.

6. Note that using population rather than GDP as a benchmark would not change the results significantly.

7. Gros and Hefeker (2002) analyze differences in monetary transmission in the context of monetary policymaking within the euro area.

8. Recently, Heinemann and Huefner (2002) have estimated reaction functions for the ECB. As there are no voting records for the ECB Governing Council, these authors had to rely on indirect ways to examine whether diverging economic developments in the euro area have affected ECB policymaking. In their ordered probit model, these authors find that the difference between euro area average and median of the inflation and output gap is significantly different from zero, albeit only at the 10 percent level.

9. Eichengreen and Ghironi (2001) use an empirical growth model based on data from the 1980s and 1990s to predict future growth for a set of accession countries that includes Turkey but excludes Bulgaria, Cyprus, and Malta. In a panel study, Crespo-Cuaresma, Dimitz, and Ritzberger-Grünwaldz (2002) find the length of EU membership to have a significant positive effect on economic growth, which is relatively higher for poorer countries. Havrylyshyn (2001) surveys the available empirical evidence on growth during transition.

10. Most studies concede that Balassa-Samuelson effects, although quantitatively important, cannot explain the entire difference in structural inflation between accession and euro area countries.

11. The Balassa-Samuelson effect is often argued as a reason that accession countries may find it difficult to meet simultaneously the Maastricht criteria on inflation and exchange rate stability. See, for instance, Szapary 2000.

12. A very different estimation procedure has been followed by Pelkmans, Gros, and Ferrer (2000). These authors have based their estimation on relative price levels in accession countries compared to that in current EMU member countries rather than on productivity growth differentials. Their results show on average an inflation differential of 3.8 percentage points between the accession countries and the euro area average because of estimated differences in the price levels.

13. See the appendix for further details and sources of the data used.

14. The weighted averages of the demand and supply shocks coefficients of correlation are 0.24 and 0.52 for the euro area countries and 0.13 and 0.11 for the accession countries (Malta and Cyprus excluded).

15. Berger (2002) provides a more formal discussion of these reform considerations. See also Baldwin et al. 2000, Baldwin et al. 2001, and Eichengreen and Ghironi 2001 concerning ECB reform.

16. The advantages of a stronger role for the centrally nominated ECB Executive Board were also discussed in the literature on the optimal institutional design of the ECB before the (virtual) euro was introduced in 1999. See, among others, von Hagen and Süppel 1994, Lohmann 1997, and Lohmann 1998; also compare Bindseil 2001. In light of the enlargement discussion, Baldwin et al. (2001) argue for full centralization, pointing to the increase in decision-making costs implied by euro area enlargement.

17. This is akin to some of the functions the General Council of the European System of Central Banks performs today. The General Council will exist as long as some EU countries remain outside the euro area. See figure 3.1.

18. Obviously, if none of the council members showed a regional bias in their decision making to begin with, bringing political and economic weights of national central bank governors in line would not hurt the euro area–wide perspective of the council either.

19. See Berger 2002 and chapter 2 for further details.

20. The organization of the International Monetary Fund's board is an example of unrestricted mandates. Even though all directors operate de facto in close collaboration with their constituencies, the Fund's Articles of Agreement do not require them de jure to consult their constituents or seek their approval before casting a vote on the board.

21. These weights would be adjusted at certain intervals to reflect changes in countries' relative GDP size.

22. Political weights have been computed by multiplying the rotation frequencies by the overall number of council seats. Based on nine selected governors and six board members, the ECB Governing Council would have fifteen members. The rotation frequencies are defined in equivalents of a permanent council seat. A frequency of 0.5, for example, indicates that a particular governor would participate in half of all ECB Governing Council meetings (e.g., the governor would occupy a council seat every second year or participate in every second meeting, depending on the specific implementation of the scheme).

23. EU commissioner Fritz Bolkenstein, who at the time of the Netherlands' decision regarding EMU membership was the leader of the liberal party in the Dutch parliament, argued that the Netherlands should not join the EMU if Italy was allowed in, given the weak fundamentals in Italy.

24. The measure is likely to favor member countries with a relatively large financial sector and a small GDP share, like Luxembourg.

References

Artis, M. J., and W. Zhang. 1999. "Further Evidence on the International Business Cycle and the ERM: Is There a European Business Cycle?" *Oxford Economic Papers* 51: 120–132.

Backé, P., J. Fidrmuc, T. Reininger, and F. Schardax. 2002. "Price Dynamics in Central and Eastern European EU Accession Countries." Working paper no. 61, Oesterreichische Nationalbank, Vienna.

Baldwin, R., E. Berglof, F. Giavazzi, and M. Widgren. 2000. "EU Reforms for Tomorrow's Europe." Discussion paper no. 2623, Centre for Economic Policy Research, London.

Baldwin, R., E. Berglof, F. Giavazzi, and M. Widgren. 2001. "Preparing the ECB for Enlargement." Policy paper no. 6, Centre for Economic Policy Research, London.

Berger, H. 2002. "The ECB and Euro-Area Enlargement." Working paper no. 02/175, International Monetary Fund, Washington, DC.

Berger, H., and J. de Haan. 1999. "A State within a State? An Event Study on the Bundesbank." *Scottish Journal of Political Economy* 46, no. 1: 17–39.

Berger, H., and J. de Haan. 2002. "Are Small Countries too Powerful within the ECB?" *Atlantic Economic Journal* 30, no. 3: 1–20.

Bindseil, U. 2001. "A Coalition-Form Analysis of the 'One Country-One Vote' Rule in the Governing Council of the European Central Bank." *International Economic Journal* 15, no. 1: 141–164.

Blanchard, O., and D. Quah. 1989. "The Dynamic Effects of Aggregate Demand and Supply Disturbances." *American Economic Review* 79, no. 4: 655–673.

Coricelli, F., and B. Jazbec. 2001. "Real Exchange Rate Dynamics in Transition Economies." Discussion paper no. 2869, Centre for Economic Policy Research, London.

Crespo-Cuaresma, J., M. Dimitz, and D. Ritzberger-Grünwaldz. 2002. "Growth, Convergence and EU Membership." Austrian National Bank, Vienna. Mimeographed.

De Broeck, M., and T. Sløk. 2001. "Interpreting Real Exchange Rate Movements in Transition Countries." Working paper no. 01/56, International Monetary Fund, Washington, DC.

Deutsche Bundesbank. 1992. Monthly report. August. Frankfurt.

Égert, B. 2002a. "Estimating the Impact of the Balassa-Samuelson Effect on Inflation and the Real Exchange Rate during the Transition." Economic Systems 26, no. 1: 1–16.

Égert, B. 2002b. "Investigating the Balassa-Samuelson Hypothesis in the Transition. Do We Understand What We See? A Panel Study." Economics of Transition 10, no. 2: 273–309.

Eichengreen, B. 1992. "Designing a Central Bank for Europe: A Cautionary Tale from the Early Years of the Federal Reserve System." In Establishing a Central Bank in Europe and Lessons from the US, ed. M. Canzoneri, V. Grilli, and R. Masson, 13–40. Cambridge: Cambridge University Press.

Eichengreen, B., and F. Ghironi. 2001. "EMU and Enlargement." University of California at Berkeley. Mimeographed.

Eijffinger, S. C. W., and J. de Haan. 2000. European Monetary and Fiscal Policy. Oxford: Oxford University Press.

"Euro Towers or Fawlty Towers?" 1998. Economist (October 31): 85–86.

European Central Bank (ECB). 1999. "The Institutional Framework of the European System of Central Banks." Monthly Bulletin (July): 55–63.

European Union. 1997. "Treaty of Amsterdam Amending the Treaty on the European Union, the Treaties Establishing the European Communities and Related Acts." Official Journal C340, 10 November, Brussels.

Eurostat. 2001. "Candidate Countries: Labour Productivity Levels and Remuneration Levels Just over 40% of EU Average." News release no. 55.

Fidrmuc, J., and I. Korhonen. 2001. "Similarity of Supply and Demand Shocks between the Euro Area and the CEECs." Discussion paper no. 14, Bank of Finland Institute for Economics in Transition, Helsinki.

Fischer, S., R. Sahay, and C. Vegh. 1998a. "From Transition to Market: Evidence and Growth Prospects." Working paper no. 98/52, International Monetary Fund, Washington, DC.

Fischer, S., R. Sahay, and C. Vegh. 1998b. "How Far Is Eastern Europe from Brussels?" Working paper no. 98/53, International Monetary Fund, Washington, DC.

Friedman, M., and A. J. Schwartz. 1963. A Monetary History of the United States, 1867–1960. Princeton: Princeton University Press.

Gros, D., and C. Hefeker. 2002. "One Size Must Fit All: National Divergences in a Monetary Union." German Economic Review 3, no. 3: 247–262.

Havrylyshyn, O. 2001. "Recovery and Growth in Transition: A Decade of Evidence." *IMF Staff Papers* 48: 53–87.

Halpern, L., and C. Wyplosz. 2001. "Economic Transformation and Real Exchange Rates in the 2000s: The Balassa-Samuelson Connection." Mimeographed.

Heinemann, F., and F. P. Huefner. 2002. "Is the View from the Eurotower Purely European? National Divergence and ECB Interest Rate Policy." Centre for European Economic Research, Mannheim. Mimeographed.

International Monetary Fund (IMF). 2002. International financial statistics. August.

Inklaar, R., and J. de Haan. 2001. "Is There Really a European Business Cycle? A Comment." *Oxford Economic Papers* 53: 215–220.

Jakab, Z., and M. Kovács. 1999. "Determinants of Real Exchange Rate Fluctuations in Hungary." Working paper no. 1999/6, National Bank of Hungary, Budapest.

Lohmann, S. 1997. "Partisan Control of the Money Supply and Decentralized Appointment Powers." *European Journal of Political Economy* 13: 225–246.

Lohmann, S. 1998. "Federalism and Central Bank Independence: The Politics of German Monetary Policy, 1957–1992." *World Politics* 50: 401–446.

Meade, E., and D. N. Sheets. 2002. "Regional Influences on U.S. Monetary Policy: Some Implications for Europe." Centre for Economic Performance discussion paper no. 523, London School of Economics.

Organisation for Economic Cooperation and Development (OECD). 2002. "Purchasing Power Parities and Real Expenditures, 1999 Benchmark Year." Paris.

Pelkmans, J., D. Gros, and J. Ferrer. 2000. "Long-Run Economic Aspects of the European Union's Eastern Enlargement." Working paper no. 109, Netherlands Scientific Council for Government Policy.

Rother, C. P. 2000. "The Impact of Productivity Differentials on Inflation and the Real Exchange Rate: An Estimation of the Balassa-Samuelson Effect in Slovenia." In *Republic of Slovenia*, Country Report no. 00/56, 26–39. Washington, DC: International Monetary Fund.

Sinn, H. W., and M. Reutter. 2001. "The Minimum Inflation for Euroland." Working paper no. 8085, National Bureau of Economic Research, Cambridge, MA.

Szapary, G. 2000. "Maastricht and the Choice of the Exchange Rate Regime in Transition Countries during the Run-up to EMU." Working paper no. 7, National Bank of Hungary, Budapest.

von Hagen, J., and J. Süppel. 1994. "Central Bank Constitutions for Federal Monetary Unions." *European Economic Review* 38: 774–782.

Comments

Alex Cukierman

The recent decision of the European Council to admit ten Eastern European countries into the EU, and by implication into the EMU, transforms the issue of reform of decision-making institutions at the (ECB) from a pure academic exercise into a practical policy issue. The chapter by Berger, de Haan, and Inklaar presents a welcome systematic evaluation of the trade-offs that will have to be faced at the ECB in view of enlargement. The basic problem is that under the current institutional structure, the Governing Council of the ECB, which is composed of the six members of the ECB Executive Board plus all the governors of the national central banks (NCBs) participating in the euro area (for a current total of eighteen members) may increase to as many as thirty-three members. Such a number appears excessive if the council is to maintain its ability to make efficient and timely decisions. Berger et al. propose a council of fifteen members. This number appears to strikes a reasonable balance between the need for representation of different countries in the euro area and the need for decision-making efficacy of the ECB Governing Council.

Given a fifteen-member council, there is a basic tension between the (politically motivated), principle of equal vote shares for each of the council members laid down in the Maastricht Treaty and the need to reflect the fact that countries within the euro area differ widely from one another in terms of both economic and financial size. Under the current system the principle of equal vote shares leads to substantial discrepancies between the voting rights of the NCB governors and the economic size of the countries they represent. Berger et al. refer to this discrepancy as a wedge between political and economic weights and quantify it by constructing a measure of the aggregate discrepancy between the vote share of each country on the Governing Council and its share in the combined GDP of the euro area. Obviously, this discrepancy is already sizable today, with only eighteen council members. Some of the centrifugal forces exercised by the NCB governors are currently mitigated by the non-negligible voting share of the Executive Board (one-third), amplified by the permanent presence of its members at the ECB headquarters in Frankfurt. But if and when the number of council members increases to thirty-three, the share of votes of the Executive Board will decrease to less than 20 percent and the likelihood that economically small countries will have political weights substantially greater than their economic weights increases, as illustrated by figure 3.2.

As the chapter clarifies, there are several options for bringing economic and decision-making power on the Governing Council more in line with one another. One is to increase the vote share of the Executive Board; another is to create groups of countries, with each group having one representative on the council, or to continue with the current system of one vote to each NCB governor on the council and to achieve better balance between economic size and voting shares by means of rotation in voting rights. Although the first option is desirable on efficiency grounds, it would require a fundamental adjustment in the Treaty of Maastricht. Such an adjustment is likely to lead to a reconsideration of other items in the charter of the ECB. This would be politically unwise so soon after the creation of the ECB, since it might endanger the hard-won level of long-run nominal stability in the euro area.

After some discussion of the relative merits of those three systems, the chapter finally opts for the last method of sharing power and evaluates alternative schemes for rotating voting shares among members of country groups. Weighted rotation appears a reasonable compromise between maintaining the efficacy of the Governing Council's decision-making process and preserving sufficient involvement of individual countries governors' in the decision-making process at the ECB. Admittedly, under rotation schemes, large countries will have voting rights over longer periods than small countries will. But the fact that representatives of all countries, even if small, will occasionally be in positions of responsibility is likely to contribute to a feeling of collective responsibility and to enhance the culture of long-run nominal stability in the euro area.

In addition to the criterion of matching economic weight with decision-making power, the chapter proposes two other criteria for evaluating the desirability of alternative rotation schemes. One is the degree of business cycle coherence across the countries represented on the Governing Council, and the other is the cross-sectional distribution of inflation rates across countries. Although Berger et al.'s simulations of the values of those two indicators for alternative rotation schemes are interesting and informative, I doubt that the indicators should be used as criteria for restructuring the ECB for a number of reasons. First, one of the objectives of the Maastricht Treaty, as reflected in the Maastricht criteria, is convergence of inflation rates. Taking the existing discrepancy of inflation rates between the euro block and the ten Eastern European prospective members as a criterion for the choice of rotation scheme is in contradiction to the principle of inflation convergence. It may introduce, following enlargement, an inflation bias into the euro area through the back door. Second, even if we abstract from this argument, the cross-country correlation among inflation rates is likely to change because of enlargement. Hence pre-enlargement inflation correlations are likely to carry little information as a guide for the choice of rotation schemes in the post-enlargement era.

To a lesser extent this argument also applies to the cross-country business cycle correlations. Entry of the ten Eastern European countries into the EU is likely to change their patterns of production and of specialization, at least in the longer run. This will alter the cross-country business cycle correlations as well. Under the presumption that it is undesirable to adjust the institutional structure of the ECB too often, it appears therefore that the current business cycle correlations are largely irrelevant for the choice of rotation scheme.

The chapter argues that since, because of the Balassa-Samuelson effect, the relative price of non-tradables in the prospective new members of EMU is likely to increase over time, one should allow for the possibility of higher average inflation in those countries. Again, there is a risk in this approach, since it implies that relative price changes that are expected to take place over the long run in the economies of the Eastern European prospective members might be accommodated to some extent by a general nominal expansion in the enlarged euro area. I doubt therefore that this consideration should be allowed to have much effect on the choice of rotation scheme.

Recently the ECB circulated a press release that outlines its official position on possible restructuring of its decision-making institutions following enlargement (ECB 2002). Like Berger et al., the ECB proposes to achieve a better match between voting and economic shares by means of rotation while preserving the principle of one vote for each voting council member.[1] But the ECB proposal envisages a council of twenty-one voting members: fifteen NCB governors plus the six members of the Executive Board. This number appears to be on the high side. A total of fifteen voting council members, as proposed by Berger et al., appears more appropriate for efficient committee work.

The ECB also proposes that all NCB governors, including those from the member countries that do not exercise voting rights, will continue to participate in the discussions of the Governing Council and attend its meetings in a personal and independent capacity. This feature of the ECB proposal strikes me as a very good idea for several reasons. First, it is likely to facilitate the building of consensus and to enhance continuity in the decision-making process in spite of rotation. Second, it is likely to contribute to a better internal flow of information and generally to strengthen the norm of collective responsibility for stability in the euro area as a whole, in spite of possibly divergent interests due to asynchronization in business cycles and other reasons. Finally, it may also contribute to a smoother transmission to individual countries' levels of the stance of monetary policy decided upon by the Governing Council.

A useful feature that might be added to the above stipulation that nonvoting NCB governors will continue to participate in council meetings and discussions is that all NCB governors (voting and nonvoting) should generally have free access at all times to the research output of the ECB, as well as to that of the research departments of individual countries' central banks. This type of information sharing enhances transparency within the system and is likely to increase the proportion of ECB decisions that are based on professional considerations rather than on political motives. Effective decision making depends not only on the weight of the ECB center, as represented by the Executive Board, in comparison to that of the NCB governors, but also on the effectiveness of continuous internal communications, and on clear understanding and consensus about what monetary policy can and cannot do. Free mutual access to central bank research departments in the euro area can significantly contribute to the building and maintenance of such a long-run consensus.

As a criterion for choice of rotation scheme, the ECB press release gives a positive weight also to the relative size of financial development of each country, as measured by total assets of the aggregate balance sheet of the country's monetary and financial institutions. In my view this makes a lot of sense, as one of the main costs of inflation is proportional to the size of nominal financial assets in the economy. Thus if the ECB allows euro inflation to increase by 1 percent, the cost to countries with a higher share of financial assets is higher. The representatives of those countries should therefore be given an appropriately higher decision-making weight in the Governing Council of the post-enlargement ECB. Such a strategy is also likely to have a positive externality for the entire euro area, because central bankers in countries with higher shares of financial assets are likely to be more conservative and therefore to have a lower inflation bias. Hence, the long-run, post-enlargement euro area inflation bias is likely to be smaller when decision-making power on the Governing Council is allocated also on the basis of the share of financial assets.

Let me conclude this comment by voicing a warning. The Treaty of Maastricht makes the ECB responsible for achieving one main objective, price stability, but the treaty does not require the ECB to engage in stabilization of output. Admittedly, the statement in the treaty that, without prejudice to its main objective, the ECB should support the economic policies of the EC can be construed as opening the door for stabilization of output or "flexible inflation targeting." But many among the drafters of the treaty might not agree with this interpretation. In spite of this, current consensus, as reflected, inter alia, in the Berger et al. chapter, appears to be that the ECB should make some contribution to the stabilization of output in the Euro area.

Following enlargement, this point of view may put the primary objective of the ECB at some risk for at least two reasons. First, as discussed in the chapter, because of the Balassa-Samuelson effect, the ten or twelve new entrants are likely to be more inflationary than current members in the long run. Second, in spite of very substantial increases in legal independence in the former socialist economies during the 1990s, the evidence regarding the effectiveness of this institutional device in bringing inflation down to the levels of the EMU is still mixed.[2]

Excessive emphasis on stabilization of output may therefore raise the inflation bias, following enlargement, through the back door. This consideration is amplified by the fact that, following enlargement, the euro area will be even more vulnerable than now to the free-rider problems inherent in its federative structure. Perhaps the time has come to think about shifting more of the burden of output stabilization to other instruments.

Notes

1. Unlike Berger, de Haan, and Inklaar, the ECB does not use either business cycle or inflation correlations across countries as a criterion for the choice of rotation scheme.

2. One reason is that the discrepancy between actual and legal independence is higher in the former socialist economies than in the euro area countries. See Cukierman, Miller, and Neyapti 2002 for details.

References

Cukierman, A., G. P. Miller, and B. Neyapti. 2002. "Central Bank Reform, Liberalization and Inflation in Transition Economies—An International Perspective." *Journal of Monetary Economics* 49 (March): 237–264.

European Central Bank (ECB). 2002. "Governing Council Prepares for Enlargement." Press release. December 20.

4   Who Needs an External Anchor?

Daniel Gros

4.1   Introduction

It is well known that highly indebted countries, or countries with weak fiscal institutions, can fall into a low credibility trap. This occurs when a government loses credibility in the eyes of the financial markets and is forced to pay a risk premium in the form of higher interest rates. The higher debt service burden that results, if inflation is kept low, makes it even more likely that authorities will abandon efforts to stabilize the situation and attempt to reduce the real value of the debt through a surprise inflation. This further increases the risk premium demanded by financial markets and can lead to a spiral of increasing interest rates until the government caves in and produces the inflation the market expects.

A country in such a situation has an interest in using an external anchor. For Central and Eastern European countries, the obvious candidate for such an anchor would be the euro, given that most of their external trade is with the euro area. Some of these countries (e.g., Estonia, Bulgaria, and Lithuania) have already de facto joined the euro area by linking their money via a currency board to the deutsche mark, or now the euro. For all the others that are also candidates for membership in the EU, a key question that remains on the table is when to enter the euro area as well. The orthodox approach to the issue of EMU membership is that countries should converge gradually first and can join the euro area only once they satisfy the Maastricht criteria on inflation and public finance. This approach, however, misses the point that the weaker countries would actually gain more from joining the EMU than countries that have already achieved price stability on their own. Fulfilment of the Maastricht criteria can be reasonably required of countries that want to have a seat on the Governing Council of the

ECB, but this should not prevent weaker countries from considering adoption of the euro unilaterally, either via a currency board (as in Estonia and Bulgaria) or via full euroization, under which euro notes and coins are fully substituted for the domestic currency (which became feasible in 2002), as discussed in Emerson and Gros 1999.

The purpose of this chapter is to show that the standard model used to explain why a country with a credibility problem might benefit from an external anchor can actually lead to the result that the relationship between the strength of fiscal institutions (in terms of their ability to sustain price stability) and the interest in joining the euro area is not monotonic. Very strong countries might benefit (as assumed under the orthodox convergence approach), but very weak countries would also benefit and should thus contemplate a different, unilateral approach.

The standard optimum currency area (OCA) approach stresses different considerations, for example, the importance of asymmetric shocks. This chapter shows that the standard OCA approach can be thought of as constituting a baseline: Countries with fewer asymmetric shocks have a stronger interest in pegging their exchange rates.[1] The public-finance arguments stressed here present an additional consideration that should also be taken into account. It remains true that, ceteris paribus, that is, for the same level of asymmetric shocks, both countries with very high and those with very low levels of public debt might have an interest in pegging their currencies to an external anchor.

The remainder of this chapter is structured as follows: the next section presents the model employed in the chapter. This is followed in section 4.3 by an examination of the equilibrium. The relationship between the interest in an external anchor and the level of public debt is then discussed in section 4.4. Section 4.5 describes briefly how an inefficient fiscal policy that allows special-interest groups to gain at the expense of society can lead to excessive inflation and shows how a country's degree of inefficiency influences its interest in adopting the euro. Section 4.6 concludes.

4.2   The Model

The model used in this chapter is entirely conventional. The starting point is a standard social-loss function, L_t, given by

$$L_t = [\alpha q_t^2 + p_t^2], \qquad \alpha \geq 0, \tag{1}$$

where p_t stands for the inflation rate and q_t stands for tax revenues as a percentage of GDP, which is equivalent to the average tax rate. High taxes and high inflation create distortions and are thus socially costly. The parameter α indicates the *relative* weight of taxes in the social-loss function. A high α could be interpreted to mean that the country's tax collection system is not efficient, that is, that it causes high distortion costs for a given revenue. The experience in Central and Eastern Europe has shown that there are indeed great differences from country to country in the ability raise taxes. In Russia, to take an extreme example, until recently, the government was not even able to raise 15 percent of GDP, whereas in Estonia government revenues amount to over 30 percent of GDP.[2] At this point it is assumed that the government reflects accurately the preferences of society in setting taxes and inflation.

The authorities in a particular country can determine inflation via their control over the money supply (or to be more precise, its growth rate), m_t, but the control is not perfect, as money demand is subject to shocks, μ_t:

$$p_t = m_t + \mu_t, \tag{2}$$

with $E(\mu_t) = 0$ and variance σ_m^2. The aim of the authorities (as usual, no distinction is made between the central bank and the ministry of finance) is to minimize social loss, subject to the expected budget constraint:

$$d(b_t) = g_t + b_t(i_t - m_t) - q_t - m_t\xi, \tag{3}$$

where b_t is the public debt-to-GDP ratio and g_t represents (non-interest) expenditure relative to GDP. The last term in this budget constraint (3) represents seigniorage revenues under the assumption of a constant-velocity money demand function, with the cash-to-GDP (or rather the monetary base–to–GDP) ratio constant and denoted by ξ. The constant-velocity assumption implies that seigniorage increases linearly with the money supply (and hence expected inflation). This assumption is not realistic, but it was chosen to show that the results do not depend on a Laffer curve for seigniorage revenues under which the revenues from the inflation tax decrease with very high inflation rates as money demand goes toward zero.

In countries with moderate inflation, seigniorage revenues can reach 3 percent of GDP, or 10 percent of overall public-sector revenues. Seigniorage can thus make a significant contribution to public-sector

Table 4.1
Seigniorage and domestic debt

	Seigniorage (change in monetary base in 1995–2000) as percentage of GDP	Domestic debt as percentage of GDP[c]
Bulgaria[a]	5.1	60.2
Czech Republic	1.7	13.2
Estonia	2.3	0.5
Hungary	1.6	47.7
Latvia	1.7	3.0
Lithuania	0.8	6.3
Poland	0.8	19.7
Romania	3.4	12.0
Slovakia	1.3	17.6
Slovenia	0.7	25.8
Cyprus	1.0	43.2
Malta	0.8	52.5
Turkey	3.1	27.6
Eurozone[b]	0.3	

Source: Author's calculations based on IFS data.
[a] Average for individual years.
[b] Only for 1999 and 2000.
[c] As defined in line 88a of the IFS data.

revenues.[3] Table 4.1 shows some crude estimates of seigniorage revenues, defined, as in the model, as the ratio of the increase in the monetary base to GDP, for the average over the period 1995–2000. There are
evidently wide differences among the candidate countries in terms of
seigniorage revenues, with values ranging from 5.1 percent of GDP for
Bulgaria (with peaks during 1996–1997 of over 10 percent of GDP) to
only 0.7 percent for Slovenia. The value for the euro zone, reported for
comparison, is, at 0.3 percent of GDP, even lower. Seigniorage is thus
definitely more important for the candidate countries than in the euro
zone.

Table 4.1 also shows the size of domestic debt. The debt-to-GDP
ratio, which plays a central role in the model, refers only to domestic
debt, because foreign (or rather foreign-currency) debt cannot be
devalued by domestic inflation. The last column in table 4.1 shows that
there is clearly still a lot of domestic public debt in candidate countries,
making the model potentially relevant.

Another real-world qualification on the model is that it is implicitly
assumed that the monetary base consists only of cash. Introducing

required reserves for commercial banks (which could be remunerated) would not change the thrust of the analysis. If required reserves are not remunerated (which is usually the case), the value of ξ would just be somewhat higher than when they are.

For the sake of simplicity, real growth is assumed to be zero. Government expenditure could be made endogenous, as in a number of other contributions on the optimal choice of taxes and inflation, but this has not been done here, as it would not affect the main results of the chapter, which concentrate on the incentive to use surprise inflation to reduce the real value of the public debt (see, e.g., Mankiw 1987).

The crucial point about the budget constraint (3) is that real interest payments, given by $b_t(i_t - m_t)$, are a function of the difference between the nominal interest rate and money supply, because the latter determines the expected future price level. The simple form of the budget constraint used here assumes implicitly that all government debt has the same maturity, equal to the length of the period of this model. Another interpretation would be that b represents only the government debt that matures in this period. Interest payments on other government debt would then be subsumed under general government expenditure. This is not a serious limitation of the model, since most emerging-market countries have a relatively short average duration of debt (and the little long-term debt that exists is indexed on short-term interest rates). The nominal interest rate, i_t, can be written as the sum of the real interest rate, r_t, required by investors and their expected inflation. The latter will be equal to $E_t(m_t)$ by equation (2):[4]

$$i_t = r_t + E_t(m_t). \tag{4}$$

The real interest rate demanded by financial markets is here assumed (as usual) to be exogenous to the country concerned, but not necessarily constant. It is affected by shocks to the world financial markets, denoted by ε_t with $E(r_t) = \rho$ and variance σ_ε^2. These shocks are observed by the financial market and by the authorities at the same time, when they converge on an interest rate on public debt:

$$i_t = \rho + \varepsilon_t + E_t(m_t). \tag{4'}$$

Authorities can thus use monetary policy and also the tax rate to accommodate interest rate shocks. Taking into account (4'), the expected budget constraint that the authorities have to observe can be rewritten as

$$d(b_t) = g_t + b_t(\rho + \varepsilon_t + E_t(m_t) - m_t) - q_t - m_t\xi. \tag{3'}$$

4.3   Equilibrium under Discretion

In the model, authorities have to make their decisions about q and m before μ occurs. They try each period to minimize the expected loss while observing their budget constraints. The first-order conditions for a minimum of (1), subject to (3′), are

$$\frac{\partial L_t}{\partial q_t} = 0 = 2\alpha q_t - \lambda_t, \tag{5}$$

$$\frac{\partial L_t}{\partial m_t} = 0 = 2m_t - \lambda_t(b_t + \xi), \tag{6}$$

where λ_t is the shadow price associated with the budget constraint (3′).

To simplify the notation, only the steady state will be considered, with a constant debt-to-GDP ratio, denoted b.[5] Conditions (5) and (6) then yield a simple relationship between money supply and tax revenues (as a percentage of GDP):

$$m_t = (b + \xi)\alpha q_t. \tag{7}$$

This equation can be substituted into the budget constraint (3′) to obtain an expression for the steady-state "tax rate." If one assumes that the public anticipates monetary policy and hence inflation correctly (remember that the interest rate shock is observed by the authorities and the financial markets at the same time), $E_t(m_t|\varepsilon_t) - m_t = 0$. The debt-to-GDP ratio remains constant on average only if

$$q_t = g_t + b(\rho + \varepsilon_t) - \xi(b + \xi)\alpha q_t. \tag{8}$$

If expenditure is constant at g, the optimal tax ratio changes only if the realization of the interest rate shock is different from zero:[6]

$$q_d = \frac{[g + b(\rho + \varepsilon_t)]}{1 + \xi(b + \xi)\alpha}. \tag{9}$$

The expected loss under discretion $E(L_{\text{disc}})$ would then be given by

$$E(L_{\text{disc}}) = \frac{\{[g + b\rho]^2 + b^2\sigma_\varepsilon^2\}}{[1 + \xi(b + \xi)\alpha]^2}\{\alpha + [(b + \xi)\alpha]^2\} + \sigma_\mu^2. \tag{10}$$

As usual the discretionary equilibrium is not the first-best for the country. The social optimum, if there are no constraints on credibility, can be calculated by using the first-order conditions (5) and (6), but without the effect of surprise inflation on debt service in equation (6).

This means that in the social optimum the relationship between taxes and money supply would be given by

$$m_{SO} = \xi aq, \tag{11}$$

which differs from the corresponding relationship (7) in that in (11), only seigniorage is a valid argument for having inflation. The optimum tax rate is then given by substituting this expression into the budget constraint (and setting the debt-to-GDP ratio constant), which yields

$$q_{SO} = \frac{[g + b(\rho + \varepsilon_t)]}{[1 + \xi^2 \alpha]}. \tag{12}$$

The expected loss under the social optimum, $E(L_{SO})$, would then be equal to

$$E(L_{SO}) = \left\{ \frac{[g + b\rho]}{[1 + \xi^2 \alpha]} \right\}^2 [\alpha + (\alpha\xi)^2] + \frac{b^2 \sigma_\varepsilon^2}{[1 + \xi_\alpha^2]^2} [\alpha + (\alpha\xi)]^2 + \sigma_\mu^2, \tag{13}$$

which is lower than the loss under discretion. In this setup, however, there is no way the country could reach this bliss point. Without an external anchor the country would be stuck at the discretionary equilibrium.

The implicit assumption behind the limitation to the alternative—discretionary equilibrium or pegging to an external anchor—is that the institutional setup of the country is such that it would be impossible to establish an independent central bank that would both be credible in financial markets and be able to react flexibly to shocks by expanding the money supply whenever required by adverse external shocks (and to do so in conjunction with the finance ministry, which would have to increases taxes (see equation (12)). This chapter makes no distinction between various forms of using an external anchor (pegging the exchange rate, instituting a currency board, or full adoption of the foreign currency). For a discussion of the choice between pegging via a currency board and via an independent central bank applied to the Baltic experience, see de Haan, Berger, and van Fraansen 2000.

4.4   Welfare Effects of the Euro

The discretionary equilibrium is clearly not a first best. The first best would consist of having an independent central bank that can credibly commit not to exploit surprise inflation to lower the real value of public debt. This is an excellent idea in theory but was not really a practical option for the countries in Central and Eastern Europe during the 1990s, when most were grappling with a myriad of problems, including containing inflation after price liberalization and establishing a two-tier banking system (with a central bank distinct from the commercial banking system). Under these circumstances another approach, namely, to peg to an external anchor, proved to be the only realistic alternative. In the past this meant (in Central Europe in particular) pegging to the deutsche mark, which has now been merged into the euro. Pegging closely to the euro (or its precursor) proved to be an acceptable second-best solution to the time inconsistency problem inherent in having an autonomous national monetary policy.

The relevant question is whether today's policymakers have more policy options to choose from than their predecessors during the early phase of transition. At face value, the answer seems to be "yes," as almost all CEECs now have delegated monetary policy to legally independent central banks. Experience suggests, however, that their factual independence might lack the strength to effectively guarantee price stability. Thus, even today, the relevant alternative to the discretionary equilibrium might be to join the euro area. This would still eliminate the credibility problem and would not be subject to the problem of speculative attacks that arise in fixed exchange rate systems.

In the EMU area prices would be determined via purchasing-power parity through the monetary policy of the ECB. It will be assumed here that the ECB maintains perfect price stability. Its independence is not in doubt, and it has a clear mandate to maintain price stability. Moreover, seigniorage is not an important source of revenue for most EU member countries, which implies that the social optimum for the EU is to set inflation to zero.

Domestic prices will then be determined by a stochastic purchasing-power condition:

$$p_t = e_t, \tag{14}$$

where e_t is the shock to purchasing-power parity, subject to $E(e_t) = 0$ and variance σ^2_{PPP}. (In this case the domestic money market adjusts passively, and the shocks to it no longer matter.)

The loss under EMU membership would then be

$$E(L_{\text{euro}}) = a(g + b\rho)^2 + ab^2\sigma^2_{\varepsilon_{\text{euro}}} + \sigma^2_{\text{PPP}}. \tag{15}$$

Joining the euro area would thus be advantageous for a country if this loss is lower than that under discretion, that is, when the country does not have an external anchor for expectations. Adopting the euro has a number of consequences that are apparent once one compares equations (15) and (10). The money demand shock is no longer relevant under the euro regime, because shocks to domestic money demand in a small participant country do not affect the euro area price level. But pegging to (or fully adopting) the euro instead of having a national currency introduces another source of shocks, namely, the shock to purchasing-power parity.

Finally, as the notation $\sigma^2_{\varepsilon_{euro}}$ suggests, it is likely that a tight pegging to a stable currency affects the risk premium on foreign debt. In particular, the large size of the euro area suggests a lower variance of shocks than for each of the euro area's constituents. Moreover, for countries with large external debt, euroization may lower the risk premium paid on foreign debt. Euroization eliminates the difference between external and internal debt, removing the government's incentive to discriminate against foreign creditors. In addition, euroization mitigates uncertainty about a country's external debt service capacity. When a country devalues its currency in reaction to an external shock, the capacity of the government to service foreign debt is usually greatly reduced, because a large part of government revenues come from taxes on non-tradable activities. A real depreciation thus also reduces the value of tax revenues in foreign currency. For example, when the price of dollars in terms of rubles increased fourfold during the Russian crisis of 1998, the Russian government's debt service capacity was initially also cut to one-fourth, because domestic prices did not jump along with the exchange rate.

All these arguments suggest that $\sigma^2_{\varepsilon_{euro}} = \phi\sigma^2_{\varepsilon_{disc}}$, with ϕ likely to be smaller than one. The difference between the losses under EMU and under the discretionary equilibrium can then be written as

$$L_{euro} - L_{disc} = a^2 \lfloor (g + b\rho)^2 + b^2\sigma^2_{\varepsilon_{disc}} \rfloor [1 + \xi(b + \xi)a]^{-2}(b + \xi)$$
$$\times \{(\xi - b) + \xi^2(\xi + b)a\} - (1 - \phi)ab^2\sigma^2_{\varepsilon_{disc}}$$
$$+ \sigma^2_e - \sigma^2_\mu. \tag{16}$$

To interpret this result, we will first examine the role of the debt-to-GDP ratio (b) and then the role of the shocks. Regarding the former, two key results emerge.

The first of these key results is well known: Countries with high public debt benefit from an external anchor, which saves them from the high inflation rates they would otherwise have to endure because the market knows that the temptation for them to use surprise inflation to reduce public-debt service is strong. The second has not been recognized so far: The relationship between the level of public debt and the cost of retaining a national currency is non-monotonic. As the debt-to-GDP ratio falls from very high levels, the welfare gain from adopting an external anchor disappears and becomes a loss for moderate debt levels. As the debt-to-GDP ratio gets close to zero, however, this loss (i.e., the disincentive to use an external anchor) starts to decline.

Both of these results can be seen by inspecting the term within braces in equation (16). This term implies immediately that the difference in welfare loss can be negative or positive depending on the sign of $\xi - b$, which is likely to be negative. The tax basis for seigniorage is the monetary base, ξ, which in most countries (including transition countries) is below 10 percent of GDP. In no country in the world does the monetary base–to–GDP or cash-to-GDP ratio exceed one; values much below the average of 0.1 for the transition countries can be found in less-developed countries with chronic high-inflation problems, but even the most stability-oriented countries never have a cash-to-GDP ratio much in excess of this value. By contrast, the debt-to-GDP ratio, b, shows much more variability (in absolute terms) and is sometimes close to 100 percent.[7] Estonia is one of the few countries without any significant public debt, so that in the case of Estonia, $(\xi - b)$ might actually be positive.

In discussing the role of the debt ratio, it is convenient to rewrite equation (16) slightly differently as

$$E(L_{\text{euro}} - L_{\text{disc}}) = \alpha^2 \lfloor (g + b\rho)^2 + b^2 \sigma^2_{\varepsilon_{\text{disc}}} \rfloor [1 + \xi(b + \xi)\alpha]^{-2} (b + \xi)$$
$$\times \{\xi(1 + \alpha\xi^2) - b(1 - \alpha\xi^2)\} - (1 - \phi)\alpha b^2 \sigma^2_{\varepsilon_{\text{disc}}}$$
$$+ \sigma^2_e - \sigma^2_\mu. \tag{17}$$

Inspection of equation (17) shows that the term within braces must change sign as b increases from zero to infinity as long as the term $(1 - \alpha\xi^2)$ is positive (which is likely, as argued earlier). This suggests that the relationship between a country's interest in joining the euro area and its debt-to-GDP ratio should be non-monotonic. As the debt ratio appears also in other terms of equation (17), however, it is not straightforward to sign the derivative.

One point, however, is clear from general considerations: When a country has no public debt, staying outside the euro area is clearly better for it, because the discretionary equilibrium is then equal to the social optimum, and by staying outside, the country can use inflation to earn some seigniorage. That is, for $b = 0$, the value of the right-hand side of equation (17) is clearly positive, as can be established by inspection. Moreover, there is clearly also one value of b for which the term within braces in equation (17) is equal to zero and hence the country is indifferent between joining the euro and staying outside: $b = \xi(1 + \alpha\xi^2)/(1 - \alpha\xi^2)$, which is larger than the cash-to-GDP ratio, and thus a realistic value. Furthermore, it is also clear that for b larger than this value, the difference in loss becomes negative. At this point all that remains to show the hump-shaped relationship between the difference in loss and b is to show that the derivative of this expression with respect to b is positive around zero. This involves some tedious algebra. The appendix shows in detail that this is indeed the case, for the case $\phi = 1$.

Having established the general presumption for a hump-shaped relationship between the difference in loss and b, it might be useful to present the relationship between the difference in welfare loss and b. Figure 4.1 shows this relationship for a particlar set of parameter values

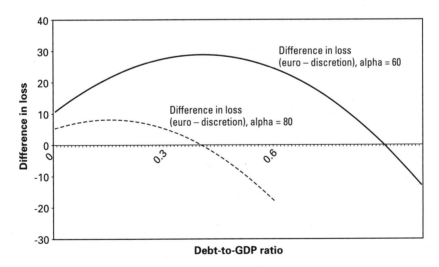

Figure 4.1
Gain or loss from entering the euro area. Difference in loss as a function of the debt-to-GDP ratio.

g (the ratio of non-interest expenditure to GDP) $= 0.3$, ξ (monetary base–to–GDP ratio) $= 0.1$, $\phi = 1$, and two values for α. It is apparent that there is an inverted U-form relationship between a country's interest in joining the euro area and its debt-to-GDP ratio. For countries with low levels of debt, the loss in the euro area is larger than that from going it alone. Such countries have an interest in staying outside, whereas very weak countries have a larger loss outside and should thus gain from joining the euro area.

The intuition behind this result is clear: For low levels of debt, the incentive to use surprise inflation is low. The market knows this and therefore expects only low inflation. It is thus possible to have an equilibrium with inflation only a little above what would be needed to get some seigniorage. In countries with high levels of debt, however, the inflation rate would be much higher than the one that would be justified for optimum seigniorage, because the market knows that the government has an overwhelming incentive to use surprise inflation.

Looking at the role of shocks, a first point to note is that neither the variance of the money demand shock nor that of the PPP shock interacts with the debt-to-GDP ratio. The relative magnitude of these two shocks just shifts the curves in figure 4.1 vertically. The standard optimum currency area approach stresses only the size of the variance of the PPP shocks. In order to make any statement about the loss from adopting an external anchor, however, one has to compare two sources of shocks: the PPP shocks and the money demand shocks that would complicate monetary management if the national currency were kept. What matters is thus the difference between these two variances.

The variance of the interest rate shock interacts, however, with b. As the net expected loss from giving up the national currency turns negative for high values of b, a higher interest rate variance would reinforce the argument for adoption of the euro. On the other hand, for very low levels of b, the size of the variance does not really affect the loss differential. Hence, for low-debt-to-GDP countries, interest rate variance does not constitute an additional argument for retaining their national currency.

Any reduction in the interest rate variance from adoption of the euro (i.e., assuming that ϕ is smaller than one) would of course reinforce the argument in favor of its adoption more, the higher b is. Figure 4.1 assumes that $\phi = 1$. Assuming that ϕ is smaller than one would lead to a new curve that would lie lower than when $\phi = 1$. The distance with the curve that assumes $\phi = 1$ would increase with the square of b.

4.5   Inefficient Fiscal Policy Institutions

This section introduces the concept of an inefficient fiscal policy process into the model. It has so far been assumed that the government makes its decision in terms of the overall level of taxation needed to finance expenditure. There are always, however, special-interest groups that plead for tax exemptions. Any tax exemption that is granted must be paid for somehow. In the setup of this model, the only alternative source of revenues is inflationary finance. Using inflation also causes a welfare loss to the special-interest group that obtains a tax exemption. As the part of any group in the overall budget will be small, however, this cost cannot fully offset the direct gain from the tax cut. Each special-interest group thus behaves as if the shadow price of a tax benefit were only $\eta\lambda$, where η is a fraction, between zero and one, that indicates the overall inflationary impact any tax benefit has on the special-interest group concerned. This fraction should be a function of various elements, for example, the share of the interest group in the overall budget, the extent to which benefits have to be shared with other groups (a tax exemption for one specific enterprise might not be possible, whereas an exemption for all enterprises in a certain category might be acceptable), and the extent to which fiscal policy decisions are centralized, so that demands by competing interest groups neutralize each other (see von Hagen and Harden 1994 for an analysis of EU member countries in this respect). Velasco (1998) uses a similar approach with two symmetric interest groups, whereas Drazen (2000, chap. 10) presents a model with a large number of competing groups that try to extract transfers from the government.

For simplicity, all shocks are set to zero in the model. (The results of the previous section show in any case that the introduction of shocks does not affect the central message of this chapter. If the influence of special-interest groups is the same throughout all areas of fiscal policy, and if all interest groups are identical in terms of their size and influence, this leads to a modified first-order condition (see equation (5)) for the setting of the overall average tax rate:

$$\frac{\partial L_t}{\partial q_t} = 0 = 2\alpha q_t - \eta\lambda. \tag{18}$$

Setting the inflation rate hits all interest groups in the same way; the first-order condition (6) is thus not affected. The resulting trade-off between taxes and inflation, however, is different:

$$p_t = \frac{(b+\xi)\alpha q_t}{\eta}. \tag{19}$$

This implies that, ceteris paribus, inflation will be higher, as all interest groups push the government to finance their benefits through inflation. As nothing changes in the remainder of the model (i.e., essentially the budget constraint), the resulting tax rate under the discretionary equilibrium is given by an equation that is identical to equation (9), except that α/η is substituted for α. This implies that the welfare loss under discretion is given by

$$L_{\text{disc, if}} = \left\{ \frac{[g+b\rho]}{1+\frac{\xi(b+\xi)\alpha}{\eta}} \right\}^2 \left\{ \alpha + \left[\frac{(b+\xi)\alpha}{\eta} \right]^2 \right\}, \tag{20}$$

where the subscript *if* stands for inefficient fiscal policy.

The loss under the euro is not affected by the inefficient policy, as special-interest groups are no longer able to have their tax benefits financed by inflationary finance. The difference in the loss between the euro regime and the discretionary equilibrium thus becomes

$$L_{\text{euro}} - L_{\text{disc}} = \left\{ \frac{[g+b\rho]}{1+\frac{\xi(b+\xi)\alpha}{\eta}} \right\}^2 \frac{\alpha^2(b+\xi)}{\eta} \left\{ 2\xi + \frac{(\xi^2\alpha-1)(b+\xi)}{\eta} \right\}. \tag{21}$$

This solution collapses, of course, to the corresponding expression for the standard case; see equation (16) or (17) if η equals one.

How does the difference in the loss expressed in equation (21) vary with the key parameter that describes the strength of the fiscal framework of a country, that is, η? As the inverse of η can vary between one and infinity, it will be convenient to analyze equation (21) by focusing on this variable. A high value of η^{-1} indicates a weak fiscal framework.

Inspection of equation (21) shows immediately that there is one value of η^{-1} for which a country will just be indifferent between joining the euro or staying out in the cold: $\eta_{\text{ind}}^{-1} = -2\xi/(b+\xi)(\xi^2\alpha-1)$, which is greater than zero under the assumptions used so far. For values of η^{-1} above this threshold, the loss from staying outside would exceed that of joining the euro area. At this threshold, the country is just indifferent between joining and going it alone, because two effects just offset each other: If the country joins the euro area, its inflation rate will be too low (zero inflation would not be optimal, since the country needs some seigniorage revenues), and outside the euro area, its inflation rate will be too high (because of the inefficiency in the fiscal process, which magnifies the usual time inconsistency problems).

Inspection of equation (21) also shows that as η^{-1} tends towards infinity the difference between the welfare losses tends toward minus infinity. Basket cases would thus have a very strong interest in using an external anchor.

The general shape of equation (21) is determined by the fact that it contains a quadratic expression in the inverse of η, and as long as the expression $(\xi^2 \alpha - 1)$ is negative, which is likely given that ξ is much smaller than one, this will result in a graph in the shape of an inverted parabola.

Figure 4.2 shows the difference in welfare loss as a function of η^{-1} for two values of g (the ratio of non-interest expenditure to GDP) assuming the monetary base–to–GDP ratio is equal to 0.1 and the debt-to-GDP ratio is a Maastricht-conforming 0.6. The function seems convex and depicts an inverted U-form relationship between the interest in joining the euro area and the strength of domestic fiscal institutions. For countries with strong, but not perfect, fiscal systems, the loss in

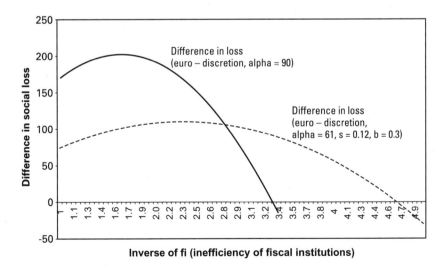

Figure 4.2
Gain or loss from entering the euro area. Difference in social-welfare loss as a function of alpha.

the euro area is larger than that from going it alone. Such countries have an interest in staying outside, whereas very weak countries have a larger loss outside and should thus gain from joining the euro area.

Another interpretation of inefficient fiscal institutions can be had by focusing on the budget constraint. One might imagine a country in which one-half of every unit spent by the government on public goods disappears. (The exact cause of this disappearance is not important in this context; it could be corruption or sheer waste.) This would imply that if one were to compare two countries that need the same level of public goods, g (say, the same number of police units), the country in which one-half of spending is wasted would have to spend spent twice as much on public goods (i.e., it would have to finance $2g$). Inspection of equation (21) shows immediately that this would not affect the sign of the difference in the loss functions, but only its magnitude. This implies that higher inefficiency, if interpreted merely as waste in public spending, would mainly affect the strength with which a country holds to its preferred exchange rate regime, but not which regime it prefers.

4.6   The Model and Reality: The Case of the Candidate Countries

The model developed here represents considerations that should inform the exchange rate regime choice of any country. The theory behind the model seems particularly relevant, however, for the countries of Central and Eastern Europe that are candidates for membership in the EU. Once they become EU members, they will also become eligible for membership in the euro area. Although membership in the euro area is subject to the Maastricht criteria, this potential for euro area membership implies that all the candidate countries have at least a medium-run prospect of being able to participate in decision making for the monetary policy governing the euro. For these countries the political cost of abandoning national monetary sovereignty is thus much smaller than for those in other emerging markets or weak economies around the world.

Do the choices of the candidate countries reflect the fundamental factors embodied in the model presented here? It seems to be the case that they do. Given the small number of observations resulting from the limited number of candidate countries, it is not possible to engage in an econometric exercise using the available data, but a quick glance at the data (see table 4.2) indicates that the countries with the highest

Table 4.2
Exchange rate regimes and public debt

	Domestic debt as percentage of GDP	Exchange rate regime (as classified by IMF 2001)
Bulgaria	60.2	Currency board
Czech Republic	13.2	Managed float (inflation target)
Estonia	0.5	Currency board
Hungary	47.7	Managed float (inflation target)
Latvia	3.0	Fixed peg
Lithuania	6.3	Currency board
Poland	19.7	Managed float (inflation target)
Romania	12.0	Managed float
Slovakia	17.6	Managed float
Slovenia	n.a.	Managed float (monetary target)

Source: IMF 2001. n.a. = not available.

and the lowest debt ratios have opted for the tightest exchange rate regimes (namely, currency boards).

Another way to look at the relationship between public debt and the exchange rate regime is provided in figures 4.3 and 4.4, which depict in each case the ratio of (domestic) debt to GDP on the horizontal axis, and on the vertical axis, two different measures of the extent to which the candidate countries have used an external anchor. Figure 4.3 uses the variability of their currencies vis-à-vis the euro,[8] and figure 4.4 shows the relationship between government debt and inflation in those countries. A polynomial trend line seems to support the hump-shaped relationship posited by the model.

4.7   Concluding Remarks

This chapter has deliberately used a standard model to derive a result that is intuitively plausible but has not been recognized so far. It is well known that countries with high levels of public debt or weak fiscal institutions may benefit from an external anchor to save them from the high inflation rates they would otherwise have to endure because the market knows that they face a strong temptation to use surprise inflation to reduce public debt service. The same model that delivers this kind of result, however, also implies that the relationship between the level of public debt in a country and the cost of its retaining a national currency is non-monotonic. As the debt-to-GDP ratio falls from very

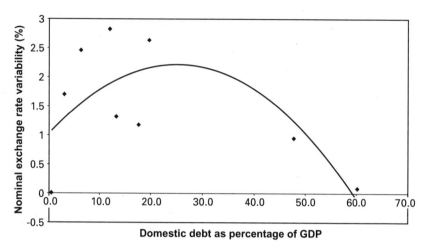

Figure 4.3
Domestic debt and ER variability in candidate countries.

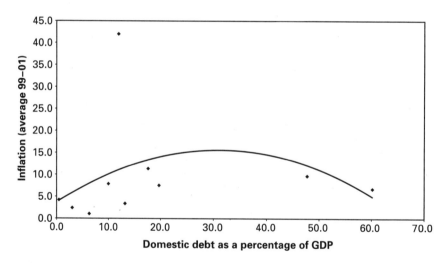

Figure 4.4
Domestic debt and inflation in candidate countries.

high levels, the welfare gain from adopting an external anchor disappears and becomes a loss for moderate debt levels. As the debt-to-GDP ratio gets close to zero, however, this loss (i.e. the disincentive to use an external anchor) starts to shrink. Indeed, a country without public debt is close to indifferent between keeping its national currency and adopting an external anchor. This implies that very strong countries might have only have a weak interest in retaining their national currency, a fate they share with very weak countries. For the Central and Eastern European countries, this would imply that one might see not only the very weak, but also the very strong, trying to join the euro area as quickly as possible (and pegging to the euro in the meantime).

The intuition behind this result is straightforward: Countries with little pressure for excessive expenditure and an efficient tax system would enjoy low inflation rates in any case and therefore have little problem with a peg to a hard currency. Countries with high levels of debt or very weak fiscal institutions would greatly benefit from an external anchor to save them from the high inflation rates they would otherwise have to endure. By contrast, countries with moderate weaknesses might be in a situation in which they need some inflation to supplement government revenues with seigniorage, but the inflation resulting from the interaction with the market, which knows about this, is still moderate.

This result is independent of the issues stressed in the usual OCA approach. It is clear that a country's likelihood of experiencing an asymmetric shock and the gains it can realize from transaction costs will be further elements in its choice of an exchange rate regime. The OCA considerations, however, are independent of the aspects discussed here. Moreover, the main difference between Estonia and Bulgaria is not that the latter is much more exposed to asymmetric shocks à la Mundell (1961), that is, shocks to export earnings or terms of trade. Both countries are vulnerable in this respect, since they have a narrow industrial base. The really important difference between them instead lies in the strength of their domestic fiscal frameworks: In Estonia there is almost no public debt, as the government has so far usually been able to balance its budget. The tax service works reasonably well, and tax rates are low, but the tax base is broad, and the (uncomplicated) tax code is actually enforced. By contrast, in Bulgaria, the public debt is very large, the government has until recently had constant difficulties in finding enough revenues to finance its expenditures and large state-owned enterprises have been a constant drain on the budget.

   The purpose of this contribution was modest: to point out that in an entirely conventional model, the relationship between debt levels and the need for an external anchor is non-monotonic. A high variability of the risk premium in the international capital market reinforces this argument. If a country starts from very low levels of debt, a high variability of the international interest rate might initially make it more attractive for the country to have flexibility in the exchange (and hence monetary) policy to enable it to finance increased debt service partially via the inflation tax. If a country starts from a high level of debt, however, a shock to the international interest rate can cause such severe credibility problems that pegging the exchange rate again becomes more attractive. The chapter also shows that a higher degree of inefficiency of the domestic fiscal-policy process can be equivalent to a higher public debt level. Pegging to a stable currency might thus be useful not only for countries with very high or very low levels of public debt, but also for those with very strong or very weak fiscal-policy institutions.

Appendix: Derivative of Equation (17) with Respect to b around the Value $b = 0$ (for $\phi = 1$)

To simplify the notation, it is convenient to take the derivative of the logarithm of the difference in the loss:

$$\partial \ln(L_{\text{euro}} - L_{\text{disc}})/\partial b = [(g + b\rho)^2 + b^2\sigma_{\varepsilon_{\text{disc}}}^2]^{-1}[2(g + b\rho)\rho + 2b\sigma_{\varepsilon_{\text{disc}}}^2]$$
$$- 2[1 + \xi(b + \xi)\alpha]^{-1}\alpha\xi + (b + \xi)^{-1}$$
$$- \{\xi(1 + \alpha\xi^2) - b(1 - \alpha\xi^2)\}^{-1}(1 - \alpha\xi^2).$$

For $b = 0$ this, reduces to

$$\partial \ln(L_{\text{euro}} - L_{\text{disc}})/\partial b = [(g)^2]^{-1}[2g\rho] - 2[1 + \xi^2\alpha]^{-1}\alpha\xi + (1 + \alpha\xi^2)$$
$$\times [(\xi)(1 + \alpha\xi^2)]^{-1} - \{\xi(1 + \alpha\xi^2)\}^{-1}(1 - \alpha\xi^2).$$

Collecting terms yields

$$\partial \ln(L_{\text{euro}} - L_{\text{disc}})/\partial b = 2g^{-1}\rho - [(1 + \xi^2\alpha)\xi]^{-1}$$
$$\times [-2\alpha\xi^2 + (1 + \alpha\xi^2) - (1 - \alpha\xi^2)].$$

The terms within the last set of square brackets just cancel one another out. This implies that around the value of zero, the derivative of the difference in the loss with respect to b is always positive.

Notes

Many thanks to Anna Maria Pinna and Peer Ritter for important research assistance.

1. This is the standard hypothesis. Berger, Jensen, and Schjelderup (2001) make the point that the covariance of shocks (domestic and foreign) might also be a key element under the standard OCA approach.

2. An alternative interpretation would be that society and/or the politicians in power dislike high taxes (for example, because their marginal voter is a household with a high marginal tax rate).

3. For an analysis of the importance of seigniorage revenues in transition countries and the relative stability of money demand, see Gros and Steinherr 1995 or Gros and Vandille 1995.

4. With pedantic notation, it would be $E_t(m_t|\varepsilon)$.

5. In a similar model, Gros (1990) shows that this should not affect the conclusions.

6. Since this chapter's focus is steady states, the time subscript will henceforth be suppressed.

7. To highlight the role played by the interest burden on public debt, Gros (1996) assumes that $\xi = 0$. This elimination of seigniorage from Gros's model was justified by the fact that seigniorage has not played a significant role in EU public finances in recent years, as shown by Gros and Vandille (1995).

8. Exchange rate variability is measured by the standard deviation of month-to-month changes, in a given year, in the logarithm of the nominal exchange rates of the respective currencies against the euro. To eliminate possible excessive short-term disruptions, the average value for 1999–2001 is used. Inflation is measured using the Consumer Price Index over the same period.

References

Berger, H., H. Jensen, and G. Schjelderup. 2001. "To Peg or Not to Peg? A Simple Model of Exchange Rate Regime Choice in Small Economies." *Economic Letters* 73: 161–167.

de Haan, J., H. Berger, and E. van Fraansen. 2000. "How to Reduce Inflation: An Independent Central Bank or a Currency Board? The Experience of the Baltic Countries." *Emerging Market Review* 2, no. 3: 218–243.

Drazen, A. 2000. *Political Economy in Macroeconomics*. Princeton: Princeton University Press.

Emerson, M., and D. Gros. 1999. *The CEPS Plan for the Balkans*. Brussels: Centre for European Policy Studies Paperback.

Gros, D. 1990. "Seigniorage and EMS Discipline." In *The European Monetary System in the 1990s*, ed. P. de Grauwe and L. Papademos, 162–177. London: Longman.

Gros, D. 1996. "Self-Fulfilling Public Debt Crises." CEPS Working document no. 102, Centre for European Policy Studies, Brussels. Reprinted in *European Monetary Union, Transition, International Impact and Policy Options*, ed. P. Welfens, 271–297. Heidelberg: Springer, 1997.

Gros, D., and A. Steinherr. 1995. *Winds of Change: Economic Transition in Central and Eastern Europe.* London: Addison/Wesley Longman.

Gros, D., and G. Vandille. 1995. "Seigniorage and EMU: The Fiscal Implications of Price Stability and Financial Market Integration." *Journal of Common Market Studies* 33, no. 2 (June): 175–196.

International Monetary Fund (IMF). 2001. Annual report. Washington, DC.

Mankiw, G. N. 1987. "The Optimal Collection of Seigniorage, Theory and Evidence." *Journal of Monetary Economics* 20: 327–341.

Mundell, R. 1961. "A Theory of Optimum Currency Area." *American Economic Review* 51: 657–675.

Velasco, A. 1998. "The Common Property Approach to the Politcal Economy of Fiscal Policy." In *The Political Economy of Reform*, ed. F. Sturzenegger and M. Tommasi, 165–184. Cambridge: MIT Press.

von Hagen, J., and I. Harden. 1994. "National Budget Processes and Fiscal Performance." *European Economy, Reports and Studies* (Commission of the European Communities, Brussels) 3: 310–418.

Comments

Margarita Katsimi

One of the main implications of the chapter by Daniel Gros is that countries with high levels of public debt and fiscal inefficiency will benefit from joining the euro area. This result is consistent with existing literature in this area (Cukierman 1992). The euro area represents a commitment environment that eliminates the inflationary bias resulting from a government's incentive to reduce the real value of debt through monetary expansion. On the other hand, in Gros's model, euro area participation entails some cost, namely, the inability to generate revenue through seigniorage. The welfare implications of euro area participation therefore depend on the trade-off between improvement in the credibility of a country's monetary policy and the elimination of seigniorage revenues. The chapter offers some useful insights into the incentives of countries to join a commitment environment and shows a non-monotonic relationship between the benefits from joining the euro area and the strength of a country's domestic fiscal institutions (or the level of debt). As a country's level of debt decreases, the government's incentive to use surprise inflation becomes weaker, so that with a certain level of debt and fiscal inefficiency, the country will be better off outside the euro area. Countries with no debt will always be better off outside the euro area, since the benefit of eliminating inflationary bias will be lower than the cost of forfeiting seigniorage creation. Moreover, the welfare loss from using an external anchor will be lower for countries with low levels of debt and a low level of fiscal inefficiency than for countries in the middle range, since the latter rely more on seigniorage revenue. The fact that high-debt accession countries have chosen fixed exchange rate regimes such as currency board arrangements (CBAs) is consistent with the model's results. Moreover, the model presented in the chapter has some interesting implications for the transition period of the accession countries to the euro area. It predicts that high-debt countries with a CBA will have an interest in joining the euro area quickly, because ERMII participation will lead to a temporary welfare loss in those countries.

The fact that strong countries like Estonia also seem to opt for an external anchor is, however, not fully explained by the model. Therefore, I think that the model could be enriched by modifying some of its basic assumptions. In that respect, a different treatment of seigniorage could strengthen the results and reveal a more interesting hump-shaped relationship, according to which both low-debt and high-debt countries will opt for a hard peg, whereas countries in the middle range will be better off in a discretion environment. Therefore, my first comment stems from the treatment of seigniorage in the model. Allowing for seigniorage revenues is a desirable feature of the model, since seigniorage is a more important source of revenues for the accession countries than for the incumbent member states. The ability to generate seigniorage revenues is an important distinction between the three environments compared in the chapter: If seigniorage revenues are not taken into account, euro area participation is equivalent to the social optimum, and therefore it is always better than discretion. In line with most theoretical models in this area, if there are no disturbances, commitment is always better than discretion. Allowing for seigniorage in the model would make its results more interesting, since it would introduce the trade-off between commitment and the loss of revenues. A complete analysis of the policymaker's incentives to increase revenues through seigniorage creation should also, however, take into account the dynamic-inconsistency aspect of seigniorage creation. The model neglects this issue by assuming a constant-velocity money demand function, so that seigniorage increases linearly with the money supply. According to the Cagan-Bailey analysis, at sufficiently high rates of inflation, the increase in inflationary expectations reduces the tax base by more than the increase in money supply. If one makes the more realistic assumption that seigniorage depends negatively on inflationary expectations, it is straightforward to show that a policymaker whose objectives are the same as in this model will have an incentive to inflate after the public has chosen the level of real money balances (Cukierman 1992). The public anticipates this behavior when it determines its money balances, so that the inability to commit monetary policy prior to the choice of real balances leads to an inefficient equilibrium.

Addressing the time inconsistency problem in seigniorage creation would imply some additional benefit from euro area participation, namely, the elimination of the inflationary bias due to the dynamic inconsistency in seigniorage creation. This would imply that, in this framework, a low-debt country may be better off using an external anchor.

My second point relates to the effect of fiscal inefficiency on the welfare loss from joining the euro area. Fiscal inefficiency in a broader sense (e.g., that due to an under-developed tax system) is also an important characteristic of the accession countries. One would expect that since countries with high levels of fiscal inefficiency rely more on seigniorage revenue, the welfare loss from joining the euro area will be higher for those countries. An inefficient fiscal system will increase the cost of raising tax revenue, leading, ceteris paribus, to a higher optimal level of seigniorage. Therefore, eliminating this possibility should be more costly to countries with high fiscal inefficiency (Grilli 1989). The chapter argues the opposite: that fiscal inefficiency increases the welfare gain from joining the euro area. This result depends on the assumption that euro area participation eliminates inefficiency. Even in the chapter, however, fiscal inefficiency should, to some extent, affect welfare within the euro area. The level of fiscal inefficiency is reflected in the model by lower tax revenue in the government's budget constraint. In the discretionary equilibrium, this will increase inflation, since the government has a stronger incentive for inflationary surprises. In the euro area, monetary growth is given, so that inflation is not affected by the level of fiscal inefficiency. Nevertheless, fiscal inefficiency will not disappear, but it will continue affecting the budget constraint of the government. As a result, the steady-state level of tax revenue in a country should still be affected by the level of fiscal inefficiency in that country, so that welfare loss in the euro area will be lower under fiscal inefficiency.

In the last decade, the incentives for a country to use an external anchor as a solution to the time inconsistency problem of monetary policy has frequently been analyzed in the literature to evaluate the welfare implications of establishing the euro area. Accession countries, however, differ in many aspects from the existing euro area member states. Gros's chapter presents a model that incorporates some important characteristics of accession countries, such as seigniorage creation and fiscal inefficiency, and produces some interesting results. In that

respect, it is a first step towards understanding the choice of exchange
rate regime in these countries.

References

Cukierman, A. 1992. *Central Bank Strategy, Credibility and Independence*. Cambridge: MIT
Press.

Grilli, V. 1989. "Seigniorage in Europe." In *A European Central Bank? Perspectives on
Monetary Unification after Ten Years of EMS*, ed. M. De Cecco and A. Giovannini, 33–58.
London: Cambridge University Press.

5

Factor Mobility, Income Differentials, and Regional Economic Integration

Michael C. Burda

5.1 Introduction

Economic integration is the current buzzword of the European Union. It is the avowed goal of the Treaty of Rome: The "four freedoms" are often linked, if not directly equated, with the notion of economic integration, and the introduction of the euro is generally seen as a means toward achieving an ever closer union. Despite this objective, it is difficult to find an exact definition of integration. Discussions of economic integration frequently confuse efficiency with equity and issues of positive with normative economics. If one is willing to accept a strictly efficiency-based notion of integration in the sense of Pareto, economic integration can be readily defined as the achievement by two or more geographic regions of the efficient production pattern made possible by their union, using as the appropriate metric world market prices for output (see, e.g., Eichengreen 1990).

This chapter adopts such an efficiency perspective for studying the role of factor mobility and accumulation in the economic-integration process. In particular, I stress the importance of adjustment costs in determining the speed of efficient economic integration, as well as the interpretation of deviations of regional factor returns in the process of dynamic adjustment to the new steady state. By focusing on efficiency in economic integration, I ignore alternative indicators of integration related to income, consumption, wages, or even GDP per capita. Strict separation of efficiency and equity issues is essential for assessing episodes of economic integration, such as the eastward enlargement of the EU. Many analysts have stressed large gaps in GDP levels per capita or in factor prices as evidence of incomplete regional or European integration and as a signal for large potential migration flows (Sinn 2000). Yet within economic trading areas such as the EU, it is possible to observe significant national differences in wages and returns to capital, along with finite and rather low rates of factor movement. According to the U.S. Bureau of Labor Statistics (2003), gross remuneration of an hour's labor (total hourly earnings) in 2001 amounted to $23.84 in Germany, $15.88 in France, $13.76 in Italy, and $10.88 in Spain. Although it is certainly possible that current wage differences reflects in part variation in human- and physical-capital endowments, it seems implausible to suggest that all of it does. So why don't French manufacturing workers move to Germany, or the Spaniards to Italy? Why doesn't capital move in the opposite direction?

Among other things, this chapter offers a framework for thinking about deviations in factor prices as reflecting equilibrium dynamic-adjustment paths toward steady states of economic integration. If costs of adjustment are important, the fact that wages in some Eastern European countries are one-tenth of Western levels will be uninformative about the extent of (efficient) economic integration in those countries. Put another way, private incentives to move factors of production are not fully reflected in observable wage or profit differentials across countries or regions. Proper consideration of adjustment costs is an important step toward putting the discussion of EU enlargement on a more empirical footing.

The chapter is organized as follows. Sections 5.1 and 5.2 define economic integration and examine the most important mechanisms for achieving it. Sections 5.3 and 5.4 present and study a formal model of the dynamics of economic integration that highlights the role of adjustment costs in competitive factor income determination. Section 5.5 discusses the relevance of mobility costs and presents some quantitative evidence on its significance. Section 5.6 concludes with some implications for European integration policy.

5.2   Making Sense of Economic Integration

Under conditions of constant returns in production, the static ideal of economic integration between two regions can be achieved under a number of different guises. First, internal accumulation of production factors such as physical or human capital can lift output per capita in poorer regions at no expense to richer ones. Second, labor can move from capital-poor regions to capital-rich ones (migration or commuting). Third, capital mobility in the form of foreign direct investment from capital-rich to capital-poor regions can occur. Finally, under the assumption of incomplete specialization and a few other technical conditions, Heckscher-Ohlin trade between the two regions can result in the equalization of factor prices in the two regions.[1]

The trade mechanism has attracted considerable attention in the discussion of European integration. In his seminal paper, Mundell (1957) stressed the equivalence, under certain conditions, of trade and factor mobility in achieving economic integration.[2] Under incomplete specialization of production patterns, convergent product market prices translate into convergent factor prices. If goods are produced by different regions with different relative factor endowments, but at common factor prices and with common technologies, regional exports will reflect a relative abundance of factor endowments. By this logic, Eastern Europe would export those goods that are less intensive in physical capital or relatively intensive in human capital or labor inputs.

Although trade-induced factor price equalization is theoretically and empirically important as a mechanism of economic integration, it is probably less relevant *within* Europe, given the similarity of overall capital intensity of production methods from country to country, the similarity of human capital endowments among countries, and the high complementarity of human and physical capital in the countries. In what follows, I will assume that any relevant "zone of incomplete specialization" is of second-order importance and approximate the efficient static allocation of capital and labor using a diagonal in the usual Edgeworth diagram; I will thus focus on the first three modes of integration and assume that production patterns are identical in the two regions. In particular, I will emphasize the two types of factor mobility.

Figure 5.1 depicts the outset of the integration process between a capital-rich west (W) and a capital-poor east (E), the union of which comprises a small open economy. Assume that both regions produce output using the constant-returns production function $F(K, L)$ employing capital (K) and labor (L). Both regions can borrow and lend at a given world interest rate r; for simplicity, labor mobility from the rest of the world is set to zero. As a result, a static steady state of the economy in figure 5.1 should lie along the capital-labor ratio, equating capital-labor ratios in both regions to that given by the slope of the factor price frontier of the economy at the world user cost of capital. Integration is represented by various adjustment paths to the diagonal. Path A in the figure suggests an adjustment in which capital locates in the east rapidly, whereas labor moves from east to west slowly; as a result the equilibrium "size" of the east is not affected by the integration process. Since the west is operating at the capital-labor ratio at

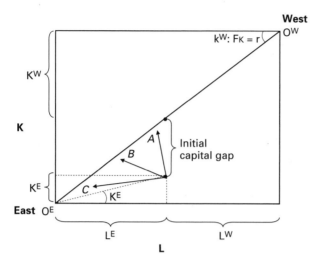

Figure 5.1
Possible paths of economic integration.

the outset, the union of the two regions imports capital from abroad. Along path B, in contrast, labor moves rapidly from the east to the west, whereas capital sluggishly moves from the west to the east and largely follows workers to the west. Path C represents a path in which investment is so small that the net evolution of the eastern capital stock is negative, leading to a "national park" in the east.[3]

The assumption of constant returns implies equality of marginal products of capital and labor for all points along the diagonal. The resting point of the economy is thus not unique; efficient production is possible at any point on the segment $O^W O^E$, with no loss of steady-state per capita productivity, since both regions are producing at the same capital-labor ratio.[4] To determine which criteria should guide society's choice for selecting the allocation of production factors, it is essential to model explicitly the dynamics of integration and thereby the transition path. That will be the task of the next section.

5.3   A Formal Model of Factor Mobility and Regional Economic Integration

5.3.1   Basic Elements

With identical production technologies in both regions, points along the diagonal of figure 5.1 are efficient in the static sense that the marginal product of capital equals the world interest rate plus economic depreciation, and the real wage can be read off the factor price frontier (the residual output after capital employed is paid its gross marginal product under competitive conditions). The indeterminacy of these potential allocations hint that an output- or welfare-maximizing trajectory for the economy will be decided by the importance of the dynamics in reaching its steady state. Let the physical-capital stocks of west and east be denoted by K^W and K^E, respectively, and assume, for simplicity, in the first instance that labor is homogeneous and supplied inelastically by households in the region of residence and that the endowment of labor in each region is normalized at the outset to one-half. We denote the population of the east by ℓ^E, so under full employment assumptions, $L^W = 1 - \ell^E$ and $L^E = \ell^E$.[5] These and other variables are defined with respect to a point in time t, but time subscripts will be suppressed whenever possible. The model is fully deterministic.

Factor mobility or adjustment costs are central to the discussion of regional integration in this model. Following a well-established and venerated tradition, I assume that capital investment costs are external and convex in the level of investment expenditures. Similarly, I assume that costs of migration are also convex in levels of migration.[6] Although not necessary for the main argument, quadratic forms of these functions are assumed for tractability. Similarly, I assume that this stylized, decentralized, competitive environment meets the conditions for an Arrow-Debreu economy, so the social planner's optimum and the decentralized market equilibrium are identical. In particular, the costs of migration are assumed to be borne fully by the migrant (there are no externalities). The skeptical reader can regard the following as a normative exercise extendable in a straightforward way to cases involving external effects.

5.3.2 Factor Mobility in the Market Equilibrium

A convenient shortcut for characterizing the competitive, decentralized equilibrium is simply to find the allocation chosen by a hypothetical social planner.[7] The task is to choose migration and investment policies in the east and west to maximize the present discounted value of national output net of migration and investment costs.[8] More formally, I will seek policies—functions of time $t \in [0, \infty)$—governing investment rates I^W and I^E in the west and east, respectively, and the net migration from west to east X to make the value of the expression

$$\int_0^\infty e^{-rt} \left[F(K^E, \ell^E) + F(K^W, 1 - \ell^E) - I^E - I^W - \frac{\psi}{2}(I^E)^2 - \frac{\phi}{2}X^2 \right] dt \quad (1)$$

as large as possible, subject to initial conditions (at $t = 0$) on factor supplies in both east and west. All workers are identical in their contribution to production. Gross and net migration flows are identical; negative values of X imply net migration from east to west. The parameters ψ and ϕ, which are both positive, capture the intensity of the relevant external adjustment costs. The regional stocks of labor and capital obey the following equations of motion:

$$\dot{K}^E = I^E - \delta K^E, \quad (2)$$

$$\dot{K}^W = I^W - \delta K^W, \quad (3)$$

$$\dot{L}^E = \dot{\ell}^E = X, \quad (4)$$

$$\dot{L}^W = -X, \quad (5)$$

where δ is the common depreciation rate of physical capital. By abstracting from adjustment costs of the western capital stock, I shift emphasis to relative adjustment costs in the east, which are driven by uncertainty over property rights, bureaucracy-related transaction costs, tax breaks, and regimes, as well as business-related public infrastructure.[9]

5.3.3 Solution and Interpretation

The solution to the model can be characterized as follows. Define q^W, q^E, and μ as the shadow values (again, with time subscripts suppressed whenever obvious) of installing an additional unit of capital in the west and an additional unit of capital in the east and of moving a worker to the east, respectively, at the optimum.[10] Denoting partial derivatives of functions with subscripts, for example, $F_K^W \equiv F_K(K^W / (1 - \ell^E), 1) = \partial F(K^W, L^W) / \partial K$, necessary conditions characterizing the optimal policy can be summarized compactly at $t = 0$:

$$I^E = \frac{q^E - 1}{\psi}, \quad (6)$$

$$X = \frac{\mu}{\phi}, \quad (7)$$

$$q^W = 1, \quad (8)$$

$$\dot{q}^E + F_K^E = (r + \delta)q^E, \tag{9}$$

$$F_K^W = r + \delta, \tag{10}$$

$$\dot{\mu} + (F_L^E - F_L^W) = r\mu. \tag{11}$$

Equations (6) and (7) relate optimal investment in the east and migration to the east as positive and linear functions of their respective shadow prices, which are sufficient statistics for determining both variables. Equations (8) and (10) give optimal behavior in the absence of adjustment costs: In the west, the capital-labor ratio continuously obeys $F_K^W \equiv r + \delta$. Since $q^W = 1$ always, I will henceforth drop the superscript for the eastern shadow value of the capital stock in place. Upon arrival, migrants from the east are immediately equipped with the same level of capital possessed by other western residents and earn the western wage, denoted by $\bar{w}$.

By definition, the two state variables in the model, k^E and ℓ^W, cannot be changed instantaneously. The hypothetical cost to the central planner of moving them from their respective optimal paths is given by the shadow values q and μ. Equations (9) and (11) can be thought of as arbitrage relations governing the dynamic behavior of those shadow prices (including capital gains or losses) and equating total returns on value in these implicit assets to their respective opportunity costs. Integrating these arbitrage conditions forward from initial conditions at time t and imposing the transversality conditions leads to the following expressions for q and μ:[11]

$$q_t = \int_t^\infty e^{-(r+\delta)s} F_K^E \, ds, \tag{12}$$

$$\mu_t = \int_t^\infty e^{-rs} (F_L^E - \bar{w}) \, ds. \tag{13}$$

Shadow prices are the present discounted values of future lifetime returns of the respective "assets." The shadow value of capital in the east, q, reflects the present discounted value of present and future marginal products of one unit of capital installed in the east, where discounting occurs using the world interest rate plus the depreciation rate. In the case of migration to the east, the shadow value μ represents the present value of the difference in future marginal products of labor between the east and west, discounted using the world interest rate.[12] In the case studied in this chapter, $\mu < 0$ will hold throughout. It follows that a wage gap will exist between the two regions that disappears asymptotically as capital accumulates in the east and labor migrates to the west.

5.4   Dynamics

5.4.1   Role of Dynamics

Constant returns in capital and labor (excluding adjustment costs) imply that marginal products in the east are scale-independent and depend only on k^E, the capital-labor ratio in the east. From (12) and (13), there is a range of absolute sizes of the eastern economy that are consistent with the same shadow value of moving capital and labor between regions, and thus with economic integration on an efficiency definition.[13] The optimal path and the steady state will depend on initial conditions k_0 and ℓ_0, as well as the constellation of adjustment costs.

The dynamics of the economy are summarized in figure 5.2, a reduced version of the familiar phase diagram in the space of the two state variables relevant for the east, K^E and ℓ^E.[14] The two loci for constancy of these two variables are given after substituting (12) and (13) in (3) and (4), respectively, and setting these equal to zero:

$$F_K^E = (r + \delta)(1 + \psi \delta K^E), \tag{14}$$

$$F_L^E = \bar{w}. \tag{15}$$

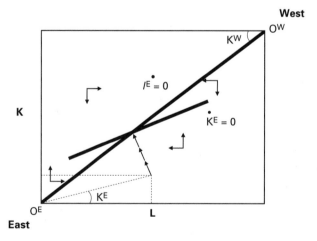

Figure 5.2
Dynamics when adjustment costs matter.

Equations (14) and (15) trace respective possible combinations of the state variables (capital and labor in the east) that are consistent with constancy of each over time. Both loci have positive slope.[15] Saddle point stability implies a unique approach by all variables to the steady state, given initial conditions. In this version of the model without relative "depreciation" or wastage of the eastern population, only the capital adjustment costs determine the steady state, whereas migration adjustment costs do not. Both types of adjustment costs will matter, however, for the particular dynamic path taken over time.

5.4.2   The Central Role of Adjustment Costs

The results of the last section established that adjustment costs are essential in determining where the economy winds up and how costly adjustment will be. It can be shown that the path taken by the eastern capital and labor stocks will depend on future (and correctly anticipated) paths of both, but also on the relative costs of adjustment. As ψ increases, capital becomes increasingly immobile, and labor bears the brunt of the adjustment. As labor immobility increases (φ goes to infinity), only capital is adjusted. Because point A in the diagram is a sink, all equilibrium paths lead to it, regardless of initial conditions.

Whereas much attention has been paid to external effects in formal models of economic integration, adjustment costs associated with moving factors of production across space have generally been neglected.[16] Overall welfare (output) in this model will depend on the transition path chosen. In particular, total output lost to adjustment costs can be written at $t = 0$ as

$$\frac{1}{2} \int_0^\infty e^{-rt} \left[\frac{1}{\psi} \left(\left[\int_0^\infty e^{-(r+\delta)t} F_K^E \, dt \right] - 1 \right)^2 + \frac{1}{\phi} \left(\int_0^\infty e^{-rt} (F_L^E - \overline{w}) \, dt \right)^2 \right] dt,$$

(16)

suggesting that the planner is "rewarded" for keeping the shadow value of the more flexible factor closer to its long-run value; this is accomplished by adjusting it more intensely. Intuitively, if capital is cheaper to adjust ($\psi \ll \phi$), it is moved more rapidly into the east, raising wages and thereby reducing the deviation of μ from its steady-state value; if labor is cheaper to move ($\psi \gg \phi$), then rapid migration removes the rate-of-return advantage in the east, thereby smoothing out the trajectory of q^E.

The consideration of adjustment costs has central implications for the behavior of observed wages and the rate of return on capital. Since factor supplies cannot move instantaneously, the factor-input ratio will be lower in the east for some time; during this period wages will be lower and returns to capital higher. The model predicts that factor price differentials are transient, persistent, and consistent with finite factor flows over time, disappearing only in the long run. Under competitive factor remuneration in the west ($F_K = r + \delta$, $F_L = \bar{w}$), (9) and (11) can be rewritten as

$$r^E = \bar{r} - \frac{\dot{q}^E}{q^E}, \tag{17}$$

$$w^E = \bar{w} + r\mu - \dot{\mu}, \tag{18}$$

respectively. Equation (17) equates the local rate of return on capital to the world rate, correcting for capital gains or losses. Since $\mu < 0$ and $\dot{\mu} > 0$, there is a persistent regional wage gap across regions ($w^E < \bar{w}$). Similarly, since $q^E > 0$ and $\dot{q}^E < 0$ along the adjustment path, $r^E > \bar{r}$. These theoretical results are consistent with both casual empirical data on persistently low wages and high rates of return in Eastern Europe, as well as finite rates of factor mobility.

5.5   The Relevance of Adjustment Costs: An Empirical Assessment

5.5.1   What Are Adjustment Costs?

Adjustment costs of labor and capital in this model give economic content to the notion that "Rome wasn't built in a day." Because migration and foreign direct investment are both costly, steady-state efficiency conditions are not sufficient to characterize optimal policies. Since all steady-state factor allocations along the diagonal in figure 5.1 are equally efficient, the path and the steady state chosen reflect the minimization of present discounted costs necessary to achieve integration. If these costs are high, regional integration is likely to take a long time. The persistence of regional adjustment in Eastern Europe would suggest that these adjustment costs are significant.

Convex adjustment costs were first invoked to explain investment behavior (Lucas 1967a,b; Treadway 1971; Abel 1982). Yet they can also be used to model migration patterns with similarly sensible results. Even in the years immediately following German unification, when eastern wages were about one-fifth of western levels and after restrictions on labor mobility were eliminated, migration rates remained finite and actually slowed in the aftermath of unification, despite the best of all imaginable circumstances for spatial mobility.[17] The convex costs of labor movement could in the German case reflect underlying population heterogeneity, which is evident in the exorbitant prices that some (but not all) migrants are willing to pay to be smuggled illegally into Europe.[18] Consistent with adjustment cost models, migration peaked at the outset of the German integration episode and fell subsequently in a monotone fashion until 1998.

The following example illustrates the transition faced by a representative household from individual heterogeneity to an adjustment cost proxy or "stand in." Suppose for the moment that migration at the individual level occurs under conditions of certainty and complete information, and further assume that the wage differential across the two regions is identical for all workers. Migration of the ith individual occurs whenever the current wage exceeds the fixed costs of migration $c(i) \geq 0$, which are distributed across workers according to a cumulative distribution $F(c)$. For distributions with concave $F(c)$, the implied inverse function mapping the cumulative fraction of those willing to change residence onto ranked private migration costs will have a convex shape, as figure 5.3 shows.[19] Convex adjustment costs are a potential stand in, provided that heterogeneity of a certain type is present.

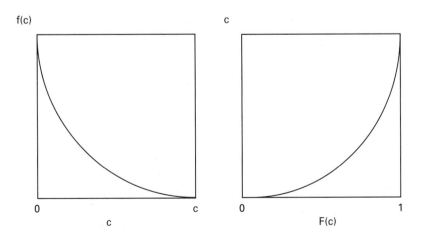

Figure 5.3
Migration costs as adjustment costs.

5.5.2 Inferring Adjustment Costs Using the Model

The model presented in the previous section allows us to calculate the adjustment costs as well as shadow values associated with the two state variables, eastern productive capital stock and Eastern employment; the costs and values calculated are consistent with recent historical experience. More concretely, we can calibrate the model for an assumed convergence path consistent with some historical episode—here, eastern Germany in the years immediately following unification[20]—along with some posited values for uncontroversial parameters and back out the adjustment costs implied by that episode. A cursory examination of the eastern German experience at the level of the federal states for 1990–1998 is given in figure 5.4. That experience appears consistent with a mobility race between capital and labor characteristic of the model presented in section 5.3.

Let us assume that the shadow value of migration at $t = 0$ is given by (13). Let us further assume that the wage equals the marginal product in both regions and that convergence occurs at constant rate over time, λ.[21] The historical record of eastern Germany in the 1990s suggests values of $r = 0.03$ and $\lambda = 0.07$ (the latter is roughly the observed rate of subsequent wage convergence). Measuring the eastern wage in units of the western equivalent results in $w_{1991}^E = 0.50$. From (13) it is easy to show that $\mu_0 = -5.0$ in 1991; that is, the shadow value of moving a worker from the east to the west in 1991 was five times the annual western wage. In equilibrium, this is also the marginal cost of migration. Now use the migration function (7) plus the observed net east-west migration in that year to calculate a value for ϕ. According to the Germany Federal Statistical Office, net migration to eastern Germany was roughly $-172,000$ in 1991.[22] The value of ϕ consistent with that migration flow in 1991 is $5/172,000$, or 0.00002907 of the square of the annual western wage per person. Put in perspective, net immigration had declined by 1998 to $-32,000$, implying a marginal cost of only 93 percent of western annual wages.

With additional assumptions, it is possible to use the model to impute a shadow value to installed capital in eastern Germany and the gross investment adjustment cost parameter ψ. An obvious problem arises in that the marginal return to capital in the east is difficult if not impossible to observe. Furthermore, extreme heterogeneity of capital goods and projects renders the average return to capital a poor indicator of the marginal return.[23] Employing a Cobb-Douglas production function calibrated on equipment capital and total employment in

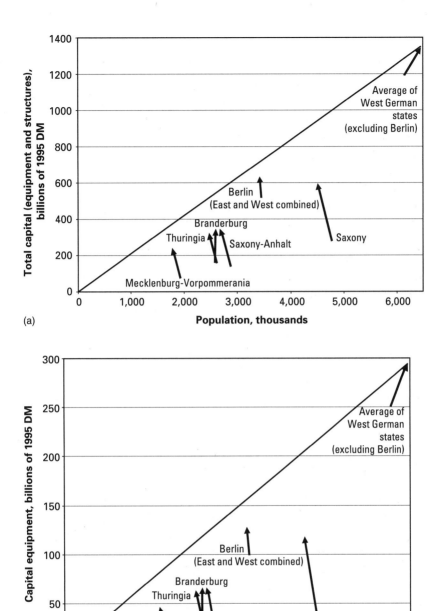

Figure 5.4
Integration of East Germany: (a) Evolution of total capital stock and population by state, 1990–1998; (b) Evolution of equipment capital stock and population by state, 1990–1998. Berlin is East and West Berlin combined.

the West German economy, I calculate that the marginal East German investment project in 1991 evaluated at East German capital and employment levels faced a rate of return of roughly 80.5 percent, compared with a rate of return of 36.6 percent in West Germany. With the same real interest rate and convergence assumptions above, plus an estimate of depreciation of 10 percent per annum, equation (12) implies a 1991 shadow value (q) of installed equipment capital in terms of current output of 4.025. According to the Statistisches Bundesamt, total gross equipment investment in eastern Germany in 1991 was DM53.2 billion or €27.2 billion, implying an adjustment cost parameter ψ of 0.147978 billion per € of real investment. The fact that equipment investment has since increased to nearly €35.7 billion in 1998 (despite cumulative investment of more than €300 billion since 1990) could be interpreted as evidence of successful policies to improve capital mobility to eastern Germany by reducing capital adjustment costs.

5.5.3 Neglected Aspects of Migration and Economic Integration

The key result of section 5.3 is that both forms of mobility represent *investment* decisions that are best spread over many periods. As a consequence, many variables can influence the relationship between the decision to migrate and the observable, contemporary wage gain from doing so. First, expectations of future convergence *alone* can vary significantly for any given current value of wage differentials. Low migration might be explained by optimistic expectations of future convergence of home wages to target region levels. Sluggish migration can also be explained by adjustment costs. Since the migration decision is binary at the individual level, adjustment costs might stand for a flat distribution of migration costs in the population, generating a low, finite flow of migrants. This last explanation is particularly plausible when age is accounted for.

There are other aspects of migration and integration that are not covered directly by the adjustment cost model. This section summarizes some of these aspects and assesses their relevance for my conclusions.

5.5.3.1 Return Migration
Return migration is an important aspect of the integration process that is not included in the model of section 5.3, since there is no reason for gross and net flows to differ from one another. As can be seen in the

surprisingly high gross rates of migration from western to eastern Germany, or from Germany to Turkey, return migration is an important aspect of the integration process and reflects heterogeneity in the migrating population with respect to age, sex, family status, wealth, and other factors.

One straightforward way of capturing return migration in the model would be to admit some form of depreciation of the eastern labor force. Another, adopted by Sinn (2000), would be to model the migration decision as resulting from a period-by-period comparison of the eastern and western wages net of a periodic cost of "having migrated" as long as the migrant is away from the home region.[24] A migrant can set this unrelenting "homesickness cost" to zero by returning to the region of origin. Although interesting, this formulation neglects the investment aspect of migration, since the costs of having migrated are paid each period. Furthermore, it predisposes the model to predict reverse migration, since the homesickness cost does not abate as long as the migrant remains in the host country. Reverse migration occurs in Sinn's formulation against a backdrop of more intensive capital formation in the east driven by higher rates of returns and lower product wages. The type of reverse migration is not borne out, however, by the long-term integration experience of the United States since the Civil War, in which net migration proved permanent and wage differentials were closed monotonically. In contrast, the German experience with Spanish and Greek migration may lend support to Sinn's model.

5.5.3.2 Nonconvex Costs of Adjustment

Although increasing marginal adjustment costs can explain time delays associated with moving production factors, their appropriateness for this purpose was questioned by Kydland and Prescott (1982, 1347–1348), who argued that short- and long-run supply elasticities should differ because of specialized inputs that are flexible only in the long run. In the case of labor mobility, one might find unacceptable the notion that convex costs are fully internal to the migrant, since migration is a binary decision.[25] There is also a literature that considers network effects that might lead to nonconvex or concave adjustment costs (see Epstein 2002). Information about the host country acquired by early migrants may also be transmitted to newcomers, who thereby supply a public good to later generations.

As a modeling strategy, convex costs have the attractive property of robustly capturing one of the most salient aspects of investment decisions: their persistence over time. Because it is difficult to map into reality, the adjustment cost framework is reminiscent of Milton Friedman's (1953) metaphor of billiard players, who know nothing about Newtonian mechanics but behave as if they do. In fact, simple observation rules out "bang-bang" investment or migration behavior in the aggregate, as well as multiple equilibria associated with a number of alternative cost functions.

5.5.3.3   Costs of Exercising the Option Value of Waiting

The notion of the option value is useful in explaining why levels of migration are low even if positive wage differentials persist. Burda (1995) and O'Connell (1997) model the migration decision as an investment project with elements of an option. Migration implies making a decision now that destroys the option of postponing migration to some later date. This additional, unobservable cost can explain why less migration occurs than expected. In an environment without uncertainty, the implied fixed cost necessary to deter migration is usually large, even for small wage differentials. Suppose the current wage gap is 70 percent, and that the migration decision is made with forty years of further lifetime income possible. As in the calibration example, suppose the wage gap shrinks at a rate of 7 percent per annum and that the discount rate is 3 percent per annum. Under these conditions, the fixed costs necessary to deter migration in a deterministic world must be roughly twenty-three times larger than the current annual wage— an implausibly large monetary figure.[26] It is natural to conclude that other factors besides present and future wage differentials are important for explaining German migration patterns in the 1990s. Real-option theory suggests that the prospect of further improvement (i.e., even faster convergence) in home labor market conditions should matter, as reflected by a high variance and persistence of the evolution of the wage differential.

According to survey data, at least Eastern Europeans do not exhibit a great willingness to migrate despite large wage differentials between Eastern and Western Europe, providing indirect support for the real-option approach to migration. Papapanagos and Sanfey (2001) report results of an extensive survey in which they found a remarkable hesitancy of Central and Eastern Europeans to migrate. Table 5.1 shows that although many have given thought to the migration option, remarkably few are set on it. This suggests that wage differentials are really only the tip of the iceberg of the data that will be necessary to resolve this issue.

Table 5.1
Attitudes toward migration among Central and Eastern Europeans

a. Considered working in Western Europe

Country	Yes (%)	No (%)	Been there already (%)
Albania	56.9	42.2	0.9
Bulgaria	25.1	73.6	1.4
Czech Republic	27.9	71.1	1.0
Estonia	32.3	65.1	2.6
Hungary	24.6	73.4	0.7
Poland	30.4	65.0	4.6
Romania	32.9	65.7	1.4
Euro-Russia	29.7	69.5	0.8

b. Likelihood of emigration by country

Country	Definitely (%)	Maybe (%)	Probably (%)	Definitely not (%)
Albania	38.0	25.1	8.3	28.6
Bulgaria	1.8	9.1	17.1	72.1
Czech Republic	0.4	3.9	12.6	83.0
Estonia	2.2	11.1	30.6	56.0
Hungary	0.8	3.2	16.5	79.6
Poland	1.4	3.4	18.7	76.6
Romania	2.8	14.2	16.4	66.6
Euro-Russia	0.6	5.8	23.2	70.4

Source: Papapanagos and Sanfey 2001.

Indirect evidence of the option value of waiting can be found in the econometric analysis of inter-German migration reported by Burda and Hunt (2001), who estimated reduced-form equations for aggregate gross migration flows in a panel of regional pairs in Germany. Table 5.2 reports their results. First, it is evident (and statistically significant) that the effect of home and source wage levels on aggregate migration are not symmetric. Second, for all but the most aggregated estimates, the impact of the home wage on migration is larger in absolute value, which supports an option value explanation of migration. Wages at home strengthen incentives to stay relative to wages in target states, presumably by virtue of the information they convey about future developments at home. This effect appears to be the strongest for young people, and all other things equal, age should affect the option value negatively.

Table 5.2
Estimated elasticities of gross migration flows to wages, Germany, 1991–1999

	Destination hourly wage (log)	Source hourly wage (log)
Full sample (all states)	1.66	−1.15
	(0.23)	(0.26)
Modified full sample[a]	0.97	−2.32
	(0.33)	(0.31)
Stratified by age[b]		
Age 18–24	1.71	−2.69
	(0.36)	(0.33)
Age 25–49	1.23	−1.58
	(0.29)	(0.27)
Age 50–64	1.32	−0.62
	(0.42)	(0.39)

Source: Burda and Hunt 2001, tables 20 and 21.
Note: Coefficients on log hourly wages from regressions of log gross bilateral migration flows between two pairs of East-West states controlling for unemployment in source and destination as well as fixed effects for time and direction-pair, East-to-West interacted with time, source, and destination unemployment.
[a] Sample aggregates city-states and omits inconsistent information in the earlier years.
[b] Estimated using gross flow data for all sources and destinations to and from Mecklenburg–Lower Pommerania and Saxony only.

5.6   Conclusions

In this chapter, I have tried to characterize regional integration as the simple outcome of regional dynamics of factors of production: capital and labor. The analysis sees integration as a mobility race between two factors of production, one that will be decided by costs of moving them, even if these costs are not relevant in the long run.[27] All the same, there is no role for direct policy interventions under the conditions considered here. If policymakers fear migration, which is perhaps another way of saying that there are external costs not reflected by market incentives, there may be a role for subsidizing capital formation in the east (or bribing workers to stay in the east). This would have to be worked out formally, since it is not a direct implication of the model.[28]

The neglect of regional trade is probably the most important limitation of the analysis presented in the chapter. If trade is driven by factor proportions and regions are incompletely specialized, the convergence in figure 5.2 will proceed not to a diagonal, but to a parallelogram with twice as many sides as goods (assuming all are traded) and angles to the horizontal axis implied by optimal factor-input proportions at world prices and the factor price equalization theorem. Within the borders of this parallelogram, factor prices are equalized and incentives for factor mobility cease. The larger the parallelogram, the more likely that integration is possible with few or no factor movements; this is the message of Mundell (1957). Although the evidence in figure 5.4 does not suggest that this effect is important in Germany, it may be significant for integration of richer EU countries with poorer ones.

Other extensions entail a broadening of the purview of the model. In particular, what is the consequence of differential initial conditions in technology for optimal investment and migration? How are the model's characteristics altered when adjustment costs are modeled explicitly in the west, or when they are characterized by constant returns in both regions, as in Hayashi 1982, Summers 1981, or Abel and Blanchard 1983? How might expected future total factor productivity growth affect the value of the migration option, under certainty and uncertainty? Explicit consideration of non-tradables and the influence these goods have on local price levels is an issue frequently noted in discussions of Central and Eastern Europe and would affect the model significantly. Finally, an important distinction between individual productivities, along the lines of migration costs modeled in the previous section, will influence the dynamic adjustment of population and integration. All these elements should be considered in a complete description of the integration process. Nevertheless, the model I have outlined stresses the premier role of labor and capital mobility as driving forces for economic integration.

The most important lesson for policy from the analysis presented in this chapter is that the integration of Europe will involve massive movements of people only in certain limiting or extreme cases. One such case is that of negligible migration costs *and* severely impaired capital mobility. This combination appears unlikely, if only because the demographic structure of the poorest economies of Eastern and Central Europe is such that those with the lowest costs of migration, young people with high skill levels, are in relatively short supply.[29] Moreover, as Buch and Piazolo (2001) have recently documented, the mobility of capital can be expected to increase significantly with the rapid adoption of the EU legal framework for capital ownership, the elimination of capital controls, and prospects for the introduction of the euro.

A second, less optimistic scenario in which European integration is accompanied by large-scale migration involves a catastrophic event, such as a war or economic crisis, in the home country that destroys the option value of waiting and unleashes large and discrete movements of population, shifting the initial conditions of the convergence process in my model. In my view, this more alarming possibility, which is related to higher moments of the wage convergence process, has received much too little attention in the discussion of EU immigration policy. In any event, it should be evident that an evaluation of European integration that is relevant for policymakers cannot proceed far without a rigorous empirical assessment of the relevance of migration and capital investment costs.

Appendix: Local Dynamics

The following analysis considers the dynamic properties of the model as approximated by the behavior of a linearized version around its steady state. Write the model in the following fashion, as four differential equations in K^E, ℓ^E, q and μ:

$$\dot{K}^E = \frac{q-1}{\psi} - \delta K^E, \tag{3'}$$

$$\dot{\ell}^E = \frac{\mu}{\phi}, \tag{4'}$$

$$\dot{q} = (r+\delta)q - F_K^E(K^E, \ell^E), \tag{9'}$$

$$\dot{\mu} = r\mu - [F_L^E(K^E, \ell^E) - \bar{w}]. \tag{11'}$$

Let $\bar{K}^E, \bar{\ell}^E, \bar{q}$, and $\bar{\mu}$ be those values that obtain when the system is at rest. The first-order linearized version of the model is

$$\dot{q} = (r+\delta)(q-\bar{q}) - F_{KK}^E(K^E - \bar{K}^E) - F_{KL}^E(\ell^E - \bar{\ell}^E), \tag{16'}$$

$$\dot{\mu} = r(\mu - \bar{\mu}) - F_{LK}^E(K^E - \bar{K}^E) - F_{LL}^E(\ell^E - \bar{\ell}^E), \tag{17'}$$

$$\dot{K}^E = \frac{1}{\psi}(q - \bar{q}) - \delta(K^E - \bar{K}), \tag{18'}$$

$$\dot{\ell}^E = \frac{1}{\phi}(\mu - \bar{\mu}), \tag{19}$$

or in matrix form:

$$
\begin{bmatrix} \dot{q} \\ \dot{\mu} \\ \dot{K}^E \\ \dot{\ell}^E \end{bmatrix} = M \begin{bmatrix} q - \bar{q} \\ \mu - \bar{\mu} \\ K^E - \bar{K}^E \\ \ell^E - \bar{\ell}^E \end{bmatrix}, \quad \text{with}
$$

$$
M \equiv \begin{bmatrix} (r + \delta) & 0 & -F_{KK}^E & -F_{KL}^E \\ 0 & r & -F_{LK}^E & -F_{LL}^E \\ \psi^{-1} & 0 & -\delta & 0 \\ 0 & \phi^{-1} & 0 & 0 \end{bmatrix}, \tag{20}
$$

and the partial derivatives of F evaluated at $\bar{K}^E, K^W$, and $\bar{\ell}^E$. The dynamics of the system can be studied by evaluating the eigenvalues of M in (20). The sum of the eigenvalues is given by the trace $(2r)$, and their product is given by the determinant $(-\phi^{-1}\delta(r + \delta)F_{LL}^E > 0)$. For stability, at least two eigenvalues must have negative real parts; for saddle point stability, exactly two must do so. Since the determinant is unambiguously positive, the model is either saddle point stable or globally stable. The eigenvalues are zeros of the polynomial in λ resulting from $|M - \lambda I| = 0$, where I is a 4×4 identity matrix, or

$$
\lambda^4 - 2r\lambda^3 + [\psi^{-1}F_{KK}^E + \phi^{-1}F_{LL}^E + r^2 - \delta^2 - r\delta]\lambda^2
$$

$$
- [\psi^{-1}F_{KK}^E + \phi^{-1}F_{LL}^E - \delta(r + \delta)]r\lambda - \delta(r + \delta)\phi^{-1}F_{LL}^E = 0
$$

Routh's theorem (Gantmacher 1986, 531) states that the number of roots with positive real parts is equal to the number of sign changes in the leading column of Routh's pattern, which turns out to be exactly two. Thus, two eigenvalues have positive real parts, which it is natural to associate with the two forward-looking variables, μ and q. The two eigenvalues with negative real parts correspond to the two state variables K^E and $\bar{\ell}^E$.

Notes

An earlier version of this chapter was presented at the CESifo Conference "Managing European Integration" in Delphi, 13–16 September 2002. I thank Sascha Becker, Helge Berger, Dirk Bethmann, Maike Burda, Jennifer Hunt, and especially my discussant Carlo Perroni for comments and discussions. The research presented in this chapter was supported by the Sonderforschungsbereich 373 of the Deutsche Forschungsgemeinschaft. I am grateful to Almut Balleer and Max Kleinert for useful research assistance.

1. The adoption of leading technologies by backward regions, driving total factor productivity to the level of leading regions, is ruled out by the assumption of shared production technologies. In the analysis that follows, I will thus ignore differences in

technologies across regions. The assumption of constant returns will rule out integration driven by agglomeration dynamics.

2. Ohlin (1933) is usually credited with first formulating the proposition. More recently, Hanson and Slaughter (2000) have shown how interstate trade may help explain factor price behavior in the United States.

3. Clearly, a central assumption is that space itself is an inessential or costless factor of production.

4. My discussant Carlo Perroni notes that any additional production factor in fixed supply, such as land, would attenuate this strong result. Although technically correct, the premise violates the assumption of constant overall returns to scale and would invalidate the central mechanisms of the model. The objective of this chapter pursues the extent to which constant returns in mobile factors imply indeterminacy in regional integration, just as constant returns in accumulable factors can lead to endogenous growth.

5. Full employment is assumed throughout for simplicity. Although the model can be modified to account for labor supply in a straightforward way, allowing for nonclearing labor markets would require significant modifications to the model and is therefore left for future research.

6. See Abel 1982 and Abel and Blanchard 1983, but also Lucas 1967b and Treadway 1971. Summers (1981) and Hayashi (1982) study the implications of adjustment costs that are convex in the rate of investment. In section 5.5, I provide a rationale for this assumption for the migration decision and offer some insights as to its importance.

7. See Mas-Colell, Whinston, and Green 1995. The assumption of perfect competition in factor markets is not an innocuous one. Rigidity in labor markets will alter the calculus of the migration decision to reflect the prospect of involuntary unemployment. This complication will be left to future research. Regional market power might even lead to better outcomes when an optimal tariff strategy is followed (Ramaswami 1968).

8. Here "output" and "utility" are synonymous. It would be straightforward to model the problem in terms of utility maximization, requiring an arbitrary weighting of eastern and western residents' utility. As long as production and consumption decisions are separable and the world interest rate is given, there is no loss of generality by focusing on the production side.

9. Some readers may object that the adjustment costs assumed here are not linear homogeneous (i.e., do not exhibit constant returns), as in Summers 1981 or Hayashi 1982. If they were, no equilibria with positive capital in both regions would exist unless all regions had identical adjustment cost functions.

10. Technically, they are the costate variables in the dynamic optimization problem and have analogues to Lagrange multipliers in static maximization analysis.

11. The transversality conditions on q^E and q^W prevent the respective shadow prices from following explosive trajectories (i.e., from rising faster than rates $r + \delta$ and r, respectively).

12. This is because labor does not depreciate, a simplification that could easily be modified to account for population attrition due to death, retirements, or return migration. I eschew explicit "depreciation" of the east population relative to the west, which seems artificial and hard to justify on a priori grounds.

13. Agglomeration effects, which are intentionally ignored, would strengthen this argument. See Puga and Venables 1996 for examples of how agglomeration effects influence the steady state in a model of economic development, and see Neary 2001 for an extensive survey of the related literature.

14. It would also be informative, but geometrically unwieldy, if not impossible, to depict the two costate variables in the same two-dimensional figure. Their instantaneous dynamic behavior can be inferred from the behavior of the two state variables.

15. The slope of the $\dot{\ell}^E = 0$ locus is the capital-labor ratio chosen given the world rate of return on capital and the fixed supply of labor, $dK^E/d\ell^E = -F^E_{KL}/F^E_{KK} > 0$, and is the slope of the isocost curve at that point. It is steeper than the $\dot{K}^E = 0$ locus with slope given by $dK^E/d\ell^E = -F^E_{KL}/(F^E_{KK} - (r + \delta)\delta\psi) > 0$.

16. It should be noted that adjustment costs are also relevant for intra-regional allocation of production factors across sectors (Mussa 1978). This issue will not be addressed in this chapter, however.

17. In fact, Hunt (2000), studying the aggregate flow patterns in regional German data, concludes that migration from East to West Germany was too low, when wage, unemployment and other differentials are taken into account.

18. For a striking description of traffic in migration passage, see "Muslim Refugees Find Growing Peril on Path to Europe" 2002.

19. Formally I require that the density function for migration costs, $f(c)$, which is defined on the compact support $[0, \bar{c}]$, have a uniformly negative first derivative. This rationalization of adjustment costs runs into the difficulty that migration takes the relevant marginal individuals out of the population, by definition, and thereby necessarily changes the distribution of fixed costs in the remaining individuals. Some stronger assumptions about return migration or population regeneration might solve this problem.

20. See Burda and Hunt 2001 for more details on the integration of East and West Germany.

21. With initial and terminal conditions w_0 and $\bar{w}$, this implies, for $s \geq 0$, $w^E_s = w^E_0 e^{-\lambda s} + \bar{w}(1 - e^{-\lambda s})$, or $w^E_s - \bar{w} = (w^E_0 - \bar{w})e^{-\lambda s}$.

22. This includes net migration from abroad to eastern Germany less migration from eastern Germany to foreign countries. Source: Statistisches Bundesamt, 2000.

23. It is important to note that the collapsing East German enterprise sector, which was still largely in state hands in 1991, required liquidity credits or outright transfers of an unprecedented magnitude, and many firms were forced to lay off bloated workforces. It appears likely that average profits were negative in East Germany in 1991. See Sinn and Sinn 1991 and Akerlof et al. 1991.

24. In fact, Sinn (2000) sets $\phi = 0$. His model thus requires a reversal of the wage gap between east and west and implies that all migration is ultimately undone as capital accumulation proceeds in the east. This "two-way" pattern can be thought of as return migration.

25. Considering migration in the family context, the metaphor has empirical validity: Migration usually begins with commuting or with the migration of a single member of the family, who gathers information and paves the way for future migration, followed by the migration of siblings, then by that of other family members, and then even by that of extended family. See Stark 1991 for a discussion of related issues.

26. The absolute gain from east-west migration is given by $\int_0^{40} e^{-0.03s}(\bar{w} - w_s^E)\, ds = (\bar{w} - w_0^E) \int_0^{40} e^{-0.1s}\, ds = 9.82(\bar{w} - w_0^E)$. Since $\bar{w} - w_0^E = 0.7\bar{w}$, the gain from migration relative to the current eastern wage is given by $9.82(0.7)\bar{w}/w_0^E = 9.82(0.7)/0.3 = 22.9$.

27. For a detailed discussion of the potential long-run effects of adjustment costs, see Abel 2001.

28. Burda and Wyplosz (1992) present a model that allows for external effects of migration due to differential human-capital endowments.

29. As noted above, Burda and Hunt (2001) find that East-West German migration responds to wage levels in sending and receiving regions, but that these effects are age sensitive, with the youngest age groups responding most elastically, as migration theory would predict.

References

Abel, A. 1982. "Dynamic Effects of Permanent and Temporary Tax Policies in a q-Model of Investment." *Journal of Monetary Economics* 9: 353–373.

Abel, A. 2001. "On the Invariance of the Rate of Return to Convex Adjustment Costs." Mimeographed.

Abel, A., and O. Blanchard. 1983. "An Intertemporal Model of Savings and Investment." *Econometrica* 51: 672–692.

Akerlof, G. A., A. K. Rose, J. L. Yellen, and H. Hessenius. 1991. "East Germany in from the Cold: The Economic Aftermath of Currency Union." *Brookings Papers on Economic Activity* 1991, no. 1: 1–105.

Buch, C., and D. Piazolo. 2001. "Capital and Trade Flows in Europe and the Impact of Enlargement." *Economic Systems* 25: 183–214.

Burda, M. 1995. "Migration and the Option Value of Waiting." *Economic and Social Review* 27: 1–19.

Burda, M., and J. Hunt. 2001. "From Reunification to Economic Integration: Productivity and the Labor Market in East Germany." *Brookings Papers on Economic Activity* 2001, no. 2: 1–71.

Burda, M., and C. Wyplosz. 1992. "Human Capital, Investment and Migration in an Integrating Europe." *European Economic Review* 36: 677–684.

Eichengreen, B. 1990. "One Money for Europe: Lessons from the U.S. Currency Union." *Economic Policy* 10: 117–187.

Epstein, G. 2002. "Information Cascades and the Decision to Migrate." Discussion paper no. 3287, Centre for Economic Policy Research, London.

Friedman, M. 1953. *Essays in Positive Economics.* Chicago: University of Chicago Press.

Gantmacher, F. 1986. *Matrizentheorie (Matrix Theory).* Translation from the Russian edition, 1966. Berlin: Springer Verlag.

Hanson, G., and M. Slaughter. 2000. "The Rybczinski Theorem, Factor Price Equalization and Immigration: Evidence from the US States." Working paper no. 7074, National Bureau of Economic Research, Cambridge, MA.

Hayashi, F. 1982. "Average q and Marginal q: A Neoclassical Interpretation." *Econometrica* 50: 213–224.

Hunt, J. 2000. "Why Do People Still Live in East Germany?" Unpublished manuscript, Yale University, New Haven, CT.

Kydland, F., and E. Prescott. 1982. "Time to Build and Aggregate Fluctuations." *Econometrica* 50: 1345–1370.

Lucas, R. E. Jr. 1967a. "Optimal Investment with Rational Expectations." In *Rational Expectations and Econometric Practice*, vol. 1, ed. R. Lucas and T. Sargent, 55–66. New York: North-Holland.

Lucas, R. E. Jr. 1967b. "Adjustment Costs and the Theory of Supply." *Journal of Political Economy* 75: 321–334.

Mas-Colell, A., M. Whinston, and J. Green. 1995. *Microeconomic Theory*. Oxford: Oxford University Press.

Mundell, R. 1957. "International Trade and Factor Mobility." *American Economic Review* 51: 321–355.

"Muslim Refugees Find Growing Peril on Path to Europe." 2002. *Wall Street Journal Europe*, May 28, p. 1.

Neary, J. P. 2001. "Of Hype and Hyperbolas: Introducing the New Economic Geography." *Journal of Economic Literature* 15: 536–561.

O'Connell, P. G. J. 1997. "Migration under Uncertainty: 'Try Your Luck' or 'Wait and See.'" *Journal of Regional Science* 37, no. 2: 331–374.

Ohlin, B. 1933. *Interregional and International Trade*. Cambridge: Harvard University Press.

Papapanagos, H., and P. Sanfey. 2001. "Intentions to Migrate in Transition Countries: The Case of Albania." *Journal of Population Economics* 14: 491–504.

Puga, D., and A. Venables. 1996. "The Spread of Industry: Spatial Agglomeration in Economic Development." Discussion paper no. 1354, Centre for Economic Policy Research, London.

Ramaswami, V. K. 1968. "International Factor Movement and the National Advantage." *Economica* (August): 309–310.

Sinn, H.-W. 2000. "EU Enlargement, Migration and Lessons from German Unification." *German Economic Review* 3 (August): 299–314.

Sinn, H.-W., and G. Sinn. 1991. *Kaltstart*. Tübingen: Mohr. Published in English as *Jumpstart*, Cambridge: MIT Press, 1992.

Stark, O. 1991. *The Migration of Labor*. Oxford: Basil Blackwell.

Summers, L. H. 1981. "Taxation and Corporate Investment: A q-Theory Approach." *Brookings Papers on Economic Activity* 1981, no. X: 67–140.

Treadway, A. 1971. "On Rational Entrepreneurial Behavior and the Demand for Investment." *Review of Economic Studies* 36: 227–239.

U.S. Bureau of Labor Statistics. 2003. "International Comparisons of Hourly Compensation Costs: Supplementary Table, 1975–2001." Available at ⟨www.bls.gov/fls.home⟩.

Comments

Carlo Perroni

In his chapter, Michael Burda argues that, in a world in which technology can spread freely across regions and all factors of production are able, in principle, to cross borders, the long-run outcome of full economic integration is theoretically indeterminate. More precisely, any interregional allocation of factors that is consistent with equality of factor proportions across regions can be supported as a long-run equilibrium. Short-run adjustment dynamics will then determine which particular long-run allocation prevails. Thus, if short-run capital relocation costs are higher than those affecting labor migration, we would expect European enlargement to produce significant and permanent eastward migration of workers; but in the reverse scenario, labor migration will be more contained, not only in the short run, but permanently. The main message we take away from Burda's chapter is that understanding short-run adjustment costs is crucial for predicting the possible long-run effects of EU enlargement.

I will direct my comments to what I consider to be the chapter's main claims: (1) short-run adjustment costs determine long-run outcomes; (2) factor return differentials that persist after integration in the short run can be used to infer adjustment costs; and (3) there is limited scope for government intervention once the process of integration is underway.

Burda's first point is based on the idea that, without adjustment costs pinning down transitional dynamics, the outcome of integration would be indeterminate. This point seems to be somewhat overstated. It clearly does not formally apply if there are interregionally immobile factors. In a neoclassical model, with constant-returns-to-scale production and perfect competition, as long as immobile inputs such as land are used in production—and no matter how dimensionally insignificant these inputs may be—there will typically be a unique long-run equilibrium allocation of the mobile factors. Thus, the conclusion that long-run outcomes are determined exclusively by short-run adjustment costs would not survive.

This is not to say that adjustment costs could not be important. Even if immobile factors pin down the long-run equilibrium, adjustment costs may still be crucial in determining factor migration in the short as well as the medium run. One could envision a scenario, however, in which, because of high short-run capital relocation costs, EU enlargement would produce an initial westward migration of workers, which would be reversed in the long run as production, and the capital and labor inputs associated with it, progressively move eastward to take advantage of the immobile factors located in the East.

On the other hand, certain other elements are missing from Burda's analysis whose inclusion would tend to strengthen his argument that adjustment costs can determine long-run outcomes. For example, there are good reasons to expect that agglomeration effects (location-based external economies of scale) will play an important role in shaping factor migration. In terms of the model presented in the chapter, economies of scale would amount to non-convexities in the aggregate production possibilities of the two regions' combined economy. These non-convexities may fully resolve indeterminacy, or they may give rise to a finite number of possible long-run equilibrium allocations. (This need not involve full migration of all factors to a single region, if non-convexities are local only to certain ranges of the production schedule.) In such a scenario, even minute variations in adjustment cost differentials across different inputs may translate into drastically different long-run outcomes.

I come now to the second claim of the chapter, namely, that short-run factor return differentials can be used to infer adjustment costs. This involves a big jump from theory to empirical prediction. It is one thing to study theoretically the effects of adjustment costs in a stylized model that abstracts from real-world complications, and quite another to interpret the factor return differential that we observe in the real world as being representative of the size of adjustment costs.

The role of immobile factors in production has been noted earlier. In addition, immobile factors may affect not only production, but also, directly, individuals who migrate. In other words, individuals may have intrinsic preferences with respect to location, which would imply permanent relocation costs for migrants. The persistence of significant inter-regional real-wage differentials that we observe within certain countries suggests that permanent relocation costs may indeed be important.

In comparison with permanent relocation costs, adjustment costs produce slower transition to a long-run equilibrium allocation but a closer convergence of long-run factor ratios across regions. Thus, if we were to interpret observed factor return differentials, in full or in part, as reflecting permanent relocation costs rather than adjustment costs, we would reach different conclusions concerning the long-run migration effects of economic integration; whether this would mean more or less labor migration in the long run is not a priori obvious.

A more flexible and powerful estimation strategy—one that allows for different components of relocation costs and uses time series and panel data for migrants—is needed before we can make inferences about the size of adjustment costs and their importance for long-run migration.

Finally, with reference to Burda's conclusion that there is little scope for policy intervention after enlargement unless migration happens to generate external effects, I should first point out that there may be policies in place that are distortionary before enlargement (such as unemployment benefits) but may become unacceptably so after barriers to migration are fully removed, thus prompting reform.

Even if we abstract from pre-existing policies, individual governments may want to adopt unilateral policies that favor their nationals. In this context, the objective pursued by individual governments at any point in time would have to be taken as promoting the ex ante expected welfare of their constituencies (maximization of aggregate ex post welfare would amount to the doubtful notion that size benefits countries even when there are no economies of scale in production.) Standard optimal tariff arguments then imply that a labor-rich region should aim at keeping the world price of labor services (which it is exporting) at a level that is above the "free trade" wage. If, in addition, non-convexities are present, the various admissible long-run equilibria may not be Pareto ranked (i.e., certain equilibria may be more favorable to one country than others). Then individual governments may have strong incentives to pursue temporary policies to "nudge" the adjustment process toward the long-run outcome they favor. Furthermore, to the extent that factor movements alter the composition (and hence the political preferences) of a region's constituency, we would also expect the political majority in that region to protect the political status quo to preserve dominance, which should translate into a systematic anti-enlargement bias.

In conclusion, Burda's analysis, although formally clean and elegant, does abstract from a number of important features of real-world markets and institutions. I should therefore caution readers against interpreting its conclusions too literally. Nevertheless, I believe that the chapter's message that short-run adjustment costs are likely to be significant in shaping migratory patterns in the medium and long run—not just the short run—is very well taken, and one that should not be overlooked in the current debate on EU enlargement.

6

The Political Economy of Migration and EU Enlargement: Lessons from Switzerland

Jaime de Melo, Florence Miguet, and Tobias Müller

6.1   Introduction

The EU is about to take in ten European states as new members, raising its population by 28 percent to 480 million. Under current EU law, the new member states would benefit from the four basic freedoms of the Treaty of Rome. This means that people, capital, goods, and services would circulate freely between those states and all others in the union. Also, under current union law, welfare payments are attributable according to country of residence. As a result, despite the results from several studies suggesting that enlargement under current rules should have small positive aggregate effects on the welfare of EU15 citizens,[1] there is fear of adjustment difficulties with respect to the free movement of persons, especially in Austria and Germany. As the EU is worried that this issue threatens to affect public support for enlargement, a flexible system of transitional arrangements has been put forward in the negotiations with candidate countries.

The EU's position is based on opinion polls that suggest that EU citizens are reluctant to further immigration. In a 1997 Eurobarometer survey (European Commission 1997), in most European countries (except Finland, Spain, and Ireland) a majority of respondents indicated that they believed that further immigration would cause problems in their own countries. Moreover, only 12 percent of respondents in the EU thought that Eastern Europeans who wish to work in the west should be accepted without restrictions. These attitudes contrast with the rather modest labor market effects that can be expected from projected migration flows under EU enlargement.

Are attitudes toward EU enlargement linked to projected migration flows or stocks? According to a number of authors (Brücker et al. 2001; Dustmann and Preston 2000), attitudes toward immigration can be explained by three factors: labor market effects, welfare take-up, and racial or xenophobic prejudice. Most studies addressing the first factor have concentrated on estimating the change in stocks that would result from CEECs' accession to the EU.[2] Such an approach, however, gives an incomplete picture of the effects of EU enlargement, since enlargement will also involve a change in the legal status of workers in the labor market. For example, the bilateral guest worker and seasonal-worker arrangements that are currently in place between several EU members and the CEECs (see Boeri et al. 2001, table 4.4), which have good reasons to exist from a political-economy perspective, will have to be abolished once those CEECs are part of the EU. With few exceptions (Bauer, Lofstrom, and Zimmerman 2000; Brücker et al. 2001, chap. 2), these political-economy aspects of the migration consequences of enlargement have been largely ignored in the current debate (see section 6.2 for a theoretical exploration of this issue).

As to immigrants' potential for welfare dependence, Fertig and Schmidt (2001) show that natives' negative perception of immigrants in this regard is not in accordance with the moderate risk of immigrants' dependence on public assistance in Germany. Nonetheless, Sinn et al. (2001) consider the problem of immigrant welfare dependence serious enough to recommend delayed integration of immigrants into the social-welfare system in the receiving countries to avoid an erosion of the welfare state through competition between receiving countries. With regard to the role of non-economic factors in shaping attitudes toward immigration, it is difficult to gauge from the few studies available whether racial prejudices significantly influence attitudes toward EU enlargement.[3]

This chapter contributes to the debate on the political economy of migration policy. It recounts the Swiss experience with immigration policy, which is pertinent for the current debate along several dimensions. First, Switzerland has throughout its history absorbed a great number of immigrants, not only before 1974 (when European countries switched to a restrictive immigration policy), but also over the last twenty years (the share of foreigners in the Swiss population rose from 14 to 20 percent between 1980 and 2000). This increase is more important, in relative terms, than the projected rise in the immigrant stock in Germany following EU enlargement. At the same time, anti-immigration attitudes seem to be less widespread in Switzerland than in other European countries, according to a recent Eurobarometer survey (European Commission 2000, see section 6.4). It is therefore worthwhile to examine more closely the characteristics of Swiss migration policy.

Second, Switzerland has carried out reforms in immigration laws and policies that are close in spirit to several of the alternatives envisaged in the debate concerning enlargement, as discussed in European Commission 2001. Of particular interest, in the Swiss case, is the interaction of economic interests with the expression of these interests via the political system. Switzerland's system of direct democracy has forced the Swiss government to conduct its immigration policy so as to avoid the adoption of restrictive propositions by popular vote.

Third, the Swiss version of direct democracy is also interesting at the empirical level. Since 1970 the Swiss electorate has voted regularly on immigration policy, and individual surveys have been carried out after most votes. From the point of view of understanding attitudes toward immigration, the attitudes revealed by these post-election surveys are in sharp contrast to attitudes drawn from survey polls, which may suffer from "hypothetical bias."

The remainder of the chapter is structured as follows. Section 6.2 reviews the political-economy dimensions of immigration policy in a direct-democracy framework, which is relevant both for Switzerland and for interpreting the results from recent polls, taking into account that Swiss migration policy has been of the guest worker type and that labor markets in Switzerland are segmented. Section 6.3 then briefly recounts how the votes on referenda and popular initiatives have shaped Swiss immigration policy over the last thirty years. Section 6.4 examines a household survey conducted in connection with the 2000 vote in Switzerland on establishing a quota (slightly below the existing level) on the stock of immigrants. That poll allows us both to estimate the probability of voters' participation in terms of individual characteristics and to predict what the outcome would have been had all voters participated (the actual participation rate was 44 percent). Although it may not be valid to infer that such predictions correspond to what is captured in opinion polls (where there are no participation costs and all participate), it might provide a first handle on how EU citizens might in fact vote, if they really were brought to the booth. Conclusions follow in section 6.5.

6.2 The Political Economy of Immigration Policy

Attitudes toward immigrants, as expressed in opinion polls and at the voting booth, can be usefully decomposed into three components: cultural preferences or social capital, implications for the functioning of the welfare state, and economic effects (fear of unemployment and/

or lower wages). Cultural-preference aspects have been examined in Hillman and Weiss 1999a, Schiff 1998, and Schiff 1999 and have been summarized in Grether, de Melo, and Müller 2001. The welfare implications of EU enlargement have recently been covered in Sinn 2000, Brücker et al. 2001, and Boeri and Brücker 2001. Here we wish to emphasize the role of economic effects in the determination of migration policies in a direct-democracy framework.[4] We consider first the political economy of skill requirements, then explore whether low-skill immigration is likely to be accepted in a direct democracy if guest worker policies are pursued.

6.2.1 Skilled or Unskilled Labor?

Following in the footsteps of Canada and New Zealand, several countries have introduced a point system to determine the eligibility of applicant migrants; such point systems correspond to one of the transitional arrangements under consideration in the accession negotiations for the CEECs. As shown by Bauer, Lofstrom, and Zimmerman (2000), cross-country evidence seems to suggest better rates of immigrant assimilation for countries that have relied on such systems.

From a theoretical viewpoint, what policies regarding skill requirements for immigrants are likely to be adopted in a direct democracy? Benhabib (1996) considers this question in a median-voter framework in which capital is distributed unequally among natives. He assumes that there is a fixed pool of potential immigrants with different capital endowments (or skill levels). His main result is that if the median capital endowment of natives k_m is smaller than some critical level k_c, a minimum skill requirement for immigration approval will defeat any other policy under majority voting with pairwise alternatives.[5]

To gain some additional insight into this issue, consider a less general setting with only two alternatives up for vote: no immigration versus admission of a fixed number of immigrants. Differences in income determine the attitude toward immigrants. Each native household is endowed with one unit of labor and a certain amount of capital, which is unequally distributed among households. If immigration lowers the household's income, the household will oppose it. If no other issue is on the political agenda, preferences are single-peaked, and the national stance toward immigration is determined by the median voter. In this framework, when will the immigration option be accepted? Consider first the simple case of a constant-returns aggregate production function $F(K, L)$ and competitive labor markets. If the number of immigrants M is small relative to the number of natives N ($L = N + M$), immigration produces the following change in income y of a resident endowed with k units of capital:[6]

$$\frac{dy/y}{dM/L} = \left(\frac{k_I - \bar{k}}{\bar{k}}\right)\left(\frac{\bar{k} - k}{\bar{k}}\right)\left(\frac{s_L(1 - s_L)}{\sigma(y/\bar{y})}\right), \tag{1}$$

where $\bar{k}$ is the country's aggregate capital-labor ratio, k_I the new immigrants' average capital-labor ratio, $\bar{y}$ per capita income, s_L the share of labor in national income, and σ the elasticity of substitution between labor and capital. Define the critical capital (or skill) level k_c as the level of capital k at which an individual is indifferent with respect to immigration. In this simple setup, the critical capital level k_c is equal to $\bar{k}$. If the distribution of capital, which should be interpreted as encompassing physical and human capital, is skewed to the right (as in figure 6.1), then the median skill level k_m is smaller than k_c, and the immigration option will be accepted if the immigrants' average skill level k_I is

$f(k)$

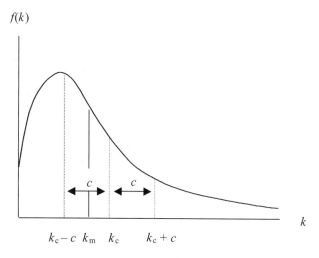

$f(k)$ density function of capital distribution
k_c critical capital level
k_m median of capital distribution
c voting costs

Figure 6.1
Skewed distribution of capital and attitudes toward immigration.

greater than the critical level k_c. By contrast, unskilled immigration ($k_I < k_c$) will be opposed.[7]

It is useful to relate this setting to the traditional analysis of immigration, which focuses on the efficiency gain ("immigration surplus") occurring with finite immigration. It should be noted, however, that the distributional changes produced by immigration are first-order effects, whereas the immigration surplus is only of the second order. As we emphasize distributional considerations in our politico-economic analysis, we neglect the efficiency gain by assuming that the immigration option that is up for vote involves only a small number of potential immigrants.

6.2.1.1 Voting Costs

The existence of voting costs might alter the above conclusion. Assume that, as in Mayer 1984, all individuals face identical voting costs, C. A voter will then take part in a vote about immigration only if the expected change in his income exceeds the voting costs, that is, if $|dy/dM| > C$. If the distribution of capital in the population is asymmetric, the outcome of the vote depends on voting costs. In particular, figure 6.1 makes it clear that if the distribution of capital is skewed to the right, it is possible that unskilled immigration ($k_I < k_c$) will be accepted by vote, even if this option is opposed by a majority of the population.[8] Indeed, among those who choose not to vote, in the example depicted in figure 6.1, a clear majority would be against unskilled immigration. The issue of participation will become prominent in the empirical analysis of section 6.4.

This first approach provides a good rationale for the recent implementation, in several European countries, of migration policies relying explicitly on skill criteria (e.g., the recent introduction of a "green card" in Germany; a similar scheme is underway in Switzerland). This simple framework is unable, however, to explain policies of temporary migration or of the guest worker type, which can be characterized as involving active recruitment of low-skill immigrants. Although these temporary migration policies were more prominent in the 1960s than they are today, they still play an important role in the current regulation of east-west migration. The remainder of this section will explore the channels through which these policies tend to decrease the critical capital level in a country, making it more likely for low-skill immigration to be accepted in a direct-democracy framework.[9]

6.2.2 Guest Workers and Temporary Migration

With the eastern enlargement of the EU, the current guest worker
policies and temporary migration schemes that apply currently to
CEEC workers will have to be abandoned for the *acquis communautaire*.[10] To understand how such a policy change would fare in a direct-
democracy framework, it is crucial to examine why guest worker
policies were adopted in the first place.

Most guest worker policies or temporary migration schemes aim at
channeling immigrants into occupations or sectors in which they do
not compete with native workers. The sectoral segregation between
natives and migrants is either the direct result of legal regulations
(e.g., work permits that limit the holders to working in certain sectors)
or the indirect outcome of differing economic incentives. We discuss
both cases in turn. To account for the structural effects of guest worker
policies, the model is expanded to two sectors (Ricardo-Viner model).[11]
The economy produces two traded goods: X (import-competing) and Y
(export-competing), using three factors: labor (L), which is mobile between the two sectors, and two types of sector-specific capital (K_X, K_Y).
We keep the assumption that capital is unequally distributed among
natives; capital owners are paid at the average return of the two
sectors. We assume furthermore that the median capital endowment
(among voters) is smaller than the average capital-labor ratio and that
immigrants are unskilled (i.e., they do not bring any capital with them
when they migrate).

6.2.2.1 Traded Goods Only

Suppose first that both goods are traded, and guest workers are confined to one sector (guest workers are not only CEEC nationals, but
also from other countries such as Turkey). In the absence of an immigration surplus, permanent immigration, which brings down real
wages, should never be observed, as it will be opposed by a majority
of voters. Guest worker immigration may occur, however, and will
be welcomed by all individuals holding capital. Indeed, suppose we
start from an initial situation in which there is already a substantial
number of guest workers in the country. Moreover, assume that all
guest workers have been confined to sector X by an exogenous segregation process that has displaced all native workers to sector Y. Such a
segregation process can be implemented (as in the case of the CEEC
workers in the EU countries) through a "rotation system" that grants

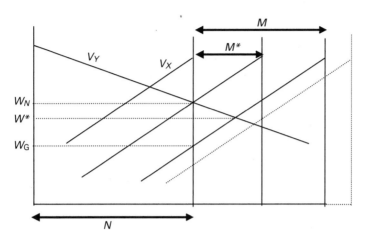

V_X marginal product of labor in sector X
V_Y marginal product of labor in sector Y
N number of native workers
M number of immigrants
M^* number of immigrants such that all natives are excluded
        from sector X

Figure 6.2
Guest workers in the Ricardo-Viner model.

only fixed-term labor contracts to immigrants and prevents them from making any change in occupation during their time of stay.

This situation is depicted in figure 6.2 where the number of guest workers (M) is larger than the critical amount of guest workers (M^*) that displaces the last native worker from sector X to sector Y $(M > M^*)$. This means that native labor (N) has become specific to sector Y and that the wage rate of natives (w_N) is higher than the wage rate of guest workers (w_G). In this case, as shown by Djajic (1997), native workers are "immunized" against additional guest worker immigration. Indeed, any additional increase in the immigrant population (represented by the dotted lines in figure 6.2) is Pareto improving for natives, as it will depress the immigrants' wage while increasing the real return to K_Y and leaving unchanged both w_N and the real return to K_X.

What if immigration policy is now put up for vote in the host country? If mass expulsion of immigrants is not an option, the median voter will prefer keeping a guest worker system to introducing the free mobility of immigrants between sectors. Specifically in the case of the expanded EU, the latter option would allow CEEC immigrants to enter sector Y and would bring the natives' wage down to w^*. At the same time, the guest worker wage would increase from w_G to w^*, attracting more immigrants from the CEECs. Thus the free movement of persons between the CEECs and EU countries would be doubly opposed by voters in those countries. By contrast, a vote on additional guest worker immigration would be successful, as it would increase capital remuneration in sector Y while leaving indifferent native workers holding no capital.

This simple framework provides a rationale for the flexible system of transitional arrangements or the establishment of fixed-quota systems as envisaged in EU Commission 2001. These conclusions are reinforced if one modifies the setup to include a nontraded sector.

6.2.2.2 Nontraded Sector
Immigrants are often confined, in the countries that receive them, to working in the lodging, restaurant, and domestic-help sectors, both in the context of European countries with guest worker systems, and currently in the bilateral EU relations with the CEECs (see Boeri et al. 2001, section 5.2). Provided that preferences are the same across household groups, the previous conclusion is reinforced if one of the two sectors produces nontraded goods. Suppose that sector is sector X, in which guest worker immigration is frequently observed, and start again from an initial situation in which all natives are employed in sector Y (now the composite traded good). With respect to the analysis of figure 6.2, the additional consequence of allowing more guest worker immigration would be a decrease in the relative price of nontraded goods (the relative supply of nontraded goods increases, whereas the relative demand is unchanged, provided immigrants share a common consumption pattern with natives). This would leave every household better off than in the traded-goods case, generating a clear majority in favor of additional guest worker immigration.[12]

The predictions of the model that voters will not vote to abandon a guest worker system in favor of the free sectoral mobility of immigrants (and a fortiori, the free movement of persons) are supported by the history of Swiss migration policy.[13]

6.2.2.3 Segmented Labor Markets
It is probably unrealistic to assume that fixed-term labor contracts are the only source of segregation between natives and immigrants.

Segregation can also be observed in the case of immigrants who face no legal barriers to inter-sectoral mobility.[14] Also, the arguments developed above do not explain why the first M^* guest workers were accepted initially. A more realistic setup, analyzed in the same Ricardo-Viner framework by Müller (2003a, 2003b), is to assume that segregation takes place because immigrants and natives face different incentives in a segmented labor market. As immigrants are likely to return to their home country, their incentives differ from the incentives of natives. Discriminatory labor market regulations, such as the preferential hiring of natives, might reinforce this effect. In the context of a dual labor market, this difference in incentives leads to discrimination against immigrants if "good jobs" are rationed in an efficiency wage setup.

The dual labor market is modeled in a standard efficiency-wage framework following Shapiro and Stiglitz (1984) and Bulow and Summers (1986). We continue to use the Ricardo-Viner small-country model with both goods traded. Y is now the primary sector offering good working conditions, with firms paying above-market clearing wages to induce workers to supply effort, and X is the secondary residual sector, in which unattractive and repetitive jobs can be monitored at no cost. As a consequence, jobs are rationed in the primary sector, and workers are queuing up for them. They can always find jobs in the secondary sector, however, in which the wage rate is set competitively. There is no unemployment.[15]

At equilibrium, the wage rate is equal to the marginal product of labor in each sector. The labor market equilibrium with and without immigration is depicted in figure 6.3. The sectoral wage differential is determined by the no-shirking constraint. As the initial equilibrium in the dual labor market is inefficient, immigration produces not only the conventional "immigration surplus" (a second-order gain, represented in the figure by the two shaded triangles, that can be neglected if immigration is infinitesimal), but also a first-order change in efficiency (represented by the rectangle) due to the expansion of primary-sector employment (for simplicity, the wage differential is assumed constant in figure 6.3).

Whether the natives can reap a share of this first-order efficiency gain depends in particular on the immigrants' incentives and on migration policy. Indeed, a distinctive characteristic of immigrants in the existing EU countries is their probability of return to their countries of origin.[16] Therefore, even if migrants are identical to natives in all other

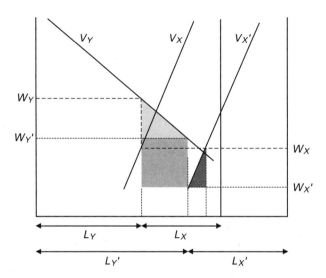

Figure 6.3
Immigration and the dual labor market.

respects, their incentive not to shirk is influenced by the probability that they will return to their home country, which depends indirectly on various aspects of the migration policy of the receiving country, such as the existence of temporary work permits and the government's attitude toward social and economic integration of immigrants. Also, firms in the receiving country are often forced by law to choose natives and "old" migrants over "new" migrants in their hiring decision.

All these factors contribute to segregation and thus to discrimination against migrants. Since competition ensures that natives and migrants are paid the same wages, discrimination is of the type "equal pay for equal work, but not equal work." Hence migrants have smaller chances of finding "good" jobs than natives and suffer from sectoral segregation. With segregation, immigration increases the natives' chances of finding a job in the primary sector and reaping a greater share of the efficiency gain represented by the shaded rectangle in figure 6.3.

These considerations suggest that the qualitative aspects of migration policy might influence political decisions concerning the desirability of further immigration. Indeed, it can be shown that a guest worker system makes a country more receptive to immigrants than a less discriminatory policy (de Melo, Miguet, and Müller 2002). In particular, an extreme guest worker policy (resulting in complete segregation) leads to a critical capital-labor ratio k_c that is smaller than the economy's average capital-labor ratio. If the distribution of capital in the economy is symmetric (or if the median capital level is not too far below the average), the median voter will therefore be in favor of immigration. Moreover, a less discriminatory policy regarding immigrant labor entails a critical capital level that is higher than in the extreme guest worker case.

Not only will the eastern enlargement of the EU create new immigration flows, but it will also improve the legal situation of CEEC nationals who are currently working in the EU under temporary migration or guest worker schemes. Such a policy change would improve the social and economic integration of immigrants and enhance their chances of finding "good" jobs in the economies of the countries that receive them. How would such a qualitative policy change fare in a popular vote? Grether, de Melo, and Müller (2001) show that if the median capital endowment among natives is below the average capital per capita, the improved integration of immigrants will be rejected by a majority of natives who fear the deterioration of their own economic situation. It should be emphasized that this is an inefficient outcome, since a policy of social integration would increase the number of good jobs at the expense of bad jobs and therefore improve the aggregate welfare of natives *and* immigrants (see Müller 2003a). Indeed, were immigrants allowed to vote, it is possible that a majority in favor of the policy change could be found.

In sum, our theoretical framework suggests three main conclusions. First, in the absence of segmented labor markets, voters will be in favor of a policy that imposes skill requirements on immigrants. Second, restricting the mobility of guest workers to nontraded sectors is likely to engender support for immigration. Third, with segmented labor markets a discriminatory migration policy, of the type used in the EU and Switzerland in the past, will obtain more support than an unrestricted migration policy, and natives are likely to oppose a shift from the former to the latter.

6.3 The Shaping of Switzerland's Immigration Policy

How does Switzerland's immigration experience compare to that of other developed countries? Table 6.1 depicts the evolution of the share of foreigners across European countries from 1950 to 1998, along with the share of EU foreigners among foreigners.[17] Switzerland stands out

Table 6.1
Foreign population in country of destination (as percentage of total population)

	1950	1960	1970	Share of EU foreigners, 1950–1970	1980	1985	1990	1998	Share of EU foreigners, 1998
North Europe									
Denmark	n.a.	n.a.	1.8[a]	n.a.	1.9	2.2	2.5	4.8	20.7
Sweden	1.8	2.5	5.0	95	5.0	4.6	4.7	5.6	40.0
Norway	0.5	0.7	2.0	n.a.	2.0	2.4	2.6	3.7	45.7
Finland	n.a.	n.a.	n.a.	n.a.	n.a.	0.0	0.4	1.6	18.4
Ireland	n.a.	n.a.	n.a.	n.a.	2.4	1.9	2.2	3.0	76.7
United Kingdom	3.4	4.5	5.7	60	3.0	3.1	3.2	3.8	40.0
Austria	11.0	n.a.	7.0	88	n.a.	4.0	4.1	9.1	13.0
Belgium	4.3	4.6	7.2	85	8.9	8.5	8.6	8.7	63.1
Netherlands	1.1	1.0	1.9	66	3.6	3.8	3.9	4.2	29.0
Switzerland[b]	6.1	10.8	17.2	96	14.1	14.6	14.7	19.0	62.0
Luxembourg	9.9	13.2	18.4	53	n.a.	26.5	26.3	35.6	87.0
France	4.2	4.6	5.3	61	6.8	n.a.	6.8	6.3	36.5
Germany	n.a.	1.2	4.5	77	5.6	5.6	7.4	8.9	25.3
South Europe									
Italy	0.1	0.1	0.2	39	0.1	0.1	1.2	2.1	13.7
Portugal	0.2	0.3	0.4	26	0.6	0.9	1.0	1.8	27.1
Spain	0.3	0.2	0.4	60	0.5	0.6	1.1	1.8	41.0
Total Europe	2.4	2.3	3.6	n.a.	3.7	3.9	4.4	5.3	n.a.

Source: Brücker et al. 2001a, table 1b.

Note: Data for 1950, 1960, and 1970 are derived from Census: They represent the share of foreign population in total population, except for the United Kingdom, where they represent the share of the foreign-born population. Data for 1980–1998 are derived from various national sources and represent foreign population share (in total population). n.a.: Not available.
[a] Percentage for 1975.
[b] Seasonal workers excluded.

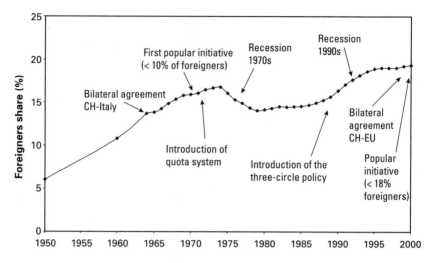

Figure 6.4
Foreign population share and migration policy in Switzerland.

from other European countries in two dimensions. First, compared with other European countries, with the exception of Austria (and Luxembourg), Switzerland had the highest initial share of foreigners in 1950 (6 percent), a lead it maintained until 1998, when the share had risen to 19 percent, whereas in Austria the share, which had started higher than Switzerland's (11 percent) actually fell over the same period. Second, although, as in all other countries, the share of EU nationals among foreigners in Switzerland has declined sharply over the last fifty years, the share of EU nationals among foreigners in Switzerland (62 percent in 1998) is still among the highest in Europe.

It is instructive to consider the history of Swiss migration policy in connection with the evolution of the foreign population share in Switzerland[18] (see figure 6.4). During the period of strong growth in the postwar period, labor shortages in Switzerland were met through immigration, with the foreigners' share in the population increasing from 5.8 to 9.1 percent between 1950 and 1960. But at the beginning of the 1960s, tensions started building, and the Swiss government issued two federal orders (in 1963 and 1964) aiming at limiting the inflow of immigrants into the country.[19]

In 1965, the first popular initiative attempting to limit the number of foreigners to 10 percent of the population (instead of the prevailing 15 percent) was launched. The initiative was later withdrawn. Confronted with this issue, in 1968, the government issued a new federal order aiming at stabilizing the stock of foreigners while at the same time making it easier for foreigners' children to become naturalized and giving leeway on exemptions to assuage economic interests. As the number of foreigners with renewable or long-term permits actually increased by close to 5 percent (instead of falling by 3 percent, as announced in the federal decree of 1968), a second initiative, also asking foreigners be limited to 10 percent of the population was launched in 1969; this time, the initiators gave up the possibility of withdrawing the initiative.

The 7 June 1970 vote on this initiative marks a watershed in Switzerland's policy toward immigrants (see table 6.2a). The initiative was the first in a series of popular initiatives taken to the polls over the next thirty years and the beginning of a policy based on a complex system of yearly quotas that is still in place today.[20] This vote also registered one of the highest participation rates (74 percent), and the proposal was rejected only narrowly, in spite of a last-ditch effort by the government to build consensus around its immigration policy by introducing further restrictions on immigration. But the system of popular initiatives (some aiming at controlling the flow of immigrants, others at improving the status of immigrants) has forced the Swiss government to compromise and to design, over the years, an effective, though not economically efficient, immigration policy.

During that period, the government was squeezed between economic interests seeking to avoid or reduce the impact of immigration quotas and the popular pressure to tighten them. Its response was to devise a complex system of quotas that gave it the flexibility to play both sides and to adjust rapidly to short-term objectives arising out of the combined pressures exerted by labor unions (pressing for binding quotas), firms (preferring loose quotas) and parts of the public (wishing to preserve cultural identity, as expressed in its xenophobic requests). For example, immigration to permit family reunification was not included in the quotas, nor was the conversion of seasonal to annual permits. These loopholes in the immigration laws led to the third popular initiative seeking to restrain immigration. The initiative's rejection, in a vote with a high participation rate, on 20 October 1974 by a two-thirds majority heralded the success of the government's give-and-take approach. One can conclude from the size of the majority that rejected the initiative that the conjunction of direct democracy and lobbying was shaping Switzerland's policy toward immigrants.

Table 6.2
Votes on immigration policy

Date	Contents	Result	Participation
a. Popular initatives[a]			
7 June 1970	Foreigners' share in population ≤ 10 percent (25 percent) in each canton (Geneva)	rejected 54%	74%
20 October 1974	Foreigners' share in population ≤ 12 percent (25 percent) in each canton (Geneva), with total in Switzerland ≤ 500,000 + Naturalizations ≤ 4,000 per year	rejected 65.8%	70%
13 March 1977	Foreigners' share in population ≤ 12.5 percent in Switzerland	rejected 70.5%	45%
13 March 1977	Naturalizations ≤ 4,000 per year	rejected 66.2%	45%
5 April 1981	Abolish seasonal-worker status + Indefinite renewal of working permits + Immigration flows to match emigration flows	rejected 83.8%	39%
4 December 1988	Immigration flows ≤ two-thirds of emigration flows (including asylum seekers) + Limit on seasonal workers and cross-border commuters	rejected 67.3%	52%
1 December 1996	Illegals cannot ask asylum seeker status + Restrictions on rights of appeal	rejected 53.7%	46%
24 September 2000	Foreigners' share in population ≤ 18 percent (including asylum seekers)	rejected 63.8%	45%
b. Referenda[b]			
6 June 1982	Counterproposal to the initiative of 5 April 1981: Indefinite renewal of working permits + Immigration flows to match emigration flows	rejected 50.4%	35%
4 December 1983	Tightening of naturalization criteria + Children of any Swiss citizen get Swiss nationality	accepted 60.8%	35%
4 December 1983	Loosening of naturalization requirements for foreigners' children, refugees, asylum seekers, and the nationless	rejected 55.2%	35%
5 April 1987	Distribution of asylum seekers across cantons + Faster admission process + Tightening of asylum law	accepted 67.3%	42%
5 April 1987	Amendment of the law regulating the stay and establishment of foreigners (e.g., imprisonment of dangerous asylum seekers or those who refuse to leave the country)	accepted 65.7%	42%

Table 6.2
(continued)

Date	Contents	Result	Participation
12 June 1994	Right of easier naturalization for young foreigners who grew up in Switzerland	rejected by cantons	46%
4 December 1994	Expanded search rights in asylum seekers' domiciles + Tightening of law on foreigners' rights	accepted 72.9%	43%
13 June 1999	Amendment of asylum law (i.e., less-restrictive provisory admission rights)	accepted 70.6%	45%
13 June 1999	Stricter criteria for asylum status + asylum seekers must be cooperative with authorities	accepted 70.8%	45%

[a] To be voted upon, an initiative must obtain 50,000 signatures (pre-1977) and 100,000 (starting in 1977). Acceptance of an initiative implies changes in the constitution.
[b] Laws or federal orders are put to vote if they obtain 50,000 signatures (1977 law).

The role of the democratic process was also evident in the 1981 vote on a popular initiative aimed at creating more equality between Swiss nationals and foreigners and eliminating the seasonal-worker status. This proposal was sharply opposed by the construction, catering, and agriculture sectors, which relied on labor from workers in this category. As these economic interests were opposed to the suppression of the seasonal-worker status but not to the equality principle, the government proposed a modification of the country's foreigners' law. As shown in table 6.2, both the popular initiative (in 1981) and the proposed law (in 1982) were rejected by the electorate. By that time, the foreign population was effectively stabilized, but as the proportion of annual permits had fallen from 70 percent in 1970 to 25 percent in 1980, flexibility in migratory policy was waning.

Only in the late 1980s, with the surge in asylum seekers and the prospects of a closer relationship with the EU, did immigration policy in Switzerland again begin to be questioned: On the one hand, distinguishing between economic and political motives for immigration was becoming difficult; on the other hand, the guest worker system appeared inappropriate if closer ties with the EU were to develop. Sensing that the European Economic Area (EEA) act would be rejected in a vote because it would call for an abolishment of the guest worker system, an immigration policy based on "cultural proximity" that was often referred to as the "three-circle policy" was adopted by the government.[21] In 1992, the referendum to join the EEA was nevertheless rejected by Swiss citizens.

The failure of the discriminatory cultural-proximity policy, Switzerland's participation in the international convention against racism in 1995, and the growing criticism of the quota system by the country's business sector led to the proposal in 1998 of a point system for immigration akin to the system in use in Canada and Australia. Although this proposal did not carry the day, the government did shift from a three-circle to a "two-circle" policy that would both accommodate the desire for closer ties with the EU (with 57 percent of the electorate accepting the proposed bilateral agreements with the EU in May 2000) and cater to anti-foreigner feelings in the population. Meanwhile, guest worker permits were cut in half to 88,000 per year during the 1990s.

What are the characteristics of the foreign population in Switzerland (now 20 percent of the total population, as noted in section 6.1) compared to that of other countries? With respect to the main categories of newly arriving immigrants, table 6.3 shows that, in 1998, Switzerland had an inflow composition similar to that of other countries: About 50 percent of immigrants were entering as workers, and 45 percent for family reunification purposes. In this table, Sweden stands out as having a large proportion of asylum seekers among its immigrant population, and France is distinguished from other countries of Europe in that the motivation for immigration to that country is less linked to work; the profile of its immigrants' reason for migrating resembles that of the United States.

Having noted that averages hide differences across nationalities, Brücker et al. (2001, 16) summarize as follows the socio-economic characteristics of immigrants in the EU. Immigrants to EU countries are concentrated in large cities and are younger than natives, with a higher proportion of males among migrants than among natives; migrants are also more than proportionally affected by unemployment. Most of these stylized characteristics apply to immigrants in Switzerland as well.[22] In the EU, immigrants generally have lower skill levels than natives, which is also the case in Switzerland if one considers immigrants from Southern Europe.[23] Brücker et al. also note that immigrants have an occupational status below that of natives with comparable skill levels. Foreigners in Switzerland have lower salaries and have lower chances of reaching upper-level positions in their firms' hierarchies than natives with comparable skill levels (Flückiger and Ramirez 2001).

Table 6.3
Immigration inflows by main categories

	Year	Workers[a]	Family reunification[a]	Asylum seekers and refugees[a]	Others[a]	Net inflow of foreigners[b]
Switzerland[c]	1998	50	45	5	0	1.1
Sweden	1997	2	55	21	22	0.4
France	1996	21	55	10	16	0.1
Italy[d]	1999	50	39	3	8	0.2
United Kingdom[e]	1998	45	50	5	0	0.4
United States[f]	1998	12	72	8	8	0.2
Canada[f]	1998	55	29	13	3	0.6
Australia[f]	1998	34	26	11	29	0.4

Sources: Brücker et al. 2001a, table 6, and OECD (2000a).
[a] As a percentage of total immigration to the country. With the exception of the United Kingdom and Switzerland, total inflows also include students, visitors, and so forth; thus the total does not sum to 100 percent.
[b] As percentage of total population in the country.
[c] Seasonal workers included.
[d] Inflow of foreigners: 1998.
[e] EU immigrants not included; inflow of foreigners: 1997.
[f] Inflows of permanent settlers.

6.4   Determinants of Attitudes and Voting Behavior

The analysis of surveys of individual voter attitudes in various countries points to the conclusion that attitudes toward immigration differ significantly among countries. Using cross-country data at the individual level from the International Social Survey Program (ISSP) for 1995, Bauer, Lofstrom, and Zimmerman (2000) find that most country dummy variables have a significant influence in their probit model, even if individual demographic and education variables are included. They conclude, rather tentatively, that sentiments toward immigrants are more favorable in countries using skill criteria in their immigration policies. By contrast, Brücker et al. (2001) work with country averages of a 1997 Eurobarometer poll to study attitudes toward immigration with respect to labor market effects, racism or xenophobia, and welfare take-up. Their strategy is to relate respondents' attitudes to country characteristics (previous growth rate, stock of foreigners, and rates of unemployment). In their sample of thirteen EU countries (Greece and Luxembourg are omitted), they find a significant positive relationship between fears that further immigration will cause problems domestically and the stock of foreign population in the country and a significant negative relationship between the unemployment rate in the country and apprehension about the negative effects of further immigration (Brücker et al. 2001, table 2.3).

How does Switzerland fit into this picture? Unfortunately, the 1995 ISSP and 1997 Eurobarometer surveys were not carried out for Switzerland. In figure 6.5, we report country averages, from a 2000 Eurobarometer survey that includes Switzerland, for the two questions in that survey that are closest to those analyzed by Brücker et al. (2001). It is striking in figure 6.5a that the inclusion of Switzerland upsets the pattern of consistently positive correlation between anti-immigration attitudes and the share of foreign population that exists in the other countries. In figure 6.5b, the negative correlation between anti-immigration attitudes and the unemployment rate reported by Brücker et al. (2001) is not reproduced for the thirteen EU member countries; it is even less well reflected if Switzerland is included. Switzerland can be considered an outlier among European countries in 2000: Having the highest foreign population share among those countries, it is the most open country toward foreigners. This result should, however, be interpreted with caution.[24]

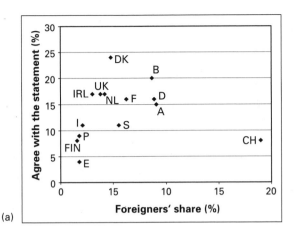

(a)

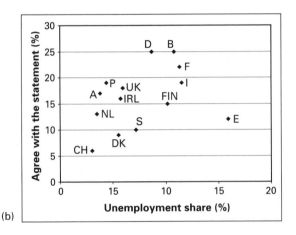

(b)

Countries:

A = Austria	E = Spain	NL = Netherlands
B = Belgium	F = France	P = Portugal
CH = Switzerland	FIN = Finland	S = Sweden
D = Germany	I = Italy	UK = United Kingdom
DK = Denmark	IRL = Ireland	

Figure 6.5
Attitudes toward immigrants: Eurobarometer survey, 2000: (a) "Other nationalities are disturbing"; (b) "Foreigners should be sent back."
  Available responses were "agree with the statement," "disagree," or "don't know." The exact wording of the questions was as follows: (a) "Do you personally find the presence of people of another nationality disturbing in your daily life?" (b) "All immigrants, whether legal or illegal, from outside the EU and their children, even those who were born in your country, should be sent back to their country of origin." *Sources:* Eurobarometer survey 2000; OECD 2000 for 1998 foreigners' share; OECD 2001 for 1999 unemployment rate.

Because of its direct democracy, Switzerland provides a unique setting for analyzing the determinants of voters' attitudes toward immigration. After each national vote (since 1983), the GfS Institute carries
out an individual-level survey (called *VOX*) asking Swiss citizens
whether and how they voted. To elucidate the motivations behind
voters' choices, the VOX polls also ask other questions concerning the
issues at stake. Analysis of the data from this survey allows us to
improve on existing studies of attitudes toward immigration (Scheve
and Slaughter 1999, Citrin et al. 1997, Espenshade and Hempstead
1996, etc.) in two respects. First, the Swiss direct-democracy context
enables us to address the issue of hypothetical bias, which hampers the
analysis of conventional survey data.[25] Since Swiss voters are aware
that if a popular initiative that is up for a vote is accepted, the proposed constitutional change reflected in the initiative will take place,
there is no hypothetical bias. Second, the information on participation
behavior provided by the survey data allows us to analyze how attitudes materialize in actual voting behavior. Indeed, the outcome of a
vote is influenced by the decision to participate in the vote. Since it is
likely that the decision to participate in a vote involving immigration
policy and a voter's attitude toward immigration are not independent
of one another, the outcome of a vote on immigration cannot accurately be inferred simply from survey questions on individuals' attitudes, as has been done in previous studies.

How can the decision to participate in a particular vote be explained
if individuals are rational? If the result of the vote (yes/no) is the only
politically relevant outcome of a referendum, then a citizen's motivation to vote is very weak, since his chances of changing the results of
the vote are extremely small (the voting paradox). As is evident from
the discussion of immigration policy in section 6.3, the voting paradox
does not apply in the Swiss context: Even if a popular initiative is
rejected, the outcome of the vote will be taken into account in later
decisions by the government.[26] Thus the decision to participate in a
popular vote can be interpreted more generally as a decision to influence the political process.

We turn now to the analysis of the Swiss vote in September 2000
on a popular initiative proposing that a limitation be imposed on the
number of foreigners in the country. The initiative proposed that
the Swiss constitution be changed to restrict the share of foreigners in
the Swiss population to a maximum of 18 percent. Some categories of
resident foreigners (e.g., academics, artists) would have been excluded

from this count, but some non-residents (e.g., asylum seekers) would have been included. According to the definition of immigrant specified in the proposed constitutional change, the share of foreigners was 19.3 percent at the time of the vote. Therefore the initiative would have forced the government to limit immigration severely. The popular initiative was rejected by 63.7 percent of voters; the participation rate in the vote was 43.6 percent. The data that we are analyzing here come from an individual-level *VOX* survey that was carried out during the two weeks following the vote and includes 1,024 Swiss citizens over eighteen years old.

6.4.1 The Econometric Model

Our econometric framework is based on the direct-democracy model with voting costs discussed in section 6.2. To account for non-economic determinants of attitudes as well, we focus on immigration-induced changes in utility rather than income. The participation and voting decisions are modeled simultaneously by defining two dichotomous variables v (where $v = 1$ denotes a positive vote) and p (where $p = 1$ denotes participation) and two latent variables v^* and p^*:[27]

$$v^* = x'\beta + \varepsilon^*, \qquad v = 1 \quad \text{if } v^* > 0, \quad v = 0 \quad \text{otherwise,} \qquad (2)$$

$$p^* = x'\alpha + z'\gamma + \xi^*, \qquad p = 1 \quad \text{if } p^* > 0, \quad p = 0 \quad \text{otherwise,} \qquad (3)$$

where equations are normalized $(\text{Var}(\varepsilon^*) = \text{Var}(\xi^*) = 1)$. The interdependence between the decision to participate in the vote and a vote in favor of the popular initiative is captured by the fact that disturbances are assumed to be correlated: $\text{Corr}(\varepsilon^* \xi^*) = \rho$. Equations (2) and (3) can be interpreted as a simplified reduced form of a structural-voting model (see Krishnakumar and Müller 2003).

In this survey only individuals who participated in the vote were asked how they had voted. Therefore, equations (2) and (3) must be estimated using a bivariate probit model with censoring: For a given individual, v is not observed unless $p = 1$. The maximum-likelihood procedure that applies in this context was proposed by van de Ven and van Praag (1981).

In constructing the variables to estimate the model, we follow the literature (see, e.g., Citrin et al. 1997 and Scheve and Slaughter 1999) by distinguishing between economic and non-economic determinants of attitudes toward immigration. Economic determinants are related to

Table 6.4
Variables of the voting model

Variables	Mean	Standard deviation
Vote	0.283	0.451
Participation	0.579	0.494
Schooling (years)	12.650	2.113
Vocational education	0.636	0.481
Wage	5.045	2.981
Retired	0.205	0.404
Age	47.769	17.074
Unemployment share (canton)	1.845	0.837
Share of foreigners (agglomeration)	19.308	6.386
French speaking[a]	0.195	0.396
Italian speaking[a]	0.067	0.250
Female	0.485	0.500
Owner	0.481	0.500
Political orientation (0–10)	4.916	1.481

Note: There are 805 observations for all variables, except for the vote (466 observations).
[a] Reference group: German-speaking individuals.

the costs and benefits of immigration at the aggregate or individual level. At the individual level, economic determinants include in particular factor endowments such as the individual's skills and capital holdings. Non-economic determinants include individuals' political ideology, attitudes toward other cultures, and attitudes toward the civil rights of immigrants.[28]

From the viewpoint of an economist, the main question is whether skill or human capital is a significant determinant of attitudes toward immigration even if one controls for political ideology and other social and demographic variables. We explore carefully the role of economic determinants by using two different measures of skills. First, as a measure of educational attainment, we constructed an indicator of years of schooling according to the five education types reported in the survey (descriptive statistics of variables are given in table 6.4). The particularity of the dual education system in Switzerland is taken into account by defining a dummy variable that takes a value of one for individuals who received most of their secondary education as vocational training (apprenticeship, etc.).

Second, we used a wider measure of skills by including also on-the-job training. The two types of skills (schooling and on-the-job training) can be aggregated into a common indicator by appealing to Mincer's concept of "potential earnings." In Mincer's framework, observed wages and potential earnings are closely linked. To construct the aggregate skill measure ("earnings"), we applied a standard Mincer wage equation to data from the Swiss wage structure survey. The *earnings* indicator was constructed using the following equation:

$$\ln(earnings) = \text{constant} + 0.04(experience)$$

$$- 0.5(experience^2/1000) + 0.09(schooling),$$

where *experience* is defined as $(age - schooling - 6)$.[29] The macroeconomic context is captured by the unemployment rate in the individual's canton of residence.[30] In addition, we use a variable measuring the share of foreigners in the population of the geographical area where the individual lives.

Among the non-economic determinants of attitudes toward immigration, we represent the political beliefs of citizens by a variable based on the individual's own judgment of his political position on a scale from 0 (left) to 10 (right). Cultural differences between the German-, French-, and Italian-speaking parts of Switzerland are captured by dummy variables for minorities. The participation equation furthermore includes dummy variables on gender and housing status (owner) and two continuous variables for age and age squared.

6.4.2 Results

We now report the results of four specifications of the voting and participation equations. Each specification includes one of the two skill measures and, in order to avoid problems of multicollinearity, either the cultural dummies or the other variables that are defined on a geographical basis (unemployed rate, share of foreigners). Indeed these variables are highly correlated since unemployment rates and the share of foreigners tend to be higher in the French and Italian speaking parts of Switzerland.

Before discussing the results in detail, it is useful to gauge the importance of the participation bias (sample selection bias) which can be done by estimating two versions of the model. First, the full model given by (2) and (3) is estimated using a bivariate probit model with censoring, as described above. Second, we ignore deliberately the selection mechanism and fit a standard probit model to equation (2),

Table 6.5
Estimation results of the voting model (specification 1)

	Probit	Probit with sample selection		
	Vote	Vote	Partici-pation	Marginal effect
Years of schooling	0.042	−0.068*	0.113***	−0.027*
	(1.17)	(1.81)	(4.72)	(1.85)
Vocational education	0.565***	0.259	0.104	0.103
	(3.60)	(1.61)	(1.01)	(1.59)
Age	−0.053**	−0.072***	0.052***	−0.028***
	(2.22)	(3.92)	(3.25)	(3.91)
Age squared/1,000	0.583**	0.640***	−0.348**	0.253***
	(2.56)	(3.53)	(2.17)	(3.49)
Unemployment rate	−0.003	0.196**	−0.323***	0.0776**
	(0.03)	(2.16)	(4.39)	(2.19)
Share of foreigners	−0.007	−0.017	0.029***	−0.007
	(0.54)	(1.54)	(2.94)	(1.55)
Female			−0.159*	
			(1.94)	
Owner			0.389***	
			(3.57)	
Political orientation	0.234***	0.151***	−0.440***	0.060***
	(5.47)	(3.71)	(4.28)	(3.59)
Political orientation squared			48.168*** (4.38)	
Constant	−1.524*	1.811**	−2.028***	
	(1.90)	(2.03)	(3.73)	
Number of observations	466	805		
Number of uncensored observations		466		
Log-likelihood	−247.82	−720.25		
Rho		−0.92***		

Note: Absolute value of z-statistics in parentheses.
*significant at 10 percent. **significant at 5 percent. ***significant at 1 percent.

using only the part of the sample that includes observations on individuals who participated in the vote.

The results in table 6.5 demonstrate that the voting and participation decisions must be estimated simultaneously to explain (1) individuals' attitudes toward immigration and (2) the mechanism that links individual attitudes to actual voting behavior.[31] Indeed, the correlation ρ between the disturbances of the voting and participation equations is significantly different from zero, and its estimate is close to −1. As a consequence, the naive probit model yields biased results and would lead one to believe that schooling and the unemployment rate are not significant determinants of attitudes toward immigration.[32]

In the complete model with sample selection, the main parameters turn out to be significant and have the expected sign: A lower education level and right-wing convictions are associated with a higher probability of accepting the popular initiative.[33] The probability of voting "yes" decreases with age until it reaches a minimum around the age of fifty-six. This age-voting profile resembles (in the negative) an age-earnings profile. One might therefore be tempted to conclude that in this regression, *age* is a proxy for labor market experience (representing another measure of skill). That this is indeed the case can be seen in table 6.6, which reports the results of the three alternative specifications. When potential earnings (*wage*) are included in the equation (specifications 3 and 4), they contribute significantly to the explanation of voting and participation behavior, and in this case no independent influence of a voter's age can be identified.

It is interesting to note that a high foreign-population share in the voter's geographical area is not associated with an anti-immigration vote (specification 3 suggests rather the opposite). The effects of the remaining explanatory variables in the voting equation are rather robust with respect to the different specifications. Individuals living in cantons with high unemployment rates tend to be more hostile to immigration. Italian-speaking Swiss are significantly more opposed to immigration, which is certainly due to the specific situation of the labor market (with many low-wage workers along the Swiss-Italian border) and the strong influence of a local right-wing party (Lega).

The estimation of the participation equation yields interesting results in its own right. First, people from the political extremes are more likely to participate in the vote than those who hold centrist beliefs. Indeed, the probability of participation is related to the political scale in a U-shaped relationship, with the minimum (4.6) close to the sample

Table 6.6
Estimation results under different specifications

	Specification 2		Specification 3		Specification 4	
	Vote	Participation	Vote	Participation	Vote	Participation
Schooling	-0.073** (2.02)	0.115*** (4.84)				
Vocational education	0.259* (1.69)	0.064 (0.62)	0.230 (1.43)	0.108 (1.04)	0.223 (1.38)	0.066 (0.63)
Wage			-0.140** (2.03)	0.176*** (3.40)	-0.150** (2.16)	0.185*** (3.60)
Retired			-1.250** (2.30)	1.460*** (3.36)	-1.291** (2.36)	1.496*** (3.45)
Age	-0.071*** (4.00)	0.050*** (3.11)	-0.042 (1.51)	0.012 (0.53)	-0.037 (1.32)	0.006 (0.26)
Age squared / 1,000	0.633*** (3.56)	-0.322** (2.03)	0.465* (1.70)	-0.093 (0.43)	0.413 (1.49)	-0.034 (0.16)
Unemployment rate			0.213** (2.40)	-0.330*** (4.49)		
Share of foreigners			-0.018* (1.68)	0.031*** (3.17)		
French speaking	0.133 (0.92)	-0.243** (2.02)			0.170 (1.17)	-0.243** (2.02)
Italian speaking	0.567** (2.37)	-0.818*** (4.27)			0.600*** (2.62)	-0.836*** (4.38)
Political orientation	0.149*** (3.83)	-0.442*** (4.36)	0.148*** (3.68)	-0.448*** (4.41)	0.144*** (3.72)	-0.450*** (4.57)

Political orientation squared	48.508*** (4.47)	48.764*** (4.48)	49.088*** (4.67)
Female	−0.141* (1.76)	−0.190** (2.33)	−0.165** (2.07)
Owner	0.367*** (3.38)	0.396*** (3.31)	0.356*** (2.72)
	1.879** (2.25)	0.986* (1.83)	0.983** (2.02)
Constant	−1.911*** (3.58)	−0.504 (1.09)	−0.307 (0.70)
Number of observations	805	805	805
Log-likelihood	−719.51	−725.16	−724.50
Rho	−0.94***	−0.94***	−0.96***

Note: Absolute value of z-statistics in parentheses.
* significant at 10 percent. ** significant at 5 percent. *** significant at 1 percent.

Table 6.7
Probability of voting in favor of the popular initiative (sample averages, in percent, specification 1)

	Entire sample (805 observations)	Subsample of voters ($p = 1$) (466 observations)
Probit without sample selection		
$P\,(v = 1)$	27.4	28.3
Probit with sample selection		
$P\,(v = 1)$	54.6	51.8
$P\,(v = 1 \mid p = 1)$		28.3

mean (4.9). Second, participation is positively related to education, a result found in many other studies (see Mueller 1989, 365). Third, the participation of Swiss is greater in geographical areas in which there are many foreigners. Finally, the young, women, tenants, and minorities are less likely to go to the polls.

Turn now to the link between attitudes toward immigration and voting behavior. The estimates of marginal and conditional probabilities can inform us about this link (table 6.7 gives the average probabilities calculated both for the entire sample and the subsample including only people who participated). The conditional probability $P(v = 1 \mid p = 1)$ represents the model's fit for the outcome of the vote (the "yes" vote in the sample, 28.3 percent, is very well predicted). The marginal probability $P(v = 1)$ indicates how people voted or would have voted, whether they participated or not. For the entire sample, the average probability of accepting the initiative is 54.6 percent. This is a startling result. Had all Swiss citizens voted, the anti-immigration initiative would have been accepted!

The large divergence between the conditional and marginal probabilities can be explained by appealing to differences in observed and unobserved characteristics between those who voted and those who did not. It turns out that observed characteristics account for only a fairly small part of this difference. The participation and voting equations show, for example, that more-skilled individuals were more likely to participate and to reject the initiative. This effect, however, is quantitatively not very important, since the marginal probability of accepting the initiative is only slightly lower in the subsample of voters (51.8 percent) than in the entire sample (54.6 percent).[34]

The main difference between the marginal and conditional probabilities is due to the negative correlation between unobserved factors (disturbances) in the two equations. In other words, individuals who were more likely to participate than others *because of their unobserved characteristics* were generally more likely to reject the popular initiative. Indeed, this fact accounts for the large difference between the marginal probability (51.8 percent) and the conditional probability (28.3 percent) in the subsample of voters.[35]

To put these results into perspective, consider what would have happened if the Swiss government had followed opinion polls to define immigration policy, as some policymakers are tempted to do today in the context of EU enlargement. According to our econometric results, a general-opinion poll would have shown that more than half of Swiss voters were in favor of the popular initiative; interestingly, two "real" opinion polls came quite close to this conclusion.[36] Instead, the clear result of the vote was interpreted as a political signal of opposition to a restrictive immigration policy.

6.5 Conclusions

Perhaps the most controversial aspect of the ongoing negotiations about EU enlargement to the east is the free mobility of persons. Fears of a large inflow of immigrants have been apparent in recent EU-wide opinion polls. These fears are in sharp contrast with studies suggesting a net welfare gain from allowing the free mobility of persons to and from the CEECs, and with other studies predicting only moderate inflows of immigrants into the current EU member countries under free mobility.

This chapter informs the debate in two areas. First, we reviewed Switzerland's long-standing experience with immigration. We found that, compared with those of EU member countries as a whole, Swiss respondents in opinion polls are relatively more favorable to immigration in spite of Switzerland's having a higher stock of immigrants. The review of the debate and votes on initiatives and referenda over the last thirty years shows that the results at the election booth have influenced government policy on immigration, which has pursued a course accommodating the conflicting interests of unions, owners of businesses in sectors that are largely non-competitive internationally, and the public at large (as expressed in the results of the votes).

The resulting flexible system of annual quotas by worker categories combined with limited mobility and exemptions allowing the progressive transfer of immigrants from temporary to permanent status has successfully absorbed a large inflow of foreigners into Switzerland. Interestingly, many of the elements of this policy that have survived repeated challenges at the polls have been employed by EU members in their current immigration policies with the CEECs.

Second, and perhaps more interestingly, we have been able to show that the results from opinion polls are probably overly pessimistic, if interpreted as reflecting what people would actually vote if asked to. Indeed, drawing on a survey for the last immigration-related vote in Switzerland, which attempted to limit the stock of immigrants to its current level, we show that the government would have been tempted to put a limit on the number of immigrants if it had listened to opinion polls. In fact, the vote clearly rejected the proposal, confirming the notion that as in the contingent-valuation methods used to assess environmental damage, opinion polls are likely to suffer from hypothetical bias.

As to lessons for the current EU enlargement, it is interesting to contrast the Swiss experience with the debate on the EU's alleged "democratic deficit." Schematically, the Swiss political system derives its political legitimacy from direct-democratic procedures ("input legitimacy"), whereas the EU's legitimacy is based on the performance and efficient functioning of the decision-making process ("output legitimacy"). The EU's quasi-exclusive reliance on output legitimacy has prompted the criticism that the EU's political process suffers from a democratic deficit. But could the eastern enlargement have been carried through if voters in Western Europe had had the opportunity to oppose particularly sensitive issues, such as the free movement of persons? The Swiss experience suggests that large immigration flows can be absorbed in the context of a direct democracy, since the foreign population share of Switzerland has tripled over a forty-year period. But in the presence of populist right-wing movements, this absorption has been a long process. A flexible system of quotas and the gradual integration of immigrants turned out to be crucial in the case of Switzerland. Therefore, the Swiss experience suggests that the proper sequencing of policies toward immigrants during the transition period could turn out to be decisive for the political acceptance of EU enlargement.

Notes

This is a shortened version of de Melo, Miguet, and Müller 2002. The authors would like to thank Helge Berger, Fabrizio Carlevaro, Riccardo Faini, Thomas Moutos, Hans-Werner Sinn, Martin Werding, and participants at the CESifo workshops on EU enlargement in Munich (13–15 December 2001) and Delphi (13–14 September 2002) for useful suggestions and stimulating comments on previous drafts of the chapter. Financial support by the Swiss National Science Foundation (Grant 12-63953.00) is gratefully acknowledged.

1. See, e.g., Boeri and Brücker (2001), Brücker et al. 2001, and Sinn et al. 2001. The last study emphasizes, for Germany, potential problems during the transitional phase.

2. Evidence, mostly based on estimates of inflows from the ten aspiring countries, suggests that the stock of people (not only workers) would rise, after accession, to 4.0 million (up from the current 830,000), with their share in the EU population rising from 0.2 to 1.1 percent. The estimates suggest that the increase in immigrant population from enlargement will be largely concentrated in Germany, which is to absorb over two-thirds of the projected immigrant inflow, with an additional 10 percent to go to Austria. Sinn et al. (2001) forecast that between 3.4 and 4.3 percent of the population in acceding countries will flow to Germany, whereas Boeri and Brücker (2001) have a lower forecast (between 1.8 and 2.4 percent). According to Sinn et al. (2001), over the next fifteen years, the stock of immigrants in Germany would increase as a result of EU expansion to between 4 and 5 percent of the native population. Boeri and Brücker (2001) estimate that over the next thirty years, the share of immigrants from the CEEC10 in the German population would increase as a result of the expansion from 0.6 percent in 1998 to 3.5 percent in 2030 and in Austria from 1.3 to 5.5 percent. (As a reference, the stock of foreigners in Switzerland has more than tripled since the end of World War II to over 18 percent of the population.) Other estimates also suggest that past immigration has had little effect on unemployment, and that any negative impact on wages would be limited.

3. Dustmann and Preston (2000) find that racial prejudice is the most important component explaining negative inclination toward immigration from populations (e.g., West Indies, Asia) that are ethnically different from that of the receiving nation. By contrast, with regard to European immigrants, the estimated contributions of welfare and job concerns to negative feelings about immigration are as strong as those of racial prejudices.

4. The median-voter model employed in this chapter is well suited to representing how citizens' preferences over immigration translate into actual migration policies. Indeed, Scheve and Slaughter (1999) find that individuals form their opinions in accord with their interests as labor force participants. Moreover, the median-voter model gives a realistic description of the Swiss political system, in which people actually vote on immigration issues, and also of representative democracies in which governments monitor closely the public's mood on immigration. In the median-voter approach, the links to the underlying economic model are more transparent than in other political-economy approaches. Alternatively, one could rely on the pressure group model, in which policy is the result of the maximization of a welfare function whose weights are often arbitrarily chosen. For examples of this approach, see Buckley 1996 and Mezza and Winden 1996.

5. By symmetry, if $k_m > k_c$, a maximum skill requirement will defeat all other policy alternatives. Such a policy, however, might be difficult to enforce in the case of non-human capital, since immigrants might be able to conceal their capital holdings.

6. Equation (1) is obtained by differentiating $y = F_L + kF_K$, with $F_{KL} = -(L/K)F_{LL} = -(K/L)F_{KK}$ and $\sigma \equiv F_K F_K/(F_{KL}F)$.

7. See also Bilal, Grether, and de Melo 2003, which deals with the case of a beta distribution of capital in a direct-democracy model with three factors and two sectors.

8. Note that the voting costs c depicted in figure 6.1 are expressed in terms of capital per capita. They are linked to voting costs C through the following expression: $c = C\bar{k}^2\sigma L/((\bar{k} - k_I)s_L s_K \bar{y})$.

9. Consider the following simple example that lowers the critical capital level k_c (relative to the case considered above). Assume that, at the moment of the vote on migration policy, unskilled immigrants make up an important share of the initial population. If these immigrants do not have the right to vote, then k_c, equal to the average capital-labor ratio of the total population, is smaller than the average capital-labor ratio of the native population. Thus the capital endowment of the (native) median voter might well be greater than k_c. This case, however, which is reminiscent of the current Swiss situation, does not provide an explanation of why the (old) immigrants were accepted in the first place. The consequences of allowing for immigrants who do not have a right to vote in a Ricardo-Viner direct-democracy model are analyzed in Grether, de Melo, and Müller 2001.

10. Currently, in EU countries, immigration from the CEECs mostly takes the form of temporary migration, regulated either unilaterally by the host country or by bilateral agreements (see Boeri and Brücker 2001, table 4.4). Through these temporary migration programs, workers from the CEECs are channeled into occupations with low skill requirements. As a result, Boeri and Brücker (2001, 56) find that, although migrants from the CEECs are highly skilled, they work in the same sectors as other foreigners (i.e., labor-intensive sectors with a high share of unskilled workers).

11. The Ricardo-Viner model is a natural framework for examining the political-economy aspects of various migration policies in an open economy. Its time frame, with short-term rents, also probably corresponds to the time frame envisaged by many voters when they form an opinion on immigration policy. For example, Hillman and Weiss (1999b) suggest that voters probably find the Heckscher-Ohlin model appealing when formulating trade policy, since it captures the indirect effect on labor of trade in goods (via embodiment in imports), and the Ricardo-Viner model when formulating immigration policy, since immigrants compete directly with domestic labor.

12. See Djajic 1997. This is all the more likely if one makes the assumption, as do Hillman and Weiss (1999b) in the context of a similar analysis applied to illegal immigrants, that domestic (and permanent- or legal-immigrant) households have stronger preferences for nontraded goods than illegal-immigrant households.

13. In 1964, Italy pressured Switzerland to renegotiate the 1948 bilateral recruiting agreement between the two countries, leading to important improvements in the legal situation of Italian immigrants in Switzerland. The revised agreement aroused much opposition in Switzerland, triggering the creation of several anti-immigration movements. In 1981, the abolition of the seasonal-worker status was also opposed by a large majority of Swiss voters (see details in section 6.4).

14. The economic performance of ethnic Germans in the German labor market seems to be similar to (or even worse than) the performance of other immigrants, although ethnic Germans do not face any legal barriers to mobility and can be assumed to have better German language skills than other immigrants (Brücker et al. 2001, 58). This points to the conclusion that these immigrants suffer from an unequal access to the high-wage segment of the labor market.

15. For the effects of immigration in efficiency wage models with unemployment, see Müller 2003b and Epstein and Hillman 2000, in which the natives' willingness to exert effort increases with the number of immigrants.

16. In 1995, average return rates among the incumbent EU countries ranged from 1.5 percent for the Netherlands to 7.8 percent for Germany, though much higher return rates are observed for particular groups (e.g., 25.6 percent return rates for Polish immigrants in Germany) and for immigrant workers certain legal categories (e.g., 10.3 percent for holders of annual work permits in Switzerland).

17. Except for those for the United Kingdom, for which the figures are based on "foreign birth," the figures in table 6.1 are based on nationality. The statistics may misrepresent "immigrant pressure" for countries with high naturalization rates, like France and the United Kingdom. In the case of Switzerland, in 1990, 20.5 percent of residents were foreign born, and the foreign population share was 18.1 percent, indicating a lower rate of naturalization than in France and the United Kingdom. In 1999, foreigners accounted for 21.1 percent of the country's population. Excluding seasonal workers, asylum seekers, and short-stay foreigners, the share was 19.6 percent; excluding international workers and foreigners born in Switzerland, it was 16.3 percent.

18. A more detailed account of the recent history of Swiss migration policy can be found in Piguet and Mahnig 2000.

19. Even before the two orders were issued, foreign labor in Switzerland was grouped into three categories according to the type of work permit the workers held: seasonal (permit A), which prohibited the workers who held them from residing in the country more than nine months per year; annual renewable (permit B); and long-term (permit C), which allowed the establishment of residence. This reflected the view (expressed in the 1931 federal law on foreigners) that as long as they were not seeking residence, foreigners were welcome. This changed, under pressure from Italy, when the bilateral accord of 1964 allowed Italians residing in Switzerland for five years to change jobs and/or occupations, and relaxed time limits for family reunification and for obtaining long-term residence permits. This accord unleashed opposition in the media, to which the government replied by implementing its quota policy prior to ratifying the accord in March 1965.

20. Since 1970, yearly quotas for immigration have been established on the basis of data on return immigrants. To appease senescent sectors of the economy threatened with the loss of workers to expanding sectors, immigrants can change jobs only after one year, and they can change the canton in which they reside only after three years, with a consultative bargaining process at the canton level in cases of an excess number of demands for permits. The yearly quota policy averted a rise in unemployment during the economic crisis of the early 1970s, with the stock of foreigners diminishing by 86,000 between 1974 and 1976. As unemployment insurance was not compulsory at the time, many foreigners did not take it, which explains why the foreign population share fell by 2 percentage points during this crisis, but not in the subsequent crisis when unemployment insurance became compulsory in the early 1980s.

21. Under the three-circles policy, no restrictions were placed on immigration by citizens of EU and the European Free Trade Area (EFTA) countries (the first circle), whereas some restrictions were imposed on immigrants from a second circle of countries with close cultural ties to Switzerland (including Canadian, U.S. and CEEC citizens), with only exceptional admission of immigrants from the rest of the world, lumped together in a third circle.

22. The statistics for Switzerland (1999) are (nationals, foreigners): mean age (41, 33); male share (47.8 percent, 53.3 percent); urban dwellers (66.5 percent, 80.1 percent); unemployment rate (1.6 percent, 5.3 percent).

23. About two-thirds of foreigners living today in Switzerland come from Southern Europe (including Turkey and the former Yugoslavia). Note, however, that a substantial percentage of the immigrants from Northern Europe are highly skilled.

24. We are grateful to the editors for the following remarks. First, to the extent that some people move randomly in a regional context without paying attention to national borders, the fact that small countries have higher shares of foreign residents can be seen as a statistical artifact. Second, Eurobarometer data are known to be rather volatile over the years. Unfortunately, we are unable to carry out comparisons over time since there has been only one Eurobarometer survey (in 2000) with questions on immigration that included Switzerland.

25. Cummings, Harrison, and Rutström 1995 and Cummings et al. 1997 discuss the reasons why intentions may differ from actual behavior in the context of contingent methods for valuing environmental goods.

26. In certain circumstances, government decisions even anticipate the outcome of a popular vote. To prevent a popular initiative from being accepted by the voters, the government makes decisions that fulfill some of the initiative's demands. One example is the introduction of immigration quotas in the early 1970s, when a xenophobic popular initiative was up for vote (see section 6.3).

27. This model draws on Krishnakumar and Müller 2003.

28. The distinction between economic and non-economic determinants is, however, controversial and cannot be made easily in practice. For example, educational attainment is a measure of general human capital and is therefore an important determinant of an individual's wage. On the other hand, political values are certainly influenced by education as well. This double nature of education explains why Scheve and Slaughter (1999) classify education as an economic variable, whereas Citrin et al. (1997) interpret it as a demographic variable. A similar ambiguity arises for age, since it can be considered a proxy for work experience but also captures differences in political attitudes between generations.

29. The coefficients in this equation are based on a sample of Swiss men, bypassing problems associated with the measure of labor market experience (women) or schooling quality (foreign workers). To adapt the wage equation to the inactive citizens in our sample, we made some additional assumptions. For students, potential earnings are computed as if they were active citizens without experience. For the unemployed and people working in their home, potential earnings are computed as if they were active, but dummy variables are added to the regression to account for (unobserved) differences in work experience (as the coefficients of these dummies turn out not to be significant in the regression, they are not reported in the results). As the retired are no longer involved in the labor market, their attitude toward immigration is influenced by other considerations (such as the impact of immigration on social security). Therefore, their potential earnings are set to zero, and a dummy for the retired is included in the voting and participation equations.

30. In a dual labor market with unemployment, Müller (2003b) shows that the lower the unemployment rate, the greater are the chances that additional immigration is beneficial for natives.

31. As the four specifications do not differ significantly with respect to the problem of sample selection, we report results from only one of them.

32. To test the robustness of these results, we analyzed in addition two auxiliary questions. Those who participated in the vote were asked whether they agreed with the following statements: (1) "There are too many foreigners in Switzerland" and (2) "The current immigration policy is too lax; it should become tougher." Both estimations confirmed the crucial role of the variables *schooling* and *political ideology* (with p-values smaller than 0.005).

33. In contrast to the finding for participation, the square of the *political ideology* variable was found to have no significant influence on the vote; it was therefore dropped from the equation of the vote.

34. If there was no correlation between the disturbances of the two equations ($\rho = 0$), the conditional probability of voting "yes" would be equal to: $P(v = 1 \mid p = 1) = P(v = 1, p = 1)/P(p = 1) = P(v = 1)$. Therefore, the average of probabilities $P(v = 1)$ calculated on the subsample of voters represents the outcome of the vote as if omitted factors were not correlated across equations.

35. The ratio between the conditional and marginal probabilities is given by $P(v = 1 \mid p = 1)/P(v = 1) = P(v = 1, p = 1)/[P(p = 1) \cdot P(v = 1)]$. This ratio is equal to one if and only if $\rho = 0$.

36. According to a poll carried out in July 2000 and commissioned by Swiss television (DSR/TSR), 40 percent of respondents were in favor of the popular initiative, 42 percent were against, and 17 percent did not have an opinion. A similar poll, commissioned by the Swiss government in May 2000, concluded that the popular initiative would be accepted (see "Un Sondage sur l'Initiative des 18 percent secoue ses Opposants," *Le Temps*, 17 July 2000).

References

Bauer, T., M. Lofstrom, and K. F. Zimmerman. 2000. "Immigration Policy, Assimilation of Immigrants and Natives' Sentiments towards Immigrants: Evidence from 12 OECD Countries." Discussion paper no. 187, Institute for the Study of Labor (IZA), Bonn.

Benhabib, J. 1996. "On the Political Economy of Immigration." *European Economic Review* 40: 1737–1743.

Bilal, S., J.-M. Grether, and J. de Melo. 2003. "Determinants of Attitudes towards Immigration: A Trade-Theoric Approach." *Review of International Economics* 11, no. 2: 253–267.

Boeri, T., and H. Brücker. 2001. "The Impact of Eastern Enlargement on Employment and Labor Markets in EU Member States." Report for the European Commission, Berlin.

Brücker, H., G. Epstein, B. McCormick, G. St. Paul, A. Venturini, and K. Zimmerman. 2001. "Managing Migration in the European Welfare State." Mimeographed.

Bulow, J., and L. Summers. 1986. "A Theory of Dual Labor Markets with Application to Industrial Policy, Discrimination and Keynesian Unemployment." *Journal of Labor Economics* 23: 376–414.

Citrin, J., D. Green, C. Muste, and C. Wong. 1997. "Public Opinion toward Immigration Reform: The Role of Economic Motivation." *Journal of Politics* 59, no. 3: 858–881.

Cummings, R. G., S. Elliott, G. W. Harrison, and J. Murphy. 1997. "Are Hypothetical Referenda Incentive Compatible?" *Journal of Political Economy* 105, no. 3: 609–621.

Cummings, R. G., G. W. Harrison, and E. E. Rutström. 1995. "Homegrown Values and Hypothetical Surveys: Is the Dichotomous Choice Approach Incentive Compatible?" *American Economic Review* 85, no. 1: 260–266.

de Melo, J., F. Miguet, and T. Müller. 2002. "The Political Economy of Migration and EU Enlargement: Lessons from Switzerland." Discussion paper no. 3449, Centre for Economic Policy Research, London.

Djajic, S. 1997. "Illegal Immigration and Resource Allocation." *International Economic Review* 38, no. 1: 97–117.

Dustmann, C., and I. Preston. 2000. "Racial and Economic Factors in Attitudes to Immigration." Working paper no. 2542, Centre for Economic Policy Research, London.

Epstein, G., and A. Hillman. 2000. "Social Harmony at the Boundaries of the Welfare State: Immigrants and Social Transfers." Discussion paper no. 2414, Center for Economic Policy Research.

Espenshade, T., and K. Hempstead. 1996. "Contemporary American Attitudes toward U.S. Immigration." *International Migration Review* 30, no. 2: 535–570.

European Commission. 1997. "Racism and Xenophobia in Europe." Eurobarometer Opinion Poll no. 47.1, Brussels.

European Commission. 2000. "Eurobarometer: Public Opinion in the European Union." Report no. 53, Brussels.

European Commission. 2001. "The Free Movement of Workers in the Context of Enlargement." Information note. Brussels. Directorate General-V.

Faini, R., J. de Melo, and K. Zimmerman, eds. 1999. *Migration: The Controversies and the Evidence.* Cambridge, UK: Cambridge University Press.

Fertig, M., and C. Schmidt. 2001. First- and Second-Generation Migrants in Germany— What Do We Know and What People Think." Discussion paper no. 286, Institute for the Study of Labor, Bonn.

Flückiger, Y., and J. Ramirez. 2001. "Positions hiérarchiques et ségrégation par origine en Suisse." In *La migration et la Suisse: Résultats du programme national "Migrations et relations interculturelles,"* ed. H.-R. Wicker, R. Fibbi, and W. Haug, 275–301. Zurich: Seismo.

Grether, J.-M., J. de Melo, and T. Müller. 2001. "The Political Economy of International Migration in a Ricardo-Viner Model." In *International Migration: Trends, Policies and Economic Impact,* ed. S. Djajic, 42–68. London: Routledge.

Hillman, A., and A. Weiss. 1999a. "Beyond International Factor Movements: Cultural Preferences, Endogenous Policies and the Migration of People: An Overview." In *Migration: The Controversies and the Evidence,* ed. R. Faini, J. de Melo, and K. Zimmerman, 76–91. Cambridge, UK: Cambridge University Press.

Hillman, A., and A. Weiss. 1999b. "A Theory of Permissible Immigration." *European Journal of Political Economy* 15: 585–604.

Krishnakumar, J., and T. Müller. 2003. "Participation and Voting Behavior in a Direct Democracy: The Case of Migration Policy in Switzerland." Forthcoming.

Mayer, W. 1984. "Endogenous Tariff Formation." *American Economic Review* 74, no. 5: 970–985.

Mueller, D. C. 1989. *Public Choice II.* Cambridge: Cambridge University Press.

Müller, T. 2003a. "Migration Policy in a Small Open Economy with a Dual Labor Market." *Review of International Economics* 11, no. 1: 130–143.

Müller, T. 2003b. "Migration, Unemployment and Discrimination." *European Economic Review* 47, no. 3: 409–427.

OECD. 2000a. "Trends in International Migration." Système d'Observation Permanente des Migrations (SOPEMI) report, Paris.

OECD. 2000b. "Main Economic Indicators." Paris.

Piguet, E., and H. Mahnig. 2000. "Quotas d'immigration: L'expérience de la Suisse." Cahiers de migration internationale no. 37, International Labor Office Geneva.

Scheve, K., and M. Slaughter. 1999. "Labor-Market Competition and Individual Preferences over Immigration Policy." Working paper no. 6946, National Bureau of Economic Research, Cambridge, MA.

Schiff, M. 1998. "Trade, Migration, and Welfare: The Impact of Social Capital." Policy Research working paper no. 2044, World Bank, Washington, DC.

Schiff, M. 1999. "Labor Market Integration in the Presence of Social Capital." Policy Research working paper no. 2222, World Bank, Washington, DC.

SIDOS. 2000. "Eurobarometer for Switzerland." Swiss information and data archive service for the social sciences, Neuchâtel.

Shapiro, C., and J. Stiglitz. 1984. "Equilibrium Unemployment as a Worker-Discipline Device." *American Economic Review* 74: 433–444.

Sinn, H.-W. 2000. "EU Enlargement and the Welfare State." Working paper no. 307, CESifo, Munich.

Sinn, H.-W., G. Flaig, M. Werding, S. Munz, N. Düll, H. Hofmann, A. Hänlein, J. Kruse, H. J. Reinhard, and B. Schulte. 2001. "EU-Erweiterung und Arbeitskräftemigration: Wege zu einer schrittweisen Annäherung der Arbeitsmärkte." Ifo Beiträge zur Wirtschaftsforschung no. 2, München.

van de Ven, W. P. M. M., and B. M. S. van Praag. 1981. "The Demand for Deductibles in Private Health Insurance: A Probit Model with Sample Selection." *Journal of Econometrics* 17: 229–252.

Comments

Riccardo Faini

There is an intriguing gap between voters' attitudes toward migration and the stance of migration policies. As Barry Chiswick and Tim Hatton (2003) have highlighted in their recent survey on the globalization of labor markets, migration policies since at least 1880 have by and large been substantially more liberal than warranted by voters' attitudes and interests. The insightful chapter by de Melo, Miguet, and Müller tackles head on the Chiswick-Hatton puzzle. The authors rely on sound theory and new empirical evidence to address what I believe is a key issue in the political economy of migration.

The authors review two main theoretical models. They first look at the Benhabib model, in which native voters differ from one another depending on their capital endowment. The model predicts under fairly plausible assumptions (namely, that the capital endowment of the median voter is lower than the economy-wide average) that voters will typically favor a minimum skill requirement for immigrants, with a view to raising the return to unskilled labor. The model is well suited to account for the growing policy bias toward skilled migrants in receiving countries. It offers no answer, however—quite the contrary—to the Chiswick-Hutton puzzle. To explain the preponderant role of unskilled immigration, the authors need to appeal to the existence of voting costs and to assume, somewhat arbitrarily, that the distribution of such costs is sufficiently asymmetric to discourage mainly the opponents of unskilled migration from going to the poll booth. Analytically, this is not a very palatable approach. Interestingly enough, though, it finds significant support in the data. The authors' evidence shows that, confronted with a proposal to shift toward a more restrictive stance on immigration policy, a majority of potential Swiss voters would have supported the proposal. When the probability of voting is taken into account, however, the support for the initiative dwindles to only 28 percent. The gap between voting attitudes and voting outcome is yet another manifestation of the Chiswick-Hatton puzzle. The econometric evidence also casts some light on the distribution of voting costs by showing that uneducated and low-income workers are more likely to oppose migration but less likely to actually vote. This could well be the end of the story. Unfortunately, as the authors point out, observed characteristics, such as income and education, play only a minor role empirically. Indeed, the correlation between voters' attitudes toward migration and their propensity to vote is almost fully accounted for by unobserved factors. In the end, therefore, the puzzle remains. Additional research on the nature, the determinants, and the distribution of voting costs is therefore badly needed.

An alternative strategy for addressing the Chiswick-Hatton puzzle stems from the observation that, particularly in Germany and Switzerland, unskilled migrants have been typically admitted under temporary labor contract schemes. The chapter offers an ingenious explanation of the popularity of the guest worker system. Suppose that labor markets are effectively segmented, with migrants being confined to the nontraded-goods sector. An increase in immigration will benefit natives on two counts: First, it will raise the return to capital; second, it will lower the price of nontraded goods. The result hinges quite crucially on the assumption that natives are not employed in the nontraded-goods sector. Moreover, as the authors themselves acknowledge, this setup does not explain why migrants are admitted into the country in the first place. This should be a key aspect in any attempts to resolve the Chiswick-Hatton puzzle. Finally, the model does not cast light on an intrinsic contradiction of the guest worker system in Switzerland. The attempt to fill what were too often permanent jobs with temporary workers (Collinson 1993) clashed with Swiss firms' desire to retain a well-trained workforce and the migrants' fear that they might be unable to return to the host country once they had left it even for a brief period. The contradiction remained latent until the mid-1970s, when Swiss migration policies shifted to a fairly tight stance. What remains to be explained is why rational voters did not perceive at the outset that the guest worker system as it stood was hardly viable in the medium run.

At a more general level, the chapter shares what I believe is one of the main shortcomings of the political-economy literature, namely, the lack of a joint analysis of trade and migration policies. The two policies are obviously related, albeit in a complex and model-dependent way.

A simple example may clarify what I have in mind. Consider the case of a labor-abundant country. Suppose that in a free-trade equilibrium the economy is fully specialized in a labor-intensive good. An inflow of migrant labor will then lead to a fall in the wage rate and therefore will face strong opposition from capital-poor workers. Suppose now that, because of protectionist trade policies, the economy ends up producing both commodities. In this case, an inflow of labor will have no impact on factor prices but will simply lead to factors' being reallocated toward the labor-intensive sector. Hence, migration will face little if no opposition. This example has many loose ends—for instance, how are trade policies determined?—but highlights the key link between a country's stance on trade and its immigration policies. Unfortunately, the Swiss data are ill suited for this purpose. First, they refer only to migration. Second, they are taken at a single point in time and are therefore incapable of capturing the effects of time-varying factors such as the evolution of the real exchange rate and the changing stance of trade policy. Still, a country's trade policy is likely to be a key factor in determining its stance on immigration. Probing into this link may well provide some further insights into the Chiswick-Hatton puzzle.

References

Chiswick, B., and T. Hatton. 2003. "International Migration and the Integration of Labor Markets." In *Globalization in Historical Perspective*, ed. M. Bordo, A. Taylor, and J. Williamson, forthcoming. Cambridge, MA: NBER and Chicago: University of Chicago Press.

Collinson, S. 1993. *Europe and International Migration*. London: Pinter.

7

Eastern Enlargement of the EU: Jobs, Investment, and Welfare in Present Member Countries

Ben J. Heijdra, Christian Keuschnigg, and Wilhelm Kohler

7.1 Introduction

Based on the Maastricht Treaty of 1992, the European Council, at the Copenhagen summit of 1993, issued a firm commitment toward an eastern enlargement of the European Union. Within a short period of time it was faced with ten membership applications from CEECs. The Luxembourg summit of December 1997 marked the beginning of formal negotiations with a first group of five CEECs. Following the Helsinki summit of 1999, negotiations were extended to the remaining applicant countries from Central and Eastern Europe, plus Malta and Cyprus.[1] The prime purpose of these negotiations was to ensure a complete adoption of all existing union legislation (*acquis communautaire*) by future member countries. But taking in as many as twelve new members requires significant change on the part of the union itself. In their summits in Nice (December 2000) and Laeken (December 2001), the EU15 heads of state therefore agreed on an institutional reform aimed at the smooth and efficient operation of an EU27. In its meeting in Brussels (October 2002), the European Council adopted a revised framework, and this adoption was followed by a formal conclusion of negotiations with all twelve countries at the Copenhagen summit of December 2002.

The negotiating progress notwithstanding, enlargement is likely to remain a cause for hot debate. Although the whole process has so far been driven primarily by political impetus, implementing enlargement will shift the balance in favor of economic concerns. Incumbent members will have to foot the bill for net financial transfers to new members, and they will face adjustment pressure that arises from extending the single market to economies featuring a well-educated labor force with relatively low wages. Economists were quick to emphasize that incumbents will also reap economic benefits from enlargement that tend to offset the burden of net payments to new members. But empirical analysis has revealed that the gains that can be expected are relatively small in size. Baldwin, Francois, and Portes (1997) have argued that the benefits of enlargement are of only minor importance for the EU15 as a whole, but potentially large for accession countries. This seems to justify the observed preoccupation of incumbents with the fiscal burden enlargement will impose on them, although we have shown in a series of papers that Austria and Germany should reap integration gains in excess of their fiscal burden (see Keuschnigg and Kohler 2002, Kohler and Keuschnigg 2001, and Keuschnigg, Keuschnigg, and Kohler 2001).

In their assumption of continuous labor market clearing, however, these early studies were probably too sanguine about employment. Given widespread unemployment in Europe, the analysis of enlargement should include *potential effects on unemployment* by means of a more realistic treatment of labor markets, particularly when migration is being examined. A further issue relates to *differences among EU15 countries*. Obviously, member countries differ a great deal from one another, in terms of both the likely fiscal burden financing enlargement will place on them and the effects they will feel from market integration. Therefore, results obtained for Germany and Austria do not directly apply for other incumbent countries. This chapter takes up the first of these issues, both theoretically and empirically.

We analyze enlargement-type integration, relying on a *search-theoretic framework* of job creation and destruction in which equilibrium unemployment is determined by firms' incentives to incur costs of search and recruitment. We combine this with forward-looking *capital accumulation*, in which growth acts as a prime transmission channel for labor market effects of enlargement. Reflecting the general concern about the effects of demographic change and population dynamics on unemployment in the EU15, we merge our search-theoretic approach to the labor market with an *overlapping-generations model* of household behavior. This is highly relevant for migration, since it allows us to show how the age structure of migrants determines the transitional effects of enlargement on employment.

The framework is then applied empirically by calibrating a multisector dynamic general equilibrium model. This allows us to quantify enlargement effects for the German economy by means of numerical solution. Our work builds on Keuschnigg, Keuschnigg, and Kohler

2001 by incorporating search unemployment (discussed in section 6.3) separately for high- and low-skilled workers. The model allows us to address a rich enlargement scenario focusing on commodity market integration, budgetary effects, and, notably, immigration from applicant countries. Among the effects considered are capital accumulation, unemployment, the government budget, income distribution, and overall welfare.[2]

The chapter is structured as follows. In section 7.2, we present a general discussion of the eastern enlargement scenario, as perceived by present member countries. Section 7.3 uses a skeletal version of our model to develop key intuitive insights on how immigration and market integration affect investment, unemployment, and welfare in an open economy. This paves the way for a deeper understanding of the numerical results reported in subsequent sections. Section 7.4 then defines the specific enlargement scenario in quantitative terms and discusses simulation results from our CGE model for Germany. Section 7.5 closes the chapter with a summary.

7.2 Features of Eastern EU Enlargement

Although similar in quantitative significance to the southern enlargement of the EU (Greece, Spain and Portugal) in the 1980s, the upcoming eastern enlargement forms an unprecedented challenge in five distinct ways. First, it involves countries that are still in transition to market economies. This is reflected by special entry conditions specified at the Copenhagen summit of 1993, requiring stable democracies, competitive market economies, and adoption of the EU *acquis communautaire*. Second, the income gaps between the accession and incumbent countries are still enormous. Given the objective of regional convergence and coherence within the EU, which draws 40 percent of EU expenditure, this large income gap is likely to generate severe strains. The gap is also mirrored in the "pre-accession aid" extended to candidate countries to support costly institution building in line with the *acquis communautaire*. Third, the expected migration flows from eastern enlargement are larger than those that occurred as a result of the southern enlargement. The CEECs have a well-educated labor force, and existing income gaps between the CEECs and the EU15 do not reflect equal differences in personal skills and human capital. In addition, the geographic proximity and cultural ties of the CEECs to the EU15 make for low "natural" migration barriers between the two groups. Hence, some EU15 countries expect large inflows of Eastern European labor, which might put their labor markets under pressure. Fourth, in some candidate countries the farming sector is very large, particularly in Poland, and productivity in those countries is often much below the EU15 level, more so than with southern enlargement of the 1980s. This has severe implications for the CAP, which aims to support farm income and draws another 40 percent of the EU budget. Finally, the number of candidates presents a problem of its own. EU institutions and rules of decision making have been designed for a union of nine to twelve countries and are inappropriate for a twenty-seven-country union. Hence, in the Nice summit of 2000, the European Council set the stage for a reform aimed at developing institutional structures that are more appropriate for the enlarged union.

Figure 7.1 presents a snapshot view of previous and upcoming enlargements. Using 1995 data, it examines various groups of countries forming the European Union at different stages of its history. Values for the group of countries forming the initial EEC in 1957 are set equal to 100. Although all ten candidates from Central and Eastern Europe will jointly enter the union in 2004, we present data for the Luxembourg group of CEEC5 countries separately from that for the remaining candidate countries. The figure shows that as it grew in size, the EU steadily became less wealthy and more agricultural. Moreover, the income gap involved in the eastern enlargement is clearly enormous, compared with that pertaining to previous enlargements. On the other hand, the incremental effect the eastern enlargement will have on the share of agriculture in GDP is not without precedent.[3]

As a result of the Europe Agreements (EAs) of the mid-1990s, non-agricultural trade between the EU15 and the CEECs is now almost tariff-free. Enlargement will do away with all remaining tariff barriers between the countries in these two groups, and it will extend the customs union as well as the EU single market (SM) to new members. As always, enhanced trade and factor movements between the new and old members are expected to entail a mixture of efficiency gains and painful adjustments. History and geography put present member countries in rather different positions with respect to these gains and pains. Figure 7.2 looks at the importance of merchandise trade between the EU15 and the CEEC10 candidates. We express all magnitudes relative to the corresponding value for the EU15 as a whole, which is set to 100. Despite the significant increase during the 1990s, trade with CEECs is still of relatively minor importance for the EU as a whole:

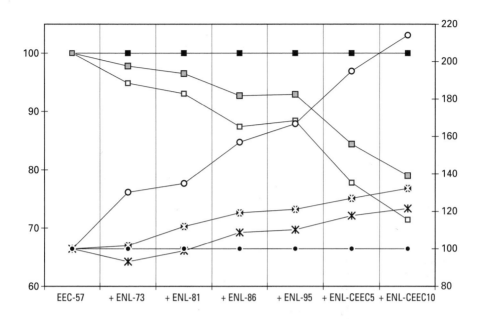

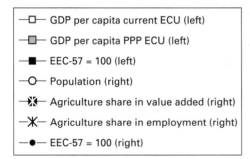

Figure 7.1
Snapshot view of European Union enlargements. *Source:* European Commission 1997.

1997 exports to CEEC10s were 1.08 percent of GDP ($= 100$); the corresponding share for imports is a mere 0.79 percent ($= 100$). The cross-country variation, however, is substantial. Thus, the export share for Portugal is less than a fifth of the EU-wide share, whereas the Austrian share is well over three times the EU15 value. On the import side, the variation is similar, ranging from 0.16 percent for Ireland to 2.71 percent for Austria, which is almost four times the EU value. The difference between EU15 countries in terms of these trade shares seems to persist as the level of east-west trade increases through time (see Kohler 2000).

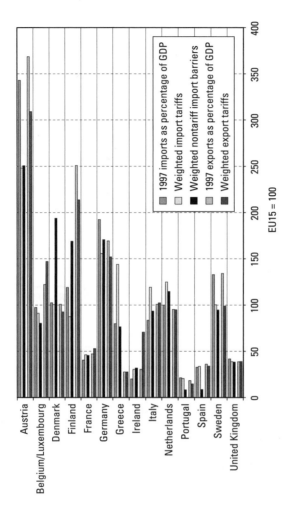

Figure 7.2
Trade shares and trade barriers for EU15 merchandice trade with CEEC10s (individual countries relative to the EU15-100 values). *Source:* Keuschnigg and Kohler 2000.

For assessing the trade effects of enlargement, it matters a great deal whether an incumbent country is more heavily exposed to new members on the export or the import side. Removal of formal barriers starts from a higher level for EU15 exports into the CEECs than for EU15 imports from those countries. Thus, pre-EA most-favored nation (MFN) tariffs on CEECs' imports into the EU15 amounted to about 7 percent on average for all goods. In contrast, EU15 exports faced average tariffs in some CEECs well above 10 percent, with Poland leading with 15 percent (see European Integration Consortium 2001). Moreover, in addition to removing all distortions (like tariffs and quantitative restrictions), the SM also saves on real resources used to overcome technical barriers (different standards, border controls, rules of origin). The expected gains from enhanced trade are therefore larger than in the textbook case of integration. They arise through different channels on the export and the import side. Under perfect competition, lower real trade costs are reflected in a direct gain to incumbents resulting from cheaper imports from new entrants, which will partly be offset by an equilibrating increase in foreign producer prices. Applying this same reasoning on an incumbent's export side, it is clear that the direct gain from lower trade costs should mainly accrue to new member countries, whereas incumbents benefit only through a rise in domestic producer prices caused by higher demand (see Kohler and Keuschnigg 2000). A priori, the gains to EU15 countries from trade enhancement are therefore more significant on the import than on the export side.

The expected gains (and pains) from trade enhancement will be larger if a country's trade is heavily concentrated in goods for which barriers are high to start with. To capture this, we have constructed weighted average tariff barriers, using each EU15 country's bilateral trade with the CEECs (again expressed as a percentage of that country's GDP) as weights.[4] For imports, we also calculate a weighted-average measure of nontariff barriers. When such structural details are taken into account, the differences among the various incumbents in terms of trade exposure are somewhat less pronounced. The Austrian measures of import barriers fall to 2.5 times the EU level (from 3.5 for the simple trade share), whereas those for Ireland, Italy, and Greece are higher than using the simple trade shares. Figure 7.2, of course, gives no more than a quick overview of cross-country differences in trade exposure to eastern enlargement. A more systematic treatment of trade effects requires a more ambitious modeling effort, to which we turn below.

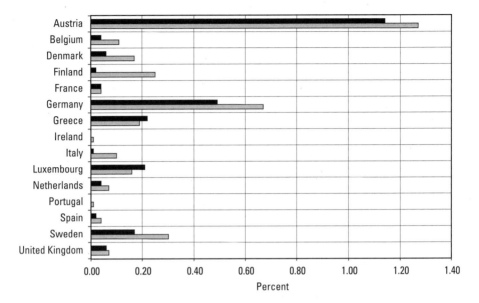

Figure 7.3
Stocks of residents and employees from CEEC10s in EU15 countries. Employee statistics unavailable for Ireland. *Source:* EIC 2001.

Differences are even more pronounced when it comes to migration. Based on recent estimates by the European Integration Consortium (2001 Part A, Table 5.5), figure 7.3 depicts stocks of residents and employees from CEEC10 countries living in EU15 countries, expressed as a percentage of the total stocks, of employees and residents, respectively, in each of those EU15 countries. The number for residents is estimated at 1.27 percent of the Austrian population, almost double the German figure (0.68 percent) which, in turn, is more than double the figures for Sweden and Finland (0.30 and 0.23 percent) (see European Integration Consortium 2001). The percentages are mostly smaller for employees than for residents. The numbers clearly indicate that Austria and Germany are likely to be the prime recipients of enlargement-induced migration.

Incumbents are also quite differently affected from country to country by the costs of enlargement. The overall cost of enlargement may be estimated from the financial framework drawn up by the European Commission and adopted at the summits of Berlin (1999) and Brussels

(2002). Taking the Berlin framework and comparing the projected appropriations for payments to the CEEC5 with the increase in each CEEC5 country's resources resulting from the appropriations, and taking 2006 (the final year of the framework) as the benchmark, one obtains an annual cost of enlargement of 10.48 billion euro in constant 1999 prices, or 0.113 percent of EU15 GNP. However, the Berlin framework assumes no direct payments to eastern farmers, and it covers only a subset of entrants (the Luxembourg CEECs plus Cyprus). It also assumes that enlargement took place in 2002. The more recent framework adopted at the Brussels summit extends to all twelve prospective member countries and includes agricultural payments, albeit at reduced levels. With enlargement taking place in 2004 rather than 2002, and assuming that agricultural payments will be phased in gradually, the projected costs for 2006 are lower in the revised framework than in the Berlin framework. Thus, commitment appropriations for 2006 are projected at 15.966 billion euro, down from 16.780 billion euro in the Berlin 1999 scenario (in 1999 prices). Payment appropriations are 11.840 billion euro, as compared to 14.220 billion euro in the Berlin scenario. The relevant comparison, however, is between the new 2006 figures and the Berlin 1999 figures for *year 3 after scheduled enlargement*, which in the Berlin scenario is 2004. With this perspective, one finds an increase by 4.356 billion (2.720 billion) euro for commitment (payments) appropriations (see European Council 1999 and European Commission 2002).

The burden imposed by enlargement on an individual member country depends on the strategy that the EU adopts to achieve a balanced budget. Obviously, there are alternative strategies, and countries take different positions regarding which strategy is preferable. In Kohler and Keuschnigg 2000, we presented individual-country burdens under three alternative scenarios: increasing own resources, downsizing return payments from the CAP, and cuts in Regional and Structural Funds (RSFs). Obviously, the more a country currently receives from RSFs, the more severely it would be hurt by a strategy for financing enlargement that heavily relies on RSF cuts.

7.3   A Model Based Analysis of Enlargement

7.3.1   *Main Transmission Channels*

Quantitative evaluation of enlargement should be based on an explicit model that incorporates all channels that theoretical work has

recognized to be important and at the same time is empirically tractable. In economic terms, enlargement involves, first and foremost,
extending market integration for commodities and factors. In empha-
sizing beneficial effects of trade and factor movements, including dynamic effects through accumulation, the theory of integration almost
always assumes full employment. This is an obvious shortcoming, especially against the background of EU economies, that we attempt to
overcome in this chapter. In doing so, we rely on the theory of search
unemployment, pioneered by Pissarides and others.[5] This theory emphasizes the role of job separation, labor market search, and costly job
creation as an important source of unemployment. A central thrust of
the chapter is that combining search unemployment with investment
and growth reveals an important channel through which enlargement-
type market integration affects unemployment.[6]

The key modeling challenge is to integrate the theory of search
unemployment with a model of investment and savings. Our approach features forward-looking investment in physical capital and
inter-temporal optimization of overlapping generations. Firms face
exogenous job destruction and costly search, whereas households face
unemployment and uncertain job tenure. When individual unemployment spells are stochastic, agents become heterogeneous with respect
to their past unemployment and savings history. In the absence of a
tractable aggregation procedure, an income-pooling assumption is un-
avoidable. Following literature on growth and unemployment, we assume perfect insurance and income pooling within the extended family
(see Aghion and Howitt 1994, and—for real business cycle models—
Andolfatto 1996, Merz 1999, and Den Haan, Ramey, and Watson 1997,
as well as Shi and Wen 1997 and Shi and Wen 1999).

Box 7.1 presents a highly stylized core version of the model that
treats a typical incumbent country as trading with other EU countries,
eastern candidate countries, and the rest of the world.[7] Consumption is
viewed as a composite good C with a corresponding price index P,
which invokes the so-called Armington assumption of product differentiation by country of origin ("home bias"). Investment I is similarly
composed of home-produced and imported goods. Given foreign pro-
ducer prices $\bar{p}^f$, a reduction in tariffs and import costs τ^f reduces domestic demand prices and thus boosts imports through a substitution
effect. If there is Dixit-Stiglitz-type product differentiation at the firm
level, then the price index P also depends on n, the total number of
varieties of the product available. Although our computational model

Box 7.1
Main Transmission Channels

We distinguish four regions: Home (H), European Union (U), Eastern accession countries (E), and the rest of the world (R). Demand for home and foreign goods, c^H and c^f, $f = U, E, R$, is derived from (homothetic) preferences

$$C = C(c^H, c^U, c^E, c^R), \qquad P = P(p^H, p^U, p^E, p^R, n), \qquad dP/dn < 0, \qquad (1)$$

where C is a consumption aggregate and P is the corresponding price index. Although the model is dynamic, we omit a time index where such an index is unimportant. Tariffs and other import barriers introduce a wedge between domestic prices and foreign producer prices $\bar{p}^f$, which are taken as given, that is, $p^f = (1 + \tau^f)\bar{p}^f$. If there is Dixit-Stiglitz-type product differentiation, P also depends on n, the overall product variety available on domestic and imported goods. In this core version, however, we assume perfect substitution among varieties and absence of any fixed cost, while retaining n as a potentially important argument in P. (We return to the special role of n in the empirical part of the chapter.) Modeling regional trade flows is completed by adding export demand functions $e^f = e^f(p^H(1 + \tau_e^f)/\bar{p}^f)$ that are downward sloping in the price of domestic exports, inclusive of export costs τ_e^f, relative to foreign demand prices $\bar{p}^f$. Total export demand is given by $\Sigma_f e^f$.

Savings and the level of consumption follow from maximization of lifetime utility of overlapping generations, responding to interest rates and reflecting the time profile of expected future wage earnings.[8] Disposable wage income is an average over wages and unemployment benefits. Introducing a time variable t, using a dot to indicate a time derivative, and indicating high- and low-skilled labor by superscript indices s and u, respectively, aggregate labor market flows are

$$\dot{U}_t^j = N_{t,t}^j + sL_t^j - [f(\theta_t^j) + \beta]U_t^j, \qquad \theta_t^j \equiv V_t^j/U_t^j, \qquad j = s, u. \qquad (2)$$

Inflows into the pool of unemployed, U_t^j, result from arrival of new dynasties (entering without a job), $N_{t,t}^j$, and a time-invariant job destruction at rate s. Outflows consist of unemployed workers dying at rate β or finding a job at a rate $f(\theta_t^j)$, which depends on labor market tightness θ^j, measured by the ratio of vacancies V^j to job seekers U^j, where $f' > 0$. Absent immigration and assuming a constant population N^j of skill type j, we have $N_{t,t}^j = \beta N^j$ and $L_t^j + U_t^j = N^j$. The steady-state unemployment rate for labor of skill type j therefore is $U^j/N^j = (\beta + s)/[f(\theta^j) + \beta + s]$, which is falling in labor market tightness θ^j. We assume that labor market risk and the probability of death are the same for both types of labor.

Output is generated by means of physical capital K and the two types of labor, L^{Ds} and L^{Du}, as well as an intermediate input. For value added Y^v, we assume a nested production function of the following kind:

$$Y^v = F[K, A(L^{Ds}, L^{Du})], \qquad L^{Dj} = L^j - \kappa V^j, \qquad j = s, u. \qquad (3)$$

Both F and A are concave and linearly homogeneous. To fill jobs, firms must post vacancies V^j and divert a part κV^j of the workforce to search and recruitment activities, leaving L^{Dj} for production. New hiring is qV^j,

Box 7.1 (continued)

since only a fraction q of vacancies can be filled at each instant. Hiring and investment I accumulate stocks according to

$$\dot{L}_t^j = q(\theta_t^j)V_t^j - (s+\beta)L_t^j, \qquad \dot{K}_t = I_t - \delta K_t, \tag{4}$$

where δ is the rate of depreciation. Investment is a composite good, in line with (1). The hiring rate declines with equilibrium labor market tightness, with $q' < 0$.

Value maximization by firms determines optimal investment, which equates the acquisition cost of new capital P with the present value of marginal capital income,

$$\frac{(1-t^Y)p^v F_K}{r+\delta} = P(p^H, p^U, p^E, p^R, n), \tag{5}$$

where F_K is the marginal productivity of capital in value added and t^Y is the income tax rate. p^v is the "value-added price":

$$p^v = [p^H - a^q P^q(p^H, p^U, p^E, p^R, n)]a^v, \tag{6}$$

where a^q and a^v are required units of the intermediate input and value added, respectively, per unit of the final good with price p^H. By analogy to (1), P^q is the price of the intermediate input. In contrast to the case in the computational model, the above equation assumes a common aggregate for consumption and investment, and it ignores installation costs that are irrelevant for the steady-state effects that we focus on in this box. The computational model also treats taxation of capital income (t^K) differently from labor income (t^L); here we assume $t^Y = t^L = t^K$. Perfect international capital mobility ties down the real interest rate r to a given world interest rate in terms of imported goods. Investment determines capital intensity and thus the real job surplus for labor of type j:

$$R^{Lj} = p^v F_{Lj}/P(p^H, p^U, p^E, p^R, n), \tag{7}$$

where $F_{Lj} = F_A A_{Lj}$ is the marginal value-added productivity of type j labor $(j = s, u)$.

The first-order condition for new vacancies equates the opportunity cost of recruitment, κR^{Lj}, and the expected present value of the firm's net-of-tax job rent:

$$\frac{(1-t^Y)(R^{Lj} - W^j)}{r+\beta+s}q(\theta^j) = \kappa R^{Lj}, \tag{8}$$

where W^j is the real wage rate for labor of type j, determined by Nash bargaining between firms and employees. The term $\kappa R^{Lj}(r+\beta+s)$ is the user cost of a unit of labor "invested" in search and recruitment activities, which is equated to the net job rent that it generates in the respective skill category of employment. Firms post vacancies until the marginal cost of recruitment in terms of foregone output, κR^{Lj}, equals the expected value of an additional vacancy, which equals the probability q of finding a worker times the expected present value of the job rent accruing to a firm. The instantaneous discount rate reflects the exogenous and time-invariant risk of job termination resulting from death, β, or job separation, s.

fully incorporates this effect, box 7.1 does not elaborate on it any further. We shall return to the variety effect when presenting and interpreting the simulation results.

The Armington assumption implies that the country's export markets are "large." This is modeled by means of regional export demand functions that are downward sloping in export prices relative to relevant foreign producer prices, where exports are subject to foreign trade barriers τ_e^f. Obviously, if such protection against the incumbent country's exports disappears, the economy should experience an export boom. With region-specific trade barriers, our model thus captures the familiar trade creation and trade diversion effects stemming from EU enlargement. With exports a function of relative prices, p^H adjusts endogenously to ensure equilibrium for home-produced goods. The model thus features terms-of-trade effects, which are a classic source of welfare effects from integration. The strength of these effects crucially depends on the price elasticities of import and export demand, which are closely related to the Armington substitution elasticities for commodity demand.

Trade effects of enlargement will have a distinct sectoral pattern that, in turn, determines the distributional impact through general equilibrium effects on factor prices. These effects are well known in principle but difficult to pin down quantitatively.[9] Focusing on a single sector, however, box 7.1 highlights a different channel that seems equally important for policy but is less well explored in theory: unemployment effects of market integration. According to the theory of labor market search, unemployment is an equilibrium phenomenon resulting from job destruction and job creation. Our computational model solves for the equilibrium rate of unemployment in two separate classes of labor, high- and low-skilled. In this way, we can shed new light on some sensitive issues regarding enlargement. Combining search unemployment with investment and savings is obviously desirable, given the importance generally attributed to dynamic effects of integration (see, for instance, Baldwin and Seghezza 1998). Box 7.1 highlights the nexus of capital accumulation and job creation.

With box 7.1, the main channels of transmission are easily identified. Integration changes trade barriers, τ^E for imports, and τ_e^E for exports, to CEECs. Any change in τ^E directly feeds into the price index P, and τ_e^E affects exports e^E, which expands demand and exerts upward pressure on p^H. These changes have direct welfare relevance through the price index P and additionally affect the intertemporal decisions highlighted in equations (5) through (8), ultimately also leading to employment effects through a change in labor market tightness. Note that the growth effect hinges not only on capital goods becoming cheaper (the P channel) but also on lower prices for intermediate inputs (the P^q channel). In other words, they are driven by changes in the acquisition price of capital relative to the price of value added p^v. The employment effects depend on how the job surplus R^{L^j} evolves relative to the wage rate for the relevant skill class. The gross wage W^j results from wage bargaining and also depends on the fiscal rules relating to wage taxation and unemployment compensation. The ultimate impact of trade integration on employment thereby also depends on fiscal policy.[10] Enlargement-induced immigration inflates the number of labor market entrants as in equation (2), leading to a dynamic adjustment of (un)employment. The specific form of adjustment depends on the time distribution of the migration inflow for different age cohorts of the labor force.

In a world of imperfect competition and scale economies, a larger single market should allow for a more extensive exploitation of economies of scale resulting from a higher degree of product differentiation. Although box 7.1 does not focus on these sources of additional welfare gains, our computational model duly takes them into account. Specifically, we assume Dixit-Stiglitz-type monopolistic competition. Despite prices featuring markups over marginal costs, because of product differentiation, free entry leads to zero profits in equilibrium where markups are dissipated by fixed costs. With fixed costs, firm size is well determined, and increased market demand is satisfied by entry of new producers with differentiated products. The introduction of new goods raises aggregate productivity, denoted by n in the equations of box 7.1, and further magnifies any expansionary effect.

7.3.2 Enlargement Effects on Present Member Countries

Putting all of these transmission channels together in a computational model, we arrive at a rich economic structure that can address the most important aspects of eastern enlargement. It is often difficult, however, to interpret results from a complex model. Before turning to numbers, we therefore resort to box 7.1 for a general discussion of the principal effects of EU enlargement on present member countries.

In dismantling import barriers τ^E, eastern enlargement reduces the domestic demand price $p^E = (1 + \tau^E)\bar{p}^E$ of goods from new member countries. Depending on the share of these goods in domestic invest-ment and intermediate inputs, this contributes to a lower price P of the composite capital good. This share is relatively small even for countries that are neighbors, like Germany and Austria, hence one should not expect overly strong effects from it. Note, however, that the relevant price to look at is the (capital goods) price index P relative to the value-added price p^v (see (5)). Since lower import prices p^E reduce the price index of the composite intermediate input P^q, they also increase the value-added price p^v, which is related to the domestic producer price as in (6). Hence, there is a second channel through which the effects of growth can act.[11] With unrestricted capital mobility, the interest rate r in (5) is given from world markets and may be assumed constant for the present purpose. Hence, with P/p^v increasing, the acquisition price of capital falls short of the present value of the marginal returns. From (5) and (6), we conclude that producers invest to accumulate capital.

A higher capital intensity raises marginal productivity of both types of labor. Together with the lower composite-goods price, this boosts the surplus from job creation according to (7). Depending on wage bargaining, workers claim a wage rate W^j, and producers appropriate a job rent $R^{Lj} - W^j$ from new hiring, as highlighted by (8). To expand the workforce, firms must search in the labor market. Depending on market tightness θ^j, a firm is able to locate a suitable worker with instantaneous probability $q(\theta^j)$; otherwise it must continue to search. Such recruitment activities require the firm to divert κ units of labor per vacancy from production. The ensuing output loss is the opportu-nity cost of recruitment. When investing in an additional vacancy, the firm thus compares the marginal cost of a vacancy, κR^{Lj}, with the expected present value of the producer rent $R^{Lj} - W^j$ that accrues with probability q, once a worker is found and production starts with the filled job (see (8)). In raising the real job surplus R^{Lj}, integration inflates the opportunity cost of recruitment, but it also strengthens the returns to job creation, that is, the expected present value of the producer rent. If wage bargaining does not fully erode the increase in the job surplus, then the producer's job rent starts to exceed recruitment costs. As pro-ducers create more jobs, labor market tightness θ^j increases. As it is increasingly difficult to fill vacancies, the hiring probability q falls and thereby reestablishes the job investment condition in (8).

In Heijdra, Keuschnigg, and Kohler 2002, we present a full treatment of wage bargaining in which unemployment benefits and labor taxa-tion affect the outcome. A key distinction arises between the case in which wages are sticky because unemployment benefits are *kept constant in real terms*, that is, indexed to prices P, and the case in which they are *indexed to net wages*. If wages are sticky, the expected present value of producer rents increases more than proportionately to the marginal cost of a vacancy. For any given labor market tightness θ^j and a corresponding hiring probability q^j, it becomes attractive to post additional vacancies. As firms expand recruitment, the respective labor market tightens, making it increasingly difficult to find appropriate workers. The hiring probability falls, reflecting $q'(\theta^j) < 0$, until the investment condition for vacancies is restored again in the new equilibrium. Tighter labor markets improve the prospects of the unemployed to find a job, as stipulated by $f'(\theta^j) > 0$. From equation (2), the outflow from unemployment starts to exceed the inflow, until a lower equilibrium unemployment rate is attained. In turn, higher employment combines with higher capital intensity to further reinforce capital accumulation and output (see equations (3) and (4)).

So far, we have taken the prices of home-produced goods p^H as given. It is not clear a priori how these prices will change, since the scenario involves a negative demand shock as domestic spending shifts to imports, while at the same time stimulating export demand. If the outcome is excess demand, then market clearing requires higher prices, which boost the marginal return to investment. They also raise the capital goods price P, but less than proportionately, since investment uses import goods as well. According to (5), investment incentives are also strengthened. A higher capital intensity boosts job rents and thereby induces firms to post more vacancies (see equations (7) and (8)). Unemployment declines and output expands. If the outcome is excess supply, then the adjustment process runs the other way. In our numerical analysis, it turns out that enlargement raises domestic-producer prices.

Imperfect competition introduces an important magnifier. An industry-wide expansion involves entry of new firms with new, differentiated products. Hence, if the domestic capital stock expands, so does the number of domestic firms and, thus, the extent of product differentiation. Keeping the number of foreign varieties constant, a rise in domestic aggregate output comes with an increase in n.[12] A larger number of varieties, in turn, reduces the cost of the composite investment/consumption good as well as intermediates, since $\partial P/\partial n < 0$, as emphasized in equation (1). By (5) and (8), such productivity gains further stimulate investment and employment. Monopolistic competition magnifies the investment response.[13]

What are the expected labor market effects from immigration? By definition, immigration must raise the unemployment rate in the very short run, since newly arriving migrants must search in the labor market and will find a job only after some transitory search period. Immigration does not, however, affect the long-run equilibrium conditions for physical capital and job vacancies (equations (5) and (8)), and it therefore fails to affect the search equilibrium in the labor market.[14] The numbers of both employed and unemployed workers expand proportionately, leaving the unemployment rate unchanged (see equation (2)). In the long run, firms expand the number of vacancies V^j in proportion to employment. As labor market tightness remains invariant, the vacancy condition in (8) is not affected. According to (5), investment accommodates increased employment at a constant capital intensity. Output expands proportionally. There would be no further effect if scale effects were absent. With monopolistic competition, however, output expansion leads to entry of new firms and a greater variety of products. Since the associated gains from variety reduce P and thereby the cost of investment goods, they strengthen investment incentives (see (5)). Job rents for both types of skills increase, along with capital intensity, triggering increased recruitment by firms. This channel implies that immigration might well reduce the long-run unemployment rate in the existing EU countries, rather than increase it, as much of the popular opinion seems to hold.[15]

The short-run adjustment for the economy path depends on the form in which immigration takes place. Starting off from a stationary domestic population, immigration can take place in either of two forms. According to what we call a *stock scenario*, immigration augments all age cohorts by the same factor, such that, after this one-time and *instantaneous* stock adjustment, the total population again remains stationary. Immigration has no transitional effects on the population's demographic structure, but of course there will be changes in employment dynamics as a result.[16] Alternatively, in a *flow scenario* of immigration, the choice of residence is restricted to new agents. While "old" agents remain locked in their country of birth, a permanently larger share of newborns world-wide locate in the home country. Thus, the number of new arrivals or young workers in present EU member countries is permanently higher and leads to a *gradual* increase in the domestic population. The flow scenario implies extended transitional effects on aggregate labor supply. Section 7.4 will compare the transitional employment effects of the two scenarios.

7.4   Simulations with a CGE Model: The German Case

Armed with this theoretical understanding of the principal channels
involved, we may now turn to an empirical analysis based on a CGE
model of the German economy. To the best of our knowledge, this
is the first multi-sectoral CGE model that combines savings and investment with search unemployment in segmented labor markets for
high- and low-skilled labor. We relegate a brief description of the computational model and calibration to the appendixes.

7.4.1   The Enlargement Scenario from a German Perspective

In political terms, Germany is a staunch supporter of enlargement. At
the same time, it is seriously concerned about unwelcome economic
effects it may experience from enlargement, particularly with respect to
migration. Germany should thus be a particularly interesting case to
look at. But even though it is more exposed to Central and Eastern European entrant countries on commodity markets, its imports (exports)
from CEEC10 countries in 1997 were a mere 1.5 percent (1.83 percent)
of its GDP. Nor are the trade barriers between Germany and the
CEECs that need to be dismantled in the face of accession particularly
high. One should not expect overly strong effects from enlargement-
induced integration of commodity markets.

   The trade and fiscal aspects of our simulation scenario largely follow
the pattern of Keuschnigg, Keuschnigg, and Kohler 2001. Table 7.1
summarizes the scenario. The first element implements the Europe
Agreements, which have removed non-agricultural tariffs on trade
between the EU15 and CEEC10. Although these agreements are not a
requirement for membership, they must surely be seen as an integral
part of the enlargement project, hence we include them in our scenario.
The next step in trade integration removes all remaining tariffs and
extends the single market to new members by eliminating technical
barriers and other obstacles to market access. In line with other studies,
we model this as a reduction in real trade costs, assuming a 5 percent
(ad valorem) average reduction by sector. This number is considerably
more conservative than the 10 percent assumed by Baldwin, Francois,
and Portes (1997). We consider only the CEEC5 countries in our scenario, whereas the 2004 enlargement will include eight CEECs (the
CEEC5 plus Latvia, Lithuania, and the Slovak Republic) plus Malta
and Cyprus. Restricting attention to the CEEC5 seems warranted, since

Table 7.1
Eastern enlargement: Policy decomposition

Policy elements		Old	New
I. Trade integration			
Europe Agreements			
German (EU) nonagricultural tariffs removed vis-à-vis CEEC10	CEEC5:	6.3%	0%
	CEEC10:	7.6%	
CEEC10 countries nonagricultural tariffs removed vis-à-vis Germany	CEEC5:	6.7%	0%
	CEEC10:	11%	
Enlargement to CEEC5 countries			
Single market			
German tariffs on farm products removed		12.2%	0%
CEEC5 tariffs on farm products removed		9.8%	0%
Internal market: Reduction of real trade costs		5.0%	0%
Repercussions from extending CAP			
Higher prices for farm imports from CEEC5 by		0.61%	
Lower subsidies for farm exports to CEEC5		8.5%	0%
Lower world prices for farm products by		2%	
II. Fiscal burden			
Higher net contribution rate (percentage of GDP)		0.595%	0.665%
III. Immigration of low-skilled labor			
Long-run increase in stock of low-skilled labor by		6.15%	
IV. Immigration of skilled labor			
Long-run increase in stock of skilled labor by		0.84%	

the other countries involved in the 2004 accession are of minor importance. Enlargement will have special implications for agriculture. Extending the CAP price support system to new members will increase import prices for farm products from new members. At the same time subsidies on an incumbent country's agricultural exports to CEECs will be abolished. Finally, on a global level, the CAP-induced supply response of eastern farmers is generally expected to lower prices on agricultural world markets. Numerical specifications for these scenario elements are provided in table 7.1. Further explanations may be found in Keuschnigg, Keuschnigg, and Kohler 2001.

The second component of our scenario captures the cost of enlargement. In section 7.2, using the official financial framework for 2000–2006, we estimated the annual cost to the EU15 arising from an enlargement to the CEEC5 at 0.113 percent of EU15 GDP. An econometric model of EU expenditure yields a somewhat higher annual cost equal to 0.184 percent of EU15 GDP (see Kohler and Keuschnigg 2001 for details). The difference between the two estimates results in part from the fact that the financial framework allows for a gradual phasing in of the core expenditure items related to the CAP and RSFs. As the phasing in does not extend beyond the first three years after enlargement, it must be seen as a lower bound for our long-run analysis. We therefore use the 0.184 percent estimate of annual costs obtained using the aforementioned econometric approach. As we argued above, the fiscal burden for a given incumbent country depends on the strategy the EU adopts for financing the expansion. We assume that the budget will be balanced by a cut in RSF payments. In this case, Germany's net contribution payments to the union will rise from 0.595 percent of its GDP to 0.665 percent.[17]

The Brussels (2002) summit indicated a certain willingness to cut into agricultural payments as well in the next financial framework, starting in 2007. Our scenario assumption should thus not be seen as reflecting a firm commitment of the EU to financing the entire cost of enlargement by means of reducing structural funds. Barring any such commitment, incorporating an extreme, but well-defined, scenario element with a clear implication is the best one can do. For Germany, which is a minor recipient of RSF payments, this scenario clearly involves an optimistic view. Almost any other combination of financing strategies that the EU might choose would probably imply that Germany would bear a higher share of the overall cost.

Estimating migration flows from CEECs to the EU15 countries after EU expansion is notoriously difficult. We rely on a recent study by the European Integration Consortium (EIC) (2001) to derive a migration scenario that is amenable to our simulation model. The details of our procedure can be found in Heijdra, Keuschnigg, and Kohler 2002. The EIC baseline projections imply an overall increase in German residents from the CEEC10 from some 550,000 in 1998 to about 2.5 million people by 2030. Assuming in line with the EIC that 35 percent of these residents will enter the German labor force, we arrive at a long-run increase in the skilled and unskilled labor force of 0.84 percent and 6.15 percent, respectively. Note that these are not simulation results from our own model, but exogenous effects constructed from extraneous information. Formally, the migration scenarios add accumulated migration inflows to the initial stocks to obtain the new steady-state levels of skilled and unskilled labor, respectively. In line with migration theory and EIC projections, we assume that migration inflows accumulate over time and augment stocks gradually.

7.4.2 Results

The entire scenario under which EU enlargement will take place is ambiguous a priori. To facilitate an easier interpretation of our results, we report the results separately for different elements of the policy scenario. Reflecting the crucial importance of wage bargaining and the pertinent fiscal policy parameters, the base case scenario presented in table 7.2 keeps unemployment benefits B^U and wage tax allowances B^L constant in *real* terms; an alternative set of scenarios presented in table 7.3 assumes that one or both of these policy instruments are indexed to net wages.[18]

7.4.2.1 Real Benefits Constant

In the case with real benefits held constant, unemployment benefits and tax allowance are indexed to the price index P. If P falls because of lower trade barriers, benefits and allowances are reduced proportionally. Table 7.2 separates steady-state effects for the trade scenario (scenario I in table 7.1) and the fiscal scenario (scenario II in table 7.1). Column 3 presents the effect of both taken together. The base case migration scenarios are covered in columns 4 and 5 (see below).

Consider now the entire scenario of column 3 (Enlargement) in table 7.2. Cheaper capital and intermediate-goods imports improve supply conditions, which adds to the downward pressure on domestic prices p^H stemming from substitution in demand. At the same time, mutual elimination of tariff and nontariff barriers boosts demand for German exports to the CEECs. Our empirical model reveals that the scenario entails a slightly more powerful leverage on the export side, as expected based on the discussion in section 7.2. Domestic producer prices therefore increase on average, although the effect is rather small compared to the reduction in price indices resulting from lower protection rates.[19] German exports to CEECs expand by about 57 percent. Higher prices reinforce the supply side expansion by strengthening investment incentives, from which the economy experiences an investment-led expansion, with capital stocks increasing by 0.63 percent. The increase in capital intensity, in turn, strengthens marginal rents to job creation, tightening labor markets and leading to a small reduction in unemployment. The reduction is slightly larger for unskilled workers than for skilled workers, albeit from a higher initial unemployment rate. With a total benchmark labor force of forty million, the reduction in the average unemployment rate corresponds to roughly 28,000 new jobs. Although the gains in employment are

Table 7.2
Long-run effects of enlargement on the German economy (Base case: Unemployment benefits and tax allowance constant in real terms)

Variables		Trade	Fiscal	Enlargement	Low	High	Migration[b]
P	Consumer price index	-0.267	-0.033	-0.310	-0.069	-0.146	-0.214
P^I	Investment price index	-0.256	-0.042	-0.164	-0.115	-0.148	-0.262
$\bar{p}$	Domestic producer prices	0.047	-0.042	0.036	0.049	-0.023	0.027
$\bar{p}^E$	Terms of trade with CEECs	7.113	-0.043	7.131	-0.091	-0.070	-0.161
E^E	Exports to CEECs	57.350	0.188	57.392	1.043	0.806	1.861
E	Total exports	4.122	0.185	4.015	0.915	0.781	1.706
U^s	Skilled unemployment rate (6%)[a]	5.944	6.001	5.935	5.912	5.977	5.890
U^u	Unskilled unemployment rate (10%)[a]	9.937	10.000	9.903	10.544	9.879	10.402
U	Average unemployment rate (6.668%)[a]	6.611	6.669	6.598	6.726	6.625	6.677
K	$\sum_j$ capital stocks	0.524	-0.019	0.630	1.330	1.164	2.513
$\bar{n}$	Number of firms	0.581	0.003	0.666	1.192	1.057	2.267
Y	Gross domestic production	0.402	-0.058	0.376	0.988	0.826	1.824
w^s	Wage rate, skilled	0.522	-0.049	0.602	1.174	0.171	1.353
w^u	Wage rate, unskilled	0.286	-0.035	0.545	-4.251	0.921	-3.389
z	Government transfers	1.167	-0.370	0.516	2.358	2.090	4.486
ω	Average disposable income	0.796	-0.201	0.536	1.771	1.511	3.308
C	Average consumption	1.065	-0.169	0.847	1.842	1.660	3.531
EV	Aggregate welfare (percentage of GDP)[b]	0.554	-0.091	0.450	0.357	0.335	0.692

Note: Figures in table represent percentage changes under EU enlargement. Trade: Trade and CAP (scenario I in table 7.1). Fiscal: Fiscal cost (scenario II in table 7.1). Enlargement: Enlargement scenario (scenarios I and II in table 7.1 taken together). Low: Immigration of low-skilled workers (scenario III in table 7.1). High: Immigration of high-skilled workers (scenario IV in table 7.1). Migration: Total immigration (scenarios III and IV in table 7.1 taken together). A bar over a variable (e.g., $\bar{p}$) denotes a weighted average of sectoral variables.

[a] Labor market variables in absolute terms; initial values provided in parentheses.

[b] Welfare effect shown relates to flow scenario of immigration. For the stock scenario, the relevant figure for migration of both types of labor is $EV = 0.948$. See section 7.3 for the definition of the two types of immigration scenarios.

Table 7.3
Long-run effects of enlargement on the German economy (Alternative fiscal policy assumptions)

Variables		Enlargement	Index	Index B^U	E/Tax	M/Tax
P	Consumer price index	−0.310	−0.299	−0.305	−0.323	−0.276
P^I	Investment price index	−0.164	−0.152	−0.152	−0.178	−0.331
$\bar{p}$	Domestic producer prices	0.036	0.038	0.035	0.034	0.013
$\bar{p}^E$	Terms of trade with CEECs	7.131	7.138	7.138	7.122	−0.203
E^E	Exports to CEECs	57.392	57.280	57.289	57.517	2.275
E	Total exports	4.015	3.945	3.951	4.095	2.100
U^s	Skilled unemployment rate (6%)[a]	5.935	6.000	6.016	5.861	5.544
U^u	Unskilled unemployment rate (10%)[a]	9.903	10.000	10.028	9.790	9.770
U	Average unemployment rate (6.668%)[a]	6.598	6.668	6.686	6.518	6.281
K	$\sum_j$ capital stocks	0.630	0.540	0.554	0.733	3.019
$\bar{n}$	Number of firms	0.666	0.583	0.598	0.759	2.730
Y	Gross domestic production	0.376	0.313	0.323	0.448	2.173
w^s	Wage rate, skilled	0.602	0.594	0.632	0.612	1.410
w^u	Wage rate, unskilled	0.545	0.579	0.638	0.503	−3.685
z	Government transfers	0.516	0.238	0.462	−0.323	−0.276
ω	Average disposable income	0.536	0.422	0.422	0.667	3.942
C	Average consumption	0.847	0.723	0.749	0.988	4.210
EV	Aggregate welfare (percentage of GDP)[b]	0.450	0.384	0.395	0.519	0.693

Note: Figures in table represent percentage changes under EU enlargement. Enlargement: Enlargement scenario (scenarios I and II in table 7.1 taken together). Unemployment benefit B^U and wage tax allowance B^L constant in real terms. Index: Both B^U and B^L indexed to net-of-tax wages. Index B^U: B^U indexed to net-of-tax wages, with B^L held constant in real terms. E/Tax: Both B^U and B^L, as well as household transfers, kept constant in real terms, with the marginal wage tax adjusting endogenously. M/Tax: Analogous to E/Tax, but applied to the joint immigration scenario. A bar over a variable (e.g., $\bar{p}$) denotes a weighted average of sectoral variables.

[a] Labor market variables in absolute terms; initial values provided in parentheses.

[b] Welfare effect shown relates to flow scenario of immigration. For the stock scenario, the relevant figure for migration of both types of labor is $EV = 0.948$. See section 7.3 for the definition of the two types of immigration scenarios.

relatively minor, workers benefit from higher wages. Wages of skilled workers, deflated by the consumer price index, are up by 0.92 percent. Note that in the German case, unlike the Austrian, goods market integration contributes to a slightly wider wage spread.[20]

As emphasized earlier, the computational model features product differentiation, with an endogenous adjustment of the number of varieties produced. Table 7.2 reveals that output expansion in this scenario occurs largely via firm entry and new varieties. The ensuing gains from diversification translate into lower price indices, stimulating investment and other final demand and magnifying the gains in output and real income. Real GDP deflated by the consumer price index is up by 0.68 percent ($= 0.37 + 0.31$). We capture the fiscal effect by assuming that the government passes on the fiscal burden of enlargement to households by cutting transfer payments. As the overall expansion swells the tax base, however, it boosts revenues from both direct and indirect taxes, even at constant tax rates. This revenue effect in the end allows for a remarkable increase (0.52 percent, or 0.82 percent in real terms) in transfers (other than unemployment benefits) to households. The fiscal returns from enlargement are thus more than enough to pay for the increase in net contributions. Wage growth, lower unemployment, and higher transfers all boost average disposable wage income, which is up by 0.85 percent in real terms. Most importantly, table 7.2 reveals that the goods market implications of enlargement promise an aggregate welfare gain that more than offsets the fiscal cost of enlargement. The net effect is measured by a Hicksian equivalent variation of almost half a percent of German GDP.[21]

Although eastern enlargement is inherently a multicountry scenario, the single-country nature of our simulation experiment treats all foreign producer prices $\bar{p}^f$ as given. Import prices from EU partner countries and new members are unlikely, however, to change under EU expansion to an extent that would invalidate the single-country approach in the present case. First, although producers in new member countries do face additional demand from other incumbent countries, they will also lose domestic demand to western suppliers who benefit from easier market access. A mutual liberalization has no clear-cut effect on import prices from the CEECs, hence keeping them constant is a reasonable approximation. Furthermore, with the exception of Austria, other EU15 countries trade far less with the CEECs than Germany. Given their rather modest trade exposure to new members, enlargement will most likely not have a significant indirect effect on prices p^U for Germany.

7.4.2.2 Alternative Fiscal-Policy Assumptions

In the alternative case of indexation, unemployment benefits B^U and wage tax allowances B^L are indexed to net wages, keeping $B^U/[W(1-t^L)]$ and $B^L/[W(1-t^L)]$ constant. Elements of both types of indexation are present in actual policy, but it is difficult to determine numerically their respective importance. We argued in section 7.3 that integration should no longer affect unemployment once B^U and B^L are both fully indexed to net wages. One should note the theoretical possibility that unemployment rates may even increase if B^U is indexed, but B^L is kept constant in real terms. Column 2 (Index) of table 7.3 depicts the case with full indexation to net-of-tax wages. This is equivalent to the case of fully flexible wages, in which integration remains without consequences for labor market tightness and unemployment. The difference in other variables between the scenario with indexation and the previous scenario with real benefits constant is hardly discernible, except for a large difference in government transfers, which are roughly halved, since indexation requires higher unemployment benefits in line with higher wages. For this reason, the gains in average disposable wage income and consumption are somewhat lower under indexation than with real benefits held constants. The welfare gain under constant benefits is partially eroded under indexation, since the shock from enlargement is now less expansionary, which tends to subdue the gains from specialization and induced capital accumulation.

The next column in table 7.3 refers to a case in which we have recalibrated the model to allow for a more progressive wage tax with higher marginal tax rates, which combine with a larger personal allowance to replicate the data on tax revenues. Column 3 (Index B^U) reexamines the enlargement shock, this time keeping the real value B^L constant, while enforcing indexation of B^U to net wages. In this scenario, unemployment rates slightly increase in response to the enlargement shock. Column 4 (E/Tax) returns to the base case scenario, in which benefits and the tax allowance are kept constant in real terms. In addition, we now also keep constant real household transfers, adjusting the wage tax instead to close the government budget. The tax base effect of expansion yields a considerable fiscal dividend in this scenario, allowing a marginal wage tax rate that is lower by about one percentage point. The lower tax burden on labor reinforces the effects of integration and further squeezes unemployment. Compared to the base case scenario in the first column, the reduction in the unemployment rate is now more than double, with employment thus created for about 63,000 people.

7.4.2.3   Immigration

Columns 4 and 5 of table 7.2 separate the results for immigration of low-skilled and high-skilled workers, corresponding to scenarios III and IV of table 7.1, and column 6 depicts the joint immigration scenario. The effects are broadly as anticipated from the above discussion. In an open economy with a constant real interest rate, immigration does not offer any long-run incentive to adjust capital intensity. Instead, the increase in manpower resulting from immigration is accommodated by means of investment to hold the capital-labor ratio constant. Given a monopolistically competitive market structure, however, with endogenous diversification, output gains come in the form of increased firm entry, with an ensuing rise in product diversity. The gains from diversity squeeze price indices, making investment goods cheaper and contributing to a higher capital intensity and higher labor rentals. With constant real benefits, higher labor rentals increase job values by more than wages, fostering incentives for labor market search. Tightening labor markets would eventually reduce unemployment rates in both skill groups if immigration had no skill bias. However, since immigration is concentrated in the low-skilled segment, we find that only high-skilled workers experience a lower unemployment rate, whereas unemployment among low-skilled workers becomes more widespread. Because of the size of the shock resulting from enlargement, the effects are much stronger than in the base scenario of column 3.

Note that the welfare gains in the migration scenario relate only to the domestic population, corresponding to what migration theory calls the "immigration surplus." This surplus is conceptually different from the aforementioned employment effects. Graphically speaking, it arises whenever incoming migrants are employed and paid according to a downward-sloping marginal-productivity curve. And it arises in a direct and undiluted way only if wages are flexible, and if there is full employment. The present model features an endogenous adjustment of the equilibrium level of unemployment. Table 7.2 singles out the employment effects of this adjustment. The welfare gain should be interpreted as incorporating the conventional immigration surplus, but also as being influenced by unemployment effects.

If an immigration-induced increase in the labor force initiates domestic expansion, because of firm entries and a larger variety of domestic goods, then one might argue that the opposite should happen in the countries that are the source of the immigrants (i.e., the new member countries), where the labor force shrinks. There are several counteracting forces, however, that justify assuming a constant variety of imported goods. First, new member countries benefit from lower import prices from incumbent member countries, which should initiate expansion in the new member countries, over and above the general catching-up process. And second, enlargement will no doubt also allow these countries to draw further foreign direct investment, which will be an additional impetus to their growth. All of this should easily compensate for the negative effect of labor outflow on the product variety generated by new member countries.

Columns 4 and 5 of table 7.2 point to strong distributional effects when immigration is concentrated either in the low-skilled or in the high-skilled sector of the labor market. The differential effect of low-skilled immigration on the unemployment rate of low-skilled workers is more than half a percentage point; at the same time the wage rate of those employed falls by more than 4 percent. In contrast, skilled workers benefit through a 1.17 percent wage increase (almost 2 percent in real terms), while their unemployment rate falls by 0.1 percentage points. Most of the enlargement shock thus translates into wages rather than (un)employment. Immigration of low-skilled workers reduces unemployment for skilled labor, while raising it for unskilled labor, as expected. But high-skilled immigration lowers unemployment for *both* types of labor. As we have argued repeatedly above, monopolistic competition implies that output gains also involve a greater product variety, leading to a higher capital intensity and, ultimately, to a tighter labor market for both types of skills. In this way, immigration that is *evenly* distributed across skills reduces the equilibrium levels of unemployment for both skill types. But immigration that is *concentrated only in one of the two skill classes* has increased unemployment in that skill class, while reducing it in the other. But it is not at all ruled out that the total expansion, together with the product variety effect, might dominate the picture, leading to a reduced level of unemployment in *both* skill classes. This is what happens in the differential scenario of immigration of only skilled labor (column M/Tax of table 7.3). In this sense, there is a complementarity between capital and skilled labor. Indeed, the capital stock increases by more than 1 percent in column 5 of table 7.2, almost as much as under unskilled migration, although the inflow is much lower in magnitude than for unskilled labor.

Figures 7.4a and 7.4b compare the transitional effects on group-specific unemployment rates for the two differential migration scenarios (the stock and flow approaches as defined in section 7.3). The

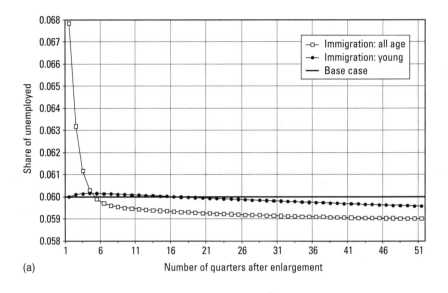

(a)   Number of quarters after enlargement

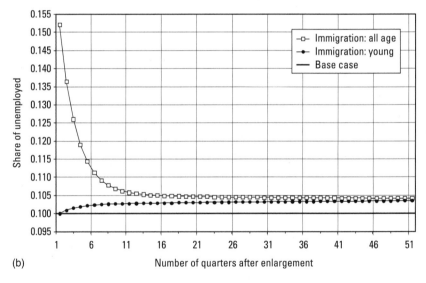

(b)   Number of quarters after enlargement

Figure 7.4
Simulation results: Immigration and unemployment of (a) skilled labor, (b) unskilled labor.

flow approach assumes a permanently higher arrival rate of *new* generations at home. The resulting adjustment process is smooth but extends over several decades until a stationary population is attained. In contrast, the stock approach assumes that immigration inflates all age cohorts proportionately without any extended demographic effects. Since all migrants find employment only by searching in the labor market, the unemployment rate shoots up instantaneously, in the stock approach, to more than double its initial value. Because of the very fast labor market dynamics in this approach, however, the long-run unemployment rate of 10.5 percent is attained (approximately) within a few quarters.[22]

7.4.2.4 Sensitivity

As in any economy-wide model, the results of our model are to some extent sensitive to parameter variation. Although the number of parameters in a detailed empirical model is large, comparative static analysis based on stylized versions of the model, as well as previous experience with simulation work, narrows down the set of sensitive parameters quite considerably. Rather than adding more simulations, we may therefore refer the reader to our earlier work for a more detailed treatment of the sensitivity issue. Generally, we can identify two sources of sensitivity: behavioral parameters and certain key specifications of the policy scenario. In Keuschnigg, Keuschnigg, and Kohler 2001 we found that scaling down the Armington trade elasticities by a factor of 0.8 reduces the aggregate welfare gains by a fourth.[23] Of course, an increase in these elasticities would yield a considerably more positive picture (see also Keuschnigg and Kohler 1996b).

As to monopolistic competition, the key parameter is the elasticity of substitution among differentiated varieties (Dixit-Stiglitz elasticity). A greater elasticity makes perceived demand for individual producers more price elastic and reduces market power. Furthermore, the external productivity gains from product differentiation, which act as important magnifiers, become smaller. We find that doubling the elasticity from the base case reduces welfare gains by a third. As regards labor market parameters, Heijdra and Keuschnigg (2000) show that the comparative static effects of enlargement are not overly sensitive to variations in the matching elasticity and the bargaining power of workers, even though these are key parameters in determining the unemployment rate. Overall, then, we may conclude that our results

are very unlikely to be reversed if we were to re-calibrate the model
with different parameter values.

Very important, but often neglected, is the sensitivity of model
results with respect to particular assumptions underlying the policy
scenario depicted in the model. For instance, the size of reductions in
real trade cost as a result of expansion is subject to much debate. We
have chosen a rather conservative estimate, that is, a 5 percent reduction on average as compared to 10 percent in Baldwin, Francois, and
Portes 1997. As evidenced by table 7.2, the reduction in real trade cost
clearly dominates the overall picture. Our results would, of course, indicate more benefits if we were to follow the more optimistic assumptions made in Baldwin, Francois, and Portes 1997. Finally, table 7.3
points to the importance of domestic fiscal-policy rules in determining
the impact of enlargement. Complete indexation of unemployment
benefits would eliminate the effects on unemployment. On the other
hand, if real benefits are kept constant and the revenue proceeds are
used to reduce the wage tax instead of cutting neutral transfers to
households, the results point to an even more beneficial enlargement.

7.5 Conclusions

Employment effects of an eastern EU enlargement are a big concern to
policymakers and the general public of present EU member countries.
Existing studies of enlargement effects do not sufficiently accommodate this concern. The purpose of this chapter was to provide a uni-
fied general equilibrium framework for investigating the employment
effects of EU enlargement, alongside the trade integration effects and
the costs of enlargement. Based on a highly stylized model that
combines search unemployment with growth, we have derived key
intuitive insights into how trade integration and immigration affect
domestic labor markets. Among other things, our results indicate that
fiscal-policy rules pertaining to unemployment and wage taxation are
important in determining the employment effects of enlargement.
Based on an empirically implemented and enriched version of our
model, we were able to trace in considerable detail the quantitative
effects of EU enlargement on the German economy.

If unemployment benefits and the wage tax allowance are kept
constant in real terms, as in our base case scenario, this installs some
degree of wage rigidity. In this case, the trade integration effect of EU
enlargement is expansionary. By raising the capital intensity of pro-

duction, trade integration also boosts the marginal productivity of labor. Job values increase by more than wages, leading firms to post more vacancies. As labor markets become tighter, unemployment declines. In a situation in which the economy suffers from excessive bargaining power of workers or is stuck with high unemployment benefits, resulting in high wages and high unemployment, trade integration yields further welfare gains, over and above the traditional ones, by stimulating employment. We also find that the effects of expansion yield a remarkable fiscal dividend that could be used to cut the wage tax, despite the need to finance higher net contributions to the EU. This reinforces the reduction in the unemployment rate.

Our results suggest that, in quantitative terms, the labor market effects of trade integration are rather modest compared to those of immigration. Looking at a scenario based on econometric projections of migration from CEECs to EU15 countries that features a concentration of immigration among low-skilled labor, our numerical results reveal that low-skilled workers in incumbent member countries will find both their wages and employment prospects directly impaired by an inflow of low-skilled workers. The high-skilled, on the other hand, will gain on both counts. Interestingly, the same does not hold true for immigration of high-skilled workers as such; in that case, both types of labor experience a lower level of unemployment, while at the same time enjoying a higher wage rate. In addition to describing these direct labor market effects, we have also provided an empirical estimate of the so-called immigration surplus amounting to 0.7 percent of GDP.

Appendix A: The Computational Model

The model presented in this chapter differs from the one used in Keuschnigg and Kohler 1996a, Keuschnigg and Kohler 1996b, and Keuschnigg and Kohler 2002 by allowing for search unemployment, but it shares other elements with the model used in those studies. A detailed presentation of the search-theoretic elements of the model can be found in Heijdra, Keuschnigg, and Kohler 2002, hence we need give only a brief verbal overview of the computational model here, specifically pointing out where it departs from the core version presented in box 7.1.

Production occurs in twelve sectors, connected by inter-industry intermediate goods. Physical capital is sector-specific in the short run, because convex installation costs imply prolonged capital dynamics. In the long run, after a prolonged period of slow adjustment, capital is fully mobile across sectors. Furthermore, firms decide on employment of high- and low-skilled workers, and on the amount of labor used for search and recruitment to maintain an acceptably low number of vacancies in the hiring process. Each firm has market power, based on product differentiation generated by preferences as in Dixit and Stiglitz 1977. Production of varieties is subject to fixed costs. Free entry determines the equilibrium number of firms within each sector through a zero profit condition. Unlike the stylized model in the analytical part of the paper, the computational model thus features an endogenous adjustment of the degree of domestic product differentiation.

The *household sector* consists of overlapping generations, as in Blanchard 1985. There are two types of households, high-skilled and low-skilled, each with a stationary population in the benchmark equilibrium. Each generation maximizes expected lifetime utility, subject to a lifetime budget constraint, in which income in each period depends on the employment status and on the wage rate and unemployment benefit. An income-pooling assumption allows us to reconcile intertemporal savings and consumption choice with labor income risk by focusing on average labor income of each generation. Wages are determined by Nash bargaining, whereby the households' objective is the differential value of being employed, and firms maximize their job rent. Job matching takes place separately in the high- and low-skilled segments of the labor market.

The *public sector* collects a number of taxes (value-added tax, excise taxes, general income tax, capital income tax, wage tax, social security contributions) and spends on government procurement as well as subsidies and household transfers (including social security expenditure), and of course contribution payments to the European Union. In the simulation runs, we enforce a constant ratio of government debt to GDP, with household transfers adjusting endogenously.

The *foreign sector* features trade in goods and services with four types of trading partners, as highlighted in box 7.1, whereby foreign producer prices are assumed constant. International capital mobility ties the domestic real interest rate to a given world interest rate. The financial wealth of the economy is thus composed of firm values, government debt, and net foreign debt, with capital market equilibrium requiring appropriate no-arbitrage conditions on all of these components.

Table 7B.1
Labor market parameters

		High-skilled $(j = s)$	Low-skilled $(j = u)$
Unemployment rate	u	0.06	0.10
Average duration of unemployment	$\frac{1}{f(\theta^j)} = \frac{1}{x_0^j}\left(\frac{U^j}{V^j}\right)^{1-\varepsilon}$	1.75 quarters	3 quarters
Average vacancy duration	$\frac{1}{q(\theta^j)} = \frac{1}{x_0^j}\left(\frac{U^j}{V^j}\right)^{\varepsilon}$	1.4 quarters	1.3 quarters
Unemployment benefits	B^U	$0.7 \times$ net wages	
Matching elasticity	ε	0.4	
Probability of death	β	$1/60$	
Average job duration	$1/s$	27 quarters	
Worker bargaining power	ζ	0.5	

Appendix B: Calibration

The model is calibrated to 1996 benchmark data for the German economy. We have largely adopted the calibration procedure described in the appendix to Keuschnigg and Kohler 1999. Given a richer treatment of the labor market in this chapter than in that work, however, there are new elements that need attention. We draw on some parameters commonly used in the real business cycle literature (see Andolfatto 1996, Burda and Weder 1998, and Mortensen and Pissarides 1999, among others). Other parameters are calibrated such that the stationary solution reproduces the benchmark data set. The model is implemented in quarterly terms to obtain meaningful lengths of unemployment spells. Table 7B.1 gives a brief overview of the calibrated labor market parameters. The matching elasticity ε with respect to the unemployed is set at 0.4 (see Broersma and Van Ours 1999 for a survey). In line with the empirical literature on search unemployment, and drawing on German evidence by Schmidt (1999), we specify the average unemployment duration $1/f$ of high- (low-)skilled labor as 1.75 (3) quarters, and the average vacancy duration $1/q$ as 1.4 (1.3) quarters. With a quarterly mortality rate of $\beta = 1/60$,[24] these values imply a certain quarterly split rate s to replicate the benchmark equilibrium. The calibrated value implies a job duration of about twenty-seven quarters for both skill types. Calibration generates a search coefficient κ such that roughly 2 (3) percent of the skilled (unskilled)

Table 7B.2
Sectoral share and elasticity parameters

	Percentage share of goods from CEECs[a]		Elasticities of substitution	
Sector	Capital goods P	Inter-mediates P^q	Capital/ labor (K/A)	High-/Low-skilled labor (L^{D^s}/L^{D^u})
1 AgrFor	0.024	0.657	0.607	0.950
2 Food	0.029	0.776	0.810	0.950
3 TexCloth	5.402	1.230	0.987	0.950
4 WoodPap	1.183	0.896	0.879	0.950
5 Chemic	0.352	0.829	0.827	0.950
6 PetrolEnergy	0.037	1.096	0.430	0.950
7 MinQuar	0.898	0.685	0.900	0.950
8 Metals	1.437	0.870	0.765	0.950
9 ConstrTransp	0.086	0.846	0.647	0.950
10 Trade	0.244	0.412	0.970	0.950
11 InsurOther	0.027	0.366	0.970	0.950
12 Public	0.003	0.320	0.970	0.950

[a] Share of imports from CEECs in total expenditure. See box 7.1 for notation.
Key: 1. Agriculture, Forestry; 2. Food; 3. Textiles, Clothing; 4. Wood, Paper; 5. Chemical; 6. Petroleum, Energy; 7. Mining, Quarrying; 8. Metals; 9. Construction, Transport; 10. Trade; 11. Insurance, Other.

labor force is absorbed in recruitment. Table 7B.2 should give the reader a minimum feeling of the sectoral disaggregation involved, as well as some key share and substitution parameters on the demand and supply sides.

Notes

We gratefully acknowledge financial support by the Austrian Science Fund (FWF grant P14702). The chapter was presented at the University of Copenhagen (EPRU), the Austrian Economic Association, the CEPR ERWIT 2000 workshop, and the CESifo 2001 workshop "Managing EU Enlargement." We appreciate useful comments by A. L. Bovenberg, M. Keuschnigg, and P. B. Sørensen, by other seminar participants and our discussants A. Belke and S. Becker, and by an anonymous reviewer.

1. Throughout this chapter, "CEECs" refers to ten countries presently negotiating for EU membership. The "CEEC5" are the countries that started negotiations in 1998, often referred to as the "Luxembourg group," namely, the Czech Republic, Estonia, Hungary, Poland, and Slovenia. The "CEEC10" additionally include the "Helsinki-group," namely, Bulgaria, Latvia, Lithuania, Romania, and the Slovak Republic.

2. In Heijdra, Keuschnigg, and Kohler 2002 we also approximate the corresponding effects for all other EU15 countries, relying on a method developed in Keuschnigg and Kohler 1996b.

3. The effect of eastern enlargement is larger in terms of employment shares than in terms of value-added shares, which reflects a productivity difference. This is probably larger than may appear from figure 7.1. ECOFIN (2001) emphasizes that both labor productivity and output per unit of land are significantly lower, compared to those of the EU15, in candidate members from Central and Eastern Europe than they were in Greece, Spain and Portugal compared to those in the EC9 prior to southern enlargement. For a more detailed comparative account of the southern enlargement, see also EIC 2001 (Part B: Strategic Report).

4. We do this on the six-digit level of the harmonized system, which comprises over 5,000 different commodities, using post–Uruguay round nominal MFN rates. Although tariffs have already been targeted by the Europe Agreements, these agreements should, in turn, be seen as an integral part of eastern enlargement.

5. See Davis and Haltiwanger 1992 for empirical evidence and Diamond 1982, Hosios 1990, and Mortensen and Pissarides 1994 for pioneering theoretical developments. Mortensen and Pissarides (1999) and Pissarides (2000) provide convenient surveys.

6. Matusz (1996), Davidson, Martin, and Matusz (1999), and Jansen and Turrini (2000) discuss trade in search and efficiency wage models without capital accumulation.

7. See Heijdra, Keuschnigg, and Kohler 2002 for a more detailed presentation of the model, including some analytical results that are particularly relevant for EU enlargement.

8. More details on the household sector, as well as the labor market, can be found in Heijdra, Keuschnigg, and Kohler 2002.

9. In Keuschnigg and Kohler 2002, we demonstrate, both theoretically and empirically, that the widespread expectation of a widening wage gap between high-skilled and low-skilled labor is not necessarily borne out in the case of EU enlargement.

10. For a theoretical treatment, see Heijdra, Keuschnigg, and Kohler 2002.

11. We shall turn to the empirical significance of these two channels in the German case below.

12. EU membership may also affect the degree of product differentiation in the new member countries. However, this effect lies beyond rigorous treatment by means of our computational model that is restricted to the German economy. Keeping the number of foreign varieties constant seems justified as a conservative research strategy, since it avoids an overly optimistic estimation of welfare effects from enlargement by means of an ad-hoc specification of some exogenous foreign variety effect.

13. See Keuschnigg 1998 for a more detailed analysis.

14. One might imagine, however, that institutional changes affect workers' bargaining power or that mismatch in the labor market increases. Both shocks would to some extent affect the long-run unemployment rate.

15. This beneficial effect of immigration should not be confused with the "immigration surplus," in which an inflow of migrants increases the income of other factors, if migrants

are employed according to a downward-sloping marginal productivity schedule. This point will be taken up again in the empirical section.

16. These are made explicit in Heijdra, Keuschnigg, and Kohler 2002.

17. In Keuschnigg, Keuschnigg, and Kohler 2001, we used the more optimistic European Commission estimate of 0.113 percent cost, in which case the German net contribution increases only to 0.645 percent.

18. With a gross wage rate W, the net wage determining the value of employment to a household is equal to $W^* = (1 - t^L)W + B^L$, where t^L is the marginal income tax rate and B^L is the tax allowance.

19. The large terms-of-trade gains vis-à-vis the CEEC5 (7 percent) are due to vanishing trade costs, which are equivalent to a terms-of-trade improvement. Note that in this case there is no offsetting terms-of-trade loss for the trading partner (CEEC5).

20. The effect on the wage spread can be understood only by investigating in more detail the structural effects of enlargement (see Keuschnigg, Keuschnigg, and Kohler 2001). For the Austrian case, see Keuschnigg and Kohler 2002 and Kohler and Keuschnigg 2001.

21. We compute the equivalent variations of lifetime wealth for each cohort and sum them over present and future generations, with due discounting and weighing by cohort size. For comparison with annual GDP, we convert the resulting wealth measure into an annuity by multiplying it by the interest rate.

22. Note that both of the scenarios depicted in figure 4 eventually end up at the same final value as reported in the "Migration" column of table 7.2, once a prolonged period of adjustment is completed.

23. The Armington elasticities directly affect the power with which the trade shock resulting from enlargement is transmitted to the home economy. Lower elasticity values make import and export demand less price elastic, which magnifies the relative price changes but dampens the quantity response.

24. An expected lifetime of fifteen years or sixty quarters may seem rather low. This parameter is not to be interpreted literally, however, since it applies equally to both young and old generations. It rather reflects disconnectedness of dynasties and discounting of future wage incomes.

References

Aghion, P., and P. Howitt. 1994. "Growth and Unemployment." *Review of Economic Studies* 61: 477–494.

Andolfatto, D. 1996. "Business Cycles and Labor Market Search." *American Economic Review* 86: 112–132.

Baldwin, R. E., J. F. Francois, and R. Portes. 1997. "The Costs and Benefits of Eastern Enlargement: The Impact on the EU and Central Europe." *Economic Policy* 24: 127–176.

Baldwin, R. E., and E. Seghezza. 1998. "Regional Integration and Growth in Developing Nations." *Journal of Economic Integration* 13: 367–399.

Blanchard, Olivier. 1985. "Debt, Deficits, and Finite Horizons." *Journal of Political Economy* 93: 223–247.

Broersma, L., and J. C. Van Ours. 1999. "Job Searchers, Job Matches and the Elasticity of Matching." *Labour Economics* 6: 77–93.

Burda, M. C., and M. Weder. 1998. "Endogenes Wachstum, gleichgewichtige Arbeitslosigkeit und persistente Konjunkturzyklen." Discussion paper, Humboldt University of Berlin.

Davidson, C., L. Martin, and S. Matusz. 1999. "Trade and Search Generated Unemployment." *Journal of International Economics* 48: 271–299.

Davis, S., and J. Haltiwanger. 1992. "Gross Job Creation, Gross Job Destruction, and Employment Reallocation." *Quarterly Journal of Economics* 107: 819–864.

Den Haan, W. J., G. Ramey, and J. Watson. 1997. "Job Destruction and Propagation of Shocks." Discussion paper no. 97-23, University of California, San Diego.

Diamond, P. A. 1982. "Aggregate Demand Management in Search Equilibrium." *Journal of Political Economy* 90: 881–894.

Dixit, A., and J. E. Stiglitz. 1977. "Monopolistic Competition and Optimum Product Diversity." *American Economic Review* 67: 297–308.

ECOFIN. 2001. "The Economic Impact of Enlargement." Enlargement paper no. 4, Directorate General for Economic and Financial Affairs. Brussels.

European Commission. 1997. *Agenda 2000*. Luxembourg.

European Commission. 2002. "Communication from the Commission: Information Note. Common Financial Framework 2004–2006 for the Accession Negotiations, Brussels, 2002." Luxembourg.

European Council. 1999. "Presidency conclusions—Berlin European Council, 24 and 25 March 1999." Berlin.

European Integration Consortium (EIC). 2001. *The Impact of Eastern Enlargement on Employment and Labour Markets in the EU Member States: Study on Behalf of the Employment and Social Affairs Directorate General of the European Commission*. Berlin and Milan.

Heijdra, B. J., and C. Keuschnigg. 2000. "Integration and Search Unemployment: An Analysis of Eastern EU Enlargement." Working paper no. 341, CESifo, Munich.

Heijdra, B. J., C. Keuschnigg, and W. Kohler. 2002. "Eastern Enlargement of the EU: Jobs, Investment and Welfare in Present Member Countries." Working paper no. 718 (7), CESifo, Munich.

Hosios, A. J. 1990. "On the Efficiency of Matching and Related Models of Search and Unemployment." *Review of Economic Studies* 57: 279–298.

Jansen, M., and A. Turrini. 2000. "Job Creation, Job Destruction, and the International Division of Labour." Discussion paper no. 2472, Centre for Economic Policy Research, London.

Keuschnigg, C. 1998. "Investment Externalities and a Corrective Subsidy." *International Tax and Public Finance* 5: 449–469.

Keuschnigg, C., M. Keuschnigg, and W. Kohler. 2001. "The German Perspective on Eastern EU Enlargement." *World Economy* 24: 513–542.

Keuschnigg, C., and W. Kohler. 1996a. "Commercial Policy and Dynamic Adjustment under Monopolistic Competition." *Journal of International Economics* 40: 373–410.

Keuschnigg, C., and W. Kohler. 1996b. "Austria in the European Union: Dynamic Gains from Integration and Distributional Implications." *Economic Policy* 22: 157–211.

Keuschnigg, C., and W. Kohler. 1999. *Eastern Enlargement to the EU: Economic Costs and Benefits for the EU Present Member States. The Case of Austria.* Study XIX/B1/9801 on Behalf of the European Commission, Brussels. Available at ⟨www.economics.uni-linz. ac.at/kohler/eu-new.htm⟩.

Keuschnigg, C., and W. Kohler. 2002. "Eastern Enlargement of the EU: How Much Is It Worth For Austria?" *Review of International Economics* 10: 324–342.

Kohler, W. 2000. "Die Osterweiterung der EU aus der Sicht bestehender Mitgliedsländer: Was lehrt uns die Theorie der ökonomischen Integration?" *Perspektiven der Wirtschaftspolitik* 1: 115–142.

Kohler, W., and C. Keuschnigg. 2000. "An Incumbent Country View on Eastern Enlargement of the EU—Part I: A General Treatment." *Empirica* 27: 325–351.

Kohler, W., and C. Keuschnigg. 2001. "An Incumbent Country View on Eastern Enlargement of the EU—Part II: The Case of Austria." *Empirica* 28: 159–185.

Matusz, S. 1996. "International Trade, the Division of Labour, and Unemployment." *International Economic Review* 37: 71–84.

Merz, M. 1999. "Heterogeneous Job-Matches and the Cyclical Behaviour of Labour Turnover." *Journal of Monetary Economics* 43: 91–124.

Mortensen, D. T., and C. A. Pissarides. 1994. "Job Creation and Job Destruction in the Theory of Unemployment." *Review of Economic Studies* 61: 397–416.

Mortensen, D. T., and C. A. Pissarides. 1999. "Job Reallocation, Employment Fluctuations and Unemployment." In *Handbook of Macroeconomics*, vol. 1B, ed. J. B. Taylor and M. Woodford, 1171–1227. Amsterdam: North-Holland.

Pissarides, C. A. 2000. *Equilibrium Unemployment Theory*, 2nd ed. Cambridge: MIT Press.

Schmidt, C. M. 1999. "Persistence and the German Unemployment Problem: Empirical Evidence on German Labour Market Flows." Discussion paper no. 31, Institute for the study of Labor (IZA), Bonn.

Shi, S., and Q. Wen. 1997. "Labour Market Search and Capital Accmulation: Some Analytical Results." *Journal of Economic Dynamics and Control* 21: 1747–1776.

Shi, S., and Q. Wen. 1999. "Labour Market Search and the Dynamic Effects of Taxes and Subsidies." *Journal of Monetary Economics* 43: 457–495.

Comments

Sascha O. Becker

The European Union faces the biggest challenge in its history in the prospect of nearly doubling the number of its members over the coming decade. Although the historic political dimension of the enlargement process of admitting a large number of former communist countries to join the union is unquestioned, the economic effects of enlargement are much harder to quantify. Incumbent countries are economically affected by enlargement along three major dimensions: first, the financing of net transfers to new members; second, trade in goods and services; and third, immigration. The chapter by Ben J. Heijdra, Christian Keuschnigg, and Wilhelm Kohler attempts to put numbers on the economic effects of enlargement within the framework of a computable general equilibrium model, thereby going beyond purely theoretical arguments about the likely effects.

CGE models provide a quantitative evaluation of the effects of the enlargement process; in particular, they enable the study of the impact of alternative government policies. Although in most policy settings economic theory provides guidelines for judging whether a particular policy will be beneficial, economic theory often cannot give a definite answer as to the size of the effects the policy will have. CGE models go beyond partial equilibrium models by permitting one to take into account interactions throughout the economy in a consistent manner. This makes CGE models a particularly suitable and powerful tool for studying the effects of EU enlargement on key economic variables under alternative policy assumptions and enlargement scenarios.

Previous research on eastern EU enlargement, starting with Baldwin, Francois, and Portes 1997, has mostly concentrated on the costs and benefits of enlargement in terms of national output. The present chapter extends the previous research and can be seen as the most comprehensive piece of work to date on EU enlargement, encompassing most of the channels previously analyzed. Its main contribution is the explicit modeling of labor market effects of enlargement that surprisingly have been neglected in much of the previous research. The chapter presents a general equilibrium model with search unemployment, separately for high- and low-skilled workers, in which the search framework is combined with capital accumulation as a prime transmission mechanism. The model is empirically implemented using a multisector dynamic general equilibrium model with exogenous trend growth of labor productivity. It is calibrated and numerically simulated, mainly for Germany, with approximate simulations also for other incumbent EU countries. The effects considered are capital accumulation, unemployment, the government budget, income distribution, and overall welfare (measured by Hicksian equivalent variation). The main results of the authors' simulations for Germany, given their assumptions about the EU's political framework, are as follows: First, the (positive) effects of mutual trade liberalization and improved market access dominate the (negative) effect of increased net transfers to the central EU budget; and second, there are only small labor market effects from trade, as compared to more pronounced effects from migration.

The most important theoretical contribution of the chapter is the introduction of unemployment into the model. Previous research simply assumed perfectly competitive markets without frictions and therefore totally disregarded unemployment. The authors model unemployment as search unemployment. Search unemployment, however, explains just one part of unemployment in countries like Germany. Germany's elevated unemployment level cannot be explained solely by search frictions in the labor market but has a sizable structural component. Wide coverage of labor contracts sets quasi–minimum wages in a large part of the economy that are further sustained by a generous welfare system that makes working unattractive for less productive workers. Furthermore, there are considerable occupational and geographic imbalances within the country. Whereas East German states have unemployment rates of up to 20 percent, the southern (West German) states are close to full employment, and in some areas firms are desperately searching for workers.

Most of the fear related to immigration following EU enlargement is actually caused by the existence of inflexible wages that do not react to an increased labor supply. Although cynical commentators see immigration as the opportunity to get rid of the rigidity in German labor markets by making the system collapse, the short- and medium-run effects of immigration may be a much higher unemployment rate, going beyond the effects predicted if unemployment is only higher temporarily, as long as immigrants search for their first job in their destination country.

Germany's institutional framework of powerful labor unions might reduce the likelihood of the predicted 4 percent drop in real wages (relative to the trend) for the low skilled. This is true unless the nature of the wage-bargaining process, in which unions fight at least to keep up with inflation, changes considerably with respect to the status quo. One way of adding (quasi–)minimum wages in the search model in order to capture downward wage rigidity was suggested by Adrian Masters (1999).

It is definitely a very valuable contribution to model labor markets at all, but future work should also consider different types of unemployment and extensions to the simple matching framework to check the robustness of the model's results with respect to the specific ways in which unemployment is modeled.

A broader issue that applies to CGE models in general is that many parameters used in the simulation are calibrated to a benchmark data set that in the present case is by definition composed of pre-enlargement data. In some cases, such (exogenous) parameters are very likely to change during the enlargement process. One particular example is recruitment search intensities: If there is an oversupply of low-skilled immigrants after enlargement, firms will probably search more intensively for skilled immigrants to bring them in line with the optimal skill intensity in their sector. The recruitment search intensities could possibly be endogenized.

Another dimension on which labor markets might be affected is the endogenous reaction of potential migrants to the labor market situation in the destination country. If, because of initial immigration of a large number of low-skilled workers to Germany, the labor market situation of all the low-skilled worsens, further potential migrants might be less inclined to migrate at all. So as an alternative to assuming migration flows to be exogenous (and possibly endogenizing firms' recruitment search intensities), using their powerful simulation tools, the authors might be able to produce their own predictions of the likely migration flows and thus endogenously determine migration flows given recruitment search intensities. Although it is clear that *something* has to be taken as exogenous in the model, in some instances it would be insightful to see how different assumptions about exogenous and endogenous forces alter the model's results or even allow for the study of further dimensions of the enlargement process.

Enlargement is to a large extent a political process. Many of the model's key parameters are set in a political decision process and are not subjected to market forces. The authors make the extreme assumption that the costs of enlargement are exclusively financed by a cut in regional structural funds given to incumbent countries. (Alternatively, net contributions to the EU budget could be increased, or there might be cuts in the common agricultural policy funds.) This assumption is probably the single most important one affecting the size and direction of the results. Surprisingly, although they perform sensitivity analyses on many other dimensions (e.g., different migration scenarios, different tax schemes, variations in model elasticities), the authors do not present results with respect to variation in this political dimension of enlargement. Although the authors think that it is precisely because there is much uncertainty around this issue that they have chosen to resort to an extreme scenario of a pure strategy relying on a cut of regional and structural funds, my understanding is that politicians in incumbent countries would be interested precisely in the likely economic effects of alternative options to balance the EU budget, and might base their decisions or negotiation strategy in the EU Council on research regarding those effects if it were available to them. The authors acknowledge that their assumption is probably the most beneficial for Germany and should therefore be interpreted as an upper bound on the likely effects of enlargement for Germany. Still, it would be interesting to see by how much their results change (all else being equal) under alternative assumptions about the way the EU budget gets balanced.

Although the model features an extended public sector, including the major taxes and spending items, the specific impact of enlargement on the public finances could have been given more consideration. Many people fear that EU enlargement may trigger immigration not only in the pursuit of higher wages, but also because of welfare systems in incumbent countries that are more generous than those in the enlargement countries. On the upside, young immigrants might have a beneficial effect on the pension systems in the incumbent countries. Many EU countries face a pension crisis caused by aging populations. Immigration of young Eastern Europeans might avert such crises.

It is clear that even the most powerful CGE models cannot explain everything at the same time, but some discussion of the importance of these effects would help the reader to assess the factors that potentially counterbalance one another when judging the economic effects of EU enlargement. On the downside, immigrants who do not find a job even after an initial search period—this relates to the discussion in the chapter about the type of unemployment—might impose a burden on the welfare system of receiving countries.

References

Baldwin, R. E., J. F. Francois, and R. Portes. 1997. "The Costs and Benefits of Eastern Enlargement: The Impact on the EU and Central Europe." *Economic Policy* 24: 127–176.

Masters, A. M. 1999. "Wage Posting in Two-Sided Search and the Minimum Wage." *International Economic Review* 40, no. 4: 809–826.

8

EU Enlargement: Economic Implications for Countries and Industries

Arjan M. Lejour, Ruud A. de Mooij, and Richard Nahuis

8.1 Introduction

This chapter explores the economic consequences of the enlargement of the EU with the CEECs. In contrast to most earlier analyses, we do not focus on existing formal trade barriers between the incumbent EU countries and the CEECs, because by the end of 2002, these barriers will be removed (at least for industry products) entirely in accordance with the Europe Agreements. Instead, we focus on further steps in the integration process that involve the accession of the CEECs to the internal market, the equalization of external tariffs in the incumbent countries and the CEECs, and free movement of labor between the two groups of countries and within the CEECs. Although these are not all the potential effects of the EU's eastern enlargement, they capture some of its main economic dimensions. Other effects of enlargement, for example, those associated with the subsequent accession to the EMU, changes in the Common Agricultural Policy, and reforms of the Regional and Structural Funds are not explored here, in part because these effects are subject to considerable policy uncertainty.

Whereas the implications of a common external tariff and the free movement of labor can be analyzed in a straightforward manner, the analysis of the accession of the CEECs to the internal market requires a more subtle approach. Previous studies have analyzed the shock this accession will pose by means of an exogenous across-the-board reduction in trade costs (see, e.g., Baldwin, Francois, and Portes 1997; Keuschnigg and Kohler 2000, 2002; Breuss 2001). Our analysis deviates from this approach in two ways. First of all, we take account of sectoral variation in trade costs, since enlargement of the internal market is likely to have disproportionate effects on some industries.[1] Second, rather than simulating a "best-guess" reduction in trade costs as a result of enlargement, we estimate gravity equations to derive the size of this shock. More specifically, for sixteen different industries, we derive from gravity equations the potential trade between the EU and the CEECs after enlargement. The estimates provide an indication of trade flows when the CEECs are full members of the EU. Comparing this potential trade with actual trade, we can derive an estimate of the tariff equivalent of the barriers to trade. These barriers are then assumed to be removed when eastern countries accede to the EU.

This chapter adopts a CGE model for the world economy, World-Scan, to explore the implications of EU enlargement in its three dimensions. The model, calibrated on the most recent version of the Global Trade Analysis Project (GTAP) database, has a number of features that make it appropriate for analyzing the impact of enlargement. In particular, the model makes an explicit distinction between, on the one hand, six regions in the EU and, on the other hand, Poland, Hungary, and the other accession countries. Moreover, the model distinguishes among 16 industries so that we are able to explore which industries will be most affected by EU enlargement. Thus, combined with the gravity approach, the model does justice to the sectoral variation in the reduction in trade costs that will result from EU enlargement.

Our simulations suggest that EU enlargement yields large gains for the CEECs and a modest welfare improvement for the EU. This conclusion is consistent with previous model simulations of EU enlargement. For instance, Brown et al. (1997) estimate welfare gains for the CEECs of between 3.8 and 7.3 percent, and of around 0.1 percent for the EU. Baldwin, Francois, and Portes (1997) find a real income gain of 1.5 percent for the CEECs and more modest effects for the EU. Breuss (2001) reports effects on real GDP of between 4 and 9 percent for the CEECs and about one-tenth of that for the EU. Our findings tend to reveal effects somewhat larger than the effects reported in those previous studies. This is because of the relatively large shock associated with the accession to the internal market, which in our study, in contrast to the previous studies, is based on empirical research.

The rest of this chapter is organized as follows. Section 8.2 discusses the main features of the WorldScan model. Section 8.3 demonstrates the shock of EU enlargement in three dimensions: the shift toward a customs union, accession to the internal EU market, and free movement of labor. Section 8.4 analyzes the implications of these shocks for both the EU and accession countries. In section 8.5, we perform sensitivity analysis on the simulations. Finally, section 8.6 concludes.

8.2   The WorldScan Model

WorldScan is a computable general equilibrium model for the world economy (see CPB 1999 for more details). The model is calibrated on the basis of the GTAP database, version 5 (Dimanaran and McDougall 2002), with 1997 as the base year. The database allows us to distinguish among a large number of regions and sectors. In particular, the database divides the EU is divided into six regions: Germany, France, the United Kingdom, the Netherlands, "South Europe" (comprising Italy, Spain, Portugal, and Greece), and "Rest of EU" (comprising Austria, Belgium, Luxembourg, Ireland, Denmark, Sweden, and Finland). The accession countries are divided into three regions: Poland, Hungary, and CEEC5 (comprising the Czech Republic, the Slovak Republic, Slovenia, Bulgaria, and Romania). Hence, the Baltic states (Estonia, Latvia, and Lithuania) are not included in the analysis of this chapter, since the data do not distinguish these countries separately or as a block.[2] The rest of the world economy is divided further into three other regions, namely, the former Soviet Union, the rest of the OECD countries, and the rest of the world (ROW). For each region, we distinguish sixteen economic sectors. These consist of agriculture, raw materials, ten manufacturing sectors, and four service sectors. As the model distinguishes only one aggregated agricultural sector, we are unable to explore the details of changes in the common agricultural policies of the EU. The appendix provides details on the countries and sectors and values for the model's key parameters.

The model relies at its core on neoclassical theories of growth and international trade. Sectoral production technologies are modeled as nested Constant Elasticity of Substitution (CES) functions. At the lower nesting, two composite inputs are produced. On the one hand, value added is produced by combining low-skilled labor, high-skilled labor, capital, and in some sectors, a fixed factor (land in the agriculture sector and natural resources in the raw-materials sector). The production of value added is modeled by means of a Cobb-Douglas technology. On the other hand, various intermediate inputs are combined to yield a second composite input. Here, we use a CES function with a substitution elasticity of 0.8. In principle, there exist sixteen intermediate inputs. Only a few intermediate inputs are important, however, in the production process for most industries. At the higher nesting, the two composite inputs (i.e., value added and the composite of intermediate inputs) are combined by means of a CES technology to yield final

Table 8.1
Trade-to-GDP ratio, distinguished by region, 1997

	EU	Rest of World	CEEC7	Total
Export share				
Hungary	0.34	0.16	0.04	0.54
Poland	0.14	0.09	0.01	0.25
CEEC5	0.26	0.15	0.02	0.44

Source: Dimanaran and McDougall 2002.

output. The substitution elasticity between the two composite inputs is 0.4.

With respect to trade, WorldScan adopts an Armington specification. In particular, commodities from different origins are imperfect substitutes for one another, which explains two-way trade between regions and allows market power of each region. The demand elasticity for manufacturing industries is set at 5.6. For service industries the elasticity is set at a lower level, for raw materials and agriculture at a higher level. In the long run, trade patterns are determined by Heckscher-Ohlin mechanisms (i.e., based on factor endowments). On the capital market, WorldScan assumes imperfect capital mobility across borders. In particular, the model includes a portfolio mechanism in which capital owners distribute their investments over regions, depending on the rates of return and the preferences in regard to asset diversification. Consumption patterns may differ across countries and depend on per capita income. If welfare levels converge, these consumption patterns also converge toward a universal pattern. We assume that the labor markets for low- and high-skilled workers clear. In the baseline, labor does not migrate.

Enlargement of the EU with seven countries (referred to as the CEEC7) implies an increase in the EU population by around 26 percent, whereas GDP will rise by a mere 4 percent. The trade patterns of the CEECs are primarily geared to the EU (see table 8.1). Table 8.2 presents the trade shares of the various sectors in terms of the total trade of a country or group of countries. This yields information about the export specialization of the country or group. We see from the table that exports in the CEECs are concentrated in four sectors: textiles and leather, machinery and equipment, transport and communication, and other services. For textiles and leather and machinery and equipment,

Table 8.2
Sectoral export as percentage of total export, 1997

	Hungary	Poland	CEEC5
Agriculture	5.1	2.2	2.2
Raw materials	0.3	6.8	0.9
Food processing	4.5	5.1	2.7
Textiles and leather	10.1	9.2	10.2
Non-metallic minerals	2.0	2.5	3.7
Energy-intensive products	8.3	5.5	6.8
Other manufacturing	3.4	10.8	8.1
Metals	1.5	5.5	6.4
Fabricated metal products	2.3	3.8	3.4
Machinery and equipment	14.3	10.5	14.8
Electronic equipment	6.4	1.8	1.0
Transport equipment	6.3	2.5	5.7
Trade services	3.9	4.8	2.1
Transport and communication	11.8	14.2	19.1
Financial services	3.1	3.4	2.0
Other services	16.6	11.6	10.9

Source: Dimanaran and McDougall 2002.

the high export shares originate in a high share of export in terms of value added in those sectors. For instance, almost all output of textiles in Hungary is exported. The high export shares of transport and communication and other services, in contrast, are due to the large size of these sectors in the CEEC economies.

Comparing the three CEEC regions analyzed in this chapter, we find that Hungarian exports are specialized relatively more than those of the other two regions in agriculture, energy-intensive products, and electronic equipment. Poland specializes relatively more than the other two regions in raw materials, other manufacturing, and trade services. The export share of the CEEC5 is relatively high, compared to that of the other two regions, in metals and transport and communication.

In exploring the economic impact of EU enlargement with World-Scan, we compare economic variables in 2020 with the results in a baseline scenario. In the baseline, GDP growth in the CEEC7, the former Soviet Union, and ROW are based on long-term projections of the World Bank (2000), which has constructed projections of GDP growth until 2010 for all developing regions. We extrapolated these projections to 2020. Thus, economic growth in Hungary and Poland is set at 4.6

percent per year, which is a bit higher than in the CEEC5 (4.3 percent) because the pace of economic reform in Bulgaria and Romania is relatively slow. For Western Europe and the rest of the OECD, GDP growth is set at about 2.1 percent, and in ROW it is set at nearly 5 percent, especially because of high growth in Asia and in particular China. In the baseline, there are no further agreements (beyond the imminent EU enlargement) on global trade liberalization between now and 2020, so that the degree of openness remains at a stable level in the scenario period.

8.3 Shock of Enlargement

This section discusses three shocks resulting from EU enlargement: (1) a gradual removal of the remaining formal trade barriers between incumbent and accession countries and between accession countries in agriculture and food processing and the adoption of the common external tariff (CET), (2) accession of the CEECs to the internal market, and (3) free movement of labor between current and new EU members. We do not analyze other potential implications of enlargement, such as CEEC accession to the EMU and changes in the Common Agricultural Policies of the EU and in EU policies with respect to the Regional and Structural Funds. Section 8.4 will analyze the economic implications of these shocks using the WorldScan model.

8.3.1 Toward a Customs Union

Accession of the CEECs to the EU implies a move from an almost-free-trade area toward a customs union. This means that all remaining bilateral formal trade barriers between the current EU members and the CEECs and between CEECs will be abolished. In 1997, these barriers were present in both agriculture and several manufacturing sectors. In accordance with the Europe Agreements, the bilateral tariffs for manufacturing products will have been removed by 2002. The abolishment of these tariffs can thus not be directly ascribed to accession to the EU. Therefore, we do not include the tariffs covered by the Europe Agreements in our analysis. Instead, we focus on the bilateral tariffs that are not covered by the Europe Agreements, namely, those in agriculture and food processing.

Apart from abolishing bilateral trade barriers, the move toward a customs union means that the external tariffs in the CEECs with re-

Table 8.3
Formal tariffs in agriculture and food processing, 1997 (% of total value of imports/exports)

	Export tariffs		Import tariffs		External import tariffs	
	Agri-culture	Food pro-cessing	Agri-culture	Food pro-cessing	Agri-culture	Food pro-cessing
Levied by CEECs						
Hungary	−2.1	−1.7	22.7	35.6	15.9	32.0
Poland	0.0	−0.3	38.4	63.3	26.7	63.3
CEEC5	0.0	−3.5	24.6	41.0	17.6	48.9
Levied by EU15					7.3	36.1
Hungary	−2.1	−5.2	17.3	33.2		
Poland	−3.0	−4.4	22.0	41.7		
CEEC5	−3.0	−5.4	9.4	30.4		

Source: Dimanaran and McDougall 2002.

spect to third countries will be set equal to the CET of the EU. This holds for both agriculture and food processing and for all manufacturing sectors.

Table 8.3 shows the bilateral export and import tariffs in 1997 between the EU and the CEECs for agricultural products and food processing. It reveals that most regions provide export subsidies. Only Poland and the CEEC5 do not give export subsidies in agriculture. Hungary provides an export subsidy of 2.1 percent of the export value in agriculture and 1.7 percent in food processing. Compared to those of the CEECs, the export subsidies of the EU are larger. The subsidy in agriculture is between 2.1 and 3 percent of the export value; in food processing it is between 4.4 and 5.4 percent. Hence, the EU stimulates its exports of agricultural and food products more than the CEECs do.

The third and fourth column of table 8.3 show the bilateral import tariffs in agriculture and food processing in 1997. We see that these tariffs are substantial, both in the CEECs and the EU. Compared to those of the EU, the import tariffs imposed by the CEECs are somewhat larger. Import tariffs in Poland are especially high, whereas Hungarian import tariffs are among the lowest. The EU levies the smallest tariffs on the CEEC5 and the highest on Polish products. These differences in EU tariffs may originate in both a different composition of agricultural export from the various countries (since the underlying

Table 8.4
External tariffs in manufacturing, 1997 (% of total value of imports)

	Hungary	Poland	CEEC5	EU
Textiles and leather	11.0	20.7	15.6	11.4
Non-metallic minerals	7.5	10.9	11.2	4.7
Energy-intensive products	5.3	11.3	7.5	3.7
Other manufacturing	5.9	12.6	9.0	2.0
Metals	0.9	12.4	6.9	1.9
Fabricated metal products	10.1	14.3	8.2	2.7
Machinery and equipment	8.9	12.5	7.6	2.8
Electronic equipment	8.0	14.4	4.9	4.2
Transport equipment	16.1	15.3	15.0	5.5

Source: Dimanaran and McDougall 2002.

products in agriculture are taxed at different rates) and differentiation in tariffs.

The last two columns in table 8.3 reveal the external tariffs in agriculture and food processing. For agricultural products, we see that the external tariff of the EU is lower than that of the accession countries. In food processing, the EU tariff is higher than in Hungary but lower than in Poland and CEEC5. Among the accession countries, Hungary imposes the lowest external tariffs.

Table 8.4 shows the external tariffs for manufacturing products. In general, the Hungarian external tariffs are relatively low but are still higher, in most instances, than the CET. The Polish external tariffs are the highest in most sectors.[3]

8.3.2 Accession to the Internal Market

The second component of EU enlargement involves the accession of the CEECs to the internal market. This will affect the economies of the CEECs and current EU members in several ways, for example, via trade, foreign direct investment (FDI), and domestic investment. Our focus in this section is on the trade effect.

CEEC accession to the internal market may increase trade between the CEECs and incumbent EU members for at least three reasons. First, a number of administrative barriers to trade between CEECs and current EU members will be eliminated or at least reduced to levels comparable to those between current EU members. Here, one can think of reduced costs of passing customs at the frontier: less time delays, less formalities, and so forth. Second and probably more important is the reduction in technical barriers to trade between the CEECs and current EU members. The single market reduces these technical barriers by means of mutual recognition of different technical regulations, minimum requirements, and harmonization of rules and regulations.[4] Finally, certain kinds of risk and uncertainty will be mitigated by the CEECs' accession to the EU. One type of risk that will be mitigated is the possibility that somewhere in the link from producer to consumer, some agent will default. This is especially important for goods moving from east to west, as export credit guarantees are less well developed in the CEECs than in the EU15. Another type of risk likely to be mitigated is political risk, a risk more relevant for goods moving from west to east (as insurance does not cover this type of risk and as democracies are thought to be less stable in the CEECs). These risks and uncertainties may form substantial impediments to trade between the CEECs and incumbent EU members under current circumstances.[5]

In discussions about the EU internal-market program of 1992, researchers had great difficulty in measuring the economic gains likely to be generated by the program. The same holds true in assessing the enlargement of the internal market with new members. Today, however, we can observe how the internal market functions by comparing the trade intensity inside the EU with the trade intensity between two otherwise equivalent countries that are not part of the EU. We follow such a procedure to measure the economic consequences of accession to the internal market by estimating gravity equations at the industry level.[6] More specifically, we follow Bergstrand (1989) in estimating the following equation:

$$X_{ijs} = \mathbf{a}_s \mathbf{Z}_{ijs} + b_s D_{ijs}^{EU},$$

where X_{ijs} stands for the log of exports from country i to j in industry s. The vector $\mathbf{Z}_{ijs}$ contains several explanatory variables, including GDP (per capita) of the exporting and importing countries, the distance between the capitals of countries, a set of dummies, and the bilateral import and export tariffs between countries.[7] The vector $\mathbf{a}_s$ contains the parameters we estimate for each sector. The variable D^{EU} is a dummy that equals unity if i and j are currently members of the EU and zero otherwise. Our main interest is in the estimated coefficient for the EU dummy, D^{EU}. For each of the sixteen industry sectors we examine in

Table 8.5
Trade increase and corresponding nontariff barrier on the basis of EU dummy

	Coefficient of EU dummy (b_s)	Trade increase (in percent)	Nontariff barrier (% of import value)
Agriculture	1.25*	249	17.7
Raw materials	−0.10	0	0.0
Food processing	0.66*	94	11.7
Textiles and leather	0.85*	134	14.5
Non-metallic minerals	0.73*	107	13.1
Energy-intensive products	0.13	0	0.0
Other manufacturing	0.08	0	0.0
Metals	−0.10	0	0.0
Fabricated metal products	0.44*	56	8.0
Machinery and equipment	0.31*	37	5.6
Electronic equipment	0.58*	79	10.0
Transport equipment	0.66*	94	11.4
Trade services	0.76*	113	17.2
Transport and communication	0.03	0	0.0
Financial services	−0.14	0	0.0
Other services	0.27*	31	6.5

*Coefficient is significant at the 5 percent level.

this study, this coefficient, b_s, is reported in the first column of table 8.5. The table reveals that in ten out of sixteen sectors, the dummy has a positive and statistically significant coefficient. Hence, in these sectors, bilateral trade is systematically higher if two countries are both members of the EU. The coefficients for agriculture and food processing are among the largest. Hence, the internal market and the common agricultural policy in the EU intensify intra-regional trade in these sectors. For textiles and leather, we also find a high and statistically significant coefficient. The dummy coefficient for raw materials is negative, but statistically insignificant, possibly because oil is intensively traded between EU members and nonmembers alike. For metals and machinery and equipment, we also find a statistically insignificant EU dummy coefficient, and the same holds true for some service sectors. This suggests that, in these sectors, trade among EU members is not significantly more intense than that between two otherwise equivalent countries that are not both EU members. The insignificant coefficients may refer either to industries in which the internal market has not progressed much or to those in which technical barriers to trade are unimportant.

How should these numbers be interpreted? For industries with an insignificant dummy coefficient, we assume that CEEC accession to the internal market has no impact on trade (section 8.5 performs sensitivity analysis with respect to this assumption). For other sectors, the dummy coefficient is used to calculate the potential trade increase from CEEC accession to the internal market. In particular, we assume that EU membership implies that the dummy would change from zero to one for bilateral trade patterns between an EU and the CEECs. Thus, potential trade can be calculated as $\exp(b_s)$, where b_s denotes the estimated coefficient for the EU dummy in (1).[8] To illustrate, the coefficient for the EU dummy in food processing is 0.66, so the potential trade is $\exp(0.66) = 1.94$, that is, almost twice the actual current trade between CEECs and EU members. The potential trade increase in food processing from CEEC accession is therefore 94 percent. The second column of table 8.5 reports the potential trade increases for all sectors.

Having determined the potential trade increase per sector as a result of CEEC accession to the internal market, the next step is to compute a trade barrier that corresponds to this potential trade increase if the barrier were removed. We do this by computing Samuelsonian iceberg trade-cost equivalents, which we refer to as nontariff barriers (NTBs). Iceberg costs are modeled as a part of the goods that melts away during the process of trade. We use the demand (or Armington) elasticities from WorldScan to infer the NTB between the EU and the accession countries that would create the potential trade increase from CEEC accession that we estimated in the previous section. This methodology implies that, once we abolish the NTBs in the WorldScan model, we arrive at the (ex ante) trade levels that correspond to the predictions from the gravity model. If the potential trade increase from CEEC accession in a particular sector is high, then the current barrier to trade in that sector must be high. If the elasticity in a particular sector is high, then (for a give trade increase) the NTB will be small, since the removal of a low barrier will not exert a large effect on trade. With a low elasticity in a particular sector, the corresponding NTB will be large.[9]

The final column of table 8.5 presents the values of the NTBs for our sixteen sectors, according to our calculations. These can be interpreted as the trade costs associated with non-membership of the CEECs in the EU internal market. We calculated weighted average NTBs across our sixteen sectors, using the sector NTBs in the final column of table 8.5

Table 8.6
Increase in export on the basis of EU dummy

	Increase in total export	Increase in export to EU15
Hungary	44%	65%
Poland	30%	50%
CEEC5	32%	52%
EU15	2%	51%[a]

Source: Authors' calculations on the basis of table 8.5.
[a] Export from the EU15 to the CEEC7.

weighted according to the output share of each sector. The weighted average NTBs we arrived at were 6.7 percent for CEEC-EU trade and 7.0 percent for EU-CEEC trade. These averages are within the range of a 5 to 10 percent reduction in real trade cost, which has been used in previous studies to simulate the impact of CEEC accession to the internal market (see, e.g., Baldwin, Francois, and Portes 1997; Keuschnigg and Kohler 2000, 2002; Breuss 2001).

The potential trade increase per sector as a result of CEEC accession can also be used to calculate the aggregate trade increase per country resulting from accession. To that end, we multiplied the existing trade shares of the sectors by the corresponding potential trade increases in those sectors, reported in the second column of table 8.5. The results are reported in table 8.6. We see that exports increase most substantially for Hungary, namely by almost 44 percent. Exports to the EU rise even more, by 65 percent. For Poland and the CEEC5, the corresponding figures are somewhat smaller, but the potential increases are still substantial. Total exports rise by approximately 30 and 32 percent, respectively, and exports to the EU by 50 and 52 percent, respectively, of their original values. The difference between Hungary and the other countries of the CEEC7 in the size of the potential trade increases exists mainly because Hungarian exports are more specialized than those in the other countries of the CEEC7 in industries with a large EU dummy, such as agriculture, textiles and leather, machinery and equipment, electronic equipment, transport equipment, and other services (see table 8.5). The aggregate increase in exports for EU countries resulting from CEEC accession is only 2 percent, which is much smaller than that for the CEECs.[10] The size of the potential increase in EU exports is much smaller than that for the CEECs because only a small fraction of the total exports of EU countries is geared to the CEECs, in contrast to the situation in the CEECs, which send a much larger share of their exports to the EU15.

The aggregate trade increases presented in table 8.6 are more or less consistent with other findings in the literature. For instance, the most recent aggregate gravity equations report an increase in bilateral trade as a result of CEEC accession, calculated using the EU dummy, on the order of 30 to 60 percent (Brenton and Gros 1997; Fidrmuc and Fidrmuc 2000). Similarly, the results of Baldwin, Francois, and Portes (1997) suggest an aggregate increase in bilateral trade resulting from CEEC accession of around 30 percent. Studies that do not explicitly refer to the EU report even higher estimates. For instance, McCallum (1995) and Helliwell (1996) suggest that a typical Canadian province trades twenty-two times more with another Canadian province than with a comparable neighboring U.S. state. This implies that borders matter substantially. In another illustration outside the context of the EU enlargement, Frankel and Rose (2000) find that joining a free-trade area triples a country's trade with other members of the free-trade area and that joining a currency union triples trade once more. This would imply that our estimates provide a lower bound on the trade effects of enlargement, especially if one believes that membership in the EMU will be the next step for the CEECs after accession to the EU.

8.3.3 Free Movement of Labor

Regarding the impact of EU enlargement on migration, we rely on a study conducted by Boeri and Brücker (2000).[11] Boeri and Brücker use historical immigration figures for Germany to estimate migration as a function of wage differentials, employment differentials, and a set of dummy variables. By substituting current wages and employment levels and assuming free movement of labor from the first day of accession, the authors compute the likely implications of EU enlargement for German immigration from the CEECs. These figures are then extrapolated to the other EU countries on the basis of historical migration patterns between the CEECs and individual EU countries.

Assuming accession in 2002 for the ten candidate member states, Boeri and Brücker predict an inflow of 335,000 immigrants to the current EU member states in the first year after accession. This flow gradually declines in subsequent years. In 2030, the stock of migrants in the current EU countries will have grown to four million, which is approximately 4 percent of the total population in the CEECs.

A nice feature of the study by Boeri and Brücker is that it gives an indication of the origin and destination of migrants. For instance, it suggests that 30 percent of all migrants from CEECs to current EU countries after CEEC accession will originate from Poland, 7.5 percent from Hungary, and the remainder from the other accession countries. These shares depend not only on the size of countries, but also on the incentives for migration, determined by wage levels and employment rates. As the income gaps between Poland and Hungary and the current EU members are smaller than those between the CEEC5 and current EU members, migration shares are somewhat lower for Hungary and Poland than their population sizes might suggest at first glance. Among migrants from the CEECs after CEEC accession, 65 percent will move to Germany, 2.5 percent to France, 4 percent to the United Kingdom, 1 percent to the Netherlands, 7.5 percent to Southern Europe, and 20 percent to the rest of Europe. Of this last group, approximately 12 percent of the immigrants will go to Austria.

We use the figures reported by Boeri and Brücker in constructing our own migration experiment. In particular, we simulate in the next section the implications of an exogenous migration impulse using World-Scan. Hence, we do not take into account endogenous feedback effects on migration (e.g., that due to wage convergence or changes in regional unemployment). Our immigration scenario in Worldscan differs from the migration flows reported by Boeri and Brücker in two important ways. First, we assume accession in 2004 for Poland and Hungary and 2007 for the other CEECs. We therefore adjust the aggregate figures derived by Boeri and Brücker according to our differentiated accession pattern. Secondly, we evaluate the implications for migration in the year 2020, whereas the estimates by Boeri and Brücker suggest that migration will continue until 2030. Hence, we do not capture the entire migration impulse reported in their study. In this way, we arrive at a total stock of immigrants in the EU of 2.4 million in 2020 (see table 8.7).[12]

8.4   Economic Impact of Enlargement

This section explores the economic implications of the three shocks discussed in the previous section by running simulations with the WorldScan model. For all three simulations, we consider the macroeconomic implications, namely, the effects on real GDP, the volume of private consumption, the equivalent variation, and the terms of trade. The equivalent variation best reflects the welfare effects of enlarge-

Table 8.7
Migration by source and destination in 2020

	Thousands of persons	Percentage of population
CEEC7	−2,400	−2.3
Hungary	−750	−2.0
Poland	−150	−2.0
CEEC5	−1,500	−3.5
EU15	2,400	0.6
Germany	1,575	2.0
France	60	0.1
United Kingdom	100	0.2
Netherlands	25	0.2
South Europe	180	0.2
Rest of EU	460	1.2

Source: Boeri et al. 2000 and authors' calculations.

ment. The effect on consumption may differ from the implications for real GDP because of terms-of-trade effects, changes in wealth, and changes in savings behavior. For the first two simulations (i.e. the customs union and the internal market), we also analyze the sectoral implications by looking at the relative changes in production in our sixteen industry sectors.[13]

In the experiments below, we assume that Poland and Hungary enter the EU in 2004 and the CEEC5 in 2007. All shocks are implemented gradually. The effects are evaluated in the year 2020, when a new stable equilibrium is achieved.[14]

8.4.1 Toward a Customs Union

In our first experiment, we simulate the implications of the elimination of bilateral tariffs reported in table 8.3 and the adoption of the CET by the CEECs. To explain the macroeconomic implications of this move toward a customs union, we first discuss the channels through which it affects the economies in WorldScan. In particular, the abolishment of formal trade barriers between the CEECs and the current EU members has two effects. First, it affects relative prices of intermediate inputs and final goods. This changes the demand for different goods from different origins, leading to trade creation and trade diversion. In particular, without import tariffs and export subsidies in agriculture and food processing, prices will better reflect relative scarcities, so that countries can better exploit the gains from trade. Trade creation will cause a reallocation in production in all countries, resulting in efficiency improvements and an associated expansion in output. The increase in bilateral trade may also come at the expense of trade with third countries, which is referred to as trade diversion.

The second effect of abolishing formal trade barriers involves the terms of trade, that is, the price of exports relative to the price of imports. In particular, the abolishment of export subsidies will reduce the supply of exports and therefore raise producer prices. This will cause a terms-of-trade gain for the country that abolishes its export subsidy on a particular product and a terms-of-trade loss for other countries that do not. In contrast, abolishing import tariffs will improve the terms of trade for countries that export their goods to the market in which the tariffs are abolished but will involve a terms-of-trade loss for the country that abolishes the tariffs. Although an improvement in the terms of trade may have adverse effects on the production of a country, it can improve welfare in that country, since it raises the value of its produced goods relative to imported goods. This welfare gain will be reflected in a higher volume of consumption.

Trade creation and terms-of-trade improvements may also raise the rate of return to capital. This will encourage savings, raise the inflow of foreign direct investment, and thus boost capital formation. This may further raise production. Moreover, changes in the external tariffs in manufacturing can affect the price of investment goods (fabricated metal products, machinery and equipment, electronic and transport equipment, and construction delivered by other services). This can increase the incentive to invest, since the cost of capital declines. The CEECs in particular import a substantial amount of investment goods, for which prices will fall.

8.4.1.1 Macro-economic Effects

Table 8.8 shows the macro-economic effects of a customs union formed between the CEECs and the current EU members. Overall, we find that the CEEC7 experience an increase in GDP and consumption of 2.5 and 2.3 percent, respectively. Welfare increases by about $US15.9 billion, which equals 1.9 percent of GDP. Consumption and GDP in the EU hardly change, but third countries benefit slightly (although this is not visible in the figures given in the table). Compared to the effects of

Table 8.8
Macro-economic impact of customs union (in percent, 2020)

	GDP	Consumption	Equivalent variation	Terms of trade
CEEC7	2.5	2.3	15.9	−0.3
Hungary	1.9	2.6	2.5	1.1
Poland	4.3	3.6	10.5	−0.9
CEEC5	1.0	0.9	2.8	−0.3
EU15	0.0	0.0	−0.8	0.0
Germany	0.0	0.0	0.9	0.0
France	−0.2	−0.2	−4.1	0.0
United Kingdom	0.0	0.1	1.5	0.1
Netherlands	0.0	0.1	0.5	0.1
South Europe	0.0	0.0	−0.3	0.0
Rest of EU	0.0	0.0	0.6	0.0
Third countries	0.0	0.0	3.2	0.0
Rest of OECD	0.0	0.0	6.9	0.1
Former Soviet Union	0.0	0.0	0.3	0.1
ROW	0.0	0.0	−3.9	−0.1

Note: GDP and Consumption in volumes; EV = equivalent variation in billions of U.S. dollars, 1997 prices; wage ratio = low-skilled wage/high-skilled wage. Figures refer to percentage changes, except for the EV which is measured in billion U.S. dollars, in 1997 prices.

the Europe Agreements, the effects of a customs union are of similar size.

Behind these aggregate figures, there are some important differences among countries. The third column of table 8.8 reveals that Poland and the CEEC5 experience a terms-of-trade loss as a result of the customs union. This loss results from the abolishment of export subsidies by the EU and the relatively large reduction in external tariffs by Poland and the CEEC5. The terms-of-trade loss shows that the change in GDP in these countries under a customs union exceeds that in consumption. The abolishment of the large initial price distortions in Poland, however, renders the Polish efficiency gains from trade creation also relatively large. Furthermore, the lower investment prices induce extra capital accumulation. Accordingly, the GDP effect in Poland is relatively large.

In contrast to Poland and the CEEC5, Hungary experiences a terms-of-trade gain, because both Hungary's current import tariffs vis à vis the EU and its external tariffs are lower than those of Poland and the CEEC5 (see tables 8.3 and 8.4). The Hungarian external tariffs are sometimes even lower than the CET of the EU (in agriculture, food processing, and metals) so that accession to the EU actually involves an increase in the Hungarian external tariff. The terms-of-trade improvement for Hungary, together with the positive effects of trade creation, are responsible for an increase in consumption and GDP by, respectively 2.6 and 1.9 percent in that country. These effects are smaller than those for Poland, partly because the initial bilateral tariffs between the EU and Hungary are lower (so that less efficiency improvements can be reaped) and partly because the price of investment goods in Hungary falls less than in Poland.

The macro-economic effects of a customs union for EU countries are relatively small. The small decline in GDP (not visible in the figures reported in the table) is due to lower export subsidies, which reduce the export of agricultural and food products from the EU. Lower export subsidies, however, are also responsible for a terms-of-trade gain for the EU. Consequently, consumption in the EU does not decline. Hence, the gains for the accession countries are accompanied by negligible welfare effects for the EU.

8.4.1.2 Sectoral Effects

Although the macro-economic effects of a customs union are modest, the implications are more significant for particular industries. Table 8.9 presents the relative changes in output for our sixteen industries as a result of the move toward a customs union.

We see in examining the figures in the table that the largest changes in output occur in agriculture and food processing,[15] because tariffs change most in these sectors. In Poland, a substantially lower external tariff in the agriculture sector as a result of accession makes imports from third countries cheaper. Consequently, we observe a shift out of agricultural production in Poland, but not in Hungary, which has already adopted lower import tariffs. Indeed, for Hungary, the positive effect of better access to the EU market dominates the effect of cheaper imports from third countries. The external tariff in the Hungarian food-processing sector also declines. Despite the cheaper imports, however, production in this sector does not fall, but instead rises, in the CEECs. The reason is twofold. First, lower tariffs in agriculture reduce the cost of an important intermediary input for food processing. This makes the

Table 8.9
Sectoral effects of a customs union

	Hun-gary	Poland	CEEC5	Ger-many	Nether-lands	South Europe
Agriculture	15.7	−0.4	0.9	−0.0	2.0	−0.4
Raw materials	−4.4	−2.0	−0.1	0.2	−0.1	−0.1
Food processing	56.2	29.9	10.6	−1.8	−1.2	−0.9
Textiles and leather	−7.8	−1.2	0.7	−0.4	−0.5	−0.2
Non-metallic minerals	−4.1	−0.5	−0.5	0.2	−0.3	−0.1
Energy-intensive products	−2.0	−0.8	−0.1	0.2	−0.2	−0.1
Other manufacturing	−4.6	1.8	−0.6	0.0	−0.3	−0.1
Metals	−3.7	−3.0	−1.0	0.2	−0.3	−0.1
Fabricated metal	−6.8	−1.7	−0.7	0.1	−0.2	−0.0
Machinery and equipment	−3.5	−1.4	−0.7	0.2	−0.2	−0.1
Electronic equipment	−0.9	−0.7	0.4	0.1	−0.3	−0.0
Transport equipment	−1.8	0.5	−0.3	0.0	−0.2	−0.3
Trade services	1.1	2.7	0.2	0.0	−0.0	−0.1
Transport and communication	−0.4	1.4	0.0	0.2	0.2	0.1
Financial services	−0.0	1.5	−0.2	0.0	−0.0	−0.1
Other services	0.7	1.7	0.3	−0.0	0.0	0.0

Note: Table presents percentage change in production in 2020 compared to baseline.

food-processing industry more competitive. Second, the removal of bilateral tariffs with the EU boosts exports to the EU. These two effects dominate the decline in tariff protection against producers from third countries and from the EU. As a result, the food-processing sector expands in all CEECs.

The external tariffs in the CEECs decline in all manufacturing sectors. The lower price of imported products exerts a small negative effect on the production of these sectors in the CEECs. Moreover, the production effect in the manufacturing sector also reflects a shift of labor and capital inputs toward food processing and, in case of Hungary, agriculture. Since the expansion of the agriculture and food-processing sectors is largest in Hungary, we also observe the largest decline in manufacturing production in that country.

In the EU countries, the sectoral implications of a customs union are much smaller than in the CEECs. The abolishment of export subsidies in agriculture and food processing, together with the lower external tariffs in the CEECs, tend to reduce EU exports to the CEECs. Indeed, EU production in food processing declines in all EU countries. In agriculture, only production in the Netherlands expands. In most manufacturing sectors in the southern EU countries and in the Netherlands, production drops slightly. In Germany, manufacturing sectors expand.

8.4.2 Accession to the Internal Market

We now explore the implications of the accession of the CEECs to the internal market by simulating a gradual abolishment of the NTBs presented in table 8.5. Since NTBs are very similar to formal import tariffs, the channels through which NTBs affect the economies in WorldScan are also similar to those through which formal import tariffs have their effects. Hence, the abolishment of NTBs changes relative prices, generates trade creation and trade diversion, changes the terms of trade, and affects the incentives to invest. There are, however, two major differences between tariffs and NTBs in regard to their effects. First, in contrast to tariffs, NTBs involve income effects, since they reflect real trade costs (e.g., waiting time at borders or the time devoted to customs formalities). In particular, NTBs are modeled as iceberg costs, the idea being that a share of the commodities melts away during the phase of trade. Removing these costs will typically cause a terms-of-trade gain in both countries involved in the trade. To understand this, note that we measure the terms of trade as the price of exports relative to imports that holds just outside the domestic border. For imports, the price includes the iceberg costs and is inclusive of c.i.f.—cost, insurance, freight—but not import taxes. For exports the price is f.o.b. (free on board) and includes export taxes but excludes the iceberg costs. Lower NTBs can thus raise the price of exports relative to imports in both countries.

The second difference between import tariffs and the NTBs is that NTBs, unlike tariffs, are symmetric between the EU and the CEECs. Hence, abolishing the iceberg tariffs implies that each sector experiences two shocks: fiercer competition on the home market as the relative price of foreign varieties falls, and a better competitive position on the foreign market.

8.4.2.1 Macro-economic Effects
The macro-economic effects of CEEC accession to the internal market are presented in table 8.10. The table reveals that indeed the CEECs

Table 8.10
Macro-economic effects of CEEC accession to internal market (in percent)

	GDP	Consump-tion	Equivalent variation	Terms of trade	Capital stock	Wage ratio
CEEC7	5.3	9.3	67.6	6.7	9.0	1.2
Hungary	9.0	13.8	13.8	7.1	15.8	1.0
Poland	5.8	9.0	27.3	6.9	9.2	1.1
CEEC5	3.4	8.2	26.5	6.7	6.5	1.4
EU15	0.1	0.2	28.7	0.6	0.2	0.0
Germany	0.1	0.4	12.0	1.2	0.3	0.0
France	0.1	0.1	2.9	0.3	0.1	−0.1
United Kingdom	0.0	0.1	1.6	0.3	0.1	0.0
Netherlands	0.1	0.4	1.7	0.5	0.4	0.1
South Europe	0.1	0.2	6.3	0.7	0.2	−0.1
Rest of EU	0.1	0.3	4.1	0.6	0.3	0.0
Third countries	0.0	0.0	−3.9	0.0	0.0	0.0
Rest of OECD	0.0	0.0	0.9	0.0	0.0	0.0
Former Soviet Union	0.0	0.0	0.2	0.1	0.0	0.0
ROW	0.0	0.0	−5.1	0.0	−0.1	0.0

Note: See figure 8.8 for an explanation of the variables.

experience a terms-of-trade gain of 6.7 percent as a result of accession, and the EU also experiences a (smaller) gain of 0.6 percent. The difference in the magnitude of the terms-of-trade effect between the CEECs and the EU is due to the large share of total CEEC trade share that trade with the EU accounts for, as compared to the much smaller share of trade with the CEECs in total EU trade.

The macro-economic implications of accession to the internal market are substantial for the CEECs. On average, GDP and consumption increase by 5.3 and 9.3 percent, respectively. The increase in GDP for Hungary is 9 percent, and GDP in Poland and the CEEC5 increases by 5.8 and 3.4 percent, respectively. For all countries, consumption growth is greater than the growth in GDP because of the terms-of-trade gain. For Hungary, the extra consumption growth due to accession to the internal market is almost 1 percent annually (between 2004 and 2020). For the CEEC5, the increase is about 0.5 percent per year (calculated, for comparability, between 2004 and 2020). Welfare increases by $US67.6 billion in the CEECs. The increase in welfare is larger for Poland and the CEEC5 than for Hungary, because of the size of the economy of the former countries. Further calculations indicate that as a percentage of GDP the equivalent variation in Hungary, Poland, and the CEEC5 rises by 11.5, 7.6, and 7.6, respectively. The average welfare gain is 8.1 for the CEEC7. For the EU, we find that welfare rises by 0.2 percent.

The macro-economic effects of CEEC accession operate through three mechanisms. First, changes in the relative prices imply that countries can better exploit their comparative advantages, which increases production efficiency and welfare. The efficiency gain induces more capital accumulation and an increase in production. Second, the terms-of-trade gain raises welfare, as the consumption volume can increase, ceteris paribus. In particular, a smaller share of GDP is used to cover trade costs and can instead be used for consumption. Third, the terms-of-trade gain as such raises the price of output relative to the cost of capital. Consequently, it raises the rate of return to investment in the CEECs. This contributes to capital formation, as shown in the fourth column of table 8.10, and increases production. These dynamic efficiency gains are important for the macroeconomic impact. Keuschnigg, Keuschnigg, and Kohler (2001) also stressed the importance of capital accumulation for the GDP effects of the EU enlargement.

The final column of table 8.10 reveals that low-skilled wages increase in the CEECs as a result of accession relative to high-skilled wages, because the CEECs have abundant low-skilled labor. Once trade barriers have been removed, the CEECs can better exploit their comparative advantages and thus specialize in sectors that are intensive in the use of low-skilled labor, such as textiles and leather and food processing. Accordingly, the demand for low-skilled labor in the CEECs increases relative to that for high-skilled labor, so that their relative wage rate rises as well. For the EU, the opposite occurs: EU countries specialize more in sectors that are intensive in high-skilled labor, so that the wage rate of low-skilled labor falls relative to that of high-skilled labor.

The macro-economic effects of accession to the internal market (table 8.10) are substantially larger than those for the customs union (in table 8.8) and for the Europe Agreements. Indeed, the GDP effects for the CEECs are about twice the size of the effects of the Europe Agreements. Measured in consumption levels, the difference is even more pronounced. The main reason for these large effects is that the shock derived in section 8.3.2 is large compared to the formal barriers to trade. Furthermore, accession to the internal market refers to a reduction in real trade costs, whereas formal trade barriers reflect distortions in relative prices accompanied by public revenues (which are recycled to the private sector).

Our results for the economic implications of accession to the internal market are also larger than those that previous studies have reported (see, e.g., Baldwin, Francois, and Portes 1997; Brown et al. 1997; Breuss 2001). These studies simulated a uniform 5 or 10 percent reduction in trade costs to explore the impact of CEEC accession to the internal market. Such a shock is no more than an eyeball view on accession to the internal market, however. In contrast, our approach is based on the empirical findings of sixteen gravity estimations. As discussed in section 8.3, the weighted average of our NTBs suggests a reduction in real trade costs as a result of CEEC accession of around 7 percent. The large effects we find as a result of accession to the internal market are mainly due to the dynamic effects of increased capital accumulation. Indeed, a major part of the GDP increases is due to additional investment associated with a higher return to capital and a lower producer cost of investment goods. These dynamic efficiency gains have not always been fully captured in previous studies.

The effects of accession on consumption and GDP for Hungary are larger than those for Poland and CEEC5 for three reasons. First, the trade shock for Hungary resulting from accession is relatively large, as Hungary has a comparative advantage in sectors that experience the largest decline in NTBs under accession (see table 8.5). Second, Hungary is relatively open, so that a larger share of its GDP is affected by the removal of NTBs. Third, Hungary expands as a result of accession in sectors that are relatively capital intensive. Accordingly, the capital stock expands substantially.

The effects of CEEC accession to the internal market for the EU countries are relatively small: EU GDP rises by less than 0.1 percent. The effect of CEEC accession differs among EU members, however. Germany and the Netherlands experience the largest gains, as they specialize in different sectors than the CEECs. Countries with export specialties in the same sectors as the CEECs, such as textiles and leather, feature smaller gains. Third countries lose from EU enlargement because of trade diversion.

8.4.2.2 Sectoral Effects

To understand the sectoral effects of enlargement of the internal market, we refer to two types of shock that can occur in any sector as a result of enlargement. First, an industry in which an NTB is abolished faces fiercer competition in the home market for its product, as the price of varieties from the EU falls relative to domestic varieties. This causes a shift in consumer demand away from domestic varieties, leading to a higher import intensity. The drop in demand for domestically produced commodities lowers the producer price, which causes a shift in resources away from the sector in which the NTB is abolished. The lower producer price also exerts an upward effect on the export intensity.

The second shock that results from the removal of an NTB is that the EU lowers its tariffs on products in the sector from which the NTB has been removed. This reduces the relative consumer price of CEEC varieties of those products in the EU, causing a higher demand for these varieties. This in turn exerts an upward effect on the CEEC producer price, which attracts resources to the sector.

Via various linkages of consumption demand, investment demand, and intermediate-input demand, enlargement of the internal market can exert an impact, through the two channels just described, on the entire sectoral structure of the CEEC economies. On balance, a sector in a CEEC is likely to expand as a result of internal-market enlargement if an NTB to trade in that sector is abolished and if that sector exports a large share of its production toward the EU. If a sector produces primarily for the home market, however, cheaper varieties from the EU may render the impact of enlargement on production in that sector negative.

In addition to the two demand effects above, the removal of NTBs also exerts a supply effect, because the resulting reduction in real trade costs changes input prices for two reasons. First, lower real trade costs reduce the price of intermediate inputs, so that production costs fall. Second, via Stolper-Samuelson factor price effects, production costs might change further.

How all these forces play out in the model depends on the details of input-output structure, comparative advantages, trade intensity of sectors, and so forth. The model consistently links these aspects and can thus tell us how the various channels ultimately affect the output structure. The results are presented in table 8.11.

In general, table 8.11 reveals that the production share in most service sectors falls in the CEECs as a result of CEEC accession to the internal market relative to food processing and textiles and leather. Also, production in the electronic equipment and transport equipment sec-

Table 8.11
Sectoral effects of CEEC accession to the internal market

	Hungary	Poland	CEEC5	Germany	Netherlands	South Europe
Agriculture	2.7	0.6	0.9	−0.4	3.5	−0.4
Raw materials	−10.8	−8.9	−5.6	0.2	0.2	0.3
Food processing	34.8	34.0	10.1	−2.6	−1.7	−0.7
Textiles and leather	34.0	47.0	52.1	3.7	2.0	−2.2
Non-metallic minerals	−2.3	−6.6	4.0	−0.4	−1.0	0.4
Energy-intensive products	−5.4	−4.0	−2.6	0.6	0.4	0.4
Other manufacturing	7.1	−2.9	−6.8	0.8	0.1	0.5
Metals	2.6	−11.7	−5.5	0.9	0.8	0.9
Fabricated metal products	−2.3	−3.3	0.3	0.3	−0.2	0.5
Machinery and equipment	22.9	−4.5	−1.0	1.0	0.6	0.9
Electronic equipment	70.3	27.5	8.4	−0.3	−0.9	−0.5
Transport equipment	68.2	29.3	42.9	−0.4	−0.7	−1.1
Trade services	7.8	7.2	2.8	0.1	0.1	0.2
Transport and communication	2.1	0.7	−4.5	0.5	0.6	0.5
Financial services	1.7	0.3	−0.5	0.2	0.2	0.1
Other services	6.1	4.0	1.9	0.2	0.1	0.1

Note: Table presents percentage change in production in 2020 compared to baseline.

tors increases substantially in the CEECs. The increases in the production of these sectors come at the expense of production in other sectors, such as energy-intensive products, raw materials, and fabricated metal products. Below, we discuss the sectoral production effects of CEEC accession in more detail.

Table 8.11 also reveals that the reduction in the NTB by 14.5 percent (see table 8.5) raises the production of textiles substantially in all CEECs, mainly because of the strong export orientation of this sector. To illustrate, Hungary exports roughly 70 percent of its total textile production.[16] Hence, the effect of increased access to the EU market for textiles dominates the effect of cheaper EU textile products on the Hungarian market.

In agriculture, output growth as a result of CEEC accession to the internal market is only marginal in the CEECs. The agriculture sector's share in total value added even shrinks. The explanation is that via

CEEC accession, the EU gains access to the CEECs' markets for agricultural products, whereas in the CEECs, the agriculture sector largely produces for the home market (the initial export ratios for Poland and the CEEC5 are less than 5 percent; for Hungary, the ratio is around 15 percent). The food-processing sector is similar in structure to the agriculture sector, although somewhat more export oriented. In a way similar to their removal in agriculture, the removal of NTBs in the food-processing sector implies a substantial reduction in trade costs. In contrast to what occurs in the agricultural sector, however, this generates a strong growth in the production of the food-processing sector. The reason for the difference in effects of NTB removal between the agriculture and food-processing sectors is that the price of the food-processing sector's most important intermediate input, namely, agricultural goods, falls substantially when NTBs in the food-processing sector are removed.

The bilateral real trade cost in the sectors machinery and equipment, electronic equipment, and transport equipment fall under accession to the internal market. This causes a substantial production increase in these sectors in Hungary, especially because these sectors are export intensive (the export share for these sectors in Hungary ranges from 70 to 85 percent of production). Since the export shares of these industries in Poland are much smaller (the shares range from 22 to 32 percent), the production increases in that country as result of internal-market accession are also smaller. In the machinery and equipment sector, production in Poland even contracts. The same holds true for the CEEC5.

In the service sectors, we observe small production increases as a result of CEEC accession. In terms of total value added, however, the shares of these four industries shrink, because real trade costs do not fall in two of the service sectors (transport and communication and financial services), and the sectors in which these costs do fall are largely non-tradable. For instance, the trade services sector includes the retail sector, and the other-services sector includes, among others, construction. These sectors have low shares in total exports. The impact on these sectors is therefore determined by the input-output links and the relative profitability of these sectors compared to agricultural and manufacturing sectors. Since most tradable sectors gain in importance under CEEC accession, we observe a shift in value added away from the service sectors. Since GDP increases in aggregate terms, however, these sectors nevertheless grow in terms of output.

In many EU countries, we observe a sectoral pattern that is opposite from that of the CEECs. Indeed, the production of food processing, electronic equipment, and transport equipment typically shrink in the EU as a result of CEEC accession. The production of textiles falls in Southern Europe and France (not reported in the table), but not in Germany and the Netherlands. The expansion in Germany, the Netherlands, and Southern European countries in the machinery and equipment sector is due to increased investment demand from the CEECs. In the Netherlands, agricultural production increases with CEEC accession, as the country is already a big exporter of agricultural products and can exploit its comparative advantage in new markets in the CEECs. Also, Dutch production in the transport and communication sector increases as a result of CEEC accession, whereas its production in the food-processing and electronic equipment sectors decreases.

So far we have not paid much attention to changes in factor markets. It is, however, worth noting that the CEECs' reallocation of production to the tradable (and unskilled-labor-intensive) sectors after CEEC accession causes the relative wage of unskilled labor to rise in all CEECs. As a consequence, production becomes increasingly skilled-labor-intensive in these countries. Production also becomes more capital intensive as the relative price of investment goods falls.

8.4.3 Free Movement of Labor

We now explore the economic implications of the migration shock presented in table 8.7. In doing so, we assume that the composition of migrants in regard to high-skilled and low-skilled workers is equal to the composition of workers in the EU. Section 8.5 performs a sensitivity assumption with respect to this assumption. Table 8.12 shows the economic implications of the migration shock.

Table 8.12 reveals that GDP per capita rises in the CEECs because of the reduced supply of labor as a result of migration to the EU countries, as capital is not perfectly mobile across countries. Hence, the lower supply of labor increases the capital-labor ratio in these countries. This raises the marginal product of labor and thereby raises wages. For similar reasons, GDP per capita in Germany and the rest of the EU decreases. Indeed, the lower capital-labor ratio causes a decline in the productivity of labor in these countries and thus a decrease in wages.[17] The effect remains small, however, because of the modest

Table 8.12
Economic effects of migration (percentage changes)

	Popula-tion	Wage ratio	GDP per capita	GDP	Consump-tion	Terms of trade
CEEC7				−1.8	−1.3	0.3
Hungary	−2.1	0.0	0.8	−1.3	−1.0	0.2
Poland	−1.9	0.0	0.6	−1.4	−1.1	0.3
CEEC5	−3.4	0.1	1.1	−2.3	−1.8	0.4
EU15				0.6	0.5	−0.1
Germany	2.0	0.0	−0.4	1.5	1.3	−0.2
France	0.1	0.0	0.0	0.1	0.1	0.0
United Kingdom	0.2	0.0	0.0	0.1	0.1	0.0
Netherlands	0.2	0.0	0.0	0.1	0.1	0.0
South Europe	0.2	0.0	0.0	0.1	0.1	0.0
Rest of EU	1.2	0.0	−0.2	0.9	0.8	−0.1

Note: GDP and Consumption measured in volumes; wage ratio = low-skilled wage/high-skilled wage.

increase in the population size. In other EU countries, immigration has a negligible impact on per capita income because of the small number of immigrants. The effect on the relative wages is negligible in all countries, because we assume that the composition of migrants in terms of skill levels is identical to that of the destination country.

The total volume of GDP drops in all CEECs by about 1.8 percent because of the outflow of labor. In Germany it increases by 1.5 percent. GDP in the other EU countries rises only slightly. The effects on consumption are smaller than those on GDP, because of changes in the terms of trade. In particular, lower wages in Germany and the rest of the EU exert a downward pressure on producer prices. The opposite holds for the accession countries. This renders the terms-of-trade effect positive for the CEECs and negative for the EU countries, with a positive effect on consumption in the CEECs and a negative effect in the EU.

The small effects of migration on GDP per capita are consistent with empirical evidence on the wage effects of immigration. In particular, Bauer and Zimmermann (1999) present a survey of the literature on the wage effects of immigration and conclude that immigrants have only a negligible negative impact on native wages.

8.5   Sensitivity Analysis

This section performs sensitivity analysis on some of the findings of the previous section. In particular, some assumptions in section 8.3.2 on the internal market can be subject to debate and thus require further elaboration. Indeed, by exploring alternative assumptions, we are able to test the robustness of our results. Furthermore, by analyzing the economic implications under extreme assumptions, this section gives us an impression of the range in which the impact of the accession to the internal market will fall. Apart from sensitivity analysis of the internal-market simulation, we also explore alternative assumptions regarding the migration effect.

To keep the presentation in this section transparent, we do not report all outcomes in the same detail as in the previous section. Instead, we concentrate on the most relevant countries for our purpose (the CEECs, Germany, the Netherlands, and Southern Europe) and the most sensitive sectors in the context of enlargement (agriculture, food processing, and textiles and leather).

8.5.1   No Internal Market for Agriculture and Food

In section 8.4.2, we simulate a removal of NTBs for all industries for which we found a significant coefficient on the EU dummy (see section 8.3.2). It is uncertain, however, how EU policy regarding the agricultural and food sectors will be applied after enlargement. One way to shed light on this is to assume a policy that somehow prevents free trade in the products from these sectors. Measures that maintain the current trade barriers—initiated by either the EU or the accession countries—might indeed be part of an agreement on the terms of accession to the EU. To get an impression of the implications of such an agreement, we simulate a removal of the NTBs in all sectors except for agriculture and food processing. The effects are presented in the second panel of table 8.13 (the first panel repeats the results from section 8.4.2).

The second panel of table 8.13 reveals that the effects on the terms of trade are smaller than in section 8.4.2, that is, smaller than when the NTBs in agriculture and food processing are also abolished. Also, the effect on consumption somewhat smaller in the CEECs than before. For the EU15, in contrast, the effects are comparable to those in section 8.4.2.

Table 8.13
Sensitivity analysis internal market simulation (percentage changes)

	Consumption	Terms of trade	Agriculture	Food	Textile
NTBs abolished (reference scenario)					
CEEC7	9.3	6.7			
Hungary	13.8	7.1	2.7	34.8	34.0
Poland	9.0	6.9	0.6	34.0	47.0
CEEC5	8.2	6.7	0.9	10.1	52.1
EU15	0.2	0.6			
Germany	0.4	1.2	−0.4	−2.6	3.7
Netherlands	0.4	0.5	3.5	−1.7	2.0
Southern Europe	0.2	0.7	−0.4	−0.7	−2.2
NTBs for agriculture and food not abolished					
CEEC7	7.0	5.3			
Hungary	10.6	5.3	−9.7	−7.6	42.7
Poland	6.1	5.0	−5.6	−5.3	56.2
CEEC5	6.6	5.6	−4.5	−4.6	52.4
EU15	0.2	0.5			
Germany	0.3	1.0	0.3	0.8	3.1
Netherlands	0.3	0.4	0.4	0.7	1.9
Southern Europe	0.2	0.5	0.4	0.2	−2.8
NTBs determined by point estimate					
CEEC7	9.7	7.0			
Hungary	14.3	7.3	2.7	35.1	34.5
Poland	9.3	7.1	0.7	34.1	47.3
CEEC5	8.6	7.0	1.0	10.1	52.5
EU15	0.3	0.7			
Germany	0.4	1.2	−0.4	−2.6	3.7
Netherlands	0.4	0.5	3.5	−1.7	2.0
Southern Europe	0.2	0.7	−0.4	−0.7	−2.2
NTBs modeled as tariffs					
CEEC7	3.9	0.7			
Hungary	6.6	1.2	6.1	41.4	50.0
Poland	3.8	0.3	3.4	40.8	62.1
CEEC5	3.0	1.1	3.2	12.8	67.3
EU15	0.1	0.0			
Germany	0.1	0.1	−0.0	−2.5	6.1
Netherlands	0.1	0.1	4.6	−1.4	3.3
Southern Europe	0.0	−0.0	0.1	−0.7	−1.5

The sectoral effects for the CEECs differ to a large extent from those in section 8.4.2. Production in agriculture and food processing no longer increases but instead decreases in the CEECs, because the NTBs imposed by the EU are not abolished, so the CEECs do not get access to the EU market. The value added to agriculture and food processing declines because low-skilled labor in the CEECs moves from agriculture and food processing toward expanding sectors, such as textiles and leather, for which the EU market is opened. Indeed, the sectoral production effects in textiles and leather are larger than in section 8.4.2.

8.5.2   Nontariff Barriers Set at Their Point Estimates

In section 8.4.2, we set the NTBs equal to zero if the coefficient of the EU dummy in table 8.5 is insignificant at the 5 percent confidence level. This cutoff point seems most natural but may be somewhat abrupt. To analyze the sensitivity of our results to this assumption, we simulate an abolishment of NTBs as they are determined by their point estimate of the EU dummy in table 8.5. If we find a negative coefficient for the EU dummy in a sector, we set it equal to zero, because higher real trade costs resulting from accession to the internal market seem implausible. The tariffs for energy-intensive goods, other manufacturing, and transport and communication are set at 2, 1, and 1 percent, respectively. As a result, the sectoral-weighted average of the NTB increases by 0.5 percent for the CEECs and 0.4 percent for the EU. Given the size of these tariffs, it is obvious that the results do not change much, as we observe from the third panel of table 8.13.

8.5.3   Nontariff Barriers Reflect Tariffs

So far, we have assumed that the NTBs imposed on trade involve real trade costs. Hence, they exert both substitution effects, by changing relative prices, and income effects. One could argue, however, that at least a fraction of the barriers that we have estimated involve no income effects. For instance, one can think of bribes that are connected to import and export licenses, exchange controls, and tax assessments. Moreover, accession to the internal market could also reduce trade insurance premiums. We therefore explore an alternative form of NTBs in which income effects are entirely eliminated. In particular, we model the NTBs as import tariffs, the revenues of which are recycled to the private sector in a lump-sum fashion. This effectively eliminates the income effects associated with the removal of real trade costs. The results are given in the final panel of table 8.13.

The results are qualitatively similar to those in the reference scenario. In quantitative terms, however, the results of the two scenarios differ substantially. The most pressing differences concern the changes in the terms of trade. If a country has export specialties in those sectors in which the price increases are largest, it will experience a terms-of-trade gain. The results in table 8.10 suggest that the CEECs typically have a comparative advantage in sectors that are substantially affected by accession to the internal market, such as textiles, machinery and equipment, and trade services. Also, the Netherlands and Germany appear to have comparative advantages such that EU enlargement exerts a terms-of-trade gain for them. Southern Europe experiences a marginal terms-of-trade loss.

The sectoral pattern differs somewhat from that in the reference scenario because of a different macro-economic picture. As the tariff reduction does not involve an income effect, but only a distortion in relative prices, the GDP and consumption effects are smaller. At a lower consumption level (as compared to the benchmark simulation), households feature a somewhat different consumption pattern, since income elasticities are not equal to unity. In particular, at lower incomes, households demand a larger share of food and agricultural goods. This explains the more positive production growth in these sectors.

8.5.4 Migration of Low-Skilled Labor

The final sensitivity analysis refers to the migration effects. Section 8.4.3 assumes that migrants from the CEECs have the same skill level as natives in the EU. It is indeed true that the skill level of workers in the CEECs is high from the perspective of those countries' economic development, that is, compared to countries at a similar level of GDP per capita. Migrants from the CEECs, however, will probably have relatively low skills as compared to natives in the EU. Moreover, because skills acquired in the CEECs are not always productive in the EU, immigrants from the CEECs to the EU15 may end up primarily in low-skilled jobs. To explore the sensitivity of our simulation to the skill composition of migrants, we run a simulation in which we assume that all immigrants from the CEECs are low skilled. This extreme assumption is intended to explore the robustness of our assumption of the

Table 8.14
Sensitivity analysis: Migration (percentage changes)

	Popula-tion	Wage ratio	GDP per capita	GDP	Consump-tion	Terms of trade
CEEC7				−1.4	−1.0	0.3
Hungary	−2.1	3.2	1.0	−1.1	−0.8	0.2
Poland	−1.9	3.1	0.9	−1.1	−0.9	0.2
CEEC5	−3.4	5.5	1.6	−1.9	−1.4	0.4
EU15				0.5	0.4	−0.1
Germany	2.0	−3.0	−0.8	1.2	1.0	−0.2
Netherlands	0.2	−0.2	0.0	0.1	0.1	0.0
Southern Europe	0.2	−0.3	−0.1	0.1	0.1	0.0
Rest of EU	1.2	−1.8	−0.4	0.7	0.6	−0.1

Note: GDP and Consumption in volumes; wage ratio = low-skilled wage/high-skilled wage.

previous section that migrants from the CEECs have the same skill level as those native to the recipient country. Table 8.14 reports the result of this alternative migration scenario.

We observe from the table that the outflow of low-skilled workers from the CEECs raises the ratio of low- to high-skilled wages in this region. Indeed, low-skilled workers in the CEECs become scarcer relative to high-skilled workers, so that the wages of the two groups tend to converge. The opposite holds for the EU countries, where the inflow of low-skilled workers reduces the wage of low-skilled workers relative to skilled workers. This observation is common to a number of empirical studies. In particular, although the aggregate wage effect of migration tends to be small, low-skilled wages are often found to respond more strongly to migration than high-skilled wages (see, e.g., Bauer and Zimmermann 1999).

Having a migrant group composed of migrants with skill levels different from those in the native population, as opposed to the group of migrants with skill levels identical to those of workers in the host country, as in the experiment in section 8.4.3, implies a different impact on GDP and consumption as well, both in the CEECs and in the EU. In particular, GDP per capita in the CEECs rises more substantially, since the ratio of skilled to unskilled people increases. The opposite effect holds for the EU. To illustrate, GDP per capita in Germany falls by 0.8

percent if all immigrants are low skilled, whereas the decline is only 0.4 percent if migrants have the same skill level as natives. The decline in the aggregate volume of consumption and production in the CEECs is, respectively, 0.3 and 0.4 percent smaller than in section 8.4.3. In the EU, the effect on GDP falls from 0.6 to 0.5 percent, and the effect on consumption falls from 0.5 to 0.4 percent. Hence, the skill composition of the immigrant group does matter in regard to the economic effects of immigration, although in macro-economic terms, the differences between the effects when the migrant group has a different skill-level composition than the native group and the effects when the migrant group is identical in skill levels to the native population are modest. The most important effects are probably related to the wage distribution: Wage differentials in the EU will become larger to the extent that immigrants from the CEECs indeed occupy low-skilled jobs.

8.6 Conclusions

This chapter explores the economic implications of enlargement of the EU with countries from Central and Eastern Europe. We consider three dimensions of enlargement: the move toward a customs union, the enlargement of the internal market, and free movement of labor. Overall, the economic implications for the accession countries tend to be significant. To illustrate, if we add together the impact of the three dimensions of enlargement studied in this chapter for the CEECs, we find that GDP per capita increases by more than 8 percent in the long run. For Hungary, the effect even exceeds 12 percent, because the relatively open Hungarian economy benefits relatively more from the accession of the CEECs to the internal market. The effects for EU countries are generally positive but modest. For instance, Dutch GDP per capita rises by a mere 0.15 percent in the long run. For Germany, the economic effects tend to be dominated by those resulting from migration, causing a slight reduction in GDP per capita.

The study suggests that, compared to the customs union and free movement of labor, CEEC accession to the internal market yields the largest economic effects. For instance, whereas the move toward a customs union and free movement of labor increase the volume of consumption per capita in the CEECs by, respectively, a little more than 2 percent and a little less than 1 percent, accession to the internal market raises consumption by more than 9 percent in the long run. Sensitivity analysis suggests that the magnitude of this effect is quite robust. Also for the EU, enlargement of the internal market yields an expansion in consumption of about 0.2 percent.

The effects reported in this study tend to be large compared to those in previous model simulations of EU enlargement. Indeed, most earlier studies report gains for the accession countries of between 1.5 and 8 percent. The large effects we find originate in the relatively large effects of CEEC accession to the internal market. In particular, the empirical approach followed in this study, as opposed to the best-guess approach followed by others, suggests that the accession of the CEECs to the internal market involves a bigger shock than is sometimes assumed. Moreover, the dynamic efficiency gains captured in our model turn out to be important.

We also find that the accession of the CEECs to the internal market yields disproportionate effects on particular industries. Indeed, industrial relocation will be required to reap the gains from trade and to exploit comparative advantages of countries. Therefore, some sectors will face a serious decline, such as energy-intensive products in the CEECs and textiles and leather in the southern part of the EU. In the CEECs, the food-processing and textiles and leather sectors are likely to expand the most.

Appendix: Regional and Sectoral Concordances for WorldScan

Table 8A.1
Country groupings

1 Hungary		
2 Poland		
3 Rest of CEEC		
4 Former Soviet Union		
5 Germany		
6 France		
7 United Kingdom		
8 Netherlands		
9 Southern Europe	Spain, Portugal, Italy, Greece	
10 Rest of EU	Sweden, Denmark, Finland, Ireland, Austria, Belgium (plus Luxembourg)	
11 Rest of OECD	United States, Japan, Australia, New Zealand, Canada, Iceland and Norway, Switzerland	
12 Rest of world	Turkey, Rest of Middle East, Morocco, Rest of North Africa, South African Customs Union, Rest of Southern Africa, Rest of Sub-Saharan Africa, Central America and Carribean, Mexico, Argentina, Brazil, Chile, Uruguay, Venezuela, Colombia, Rest of South America, All regions in Asia	

Table 8A.2
Sectoral groupings

1 Agriculture	Paddy rice, wheat, grains, cereal grains, nongrain crops, vegetables, oil seeds, sugar cane, plant-based fibers, crops, bovine cattle, animal products, raw milk, wool, forestry, fisheries
2 Raw materials	Oil, gas, coal, minerals
3 Food processing	Processed rice, meat products, vegetable oils, dairy products, sugar, other food products, beverages, and tobacco
4 Textiles and leather	Textiles, wearing apparel, leather products
5 Non-metallic minerals	
6 Energy-intensive products	Chemicals, rubbers and plastics, petroleum and coal refinery
7 Other manufacturing	Other manufacturing, lumber and wood, paper, printing and publishing
8 Metals	Nonferrous minerals, Ferrous minerals
9 Fabricated metal products	
10 Machinery and equipment	
11 Electronic equipment	
12 Transport equipment	Other transport industries, motor vehicles and parts
13 Trade services	
14 Transport and communication	Other, sea and air transport, communication
15 Financial services	Insurance, other financial services
16 Other services	Construction, other business services, electricity, gas manufacturing and distribution, water, recreational services, government services

Table 8A.3
Key elasticity values

Substitution elasticities in the production functions	
Composite 1: CES [unskilled labor; skilled labor; capital]	1
Composite 2: CES [intermediate input]	0.8
Value added: CES [composite 1; composite 2]	0.4
Armington elasticities	
Agriculture	7
Manufacturing	5.6
Raw materials	10
Services	4

Notes

All three authors are with CPB Netherlands Bureau for Economic Policy Analysis. De Mooij is also affiliated with Erasmus University Rotterdam, CESifo, and Tinbergen Institute. Nahuis is also affiliated with Utrecht University. We are grateful to Paul Brenton, Joe Francois, Rajshri Jayaraman, Jacques Pelkmans, Christian Keuschnigg, and an anonymous reviewer for helpful comments.

1. Keuschnigg, Keuschnigg, and Kohler (2001) also differentiate the reduction in trade costs between industries on the basis of nontariff barriers reported by the OECD.

2. In fact, the Baltic states are included in the data for the former Soviet Union.

3. The external tariffs in the raw-materials and service sectors are negligible and therefore not reported.

4. For a detailed discussion of these approaches and their effect on trade, see Brenton, Sheehy, and Vancauteren 2001.

5. Conforming with the internal-market *acquis communautaire* may also involve costs for CEEC producers, especially in regard to environmental norms and labor market regulation (safety and health). These costs are not included in the analysis presented in this chapter. The EU may compensate the CEECs for part of these costs, however, through the Regional and Structural Funds. Transfers and costs may thus cancel one another out.

6. The gravity model is rarely used at the industry level. Bergstrand 1989 is an exception. Bergstrand derives a gravity equation for a multi-industry world that also allows for intra-industry trade. He uses one-digit Standard International Trade Classification (SITC) industry level data from the 1960s and 1970s, and his estimates yield plausible results.

7. After the work by McCallum (1995), the appropriate estimation of border effects is discussed intensively. Anderson and van Wincoop (2001), for example, argue that a trade theory–based specification includes not only bilateral trade barriers (distance, dummies, etc.) but also two measures for multilateral openness to trade of both countries. The intuition for including the latter variables is that *relative* barriers to trade matter. For small trade blocs, the estimated border barriers tend to be biased upward if the multi-lateral variables are omitted. Though our CEEC bloc is relatively small, it is impossible to say a priori how omission of multi-lateral variables would affect our results, as we estimate at the industry level. Extending the work of Anderson and van Wincoop to a multi-industry setup is fairly complicated and would require very restrictive assumptions. Nahuis (2002) is more elaborate on the econometric specification.

8. Bilateral exports will become $\exp(b_s)$ times the initial exports if accession countries become EU members (i.e., if D^{EU} becomes one). From this, we subtract $\exp(0) = 1$ to arrive at the potential trade increase from CEEC accession.

9. Lejour, de Mooij, and Nahuis 2001 reports this procedure in more detail.

10. There are two ways to calculate this number, namely, relative to the initial level of trade inclusive or exclusive of intra-EU trade. The 2 percent refers to the increase inclusive of intra-EU trade. If we were to use the trade data exclusive of intra-EU trade, we would arrive at a trade increase for the EU countries as a result of CEEC accession of approximately 5 percent.

11. See Sinn and Werding 2001 for more results and a critical discussion on the findings by Boeri and Brücker.

12. This figure is close to the consensus estimate reported by Bauer and Zimmerman (1999). On the basis of a literature review and some calculations, these authors estimate the migration effect of EU enlargement at around three million people after fifteen years.

13. To put the effects of these three shocks into perspective, we also perform a simulation of the Europe Agreements, that is, the removal of formal bilateral trade barriers in manufacturing between 1997 and 2002. The results of this simulation suggest that the Europe Agreements exert a positive effect on GDP of, on average, 2.6 percent in the CEECs and 0.1 percent in the EU (see Lejour, de Mooij, and Nahuis 2001).

14. Given the neoclassical growth structure of the model, the year 2020 does not represent the steady-state outcome of the model. As the results of simulations with a longer time span (until 2050 and 2100) are very similar, the outcome for 2020 has approached the steady state closely.

15. Note that our high level of aggregation of the agriculture and food-processing sectors does not do justice to the underlying differences in the product categories that make up each sector. Stolwijk (2000) concludes on the basis of a scenario study for the Netherlands that the CEECs are likely to gain in sectors that are abundant in land and labor and that enlargement offers opportunities for the Dutch skill-intensive industries in food processing.

16. The baseline data refer to data from the initial calibration. Compared to this initial calibration, the simulations of the Europe Agreements and the customs union have changed these trade intensities. The effects presented in this section are relative to a path in which the customs union is already implemented.

17. Migration also increases the rate of return on capital, which creates a migration surplus. The higher rate of return to capital, however, does not raise the capital stock sufficiently to prevent a decrease in GDP per capita, since capital is not perfectly mobile. For this reason, our results on the GDP effect of immigration differ from those of studies in which capital is perfectly mobile.

References

Anderson, J. E., and E. van Wincoop. 2001. "Gravity with Gravitas: A Solution to the Border Puzzle." Working paper no. 8079, National Bureau of Economic Research, Cambridge, MA.

Baldwin, R. E., J. F. Francois, and R. Portes. 1997. "Costs and Benefits of Eastern Enlargement: The Impact on the EU and Central Europe." *Economic Policy* 24: 127–176.

Bauer, T., and K. F. Zimmermann. 1999. *Assessment of Possible Migration Pressure and Its Labor Market Impact Following EU Enlargement to Central and Eastern Europe.* Report for the UK Department for Education and Employment. London.

Bergstrand, J. H. 1989. "The Generalized Gravity Equation, Monopolistic Competition, and the Factor-Proportions Theory of International Trade." *Review of Economics and Statistics* 71: 143–153.

Boeri, T., and H. Brücker. 2000. *The Impact of Eastern Enlargement on Employment and Labor Markets in the EU Member States.* Report for the European Commission. Berlin.

Brenton, P., and D. Gros. 1997. "Trade Reorientation and Recovery in Transition Economies." *Oxford Review of Economic Policy* 13: 65–76.

Brenton, P., J. Sheehy, and M. Vancauteren. 2001. "Technical Barriers to Trade in the European Union." *Journal of Common Market Studies* 39: 265–284.

Breuss, F. 2001. "Macroeconomic Effects of EU Enlargement for Old and New Members." Working paper no. 143/2001, Österreichisches Institut für Wirtschafts-forschung. (WIFO), Vienna.

Brown, D., A. V. Deardorff, S. Djankov, and R. M. Stern. 1997. "An Economic Assessment of the Integration of Czechoslovakia, Hungary and Poland into the European Union." In *Europe's Economy looks East: Implications for Germany and the European Union*, ed. S. W. Black. New York and Melbourne: Cambridge University Press.

Central Planning Bureau (CPB). 1999. *WorldScan: The Core Version*. The Hague: Central Planning Bureau.

Dimaranan, B. V., and R. A. McDougall. 2002. *Global Trade, Assistance, and Production: The GTAP 5 Data Base*. Center for Global Trade Analysis, Purdue University, Lafayette, IN.

Fidrmuc, J., and J. Fidrmuc. 2000. "Integration, Disintegration and Trade in Europe: Evolution of Trade Relations during the 1990s." Working paper no. 2000-12, Center for Economic Research, Tilburg, the Netherlands.

Frankel, F. A., and A. K. Rose. 2000. "Estimating the Effect of Currency Unions on Trade and Output." Working paper no. 7857, National Bureau of Economic Research, Cambridge, MA.

Helliwell, J. 1996. "Do National Borders Matter for Quebec's Trade?" *Canadian Journal of Economics* 29: 507–522.

Keuschnigg, C., M. Keuschnigg, and W. Kohler. 2001. "The German Perspective on Eastern EU Enlargement." *World Economy* 24: 513–542.

Keuschnigg, C., and W. Kohler. 2000. "Eastern Enlargement of the EU: A Dynamic General Equilibrium Perspective." In *Using Dynamic General Equilibrium Models for Policy Analysis*, (Contributions to Economic Analysis no. 248), ed. Glenn W. Harrison, Svend E. Hougaard Jensen, Lars Haagen Pedersen, and Thomas F. Rutherford, 119–170. Amsterdam: North-Holland.

Keuschnigg, C., and W. Kohler. 2002. "Eastern Enlargement of the EU: How Much Is It Worth for Austria?" *Review of International Economics* 10: 324–342.

Lejour, A. M., R. A. de Mooij, and R. Nahuis. 2001. "EU Enlargement: Economic Implications for Countries and Industries." Working paper no. 585, CESifo, Munich.

McCallum, J. 1995. "National Borders Matter: Canada-U.S. Regional Trade Patterns." *American Economic Review* 85: 615–623.

Nahuis, R. 2002. "One Size Fits All? Accession to the Internal Market: An Industry Level Assessment of EU Enlargement." Discussion paper no. 14, Central Planning Bureau (CPB), The Hague.

Sinn, H. W., and M. Werding. 2001. "Immigration Following EU Eastern Enlargement." CESifo forum vol. 2, 40–47, CESifo, Munich.

Stolwijk, H. 2000. "The Dutch Food and Agricultural Sectors and the Enlargement of the EU." Report no. 2000/1, 39–42. Central Planning Bureau (CPB), The Hague.

World Bank. 2000. *Global Economic Prospects*. Washington, DC: World Bank.

Comments

Rajshri Jayaraman

The chapter by Lejour, de Mooij, and Nahuis is concerned with the macroeconomic consequences of European Union enlargement. In particular, it is interested in the effect on real GDP, the volume of private consumption, and terms of trade of three separate policy changes accompanying accession: the equalization of external tariffs, accession to internal markets, and the free movement of labor. It considers changes across variables and policies in sixteen different sectors for seven Central and Eastern European countries and fifteen EU countries, using WorldScan, a computable general equilibrium model of the world economy.

Its main findings are threefold. First, the CEEC7 experience large gains from accession to internal markets, smaller gains from adoption of a common external tariff, and small losses from labor migration.[1] Second, the EU15 experience some negligible changes from the adoption of a common external tariff and accession to internal markets and some gains from labor migration. Finally, changes in production vary widely from sector to sector, with rather dramatic expansions and contractions among sectors in the CEEC7.

There are numerous merits to this chapter, three of which I will mention here. First, it takes a novel approach to analysis of accession to internal markets. Rather than assume across-the-board reduction in trade costs, the authors take into account sectoral variations in trade costs and actually attempt to derive the size of the reduction in trade costs by estimating gravity equations. Second, it has a rich sectoral analysis, made possible by the GTAP database: Whereas standard trade models would lead us to expect sectoral variation in response to changes in trade policy, through this chapter, we are able actually to confirm or reject our theoretical priors. Finally, the chapter presents a positive analysis of different policies following from expansion and as such gives us some idea about what to expect upon expansion, in terms of the three variables analyzed.

That being said, the chapter is less elaborate in describing the underlying analytics than it perhaps should be. Many economists are somewhat skeptical of simulation exercises, particularly in the context of a general equilibrium framework, because of the degree of structure such exercises involve. The authors would go a considerable way in allaying such skepticism if they gave the reader a better idea of the animal with which she's dealing. In particular it would help to (1) know the structure of the CGE model employed, (2) be told what equations are being estimated in the tables described in the text, (3) have some justification for the choice of the calibration parameters, many of which positively invite suspicion, and importantly, (4) have some qualification of the results (how seriously should we take the estimates?).

Happily, these issues are easy to address. The other area in which the chapter falls short is in motivating the exercise or discussing the ramifications of its findings. Whether the authors should do so or not is, of course, open to debate. On the one hand, resisting the urge to pontificate may well be perceived as a strength, from the point of view of those well versed in the issues: It provides such an audience evidence that either confirms or refutes their priors without the cumbersome imposition of authorial intervention in interpretation. Having scoured all the tables and their descriptions, however, a non-specialist may be found asking, "Why do I care?"

In fact, there are innumerable reasons why one should care about the "economic implications for countries and industries" of EU enlargement from a policy perspective. Perhaps the most pertinent is that it should help to answer the question "Should the EU be expanded?" This is a normative, welfare-type question, and for economists, the general answer to this question is, "Yes, if it is efficient to do so."

That's easy for me to say. This is obviously a grand question, and one needs to be careful about how far one is willing to go in addressing it on the basis of one simulation exercise. Still, this chapter could suggest a tentative answer, particularly as the authors point out that the effect on private consumption is closely related to real disposable income of private households, and therefore, best reflects the welfare effects of enlargement.

Whether or not one believes the actual numbers, or even their general efficiency implications, the fact that this chapter considers the impact of a variety of different policies across a number of different countries highlights a couple of important (if obvious) nuances regarding EU enlargement. Accession to the EU involves the wholesale adoption of a *bundle* of policies. The direct effect of some of these policies is beneficial to some countries, others less so. Furthermore (and again, even permitting a healthy dose of skepticism regarding the actual numbers), the evidence presented in the chapter suggests that any given policy can have vastly different effects not only across countries, but across sectors within any given country. This appears to be particularly true of CEEC7 countries, in which the expansion of some sectors is as dizzying as the contraction of others.

Even in the absence of any conclusive answer to the question of whether to enlarge, these two qualifications to the general process of enlargement have important ramifications for the political economy of enlargement, which is really at the heart of the implementation of a process that many view as inevitable. This chapter can give some positive guidance regarding what to anticipate in intercountry negotiations as well as normative guidance for domestic policy to ease the transition. For instance, as we have already seen in the process of the recent Polish negotiations, countries that anticipate that suffering will arise from certain dimensions of accession will want to "unbundle" the EU accession policy package through clauses or exemptions. Similarly, the CEEC7 would do well to figure out who the biggest losers in the adjustment process will be and perhaps to compensate them accordingly, so as to avoid unrest of the kind that, for example, has accompanied many of the International Monetary Fund's structural adjustment programs.

One the one hand, it is a bit of a pity that a chapter so rich in data doesn't offer more analysis of the ramifications of its empirical findings for what is arguably *the* most pressing policy issue in Europe today: Should the EU expand eastward, and if so, how? On the other hand, by the same token, since its empirics are so elaborate and so thoughtful, this chapter offers a wealth of data for those who are interested in exploring these and similar questions themselves.

Note

1. The losses to the CEECs may from labor migration actually be smaller if one takes account of migrants' remittances.

9   The Political Economy of EU Enlargement: Or, Why Japan Is Not a Candidate Country

Antonis Adam and Thomas Moutos

9.1   Introduction

The planned eastward enlargement of the European Union is seen by many observers as both a historic opportunity and the greatest challenge the EU has faced so far. It will involve (in absolute terms) the biggest increase in the EU up to this point in the number of countries, in population size, and in surface area. In December 1997, at its summit in Luxembourg, the European Council launched the process that will make possible the accession of the following thirteen countries: Cyprus, the Czech Republic, Estonia, Hungary, Latvia, Lithuania, Malta, Poland, the Slovak Republic, Slovenia, Bulgaria, Romania, and Turkey. By February 2000 accession negotiations had been formally opened with all of the above countries except Turkey. In December 2002, at the Copenhagen European Council, the accession negotiations with the first ten countries were concluded, and it is expected that these countries will become EU members in May 2004.[1]

Professional opinion regarding the trade-related effects of enlargement on the current EU member states is unanimous: In addition to geopolitical benefits, the EU is expected to reap economic benefits from enlargement as well (see, e.g., Rollo and Smith 1993; Hamilton and Winters 1992; Baldwin 1994). Moreover, the studies assembled in Faini and Portes 1995a lead them to conclude that "it is virtually impossible to find significant negative effects of opening trade with the CEECs at the national, regional and sectoral levels" (Faini and Portes 1995b, 16). Some back-of-the-envelope calculations performed by Baldwin, Francois, and Portes (1997) suggest that the distribution of economic benefits among the fifteen countries that are currently EU members is more or less proportional to each country's share in the aggregate GDP of the EU15. The biggest (absolute) gains are expected to be experienced by Germany, France, the United Kingdom, Italy, and Spain, with Portugal being the only country that is not expected to benefit (it is estimated that it will incur a very small loss). On the basis of these projections, Faini and Portes (1995b) note "a striking paradox": Even though the trade effects of enlargement are expected to be benign, policymakers in the EU have continued to restrict access for products from the CEECs. Accordingly they urge policymakers not to "hesitate to take advantage of the historic opportunities created by the 1989 revolution in Central and Eastern Europe." (Faini and Portes 1995b, 17).

In this chapter we argue that the trade-related intercountry distributional consequences of EU enlargement may not be so benign. Our argument is based on a model of intra-industry trade in vertically differentiated products (see Falvey 1981 and Eaton and Kierzkowski 1984 for early models of vertical differentiation). In this model, differences in technology among the incumbent countries interact with the technological capabilities of the candidate countries to determine both the intercountry and intracountry distribution of benefits and costs of enlargement.

It is usually thought that the opening of intra-industry trade between two countries imposes very few adjustment costs on the industry in either country. This sanguine view regarding intra-industry trade is a consequence of the assumption that trade is conducted in horizontally differentiated products. In models that incorporate this view, the opening of trade between two economies results in an increase in the number of varieties consumed by households (relative to autarky). This increase in the number of varieties consumed can be associated either with an increase in the scale of production of each variety (in which case the number of varieties produced in each country declines), or with no change in the scale of production and the number of varieties produced by each country. The same logic applies if a customs union (CU) between a number of countries expands to include one or more countries. Accordingly, import competition (at worst) requires workers only to move between firms (or assembly lines) within the same industry.[2] If, instead, trade involves the exchange of vertically differentiated products, the effects of CU enlargement on the incumbent members can be asymmetric.[3] One (incumbent) country may enjoy increased access to the joining country's market without having to face a displacement of domestic production by imports, whereas another (incumbent) country may have to face increased import penetration. As we demonstrate in section 9.3, low-income (and technologically lagging) incumbent countries would prefer that enlargement be directed toward high-income (and technologically advanced) countries, which have comparative advantage in producing high-quality varieties of differentiated products. By the same token, high-income incumbent countries will prefer that enlargement be directed toward countries that have comparative advantage in producing low-quality varieties, thus avoiding the head-on competition that enlargement toward a high-income (and technologically sophisticated) country would imply.

The above argument rests on—among other things—two premises (in the specific case of EU enlargement): first, that trade between the EU countries and the CEECs is conducted almost exclusively in vertically differentiated products, and second, that there are significant differences among EU countries with respect to vertical specialization. We provide detailed (and direct) evidence in support of the second premise in section 9.4. As far as the first premise is concerned, it is clear that it cannot be taken as a literal representation of actual trade patterns but must instead be viewed as a simplifying assumption whose relevance depends on whether trade in vertically differentiated products is an important and growing category of trade between the EU and the CEECs. The evidence (see Freudenberg and Lemoine 1999) is clear that trade in vertically differentiated products is by far the fastest-growing trade category between the EU12 and the CEECs (between 1993 and 1996 the share of two-way trade between these two groups in vertically differentiated goods increased by 4.4 percentage points, the share for horizontally differentiated goods increased by 0.4 percentage points, and the share of one-way trade decreased by 4.8 percentage points). With respect to the importance of vertical versus horizontal two-way trade, Freudenberg and Lemoine calculate that in 1996, the real value of trade in vertically differentiated goods was five times larger than trade in horizontally differentiated goods. We thus have some confidence that the theoretical structure we assume in this chapter describes an important part of actual trade patterns.

In the rest of the chapter, we first provide a brief review of the literature explaining why countries may want to form (or join already existing) CUs. We then present a simple model of trade in vertically differentiated products to examine the intracountry and intercountry consequences of enlargement (section 9.3). In section 9.4, we present evidence in support of our basic assumptions regarding the relative position of EU countries, the CEECs, and Japan on the quality ladder based on the analysis of unit value data for about 1,500 products. We

also present the results of some econometric testing of the main implication of our model (i.e., that an incumbent country's net exports increase only if enlargement is directed toward countries on the opposite
side of the technological spectrum) by looking at the effects of previous
enlargements. We find that the data provide considerable support for
our model. In the chapter's final section, we summarize our findings
and discuss possible extensions of the chapter.

9.2   Why Do Countries Form (or Accede to) Customs Unions?

A basic question that any analysis of the effects of customs union formation (and enlargement) must face is why countries do not engage in
unilateral trade liberalization. After all, a basic premise of international
trade theory is that small countries that face perfectly competitive
markets will be better served by a unilateral reduction in their tariffs
than by agreements for reciprocal liberalization involving only a limited number of countries.[4] Answers to this question vary depending on
the perspective one wants to adopt. Corden (1984, 121), following
Viner (1950), submits that "in the main, unions are formed for non-
economic reasons ... so that the role of the economist is simply to analyze the incidental economic effects."

Among noneconomic reasons, security considerations have been
cited by many authors as an important factor in the desire for regional
integration. The "founding fathers" of the European Community,
Robert Schuman and Jean Monnet, aimed at economic integration in
the belief that it would make war "materially impossible," hoping that
the interlocking of steel, coal, and other strategic industries would
leave the community's member countries unable to wage war against
each other (see Milward 1984).

Political scientists have argued that negotiations on trade issues between political elites help build trust, which is subsequently used for
mutually beneficial collaboration in other policy areas (see also Viner
1950, 87). The examples usually cited in this respect include the Zollverein of 1834 (a CU among the numerous German principalities that
eventually led to political unification in 1871) and the CU formed
between Moldavia and Wallachia in 1847, which paved the way for
the creation of Romania in 1881. There are also examples, however, in
which policy-induced integration triggered conflict (the U.S. Civil War
and the creation of Bangladesh when East Pakistan broke free from
West Pakistan being the most prominent ones). These examples illus-

trate that tariff preferences that induce regional trade may create large income transfers within the region and concentration of industry in one location. Thus, there is a need for regional integration to be paired with side payments to the disaffected areas if conflict is to be avoided.[5]

Assuming a purely economic perspective, the answer to the question of why countries do not liberalize trade unilaterally hinges on terms-of-trade effects (see, for example, Mundell 1964; Vanek 1965; and Kemp 1969). Countries hope that by banding together to negotiate an agreement with common external barriers they, will increase their bargaining power vis-à-vis third countries (Arndt 1968, 1969). For many observers, the countries involved in the formation of the EC in the 1950s had this idea in mind, especially in connection with acquiring leverage in their negotiations with the United States.[6] Riezman (1985) demonstrates that CU formation may result (by appropriate setting of the common external tariff) in higher welfare for the countries involved compared to what they could achieve in a free-trade equilibrium. Nevertheless, imposition of "optimal tariffs" is in practice one of the less-used instruments of trade policy (according to Perroni and Whalley's 2000 calculations, the (Nash)-optimal tariff rate for the United States is about 500 percent, and for the EU about 900 percent). Arguments regarding infant industries, employment, and adjustment costs appear to be more important determinants of trade policy. Moreover, the frequent use of competitive devaluation policies (which aim at causing the terms of trade to deteriorate) by many countries places in doubt the real-world relevance of the terms-of-trade argument as a motivating factor in CU formation.

Another motive—which also hinges on the terms-of-trade argument —is that countries (especially small ones) wish to buy insurance against an outbreak of protectionism in the future (see Whalley 1998). Such protectionism could take either the form of a tariff war or, more plausibly, the use of administered protection (like quantitative restrictions, import surveillance, antidumping and countervailing duties, and safeguard measures). The gains for small countries from participating in CUs arise not only from having continued and preferential access to the other CU members' markets, but also from the fact that the tariff against nonmembers rises. It is obvious from this line of argument that small countries will be endeavoring to form partnerships with large countries, and that large countries will be able to extract side payments from small ones. There is indeed some evidence that this has happened.

Ethier (1998) and Whalley (1998), for example, report that in forming NAFTA, Canada and Mexico made implicit side payments in the form of changes in domestic policies that were favorable to the United States. Also, the EAs involve very few "concessions" by the EU. A number of "sensitive" EU sectors are exempt from the EAs, these being the sectors in which the CEECs have comparative advantage (see Lavigne 1995). Moreover, the candidate countries have been forced to undertake domestic reforms that have been to the interest of the EU.

It must, however, be stated that sometimes governments have used integration agreements as a commitment mechanism that helps to lock in domestic reforms. This may prove particularly helpful when a particular country has no track record of reform or, worse, when it has a history of reversing reforms that have been implemented. The hope in using integration agreements in such cases is that binding the country to an international trade treaty makes any future reversal of domestic policy reform more difficult to implement. Mexico's decision to enter NAFTA is frequently discussed in such terms (Tornell and Esquivel 1997), as well as Greece's decision to seek membership in EMU (Pagoulatos 2000), and the decision of the CEECs to apply for accession to the EU (Fernandez and Portes 1998).[7] Existing members of a regional group may also be able to influence the domestic economic policies and political institutions of prospective members by demanding that they undertake domestic reforms prior to accession. The EU at the 1993 Copenhagen European Council made it clear to candidate countries for EU membership that satisfaction of economic and political criteria is a prerequisite for the opening of accession negotiations.[8]

A distinguishing feature of preferential trade agreements (PTAs) is that they discriminate against third parties. In this way they generate rents for certain domestic agents, who become strong supporters for their formation and maintenance. Import-competing firms that face intense competition from competitors located outside the agreement area and export-oriented industries that stand to benefit from preferential access to the markets of the other agreement members will be among the staunchest supporters of regional integration. For these agents regional integration may appear more attractive than unilateral (nonpreferential) liberalization, since a PTA limits the international competition to which the import-competing firms are subjected and secures to export-oriented firms improved (relative to nonmembers) market access to partner countries' markets. For these reasons PTAs hold some appeal for governments that must strike a balance between promoting a country's aggregate economic welfare and accommodating interest groups whose support the governments need to remain in office. Indeed, a number of authors have argued that usually only those trade agreements that involve a significant amount of trade diversion are politically sustainable (see, for example, Grossman and Helpman 1994; Grossman and Helpman 1995; and Krishna 1998), because when a PTA is formed, domestic firms benefit from preferential access to the partners' markets but lose from giving a similar access to partners in the domestic market. In the absence of trade diversion, this increased penetration of one another's market is close to being a zero-sum game: It is not likely that firms from all partner countries will gain from it. Thus, an agreement in these circumstances has little chance of coming into effect. If by making the PTA, trade is diverted away (in all partner country markets) from the rest of the world firms, however, then it becomes more likely that firms from *all* countries gain from the agreement, and it is supported by all partner countries.

The predominance of key producer interests—emphasized in the previous paragraph—has been for many observers the most important factor behind the formation of the European Economic Community (EEC) and its subsequent evolution (see Lynch 1997 and Moravcsik 1998 for extensive arguments in support of this view; for an opposite argument, see Parsons 2000).[9] In this chapter we argue that this view may also explain why the EU has taken decisive steps toward enlargement to the east, despite the widespread uneasiness among the population of incumbent EU countries about this prospect. As we explain in the following section, enlargement to the east offers to technologically advanced EU firms the possibility of expanding their market share in the acceding countries' markets without having to sacrifice their market share in EU countries: The increased imports from the candidate countries will substitute for the domestic sales of less technologically sophisticated EU firms, rather than for the domestic sales of technologically advanced firms.

9.3 The Model

We construct for the purposes of this chapter the simplest possible model capable of highlighting the issues we wish to emphasize. The model is partial equilibrium in nature and assumes the existence of two goods and four countries. The first good is a nontraded homogeneous good, whereas the second good is a vertically differentiated product that is internationally traded. Among the four countries, two are assumed to belong to a CU, and each of the other two countries applies (and receives) non-preferential treatment in its trade with the other three countries. The latter two countries are assumed to represent the rest of the world. For ease of exposition, we identify the two CU members as Germany (D) and Greece (G), and the two ROW countries as one from the candidate CEECs (E) and one from the non-EU high-income countries (i.e., Japan, the United States, and so on), which we denote by S. (The reasons for splitting the ROW into two different groups of countries will become apparent later in the chapter.)

9.3.1 Technology and Supply Relationships

Each of the four countries is assumed to produce a homogeneous non-traded good and (some) varieties of the vertically differentiated good. Given our interest in international trade, we use the homogeneous good as the numeraire and set its price equal to unity in each country. We assume that perfect competition prevails in the production of the homogeneous good and that it is produced with labor as the only input under constant returns to scale (thus, exogenous productivity differentials across countries are reflected in wage differentials). We also assume that there is labor mobility within each country and labor immobility across countries. Finally, we assume that the exchange rate for all countries involved is fixed and equal to one.

We start our analysis by assuming that within each country the vertically differentiated product, Y, is produced under perfectly competitive conditions by identical firms. (This assumption is not necessary for our analysis, but it greatly simplifies it; we discuss later the case of infra-marginal firms.) This good is differentiated according to quality, which is measured by an index Q in the range $[1, \infty]$. We assume that there is perfect information regarding the quality index. We further assume that production costs in all countries depend on quality and that each unit of a given quality is produced at a constant cost (which differs across countries). We capture the above assumptions by writing the production function for Germany as

$$Y_D(Q) = \frac{L_D}{\gamma_D Q^{\varepsilon_D}}, \quad \text{with } \gamma_D > 0, \quad \text{and} \quad \varepsilon_D > 1, \tag{1}$$

where $Y_D(Q)$ denotes the number of units of quality Q produced in Germany, L_D stands for the (effective) units of labor used in the production process, and γ_D and ε_D are parameters. Our assumption that $\varepsilon_D > 1$ implies that although costs per unit in terms of quantity are constant, increases in quality are associated with more than equiproportional increases in unit costs. This assumption is motivated by the fact that increases in quality—for a given state of technological capability—require the employment of an increasing number of workers. These workers must be allocated not only to the production of a higher number of features attached to each good (e.g., electric windows, air bags, ABS, security devices, and so on in the case of automobiles) that directly absorb labor, but also to the development and refinement of these features as well. We assume that these endeavors are subject to diminishing returns (see Flam and Helpman 1987 for a similar assumption).

Equation (1) implies that the average cost at which each unit of quality Q will be produced by German producers is

$$AC_D(Q) = w_D\gamma_D Q^{\varepsilon_D}, \tag{2}$$

where w_D is the German wage rate (common to both sectors). We now assume that Germany has an absolute advantage in the production of every quality level of the differentiated good over Greece, and that its comparative advantage (CA) lies in the production of high-quality varieties of the differentiated good. These assumptions are reflected in the production function for Greece:

$$Y_G(Q) = \frac{L_G}{\gamma_G Q^{\varepsilon_G}}, \tag{3}$$

with $\gamma_G > \gamma_D$, and $\varepsilon_G > \varepsilon_D$.

According to equation (3) the average cost at which each unit of quality Q will be produced by Greek producers will be

$$AC_G = w_G\gamma_G Q^{\varepsilon_G}, \tag{4}$$

where w_G is the Greek wage rate. Under these conditions it is obvious that if the wage rates (per effective unit of labor) were equal in the two countries, Greek producers would not be able to produce any varieties at a lower cost (price) than their German counterparts. For this reason, we assume that wages in Greece are sufficiently lower than German wages (i.e., that $w_D \gg w_G$) to enable Greek producers to produce at least some low-quality varieties (those ones in which the country has CA) at a lower cost than German producers.

With respect to the two ROW countries, we assume that S is the most technologically sophisticated country in the world, whereas E is less technologically sophisticated than Greece. This stark assumption is made as a way of capturing the different levels of technological sophistication between S and E, by placing them on the opposite sites of technological sophistication relative to Germany and Greece (the evidence presented later in the chapter is supportive of this assumption). The production functions for S and E are written as

$$Y_S(Q) = \frac{L_S}{\gamma_S Q^{\varepsilon_S}}, \tag{5}$$

with $0 < \gamma_S < \gamma_D$, and $1 \leq \varepsilon_S < \varepsilon_D$, and

$$Y_E = \frac{L_E}{\gamma_E Q^{\varepsilon_E}}, \tag{6}$$

with $\gamma_E > \gamma_G$ and $\varepsilon_E > \varepsilon_G$, and the associated average cost functions as

$$AC_S(Q) = w_S \gamma_S Q^{\varepsilon_S} \tag{7}$$

and

$$AC_E(Q) = w_E \gamma_E Q^{\varepsilon_E} \tag{8}$$

Again, our assumptions about technology dictate that a necessary condition for each country to be able to produce some varieties of the differentiated good at a lower cost than the other countries is that wages are lowest in E and highest in S, that is, $w_S > w_D > w_G > w_E$. In figure 9.1 we depict the relationship between average cost and quality for the four countries. The assumption that E has the lowest wage among the four countries allows it to produce at the lowest cost all varieties with quality in the range $[1, Q_{EG}]$. This is a manifestation of the assumption that E has comparative advantage in low-quality varieties of the differentiated good.

We define Q_{EG} as the market-dividing quality level between E and G producers. On the other hand, S will be the least-cost producer for varieties with quality greater than Q_{DS}; that is, S has comparative advantage in very high-quality varieties.

Similarly, Greece's and Germany's comparative advantage is restricted to middle-quality varieties and high-quality varieties, that is, those with quality in the ranges $[Q_{EG}, Q_{GD}]$ and $[Q_{GD}, Q_{DS}]$, with Q_{GD} and Q_{DS} being the market-dividing quality levels between Greek and

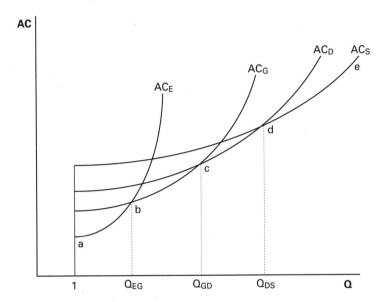

Figure 9.1
Relation between quality and cost.

German producers and German and *S* producers, respectively. From figure 9.1 it also becomes obvious that only those foreign producers that have comparative advantage in supplying contiguous (in terms of quality) varieties pose a competitive threat to a particular country's producers.

The above representation of technological differences between countries is an attempt to capture the "average" differences in terms of vertical product specialization among the countries involved. It is obvious, and the empirical evidence presented in section 9.4 verifies this, that there are some products for which the CEECs may have comparative advantage in producing higher-quality varieties than the EU countries or the ROW, mainly because of the transfer of technology through foreign direct investment from (mainly) EU countries. In many cases FDI is associated with the international fragmentation of the production process (see Jones 2000 and Jones and Kierzkowski 2001). In these instances, a country may acquire a comparative advantage in producing high-quality varieties of some intermediate inputs (components), without necessarily having comparative advantage in the production of high-quality varieties of other components or of the final product. There is indeed evidence that such processes are at work in some CEECs, but as yet (circa 1999), the contribution of FDI to the upgrading of domestically produced varieties has not raised average quality to the level observed in the least technologically advanced EU countries (see table 9.1).[10] There is also some evidence that the FDI flows from EU countries to the CEECs have, after a significant rise in the middle of the 1990s, returned to their levels early in that decade (see the OECD's Foreign Direct Investment database for more details).

9.3.2 Preferences and the Structure of Demand

Households in all countries are assumed to have similar preference structures and to be endowed with one unit of labor, which they offer inelastically. There are, however, differences in skill among households (both within and across countries), which are reflected in differences in the endowment of each household's effective labor supply. This is in turn reflected in differences in income across households. We assume that firms (within a county) pay the same wage rate per effective unit of labor, thus the distribution of talent across firms does not affect unit costs. For simplicity, we assume that incomes are uniformly distributed within each country. We also assume that the differences in productivity across countries are reflected in differences of per capita income among them, with S being the country with the highest (per capita) income, followed in order by $D, G,$ and E.

Following Rosen (1974), Gabszewicz and Thisse (1979), and Flam and Helpman (1987), we assume that the homogeneous good can be consumed in every desirable quantity, whereas the quality-differentiated product is indivisible, and households can consume only one unit of it. Thus we write the utility function as

$$U = F(H, Q),$$

where H stands for the consumption (measured in physical units) of the homogeneous good and Q is the quality index of the vertically differentiated product. We assume that both goods are normal, that is, that an increase in household income, ceteris paribus, results in the household's purchasing more units of the H good and a higher-quality (higher-priced) variety of the differentiated good.

Under conditions of free (and costless) trade, perfect competition implies that the price of each quality (variety) of the differentiated good will be equal to the lowest cost of producing this good in the four countries:

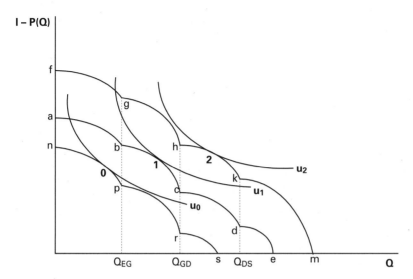

Figure 9.2
Incomes and the choice of quality.

$$P(Q) = \min\{w_E \gamma_E Q^{\varepsilon_E}, w_G \gamma_G Q^{\varepsilon_G}, w_D \gamma_D Q^{\varepsilon_D}, w_S \gamma_S Q^{\varepsilon_S}\}. \tag{9}$$

Equation (9) implies that the price schedule (as a function of quality) has a kink at the market-dividing quality levels Q_{EG}, Q_{GD}, and Q_{DS}. This price schedule is depicted as the kinked schedule *abcde* in figure 9.1. This further implies that the budget constraint of a typical household will also be kinked (i.e. non-differentiable) at the corresponding market-dividing quality levels. In figure 9.2 we depict the budget constraints of three different households within the same country. Denoting by I the household's income, $I - P(Q)$ measures the units of the homogenous good that can be consumed as a function of the quality of the differentiated good purchased by the household. The budget constraint of a middle-income household is depicted as the schedule *abcde*, with the maximum utility achieved on indifference curve u_1 at point 1. In this particular example, the household chooses to buy a middle-quality variety, which Greek producers offer at the lowest price. A household's income determines the variety it desires, and indirectly, the country of origin of this particular variety. In figure 9.2 we also show the budget constraints of a wealthier (poorer) household. This is depicted by the kinked schedules *fghkm* (*nprs*), with point 2 (0) being now the point of maximum attainable utility on indifference curve u_2 (u_0). The higher-income household chooses to consume a high-quality variety, which is offered at the lowest cost by German producers. On the other hand, the low-income household consumes a low-quality variety, which is offered at the lowest cost by E's producers. Note that even if this household wanted to spend all its income on the differentiated product, it could not afford the varieties that are offered at the lowest cost by S's producers. Given our assumption about the intercountry income distribution among E, G, D, and S, it follows that households in S will consume (on average) the highest-quality varieties, whereas households in E will (on average) consume the lowest-quality varieties.[11] This observation further implies that whereas, for example, the majority of consumers in G would prefer the elimination of tariffs on imports from E, the majority of consumers in D would prefer that imports from S receive preferential treatment, instead.

9.3.3   The Effects of a Customs Union

International trade among the four countries will involve the exchange of different-quality varieties, since, for example, there will be some low-income Germans wishing to consume low-quality varieties produced at the lowest cost in E, and some very high-income households in E wishing to buy varieties that are produced at the lowest cost in S. The distribution of income thus plays a crucial role in the analysis of this chapter in that households with identical preference structures may nevertheless consume varieties produced in different countries if they have different incomes (see also Falvey and Kierzkowski 1987 and Flam and Helpman 1987 for models with similar features). The within-country income inequality assumed in this chapter implies that even though there is a single factor of production, households will differ in their preferences as to the direction of trade liberalization.

We start our analysis by assuming the existence of a CU between Germany and Greece. We assume that there are no technical, regulatory, or other cost-increasing trade barriers within the CU (it took the EU more than thirty years after its inception for this assumption to approximate reality, even in the trade between Germany and France), but that there is a common external tariff (CET) that is applied on imports from either E or S. We assume away the existence of (differential) transport costs among the four countries and of any other trade barriers, except the per-unit CET, t. In figures 9.3a and 9.3b, we depict the consequences of an enlargement of the CU between D and G to include E. Before the enlargement, the price schedule and the budget constraint

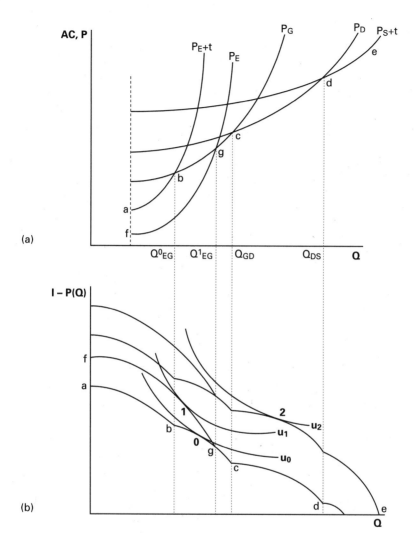

Figure 9.3
(a) CU effects on market share (*E* acceding); (b) CU effects on household welfare.

facing consumers in D and G are depicted by the kinked schedule *abcde* in figures 9.3a and 9.3b, respectively. The curves $P_E + t$ and $P_S + t$ in figure 9.3a depict the tariff-inclusive prices that producers in E and S charge to D's and G's consumers before enlargement. Under these circumstances, the range of varieties that E will be exporting to D and G will be up to Q_{EG}^0, whereas S will be exporting to D and G all varieties with quality greater than Q_{DS}. After the accession of E to the CU, the price schedule and the budget constraint facing D's and G's consumers are given by the kinked schedule *fgcde* in both panels of the figure. The range of varieties that E now exports to D and G expands up to Q_{EG}^1, whereas the range of varieties that G supplies at the lowest cost in D's and G's market diminishes by the same amount (e.g., distance $Q_{EG}^0 Q_{EG}^1$). In figure 9.3b, the drop in the prices of low-quality varieties results in utility gains for low-income (and possibly middle-income) households, and no change in the welfare indicator of high-income households, if we assume that the government does not reduce its lump-sum transfers to make up for its loss of tariff revenue.[12] We note that at this moment, in their role as consumers, low-income households in both D and G stand to gain from the enlargement, whereas high-income households do not expect such gains. Nevertheless, such unanimity of interests between the low-income households in D and G may not likely be observed once we realize that, at least the short run, the job prospects of low-income households in D will definitely improve from the enlargement, whereas the job prospects of the same type of households in G may deteriorate.

In figure 9.4 we depict the consequences of enlargement for E's market. G's export share in this market increases at the expense of local production: The range of Greek exports increases by the distance $Q_{EG}^0 Q_{EG}^1$. D's export share in E's market also increases, at the expense of S's exports, by the distance $Q_{DS}^0 Q_{DS}^1$. If we draw a diagram similar to figure 9.3b, it becomes evident that mainly the middle- and high-income households in E will be the beneficiaries of the country's accession to the CU. Moreover, if the reduction in tariff revenue in E as a result of accession is partly "financed" by a cut in government transfers to the low-income households, these households may be made worse off by the country's accession to the "rich man's" CU.

In summary, the enlargement of the CU to include E results in an increase of Greek and German exports to E and an increase of E's exports to G and D. The increase in E's exports, however, comes at the expense of Greek producers only. Higher sales of E's products in the Greek

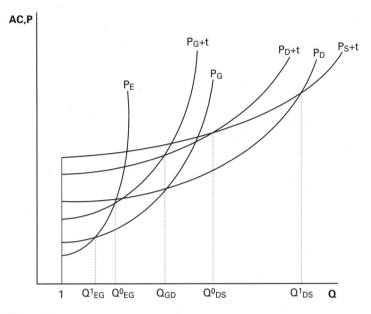

Figure 9.4
CU effects on market shares (E acceding).

market displace only domestically produced varieties there: German exports to the Greek market do not decline. Similarly, higher exports of E's products to Germany do not displace German firms' sales: They just displace Greek exports from the German market. Nevertheless, in this stylized model in which price equals average cost for all firms, neither Greek nor German producers have any interest in resisting or supporting E's accession. The model could be easily amended, however, to accommodate the existence of (economic) profits in two ways. First, we could maintain the hypothesis of a large number of firms, so that each one is a price taker, with some of them being more productive than others (a model of pure competition). The more productive firms will be earning profits in equilibrium (infra-marginal firms), and they will be interested in an expansion of demand, which would allow higher cost firms to enter the industry, thereby raising the equilibrium price above the average cost of infra-marginal firms and allowing them to increase their profits further. Second, and more realistically, we could consider a model of oligopoly in which firms choose the price-quality combination that maximizes profits. In this model, the elimination of tariffs on imports from E results in reductions in the prices that

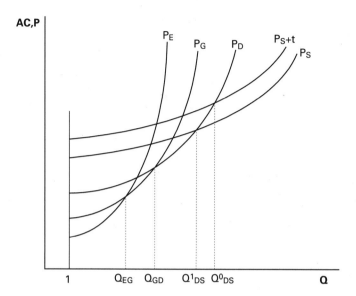

Figure 9.5
CU effects on market share (S acceding).

$G, D,$ and S firms charge to consumers in the incumbent countries in an effort to maintain their market share. Despite these complications, the prediction of the competitive model (that Germany's net exports increase if E accedes to the CU) remains intact.

This asymmetric impact of enlargement to include E is reversed when the CU expands to include S, instead. In figure 9.5 the effects of such an enlargement on the distribution of sales in D's and G's market is displayed. Initially, the market segments that producers of the four countries serve are given by $1 \leq Q \leq Q_{EG}$ for E, $Q_{EG} \leq Q \leq Q_{DS}$ for G, and $Q_{GD} \leq Q \leq Q_{DS}$ for D, with all varieties with quality higher than Q_{DS}^0 being captured by S. The accession of S into the CU implies that its exports to D and G increase; its market segment increases by $Q_{DS}^0 Q_{DS}^1$.

This increase is accomplished, however, at the expense of German producers only, who suffer a decline both in their domestic-market sales and in their exports to Greece. Both D and G will obviously increase their exports to S's market. Germany will do so at the expense of S's producers, whereas Greece's exports will increase at the expense of E's exports. The intracountry distributional consequences are also reversed in this case. Low- and middle-income households in the incumbent countries are expected to lose from the enlargement, whereas in S low- and middle-income households will benefit from acceding to a "poor man's" CU. The above analysis implies that both the intra- and intercountry effects of CU enlargement depend on whether it is directed toward countries with lower or higher technological capabilities than the incumbent countries. As far as the intracountry effects are concerned, incumbent country households (in their role as consumers) prefer that enlargement be directed toward countries that have comparative advantage in varieties that they are consuming. On the other hand, producers prefer that the acceding countries have comparative advantage in varieties that are far removed from the quality spectrum in which the producers themselves specialize.

The above analysis has been partial equilibrium in nature, since it has paid no attention to the repercussions that would be set in motion by the creation of a trade imbalance. Since our analysis tries to focus on the preferences of individual producers in regard to enlargement, however, it is reasonable to assume that producers care only about the prospect of higher profits. Moreover, even if (somehow) producers had a general equilibrium awareness and could perceive the possible future rise in their (relative) costs as domestic wages, the exchange rate, or both adjust to keep the balance of payments in equilibrium, they would still regard an (effectively) non-reciprocal opening of foreign markets to their products (which the Eastern enlargement affords to technologically advanced EU firms) as preferable to a reciprocal opening of domestic and foreign markets.

9.4 Empirical Evidence

In this section we first present some evidence in support of our basic assumptions regarding the differences in technological sophistication and the resulting differences in comparative advantage between the CEECs, the EU countries, and Japan. We also present some econometric evidence, based on aggregate data, that provides some support for our conclusion regarding the differential impact of trade flows on countries of different technological sophistication as a result of previous EU enlargements.

Our hypothesis that the CEECs have comparative advantage in producing low-quality varieties relative to the EU countries is examined by constructing measures of export quality for the CEECs relative to each EU country. We approximate the quality of exports using the unit values of total exports of Hungary, Poland, the Czech Republic, and Slovakia relative to the unit value of each EU country's exports. For this purpose we use five-digit data from the OECD's "SourceOECD—Trade by Commodities" database for all SITC (second revision) categories (they involve 1,473 products). The data are for 1999, and the EU countries considered here are Denmark, France, Germany, Greece, Ireland, Italy, the Netherlands, Portugal, Spain, and the United Kingdom. Following Greenaway, Hine, and Milner (1995), we consider the varieties of a particular product exported by CEE country j to be of relatively high quality if their unit values are at least 15 percent higher than the unit values of the varieties exported by EU county i. Similarly, varieties of a product are characterized as of low quality if their unit value in country j is at least 15 percent less than the unit values of country i. If the relative unit values are within a 15 percent range of one another, then the varieties will be considered of equal quality. We then calculate the share of high-quality exports (relative to country i) in the total trade of country j.[13]

The logic behind this methodology is that differences in relative unit values reflect differences in relative qualities. Since our data are fairly disaggregated, it is likely that differences in prices will truly reflect differences in quality. Also, since we are using total world trade for each country, it is rather improbable that differences in prices among countries reflect differences in market power across countries.

Table 9.1 shows that the exports of each CEEC country are concentrated in lower qualities than every EU12 country. There are, however, large variations among countries. The most technologically advanced among the group of CEECs are Hungary and the Czech Republic, the quality of whose exports is slightly below the average quality of exports from Greece, Spain, and Portugal. The least technologically advanced is the Slovak Republic, with more than 90 percent of its total exports in goods whose quality is lower than the quality supplied by every EU country. There is also ample evidence that, with the exception of Estonia and Slovenia, which are similar to Hungary in terms of technological sophistication, the rest of the candidate countries (Latvia, Lithuania, Bulgaria, and Romania) specialize in the production of lower-quality varieties.

The EU countries facing higher levels of competition from the CEECs are Greece, Italy, the Netherlands, Spain, and Portugal, countries to which the CEECs have the highest share of their exports in product varieties of higher or the same quality. In table 9.1, we present the same calculations for Japan, showing that only 23 percent of Japan's exports are in lower-quality varieties than the EU12 average

Table 9.1
Relative export unit values (in percent) of CEECs and Japan to EU12, 1999

Country	Low quality	Same quality	High quality
a. Hungary			
Denmark	77.71	13.09	9.20
France	73.17	9.51	17.33
Germany	77.80	8.07	14.13
Greece	60.33	14.97	24.70
Ireland	74.89	10.21	14.90
Italy	67.10	12.35	20.54
Netherlands	67.58	14.86	17.55
Portugal	60.04	20.30	19.66
Spain	57.89	18.20	23.90
United Kingdom	75.80	8.86	15.34
b. Czech Republic			
Denmark	75.11	10.10	14.80
France	63.31	18.40	18.28
Germany	72.70	11.14	16.16
Greece	47.20	20.47	32.33
Ireland	69.04	11.00	19.97
Italy	60.48	15.89	23.63
Netherlands	59.54	13.67	26.78
Portugal	57.14	19.66	23.21
Spain	54.28	15.37	30.35
United Kingdom	67.47	13.46	19.07
c. Slovak Republic			
Denmark	99.44	0.02	0.54
France	99.69	0.12	0.18
Germany	99.55	0.14	0.30
Greece	97.81	0.02	2.17
Ireland	99.58	0.11	0.30
Italy	99.68	0.01	0.31
Netherlands	96.31	0.32	3.38
Portugal	99.29	0.07	0.63
Spain	99.46	0.12	0.42
United Kingdom	99.66	0.06	0.28
d. Poland			
Denmark	77.87	4.97	17.16
France	75.09	11.31	13.60
Germany	74.92	19.02	6.07
Greece	63.69	17.46	18.85

Table 9.1
(continued)

Country	Low quality	Same quality	High quality
Ireland	81.10	11.94	6.96
Italy	73.21	12.97	13.82
Netherlands	65.01	15.59	19.40
Portugal	60.24	27.78	11.99
Spain	65.51	19.46	15.03
United Kingdom	74.44	12.68	12.88
e. CEEC average			
Denmark	91.64	1.00	7.36
France	87.43	3.94	8.63
Germany	90.97	5.74	3.29
Greece	82.64	7.40	9.96
Ireland	90.69	6.00	3.32
Italy	83.38	7.18	9.45
Netherlands	81.35	5.92	12.73
Portugal	77.45	7.98	14.57
Spain	84.01	7.79	8.20
United Kingdom	87.23	8.59	4.18
Total EU	86.48	4.73	8.79
f. Japan			
Denmark	40.48	11.88	47.64
France	22.36	13.51	64.12
Germany	27.37	16.26	56.37
Greece	25.08	7.42	67.50
Ireland	41.17	15.39	43.45
Italy	20.49	13.99	65.52
Netherlands	33.05	13.55	53.40
Portugal	20.85	11.21	67.94
Spain	20.62	8.90	70.48
United Kingdom	26.14	14.03	59.83
Total EU	23.34	14.86	61.80

Note: Belgium and Luxembourg not included due to missing data.

(the average for the four CEECs included in the table is 86 percent), whereas 62 percent of its exports are in higher-quality varieties than the EU12 average (the relevant number for the four CEECs included in the table is 9 percent). In fact, there no EU12 country has a higher share of its exports in high-quality varieties than Japan. We also calculate the relative positions of Greece, Portugal, and Spain on the quality ladder during their time of accession. Table 9.2 presents the results of these calculations.

It is obvious from tables 9.1 and 9.2 that the economies of Greece, Portugal, and Spain had very similar features during the time of their accession, producing product varieties of lower quality than the EU average. Since the eastern enlargement involves countries that specialize (on average) in the production of even lower-quality varieties, compared to the EU12 average, than the countries of the 1981 and 1986 enlargements, we expect that the effects for the incumbent countries will be in the same direction, and possibly stronger in their differential impact, than those observed as a result of the 1981 and 1986 enlargements.

Before proceeding with our econometric investigation, it is worth presenting some raw evidence that is in agreement with another prediction emanating from our theoretical framework, namely, that the decline in the share of Greek exports to the EU countries as a result of the Europe Agreements will be, ceteris paribus, more pronounced for products in which Greece has comparative advantage in low-quality varieties. In table 9.3 we present the percentage changes (between 1993 and 1998) in the export shares of Greece, the EU9 countries[14] and three CEECs (the Czech Republic, Hungary, and Poland) in the total exports of these (groups of) countries to the EU10 (the EU9 plus Greece). The first column of the table depicts the percentage changes in the share of each country (group) for all commodity groups. The three CEECs managed to increase their share by about 87 percent (their share increased from about 2.5 percent in 1993 to about 4.7 percent in 1998), whereas during the same period, Greece's share declined by about 26 percent (from about 1 percent to about 0.7 percent), and the EU9 share declined by about 2 percent. These changes in market share were most likely due to the Europe Agreements.

In table 9.3 we also present changes in market shares by splitting the total number of commodities into three groups. We use data for all (six-digit) SITC product groupings, which involves about 5,400 product classifications, and we categorize them into three quality

Table 9.2
Relative export unit values (in percent) of Greece, Portugal, and Spain to EU countries at
the time of their accession

Country	Low quality	Same quality	High quality
a. Greece, 1980			
Denmark	76.82	13.12	10.05
France	65.68	20.53	13.79
Germany	61.16	20.33	18.51
Ireland	52.60	26.99	20.40
Italy	41.00	35.82	23.18
Netherlands	47.81	35.49	16.70
United Kingdom	72.19	18.42	9.39
Total EU	53.19	29.34	17.47
b. Spain, 1985			
Denmark	67.35	17.45	15.20
France	51.89	33.45	14.66
Germany	62.33	24.36	13.31
Greece	34.99	30.35	34.65
Ireland	63.08	16.80	20.12
Italy	42.77	38.83	18.40
Netherlands	46.91	35.81	17.28
United Kingdom	63.41	24.50	12.09
Total EU	52.88	33.61	13.51
c. Portugal, 1985			
Denmark	67.85	19.69	12.46
France	64.96	25.18	9.86
Germany	62.17	29.07	8.76
Greece	35.40	30.41	34.19
Ireland	57.01	19.83	23.16
Italy	65.07	19.60	15.33
Netherlands	50.70	31.25	18.05
United Kingdom	61.41	27.35	11.24
Total EU	56.75	27.63	15.62

Table 9.3
Percentage changes in market share, 1993–1998

	All commodities	Low quality	Same quality	High quality
Greece	−26.30	−29.01	−26.33	−12.73
EU9	−2.00	−1.65	−1.63	−2.72
CEECs	87.01	79.18	75.59	104.33

groups (low, same, and high) according to Greece's relative (to the EU9) export unit values, using the procedure described earlier.[15] Each product is classified into one of the three categories for the year 1995 (a year in the middle of our time sample), to avoid as much as possible the switching of some products from one category to another during the period. (We have verified that changing the base year from 1995 to either 1993 or 1998 has no significant effect on the results.) After categorizing the industries, we add the value in exports in each category to obtain the total exports of low-, same-, and high-quality products and then calculate the percentage change in the export shares of each category for the three (groups of) countries. We see that the changes are in agreement with our theoretical priors. That is, among its exports, Greece suffered the largest decline (about 29 percent) in its exports of products in which Greece's export unit values were lower than the EU9 average (Greece was an exporter of low-quality varieties of these products) and had the smallest decline (about 13 percent) in those products for which Greece's export unit values were higher than the EU9 average (Greece was exporting high-quality varieties of these products). In contrast, the EU9 experienced the largest decline among their exports in the products in which Greece's comparative advantage lay in high-quality varieties (by construction of the three categories, the EU9 had comparative advantage and were exporting low-quality varieties of these products). It is also worth noting that the CEECs experienced the largest percentage increase in their share of exports in the commodity group in which Greece had comparative advantage in (and was exporting) high-quality varieties. This is understandable if the trade pattern of the CEECs is closer to Greece's than to the EU9, since in that case the rise in CEEC exports would be expected to be higher in products for which the CEECs have comparative advantage in high-quality varieties, given that for these varieties there is relatively high demand among the affluent EU9 households.

In the rest of this section, we estimate an aggregate net-exports equation for each country to find out to what extent eastern enlargement can be expected to exert differential effects on the incumbent EU countries. As noted earlier, one may expect that the adjustment of wage rates and exchange rates subsequent to enlargement in order to restore balance-of-payments equilibrium may diminish through time, so that no such effects can be uncovered by the data. Macroeconomic adjustments subsequent to customs union enlargement usually have long gestation periods, however. In such cases, one may expect that the effects identified earlier of customs union enlargement on an incumbent country's net exports will be observed in the data.

Our interest is in establishing whether the trade pattern of the EU countries underwent a regime switch as a result of the 1981 (Greece) and 1986 (Spain and Portugal) enlargements. From the analysis of the previous section we would expect that, ceteris paribus, only the countries that were not contiguous in the qualities of the product varieties they offer to the acceding countries experienced an increase in their net exports as a result of the enlargements. The accession of Denmark, Ireland, and the United Kingdom in 1973 does not give us the opportunity to test this prediction, since the acceding countries were offering product varieties that covered the whole quality spectrum (Ireland was offering mainly low-quality varieties, whereas the United Kingdom and Denmark were offering mainly middle- and high-quality ones).

We conduct regressions on annual data for 1960–1998 for eight EU countries that were EU members before the Iberian accession (namely, Denmark, France, Germany, Greece, Ireland, Italy, the Netherlands, and the United Kingdom). We exclude Belgium and Luxembourg because of missing data from their series. The estimated equation is

$$NX_t = a + \beta \mathbf{X}_t + \gamma D + e_t,$$

where e_t is an i.i.d. error, NX_t is real total net exports of country i, D are intercept dummies, and $\mathbf{X}_t$ is the vector of explanatory variables. In common with the empirical literature on net exports (see Rose 1991), we use as explanatory variables the logarithms of domestic GDP, world GDP, and real exchange rates (RERs).

We use dummies to capture the effects of previous enlargements. Our prime interests, for the reasons mentioned above, are the enlargements of 1981 and 1986. These two events may cause a regime switch and a change in the slope and intercept coefficients.[16] The same effect, however, may also be produced by the 1973 enlargement. In addition to these enlargements, starting from 1990, a number of events altered existing patterns of international trade, including the extension of the Generalized System of Preferences concessions to the CEECs, the re-unification of Germany, and the Europe Agreements between the EU and the CEECs (most of which went into effect after 1994). A priori, it is difficult to form an opinion about the joint effects of these changes. Moreover, these effects are not likely to be picked up by the data, since there are very few observations after 1991 (when the results of these effects may have been strong enough to show up).

The data we use for real domestic GDP and real world GDP were obtained from the CHELEM (Harmonized Data for International Trade and World Economy) database, our real net-exports data were taken from the OECD's Main Economic Indicators, and the real exchange rate data were taken from the International Monetary Fund's International Financial Statistics. All variables were tested for stationarity, using the augmented Dickey-Fuller test. For all countries the variables were found to be nonstationary, with the exception of the real net exports (dependent variable) for Ireland and France. After that the equations were tested for cointegration using the Engle-Granger test. None of the equations were found to be co-integrated.[17] To see whether this absence of co-integration was due to the structural break in the sample (see, e.g., Maddala and Kim 1998), we split the whole sample into two subsamples, one before and one after the expected (according to our theory) break. No significant evidence of a co-integrated relation was found even in the subsamples. (Since the results of these tests are similar to the ones produced by Rose 1991 and are not crucial for our results, we do not present them here, but they are available upon request.) As a result the analysis is conducted by taking the first differences of the non-stationary series.

Our strategy with respect to the regime-switching dummies was as follows: We first estimated the equation without the dummies. We then performed Cusum and Cusum squares tests to check the stability of the coefficients. When one of these tests showed instability, we performed Chow breakpoint tests for the relevant years. Whenever we established that indeed, at the time of enlargement, a break point existed, we included the particular dummies (intercept dummy).

In table 9.4 we present the results of the econometric testing we conducted.[18] First, we note that the 1973 enlargement had no effect on the incumbent countries of the EU, a result that is consistent with our theoretical framework. Second, we find that Greece's accession in 1981

Table 9.4
Main results of econometric testing

	Denmark	France	Germany	Greece	Ireland	Italy	Netherlands	United Kingdom
Constant	19.29**	86.99***	12.20***	6.21*	-9.45	35.12***	-1.22	2.71
GDP	-533.62***	-991.9*	-369.45***	-105.07**	354**	-780.58***	-90.94***	-274.95**
World GDP	54.45	-762.68***	50.57	-17.55	-250.59***	99.15*	133.45***	-10.49
Real Exchange Rates	-66.64	166.0961	201.39**	-30.18	192.30*	-148.82**	-31.77	160***
Dummy								
1974	-5.21				-15.98*			
1981				6.17	17	-11.67*		
1986		-70.88**	12.04**	-7.19**	54.30***			
R^2	0.44	0.46	0.45	0.33	0.77	0.54	0.80	0.35

* statistical significance at 10 percent. ** statistical significance at 5 percent. *** statistical significance at 1 percent.

resulted in a (statistically) significant reduction of net exports for Italy only, a result explained both by Greece's small size and the fact that Italy was the most contiguous country to Greece in terms of quality of product varieties in 1981 (see table 9.2a). Third, we observe that the Iberian accession in 1986 resulted in (statistically) significant positive effects on the net exports of Germany and Ireland and negative effects on the net exports of France and Greece. The contrasting effects on the net exports of Germany and Greece (two countries that occupied opposite positions in terms of vertical specialization vis-à-vis Spain and Portugal in 1986; see tables 9.2b and 9.2c) also provide some support for the notion that our predictions regarding the differential effects of the eastern enlargement may not be too wide of the mark.

Nevertheless, the results of our analysis are not entirely supportive of our framework. The positive effect on Ireland's net exports as a result of the Iberian accession is rather difficult to explain if we restrict our attention to Ireland's low place in the quality ladder in 1985. Yet as table 9.1e reveals, between 1985 and 1999, Ireland improved its position on the quality ladder (mainly through the attraction of a significant amount of FDI flows) so much that it shared with Germany the highest place on the quality ladder in 1999. The negative effect of the Iberian accession on France's net exports is more difficult to explain within our framework (since France's position was in the top half of the quality spectrum in both 1985 and 1999), and for this reason we must conclude that our results, although broadly supportive of our hypothesis, cannot be regarded as the last word on the issue.

9.5 Concluding Remarks

In this chapter, we have argued that the effects of CU expansion may vary significantly among the incumbent countries, and that a primary determinant of how the effects are spread among them is whether the expansion is directed toward countries with higher or lower technological sophistication than the incumbent ones. We have also argued that among EU firms, those that are technologically advanced (i.e., those residing in high-income countries) may stand to gain more from the planned eastern enlargement than from a multilateral opening of the markets. In contrast, less technologically sophisticated firms (usually residing in low-income EU countries) would prefer that opportunities for market access with high-income countries were enhanced.

The mechanism behind the (possibly) asymmetric effects of the eastern enlargement identified in this chapter is by no means the only one.

Another (potentially complementary, and in the long-run more important) mechanism through which the enlargement could produce significant changes in existing trading patterns is the intensification of the ongoing process of reorientation of FDI away from the southern EU members toward the new entrants (indeed, from 1992 to 1999, the volume of FDI going to the CEECs relative to the volume received by the southern EU members [defined here as Greece, Spain, and Portugal] has increased by a factor of six; see the OECD's Foreign Direct Investment database for more details). It is gradually becoming possible to study the influence of FDI flows on quality upgrading and the changing trade patterns at a disaggregate level as the available data relating to these changes accumulate.

From a political-economy perspective, this chapter seems to suggest that after the first wave of candidate countries has entered the EU, the decision to expand further to the east and to the south will be slightly more complicated. Key producer interests in the technologically advanced EU countries will still prefer to give "preferential access" to the EU markets to firms in the (second-wave) candidate countries in exchange for receiving similar treatment in those countries' markets. But the coalition against further expansion will by then have grown stronger, since not only the southern EU countries, but the newly admitted countries (and their producer's) as well, will be potential opponents of further expansion—in addition to those countries disaffected by immigration or reduced access to existing side payments (i.e. CAP, structural funds, etc.). The development of complicated schemes for further side payments (including political ones) will then be a crucial factor in determining the possibility of further EU enlargement.

Notes

This chapter is based on a paper presented at the CESifo-Delphi Conference "Managing EU Enlargement" in Munich in December 2001. We wish to thank Helge Berger, Heather Gibson, Sarantis Kalyvitis, Euclid Tsakalotos, Spyros Vassilakis, the conference participants, and especially, our discussants, Ronald Jones and Margarita Katsimi, for many helpful comments and suggestions. The comments of an anonymous reviewer also helped us in revising the paper. The usual disclaimer applies.

1. The Copenhagen Council also decided to continue accession negotiations with Bulgaria and Romania, with both countries expected to join the union after 2007. It was also decided that if the European Council in December 2004 decides that Turkey fulfills the Copenhagen political criteria, the EU will open accession negotiations with Turkey without delay.

2. In contrast, inter-industry trade in homogeneous goods requires the reallocation of workers from one industry to another, possibly involving lower wages if the imported goods are labor intensive.

3. A considerable body of evidence testifies to the importance of vertical intra-industry trade (see, for example, Greenaway, Hine, and Milner 1995; Schott 2001; and Malley and Moutos 2002). The accumulating evidence suggests that vertical intra-industry trade is quantitatively more important than horizontal intra-industry trade.

4. It must, however, be mentioned that in the absence of complete insurance, risk-averse individuals may not prefer full trade liberalization. Consider, for example, a policy that, by restricting trade, guarantees to all workers an income equal to 100. Consider also a policy of free trade that is expected to increase the incomes of those with employment to 120, whereas those who are unemployed receive an income of 30. Let each worker perceive that she has an 80 percent chance of being among those employed. This makes the expected income of each worker under free trade be higher than under the trade-restricting policy by 2 percent. If the utility function displays a modest degree of risk aversion (e.g., $U = Y^{0.7}$), then the workers will vote in favor of the trade-restricting policy, since the utility of the sure thing is greater than the expected utility under free trade.

5. According to Tsoukalis (1993), the EU has always been careful to diffuse tensions by accommodating member states when they signaled that an EU policy would cause them major harm (as in the case of Spain and Portugal, which were granted gradual adjustment on some issues, or in the case of the United Kingdom regarding the budget rebate).

6. Moravcsik (1998) claims that the creation of the EC induced the United States to commence the Dillon (1959–61) and subsequently the Kennedy (1963–67) and Tokyo (1974–79) Rounds of GATT negotiations. Meunier (2000) also reports that the pro-European camp in France used the slogan "Let's unite. And the world will listen to us" during the campaign before the 1992 referendum on the Maastricht Treaty on European Union.

7. The recent experience of countries using accession to a regional group to stimulate economic and political liberalization in the countries seeking accession is unique by historical standards. In 1976 Chile, for example, withdrew from the Andean Pact because it wanted to implement a reform package that this agreement prohibited (Nogues and Quintanilla 1993).

8. Existing members of a regional group are often happy to assist a candidate country in the implementation of reforms. For example, the United States made it clear to Mexico in the negotiations surrounding NAFTA that by consolidating the reforms it had undertaken in the previous years, Mexico would have a stronger claim on U.S. financial assistance (Francois 1997). The EU has also adopted this attitude with the candidate countries. For both the EU and the United States, the motivation for this attitude has been related to emigration. By making reforms in Mexico and in the candidate countries more credible, they hoped to raise the growth rates of these countries, thereby reducing immigration pressures.

9. Moravcsik explains, for example, why a "small Europe" customs union (with provisions for agriculture, atomic energy, and supra-national institutions) came into effect rather than a pan-European free-trade area, on the basis of producer interests, the distribution of relative power, and the desire for future elaboration and implementation of policy.

10. In any case, the above observations imply that the presence of another factor (in addition to labor) may be an important determinant of comparative advantage for some products. The presence of organizational (or entrepreneurial) capital may be the most important factor in the case of vertically differentiated products. We expect that no significant change to our conclusions will result from the introduction of such a factor into our analysis (see also the discussion in section 9.3.3).

11. From figure 9.2 we can also deduce that there will exist some households with income levels and preference structures such that there is more than one point of tangency between their highest indifference curve and their budget constraint. Such households will be indifferent between buying, for example, D-produced and S-produced varieties. We abstain from further discussion of such cases since they do not, in any way, influence the results of our analysis.

12. For a political-economy analysis of the role of tariff revenue in a median-voter model with both homogeneous goods and vertically differentiated products, see Moutos 2001.

13. In many cases a country does not export in some of the product categories, so for each country, the total number of products used to construct the index may be smaller than the total number of categories available. The calculated values are normalized to sum to one.

14. The EU9 includes the United Kingdom, Ireland, Denmark, Germany, Italy, the Netherlands, France, Spain, and Portugal. Our data start from 1993, so we haven't included Austria, Sweden, and Finland, because their accession to EU had just then been completed. Moreover, we haven't included Belgium and Luxembourg, because after 1995, they started presenting international trade commodity data as a single country, and there is no evidence that data prior to 1995 were collected and classified in the same way as after 1995.

15. This more detailed classification involves data only for 1990–1998.

16. We estimated the equation allowing for a change in the slope coefficients (slope dummies). In most equations these slope dummies were found to be insignificant. Slope breaks were found to be significant only in the estimated equations for Greece, Denmark, and Ireland, but even in these cases, there was no change in the results for the intercept dummies.

17. Since we are interested in hypothesis testing, we adopted a strict test for stationarity, testing the null of no cointegration at the 1 percent level of statistical significance using the augmented Dickey-Fuller test for cointegration and the critical values provided by MacKinnon (1991).

18. As is well known, there is simultaneous determination of some of the right-hand-side variables and of the trade balance. Following standard practice (see Rose 1991) we have also estimated the equations using instrumental variables. Since the results turned out to be the same in both cases, we have chosen to present the results of the most efficient estimator, which is the ordinary least squares.

References

Arndt, S. 1968. "On Discriminatory Versus Non-preferential Tariff Policies." *Economic Journal* 78: 971–979.

Arndt, S. 1969. "Customs Union and the Theory of Tariffs." *American Economic Review* 59: 108–118.

Baldwin, R. 1994. *Towards an Integrated Europe.* London: Centre for Economic Policy Research.

Baldwin, R., J. Francois, and R. Portes. 1997. "The Costs and Benefits of Eastern Enlargement: The Impact on EU and Central Europe." *Economic Policy* 24: 127–176.

Corden, W. M. 1984. "The Normative Theory of International Trade." In *Handbook of International Economics*, vol. 1, ed. R. Jones and P. Kenen, 63–130. Amsterdam: North-Holland.

Eaton, J., and H. Kierzkowski. 1984. "Oligopolistic Competition, Product Variety, and International Trade." In *Monopolistic Competition and International Trade*, ed. H. Kierzkowski, 69–83. Oxford: Oxford University Press.

Ethier, W. 1998. "The New Regionalism." *Economic Journal* 108: 1149–1161.

Faini, R., and R. Portes, eds. 1995a. *EU Trade with Eastern Europe: Adjustment and Opportunities.* London: Centre for Economic Policy Research.

Faini, R., and R. Portes. 1995b. "Opportunities Outweigh Adjustment: The Political Economy of Trade with Central and Eastern Europe." In *EU Trade with Eastern Europe: Adjustment and Opportunities*, ed. R. Faini and R. Portes, 1–18. London: Centre for Economic Policy Research.

Falvey, R. 1981. "Commercial Policy and Intra-industry Trade." *Journal of International Economics* 11: 495–511.

Falvey, R., and H. Kierzkowski. 1987. "Product Quality, Intra-industry Trade and (Im)perfect Competition." In *Protection and Competition in International Trade: Essays in Honor of W. M. Corden*, ed. H. Kierzkowski, 143–161. Oxford: Basil Blackwell.

Fernandez, R., and J. Portes. 1998. "Returns to Regionalism: An Analysis of Nontraditional Gains from Regional Trade Agreements." *World Bank Economic Review* 12: 197–220.

Flam, H., and E. Helpman. 1987. "Vertical Product Differentiation and North-South Trade." *American Economic Review* 77: 810–822.

Francois, J. 1997. "External Bindings and the Credibility of Reform." In *Regional Partners in Global Markets*, ed. A. Galal and B. Hoekman, 35–48. London: Centre for Economic Policy Research.

Freudenberg, M., and F. Lemoine. 1999. "Central and Eastern European Countries in the International Division of Labour in Europe." Centre d'Etudes Prospectives et d'Informations Internationales. Working paper no. 1999-05, CEPII.

Gabszewicz, J., and J. Thisse. 1979. "Price Competition, Quality and Income Disparities." *Journal of Economic Theory* 20: 340–359.

Greenaway, D., R. C. Hine, and C. R. Milner. 1995. "Vertical and Horizontal Intra-industry Trade: A Cross-Industry Analysis for the United Kingdom." *Economic Journal* 105: 1505–1519.

Grossman, G., and E. Helpman. 1994. "Protection for Sale." *American Economic Review* 84: 833–850.

Grossman, G., and E. Helpman. 1995. "The Politics of Free-Trade Agreements." *American Economic Review* 85: 667–690.

Hamilton, C., and A. Winters. 1992. "Opening up Trade in Eastern Europe." *Economic Policy* 14: 77–117.

Jones, R. 2000. *Globalization and the Theory of Input Trade.* Cambridge: MIT Press.

Jones, R., and H. Kierzkowski. 2001. "A Framework for Fragmentation." In *Fragmentation: New Production Patterns in the World Economy*, ed. S. Arndt and H. Kierzkowski, 17–35. Oxford: Oxford University Press.

Kemp, M. 1969. *The Pure Theory of International Trade and Investment.* Englewood Cliffs, NJ: Prentice-Hall.

Krishna, P. 1998. "Regionalism and Multilateralism: A Political Economy Approach." *Quarterly Journal of Economics* 113: 227–251.

Lavigne, M. 1995. *The Economics of Transition.* London: Macmillan.

Lynch, F. 1997. *France and the International Economy: From Vichy to the Treaty of Rome.* New York: Routledge.

Mackinnon, J. 1991. "Critical Values for Co-integration Tests." In *Long Run Economic Relationships*, ed. R. F. Engle and C. W. J. Granger, 267–276. Oxford: Oxford University Press.

Maddala, G. S., and I. M. Kim. 1998. *Unit Roots, Cointegration and Structural Change.* Oxford: Cambridge University Press.

Malley, J., and T. Moutos. 2002. "Vertical Product Differentiation and the Import Demand Function: Theory and Evidence." *Canadian Journal of Economics* 35: 257–281.

Meunier, S. 2000. "What Single Voice? European Institutions and EU-U.S. Trade Negotiations." *International Organization* 54: 103–135.

Milward, A. 1984. *The Reconstruction of Europe, 1945–51.* Berkeley University Press, Berkeley.

Moravcsik, A. 1998. *The Choice for Europe: Social Purpose and State Power from Messina to Maastricht.* Ithaca: Cornell University Press.

Moutos, T. 2001. "Why Do Poor Democracies Collect a Lot of Tariff Revenue?" *Economics and Politics* 13: 95–112.

Mundell, R. 1964. "Tariff Preferences and the Terms of Trade." *Manchester School of Economic and Social Studies* 32: 1–13.

Nogues, J., and R. Quintanilla. 1993. "Latin America's Integration and the Multilateral Trading System." In *New Dimensions in Regional Integration*, ed. J. de Melo and A. Panagariya, 278–313. London: Centre for Economic Policy Research.

Pagoulatos, G. 2000. "Economic Adjustment and Financial Reform: Greece's Europeanization and the Emergence of a Stabilization State." *South European Society and Politics* 5: 191–214.

Parsons, G. 2000. "Domestic Interests, Ideas and Integration: Lessons from the French Case." *Journal of Common Market Studies* 38: 45–70.

Perroni, C., and J. Whalley. 2000. "The New Regionalism: Trade Liberalization or Insurance?" *Canadian Journal of Economics* 33: 1–24.

Riezman, R. 1985. "Customs Unions and the Core." *Journal of International Economics* 19: 355–365.

Rollo, J., and A. Smith. 1993. "The Political Economy of Eastern European Trade with the European Community: Why So Sensitive?" *Economic Policy* 16: 140–181.

Rose, A. 1991. "The Role of Exchange Rates in a Popular Model of International Trade: Does the Marshall-Lerner Condition Hold?" *Journal of International Economics* 30: 301–316.

Rosen, S. 1974. "Hedonic Prices and Implicit Markets: Product Diffrentiation in Pure Competition." *Journal of Political Economy* 82: 34–55.

Schott, P. K. 2001. "Do Rich and Poor Countries Specialize in a Different Mix of Goods? Evidence from Product-Level US Data." Working paper no. W8492, National Bureau of Economic Research, Cambridge, MA.

Tornell, A., and G. Esquivel. 1997. "The Political Economy of Mexico's Entry into NAFTA." In *Regionalism versus Multilateral Trade Agreements*, ed. T. Ito and A. Krueger, 25–55. Chicago: University of Chicago Press.

Tsoukalis, L. 1993. *The New European Economy: The Politics and Economics of European Integration*. Oxford: Oxford University Press.

Vanek, J. 1965. *General Equilibrium of International Discrimination: The Case of Customs Unions*. Cambridge: Harvard University Press.

Viner, J. 1950. *The Customs Union Issue*. Lancaster, PA: Carnegie Endowment for International Peace.

Whalley, J. 1998. "Why Do Countries Seek Regional Trade Agreements?" In *The Regionalization of the World Economy*, ed. J. Frankel, 63–89. Chicago: University of Chicago Press.

Comments

Ronald W. Jones

Much has been, and will be, said about the forthcoming projected enlargement of the European Union as countries to the east knock at the door seeking admission. The chapter by Adam and Moutos is an important addition to this literature and focuses on the *distributional* effects of such accession, especially the intercountry effects on present members, as well as on the effects on income groups within such countries. The defining characteristic of the study conducted by Adam and Moutos is that traded commodities exhibit vertical differentiation. Although early modeling of product-differentiated traded items focused on horizontal differentiation, Adam and Moutos claim that two-way trade in vertically differentiated products represents the fastest-growing category of trade between the EU12 and members of the CEEC (applicant) group.

The authors' modeling efforts point to an important asymmetry, namely, that high-income countries prefer union with low-income countries and vice versa. These preferences are more strongly held by producers and potential exporters than by consumers. Certainly if there are elements of imperfect competition, producers would most prefer the addition of new consumers without an accompanying collection of foreign producers of like-quality commodities, and this will most likely occur if the entrants have per capita income levels significantly lower than (or higher than) those of member nations. This asymmetry points to the rationale of the chapter's subtitle, "Why Japan Is Not a Candidate Country." EU countries are, on average, higher-income countries than those found in the CEEC group, but have per capita incomes that are much closer to (or lower than) Japan's. Producers of high-quality products in France and Germany, say, might not relish the prospect of a preferential lowering of trade barriers to an advanced country such as Japan. By the same argument, the countries at the lower end of the income scale in the EU might most be wary of enlargement to applicants from the east.

If producers tend to favor union with countries at the other end of the income scale from their own countries, how about consumers? Typically consumers benefit from heightened competition, and competition is what can be expected when new entrants produce goods of similar quality to local producers. This kind of asymmetry brings to mind a quite general underlying question in the theory of international trade: Is (beneficial) international trade encouraged more in a group of countries that are dissimilar in their factor endowments and technology or in a group of countries that are fairly similar in these characteristics? Classical and neo-classical international trade theory emphasize the former view—that greater gains can be realized if trade is opened up among countries with wide variations in capital-labor endowment ratios and technologies—whereas "new trade theory" points to greater gains if countries are fairly similar in these respects, an argument going back earlier to economists such as Staffan Burenstam-Linder (1961), who expected heightened trade among countries with similar per capita incomes and tastes. Of course, issues of returns to scale and the distinction between horizontally and vertically differentiated products (emphasized by Adam and Moutos) are of importance in making these comparisons.

At several points in the chapter, the authors stress the comparison between regional integration and the option of a *unilateral* reduction in trade barriers. Although the theoretical advantages to small countries of unilateral moves in the trade area are often stressed, the relevant comparison to regional unions seems to be that of *multilateral* reductions in trade obstacles. And of course, much has been written on this issue from the point of view of world welfare—whether regional blocks are an impediment (stumbling block) to eventual free trade.

I agree with the authors' assertion as to the importance of vertically differentiated goods in international trade but would prefer not to restrict attention to these traded items as final consumer goods. Adam and Moutos's model of consumer goods trade does indeed succeed in making their point about producers in one country being more threatened by accession of new countries with levels of quality similar to those in the producers' own country represented in their production array. Such modeling helps as well to point out that within a country, the consequences of such trade on individual welfare will differ for residents with low and high per capita income. What is left out of the model presented in this chapter, in my opinion, is the importance of trade in intermediate goods and foreign investment. In particular, recent lowering of the costs of communication and transportation, as well as greater knowledge of potential suppliers in other countries and increased scales of production, all conspire to encourage a *fragmentation* of vertically integrated production processes so that, say, more labor-intensive segments of a production process can be relocated in low-wage countries (see Jones and Kierzkowski 1990). Inter alia, this suggests that gains can be realized by locating such labor-intensive fragments in countries of the CEEC group, even if the final emerging consumer good is of high quality and would, without such fragmentation, be produced entirely in the high-income country in the EU.

The empirical work presented by Adam and Moutos serves to corroborate their theoretical conjectures. Commodities are put into three categories, depending on whether each acceding country's exports are of low quality, high quality, or roughly the same quality as each of ten of the countries of the current EU. Almost all the exports of countries such as the Slovak Republic to each of the EU countries fall into the low-quality group, whereas over 30 percent of the exports to Greece of countries like the Czech Republic are in the high-quality group. Indeed, this figure compares with the lower ones of 15 percent and 16 percent for Denmark and Germany, respectively. Japan is taken as a comparison for hypothetical entry purposes. Japanese exports to each of the countries in the EU group other than Denmark fall into the high-quality range over 50 percent of the time. These and other figures support the kinds of remarks Adam and Moutos make regarding the difference between the response of Greece, on the one hand, and that of Germany, on the other, to potential entry of one of the CEEC group or of a country such as Japan. Their calculations surrounding these remarks are interesting.

Most of the results presented in the chapter will not be surprising. What the chapter accomplishes, however, is a more focused investigation of the asymmetric effects of potential entry of CEEC countries in disturbing incomes and trade patterns in various countries within the EU. Adam and Moutos's arguments tend to support the view that for the EU, greater gains will accrue to the higher-income countries in a world in which vertical quality differentiation among traded commodities is an important characteristic.

References

Burenstam-Linder, S. 1961. *An Essay on Trade and Transformation*. Stockholm: Almqvist and Wiksell.

Jones, R. W., and H. Kierzkowski. 1990. "The Role of Services in Production and International Trade: A Theoretical Framework." In *The Political Economy of International Trade*, ed. R. Jones and A. Krueger, 31–48. Oxford, UK: Blackwell.

Authors and Commentators

Antonis Adam
Athens University of Economics
and Business

Richard Baldwin
Graduate Institute of International Studies, Geneva

Sascha O. Becker
CES, CESifo, and IZA

Helge Berger
International Monetary Fund,
Free University Berlin and CESifo

Michael C. Burda
Humboldt-Universitt zu Berlin,
CEPR, CESifo, and IZA

Alex Cukierman
Berglas School of Economics and
CEPR

Riccardo Faini
Università di Roma Tor Vergata
and CEPR

Daniel Gros
Centre for European Policy
Studies (CEPS) and CESifo

Jacob de Haan
University of Groningen and
CESifo

Ben J. Heijdra
University of Groningen and
OCFEB

Robert Inklaar
University of Groningen

Rajshri Jayaraman
CES, CESifo, and IZA

Ronald W. Jones
University of Rochester

Margarita Katsimi
Athens University of Economics
and Business and CESifo

Christian Keuschnigg
University of St. Gallen
(IFF-HSG), CESifo, and CEPR

Wilhelm Kohler
Johannes Kepler University Linz

Arjan M. Lejour
CPB Netherlands Bureau for Economic Policy Analysis

Jaime de Melo
University of Geneva and CEPR

Florence Miguet
University of Geneva

Tobias Möller
University of Geneva

Ruud A. de Mooij
CPB Netherlands Bureau for Economic Policy Analysis, Erasmus University Rotterdam, Tinbergen Institute, and CESifo

Thomas Moutos
Athens University of Economics and Business and CESifo

Richard Nahuis
CPB Netherlands Bureau for Economic Policy Analysis and Utrecht School of Economics

Carlo Perroni
University of Warwick

Index

Abel, A., 117
Accession countries. *See also* Specific
  country
  average growth rate and, 37
  Balassa-Samuelson effect and, 37, 39
  business cycle and, 39–41
  currency anchoring and, 73–94
  customs union and, 222–224, 231–236,
    262–263 (*see also* Customs union)
  data sources for, 59–62
  eastern EU enlargement and, 173–210 (*see
    also* Eastern EU enlargement)
  exchange rate model and, 74–94
  income gaps and, 175
  inflation and, 36–39
  internal markets and, 224–229, 236–243,
    245–247
  migration and, 243–244, 248–250
  pooling and, 48
  representation and, 44–45
  rotation schemes and, 45–55
  transition economies and, 36–39
  vote-weighting and, 43–44
  WorldScan model and, 219
Adam, Antonis, 8–9, 261–295
Adjustment costs, 125–126
  Cobb-Douglas function and, 110, 112
  convex, 108–109
  description of, 108–109
  dynamics and, 106–108, 118–119
  Germany and, 108–112
  inference of, 110–112
  migration effects and, 112–116
  nonconvex, 113–114
  waiting option and, 114–116
Agglomeration, 5–6, 121n13
  adjustment costs and, 107–119, 125–126

Aggregation
  capital-labor ratio and, 133, 140
  economic effects and, 261–262
  shocks and, 40–41
  trade and, 229
Aghion, P., 182
Agriculture, 181
  Common Agricultural Policy, 2–3, 12–20,
    22–23, 176, 192
  customs union and, 234–236
  internal market accession and, 242, 245–
    247
Amsterdam Treaty, 14, 23–24
Andolfatto, D., 182
Armington assumption, 182, 185, 220, 227
Arndt, S., 265
Arrow-Debreu economy, 103
Australia, 17
Austria, 187, 196
  eastern EU enlargement and, 174
  migration and, 230
  rotation schemes and, 52
  WorldScan model and, 219
Autarky, 262–263

Balassa-Samuelson effect, 37, 39, 63n11, 69
Baldwin, Richard E., 2–3
  ECB restructuring and, 33
  EU management and, 11–27, 174, 185,
    190, 211, 228–229
  political economy and, 261
Bangladesh, 264–265
Bank of England, 17
Bauer, T., 130, 132, 148, 244
Becker, Sascha O., 7, 211–215
Belgium, 52, 219
Benhabib model, 169

Berger, Helge, 1–10
  ECB and, 29–66
Bergstrand, J. H., 225
Blanchard, O., 117
Boeri, T., 130, 132, 137, 229–230
Brenton, P., 229
Breuss, F., 228
Broersma, L., 205
Brücker, H., 129, 132, 148
Buch, C., 117
Budget constraints, 74, 77
  CAP spending and, 22
  customs union model and, 272–279
  equilibrium and, 78–79
  reduction of, 22–23
  structural spending and, 20–21
Bulgaria, 261
  currency anchoring and, 73, 74, 91
  ECB and, 29
  WorldScan model and, 219
Bulow, J., 138
Bundesbank, 17
  governance of, 34
  jurisdiction extension and, 45
  Zentralbankrat and, 32–33
Burda, Michael C., 5, 99–123
Business cycles, 39
  eastern EU enlargement and, 182
  rotation and, 54–55
  shocks and, 40–41

Cagan-Bailey analysis, 96
Canada, 17, 132, 229, 266
Capital. See also Labor
  dynamic analysis and, 106–108, 118–119
  factor mobility and, 100–106
  social, 131–140 (see also Migration)
  transmission channels and, 181–186
  venture, 20–21
  WorldScan model and, 219–222
Central and Eastern European Countries
  (CEECs), 8–9
  CGE model and, 190–202
  customs union and, 222–224, 231–236,
    250, 262–289
  eastern EU enlargement and, 173–210 (see
    also Eastern EU enlargement)
  guest workers and, 135–140
  industry barriers and, 217
  internal market accession and, 224–229,
    236–243, 245–247, 257
  migration and, 130, 159–160, 180–181

product restriction and, 262
reform completion and, 13
vertical trade and, 263
welfare effect and, 80
WorldScan model and, 219–222, 230–250
  (see also WorldScan model)
Centralization, 41–43
Charter of Fundamental Rights, 18
CHELEM (Harmonized Data for Interna-
  tional Trade and World Economy), 287
Chiswick, Barry, 169–171
Chow breakpoint tests, 287
Citrin, J., 151
Cobb-Douglas production function, 110,
  112, 219
Committee on Economic and Monetary
  Affairs, 19–20
Common Agricultural Policy (CAP), 2–3
  eastern EU enlargement and, 192
  migration and, 176
  spending and, 22
  subsidies and, 22–23
Computable general equilibrium (CGE)
  model, 7–8, 211, 213–214
  alternative fiscal policy assumptions and,
    197
  Germany and, 190–202
  GTAP database and, 218
  migration and, 198–201
  real benefits and, 193–196
  sensitivity factors and, 201–202
Constant Elasticity of Substitution (CES)
  functions, 219–220
Consumer Price Index (CPI), 61
Consumption, 182–184
  enlargement effects and, 230–244
Corden, W. M., 264
Coricelli, F., 39
Council of Ministers
  decision making by, 14–17
  Treaty of Nice and, 23–24
Cukierman, Alex, 3–4, 67–72
Currency. See Monetary policy
Currency board arrangements (CBAs), 95–
  96
Customs union
  autarky and, 262–263
  common external tariff (CET) and, 222–
    223
  concessions and, 266
  data sets for, 279–289
  incentives for, 263–267

macro-economic effects and, 232–234
model for, 267–279
political issues of, 264–267
production quality and, 272–279
protectionism and, 265–266
sectoral effects, 234–236
supply relationships and, 268–272
war and, 264–265
WorldScan model and, 222–224, 231–236, 250
Cyprus, 1, 173, 261
business cycle and, 40
ECB and, 29
migration and, 181
Czech Republic, 1, 261
Balassa-Samuelson effect and, 39
ECB and, 29
rotation schemes and, 52
WorldScan model and, 219

Debt. *See also* Shocks
GDP ratio and, 83–84, 89–91
welfare effect and, 79–84
Decision-making. *See* Governance
Den Haan, W. J., 182
Denmark
ECB and, 29, 32
rotation schemes and, 52
WorldScan model and, 219
Dickey-Fuller test, 287
Dimanaran, B. V., 218–219
Dixit-Stiglitz analysis, 182–183, 201
Domino theory, 24–25
Drazen, A., 85
Duisenberg, Wim, 19–20
Dustmann, C., 129
Dynamics, 106, 118–119
adjustment costs and, 107–108
equilibrium and, 106–108, 118–119, 174–175, 181–189, 203–206
saddle point stability and, 107

Eastern EU enlargement, 207–210, 297–299
alternative fiscal policy assumptions and, 197
CAP and, 192
CGE model and, 190–202
controversies over, 173–174
customs union model and, 272–289
effects on present member countries, 186–189
features of, 175–181

GDP and, 177, 192
general equilibrium model for, 174–175, 181–189, 203–206
German perspective and, 190–202, 212–215
migration and, 198–201
real benefits and, 193–196
shocks and, 107
transmission channels, 181–186
Turkey and, 261
unemployment and, 174–175, 188, 197, 199–203, 207n3
Eaton, J., 262
Economic and Monetary Union (EMU), 17
Economic issues
accession negotiations and, 12–13
Balassa-Samuelson effect and, 37, 39, 63n11, 69
business cycles and, 39–41, 54–55, 182
Common Agricultural Policy (CAP) and, 2–3, 22
Copenhagen negotiations and, 1–2
customs union and, 222–224, 231–236
European Central Bank (ECB) and, 3–4, 17–20
Hodrick-Prescott filter and, 40
industry barriers and, 217
integration and, 99–123 (*see also* Integration)
labor influx and, 5–6 (*see also* Labor)
political issues and, 43–48
poor members and, 11
shocks and, 40–41 (*see also* Shocks)
structural spending and, 20–21
transition economies and, 36–39
Economic models
adjustment cost, 107–116
Balassa-Samuelson effect and, 37, 39, 63n11, 69
Benhabib, 169
business cycle, 39–41, 54–55, 182
calibration and, 205–206
CES functions, 219–220
CGE, 7–8, 190–202, 211, 213–214, 218
charity, 20–21
Chiswick-Hatton, 169–171
currency anchoring, 74–88
customs union, 267–279 (*see also* Customs union)
direct-democracy, 151
domino theory and, 24–25

Economic models (cont.)
  dynamic general equilibrium, 174–175,
    181–189, 203–206
  econometric, 151–153
  exchange rate, 74–94
  factor mobility, 102–106
  Hodrick-Prescott filter and, 40, 60–61
  production and, 203–204
  project evaluation and, 21
  Ricardo-Viner, 135, 138
  venture capital, 20–21
  WorldScan, 7–8, 219–222, 230–250 (see
    also WorldScan model)
Eichengreen, B., 63n9, 99
Engle-Granger test, 287
Epstein, G., 113
Equilibrium
  CGE model and, 190–202
  customs union and, 250, 268–289 (see also
    Customs union)
  discretionary, 78–84, 97
  dynamics and, 106–108, 118–119, 174–
    175, 181–189, 203–206
  exchange rate model and, 74–94
  factor mobility and, 102–106
  OCA approach and, 74–94
  saddle point stability and, 107
  segmented market and, 137–140
  social-loss and, 78–79
  WorldScan model and, 219–222, 230–
    250
Estonia, 1, 261
  currency anchoring and, 73–74, 91
  ECB and, 29
  shocks and, 41
  WorldScan model and, 219
Ethier, W., 266
Euro, 19
  adoption of, 29
  external anchors and, 73–94
  transition economies and, 36–37
  welfare effect and, 79–84
Europe Agreements (EA), 176
European Central Bank (ECB), 3–4, 64–66
  centralization and, 41–43, 57
  data set of, 59–62
  decision making issues and, 30
  Executive Board, 29, 41–44
  GDP aggregation and, 31, 34
  governance issues and, 17–20, 29–41
  Governing Council, 29–30, 33–34, 36–37,
    41–42, 58–59, 70–71

  independence and, 42
  information and, 42
  jurisdiction extension and, 45
  Maastricht Treaty and, 29, 73–74
  main problems of, 32–41
  political power and, 30–31, 33–48, 58, 67–
    69
  reform of, 19–20, 55–57
  representation and, 44–45
  rotation and, 45–55
  shocks and, 40–41
  structure of, 29–32
  transition economies and, 36–39
  Treaty of Nice and, 29
  voting and, 29, 43–44
  welfare effect and, 80
European Economic Area (EEA), 145
European Union (EU), 10, 26–27
  2004 elections and, 12
  Brussels summit of, 173
  business cycle and, 39–41
  Common Agricultural Policy (CAP) and,
    2–3, 12–20, 22–23, 176, 192
  Copenhagen summit and, 1–2, 173, 175,
    261, 290n1
  Council of Ministers, 14–17
  customs union and, 262–269, 272–289 (see
    also Customs union)
  domino theory and, 24–25
  eastern enlargement of, 173–210 (see also
    Eastern EU enlargement)
  expansion consequences, 1, 7–9, 11–24
  factor mobility and, 5–6, 102–106, 126–
    127
  guest workers and, 135–137
  Helsinki summit of, 173
  inclusion pressures and, 25–26
  institutional structure and, 14
  Luxembourg summit and, 173
  migration and, 129 (see also Migration)
  objectives of, 1–2
  poor members and, 11
  transition economies and, 36–39
  vertically differentiated trade and, 263
Exchange rate model
  basic description of, 74–77
  case study of, 88–89
  currency anchoring and, 74–88
  discretionary equilibrium and, 78–84
  inefficient policy effects and, 85–88
  OCA approach and, 74–94
Export. See Trade

Factor mobility, 5–6, 102–106, 126–127
Faini, Riccardo, 6, 169–171, 261–262
Falvey, R., 262
Fernandez, R., 266
Ferrer, J., 37, 39, 63n12
Fertig, M., 130
Fidrmuc, J., 229
Finland, 52, 219
Flam, H., 272
Food, 242, 245–247
Foreign direct investment (FDI), 224
France, 219, 262
Francois, J. F., 174, 190, 211, 217, 228, 229, 261
Frankel, F. A., 229
Freudenberg, M., 263
Friedman, Milton, 33, 114

Gabszewicz, J., 272
Gantmacher, F., 119
GDP (Gross Domestic Product), 1, 11, 230
  aggregate effects and, 40–41, 261–262
  customs union and, 286
  debt ratio and, 83–84, 89–91
  ECB and, 31, 34
  enlargement effects and, 177, 192, 230–244
  exchange rate model and, 74–94
  GGDC data and, 59, 61–62
  integration and, 99–100
  internal market accession and, 224–229, 236–243, 245–247
  political issues and, 43–48
  rotation schemes and, 45–55
  seigniorage and, 75–76
  shocks and, 40–41
  structural spending and, 21
  vote-weighting and, 43–44
Germany, 7, 9, 187
  adjustment costs and, 108–112
  aggregate effects and, 262
  Bundesbank, 17, 32–34, 45
  CGE model and, 190–202
  Chiswick-Hatton model and, 170
  customs union model and, 268–289
  eastern EU enlargement and, 174, 212–215
  green cards and, 134
  migration and, 111–112, 114–116, 230, 243–244
  monetary policy of, 32–41
  WorldScan model and, 219

GfS Institute, 150
Ghironi, F., 63n9
Global Trade Analysis Project (GTAP), 218–219, 257
Governance. *See also* Political issues
  Arrow-Debreu economy and, 103
  Bundesbank and, 32–34
  centralization and, 41–43
  Council of Ministers, 14–17
  credibility and, 73
  domino theory and, 24–25
  ECB and, 17–20, 29–41, 55–57
  exchange rate model and, 74–94
  independence and, 42
  inefficient fiscal policy and, 85–88
  information and, 42
  jurisdiction extension and, 45
  political power size and, 43–48
  reform and, 15–16, 19–20 (*see also* Reform)
  representation and, 44–45
  rotation and, 45–55
  Treaty of Nice, 14–17, 23–24
  U.S. Federal Banking system and, 32–34
  vote-weighting and, 43–44
Gravity approach, 218
Greece, 8–9, 148, 179
  business cycle and, 40
  customs union model and, 268–289
  euro and, 29
  management issues and, 16, 23
  rotation schemes and, 52
  shocks and, 41
  WorldScan model and, 219
Greenaway, D., 280
Grether, J.-M., 132
Grilli, V., 97
Groningen Growth and Development Centre (GGDC), 59, 61–62
Gros, Daniel, 4, 37, 39, 63n12, 73–94, 229
Grossman, G., 266–267
Guest workers, 135–140

Haan, Jakob de, 29–66
Halpern, L., 39
Hamilton, C., 261
Harden, I., 85
Hatton, Tim, 169–171
Hayashi, F., 117
Heckscher-Ohlin mechanisms, 101, 220
Heijdra, Ben J., 7, 173–210

Heinemann, F., 63n8
Helliwell, J., 229
Helpman, E., 266–267, 272
Hillman, A., 132
Hine, R. C., 280
Hodrick-Prescott filter, 40, 60–61
Household sector, 204
  customs union model and, 272–279
  demand structure and, 272–274
Howitt, P., 182
Huefner, F. P., 63n8
Hungary, 1, 261
  ECB and, 29
  migration and, 230
  shocks and, 41
  WorldScan model and, 219 (see also
    WorldScan model)
Hunt, J., 115
Hypothetical bias, 6

Immigration. See Migration
Inclusion pressures, 25–26
Independence, 42
Inflation, 69
  Cagan-Bailey analysis and, 96
  data sources for, 60
  exchange rate model and, 74–94
  external anchors and, 73–94
  Maastricht Treaty and, 73–74, 87
  optimal, 87
  price liberalization and, 80
  rotation schemes and, 54–55
  seigniorage and, 75–76
  structural, 51
  surprise, 73, 78–79
  taxes and, 85–86
  transition economies and, 36–39
  welfare effect and, 79–84
Information, 42
Inklaar, Robert, 29–66
Institutional structure
  inefficient fiscal policy and, 85–88, 97
  reform of, 14 (see also Reform)
Integration, 120–123
  adjustment costs and, 107–116
  dynamics role and, 106–108, 118–119
  eastern EU enlargement and, 173–210
    (see also Eastern EU enlargement)
  factor mobility model and, 102–106
  migration and, 112–118 (see also
    Migration)
  Treaty of Rome and, 99

understanding of, 100–102
  waiting option and, 114–116
Interest rates, 73
Intergovernmental Conference (IGC), 12,
  14, 18–19, 24
International Monetary Fund (IMF), 59,
  64n20, 287
International Social Survey Program
  (ISSP), 148
Ireland, 16, 23, 219
Italy, 219, 262

Japan, 9, 297
  customs union and, 263–264, 279–289
Jayaraman, Rajshri, 8, 257–259
Jazbec, B., 39
Jones, Ronald W., 9, 271, 297–300

Katsimi, Margarita, 95–98
Kemp, M., 265
Keuschnigg, Christian, 7, 173–210, 217, 228
Kierzkowski, H., 262, 271
Kim, I. M., 287
Kohler, Wilhelm, 7, 173–210, 217, 228
Krishnakumar, J., 151
Kydland, F., 113

Labor
  adjustment costs and, 107–116
  agriculture and, 181
  continuous market clearing and, 174
  customs union model and, 268–272
  dynamics and, 106–108, 118–119
  enlargement effects and, 181–189, 198–
    201, 211–215
  factor mobility and, 5–6, 102–106, 126–
    127
  guest workers and, 135–140
  migration and, 99, 112–118, 126–127, 131,
    189, 198–201 (see also Migration)
  Mincer wage and, 153
  segmented markets and, 137–140
  skill level and, 132–134, 169–170, 175–
    176, 185, 198–200, 205–206, 219
  supply relationships and, 268–272
  unemployment and, 174–175, 202–203
Laffer curve, 75
Latvia, 1, 29, 190, 219, 261
Lejour, Arjan M., 7–8, 217–255
Lemoine, F., 263
Lithuania, 1, 190, 261
  currency anchoring and, 73

ECB and, 29
WorldScan model and, 219
Lofstrom, M., 130, 132, 148
Luxembourg, 148
migration and, 181
summit of, 173
WorldScan model and, 219
Lynch, F., 266–267

Maastricht Treaty, 17, 19
centralization and, 42–43
eastern enlargement and, 173
ECB restructuring and, 29, 67, 69, 71
inflation and, 73–74, 87
McCallum, J., 229
McDougall, R. A., 218–219
Macro-economic effects
customs union and, 232–234
internal market accession and, 236–239
Maddala, G. S., 287
Malta, 1, 29, 173, 261
Markets
CGE models and, 7–8, 190–202, 211, 213–214, 218
continuous labor clearing and, 174
customs union and, 222–224, 262–289
eastern EU enlargement and, 180–189
(see also Eastern EU enlargement)
exchange rate model and, 74–94
factor mobility and, 102–106
imperfect competition and, 186, 188
industry barriers and, 217
inflation and, 73
internal market accession and, 224–229, 236–243, 245–247, 257
labor tightness and, 186
migration and, 189 (see also Migration)
NAFTA and, 266
product restriction and, 262
segmented, 137–140
WorldScan model and, 230–250 (see also WorldScan model)
Masters, Adrian, 213
Mayer, W., 134
Meade, E., 36
Melo, Jaime de, 6, 129–167
Merz, M., 182
Mexico, 266
Migration, 6, 99, 166–167
CAP and, 176
CEEC and, 130, 159–160, 180–181
CGE model and, 198–201

domestic expansion and, 198–199
eastern EU enlargement and, 189
economic integration and, 112–116
estimation of, 129–130
factor mobility and, 102–106, 126–127
Germany and, 111–112, 114–116
green cards and, 134
guest workers and, 135–140
homesickness cost and, 113
hypothetical bias and, 6
immigration surplus and, 198
inflow accumulation and, 192
integration and, 117–118
job changes and, 163n20
natural barriers to, 175–176
nontraded sector and, 137
opinion polls on, 129
point system and, 132–134
political economy of, 131–140
return, 112–113
shocks and, 229–230, 243–244, 248–250
stock scenario and, 189
Switzerland and, 130–131, 140–165
unemployment and, 131–132, 198–201
voters and, 131–134, 148–159, 161n4, 169–171
VOX polls on, 150
welfare effects and, 129–132
Miguet, Florence, 6, 129–167
Milner, C. R., 280
Mincer wage, 153
Moldavia, 264
Monetary policy. See also Economic issues; Governance
customs union and, 262–289
eastern EU enlargement and, 173–210
external anchors and, 73–94
Germany, 32–41
inefficiency effects and, 85–88, 97
integration and, 99–123
jurisdiction extension and, 45
migration and, 131–140 (see also Migration)
NAFTA, 266
OCA approach and, 74–94
protectionism and, 265–266
rotation schemes and, 45–55
U.S., 32–41
welfare effect and, 79–84
Monnet, Jean, 264
Mooij, Ruud A. de, 7–8, 217–255
Moravcsik, A., 266–267, 291n9

Most-favored nation (MFN) tariffs, 179
Moutos, Thomas, 1–10, 261–295
Müller, Tobias, 6, 129–167
Mundell, R., 91, 101, 117, 265

NAFTA (North American Free Trade Agreement), 266
Nahuis, Richard, 7–8, 217–255
National central banks (NCBs), 67–70
Netherlands, 52, 219
New Zealand, 17, 132
Nontariff barriers (NTBs), 246
  agriculture and, 245, 247
  Armington elasticities and, 227–228
  import tariffs and, 236
  point estimates and, 247
  reflection and, 247–248
  sectoral effects and, 239–242

O'Connell, P. G. J., 114
OECD countries, 30, 219, 272, 280, 287, 290
Optimum currency area (OCA) approach
  equilibrium and, 78–79
  exchange rate model and, 74–94
  GDP and, 75–76
  inefficient fiscal policies and, 85–88
  welfare effects and, 79–84

Pagoulatos, G., 266
Pakistan, 264–265
Papapanagos, H., 114
Pareto optimality, 127, 136
Parsons, G., 266–267
Pegging. See Exchange rate model; Monetary policy
Pelkmans, J., 37, 39, 63n12
Perroni, Carlo, 5–6, 120n4, 125–128, 265
Piazolo, D., 117
Pissarides, C. A., 182
Poland, 1, 179, 261
  ECB and, 29
  migration and, 230
  rotation schemes and, 52
  WorldScan model and, 219 (see also WorldScan model)
Political issues. See also Governance; Reform
  accession negotiations and, 12–13
  Amsterdam Treaty, 14, 23–24
  Common Agricultural Policy (CAP) and, 2–3, 12–23, 176, 192
  Council of Ministers, 14–17

customs union and, 264–267, 272–290
ECB and, 30–48, 58, 67–69
efficient decision making and, 14–15
equal vote shares and, 67–70
jurisdiction extension and, 45
Maastricht Treaty, 17, 19, 29, 42–43, 67, 69, 71, 73–74, 87, 173
migration and, 6, 131–140 (see also Migration)
NAFTA, 266
protectionism and, 265–266
PTAs and, 266–267
rotation and, 45–55
subsidies and, 22–23
Switzerland and, 140–159
Treaty of Nice, 3, 14–17, 23–24, 29, 43–44
Treaty of Rome, 99
veto power and, 12
vote-weighting and, 43–44
Portes, J., 266
Portes, R., 261–262
  eastern enlargement and, 174, 190, 211
  economic implications and, 217, 228–229
Portugal, 16
  aggregate effects and, 262
  business cycle and, 40
  loss of, 262
  rotation schemes and, 52
  subsidies and, 23
  WorldScan model and, 219
Preferential trade agreements (PTAs), 266–267
Prescott, E., 113
Preston, I., 129
Price
  customs union model and, 272–279
  enlargement effects and, 181–189
  factor mobility and, 102–106
  internal market accession and, 224–229, 236–243, 245–247
  real benefits and, 193–196
  shadow values and, 106–108
  stochastic purchasing power and, 80
  trade barriers and, 222–224, 231–236, 250
  welfare effect and, 79–84
Production, 5–6. See also Labor
  business cycle and, 39–41
  Cobb-Douglas, 110, 112, 219
  computational modeling and, 203–204
  customs union and, 222–224, 268–289
  demand structure and, 272–274

enlargement effects and, 181–189
factor mobility and, 102–106
guest workers and, 135–140
industry barriers and, 217
internal market accession and, 224–229,
    236–243, 245–247
marginal, 184
mobility factors and, 101–106
nested function for, 183
quality and, 271–289, 297–298
sectoral technologies and, 219
Project evaluation, 21
Protectionism, 265–266, 291n4
Public sector, 204

Ramey, G., 182
Real exchange rates (RERs), 286
Reform
  Bundesbank and, 32–33
  CEEC and, 13
  centralization and, 41–43
  Duisenberg and, 19–20
  ECB and 17–20, 29–66 (see also European
    Central Bank (ECB))
  independence and, 42
  information and, 42
  institutional, 14
  jurisdiction extension and, 45
  NAFTA and, 266
  political power size and, 43–48
  representation and, 44–45
  rotation and, 45–55
  vote-weighting and, 43–44
Representation, 44–45
Ricardo-Viner model, 135, 138
Riezman, R., 265
Rollo, J., 261
Romania, 261
  ECB and, 29
  rotation schemes and, 52
  WorldScan model and, 219
Rose, A., 229, 287
Rosen, S., 272
Rotation, 46
  asymmetric, 45, 48
  cycle correlations and, 54
  inflation and, 54
  pooling and, 48
  schemes for, 48–55
  size issues and, 48, 50–52
Routh's theorem, 119
Russia, 39

shocks and, 79–84
WorldScan model and, 219

Safety devices, 269
Sanfey, P., 114
Scheve, K., 151
Schiff, M., 132
Schmidt, C., 130, 205
Schuman, Robert, 264
Schwartz, A. J., 33
Sectoral effects, 251–252
  customs union and, 234–236
  internal market accession and, 239–
    243
Seghezza, E., 185
Seigniorage, 4
  GDP revenues and, 75–76
  generation of, 96
  inflation and, 75–76
  welfare effect and, 82
Shapiro, C., 138
Sheets, D. N., 36
Shi, S., 182
Shocks, 40–41
  customs union and, 222–224, 231–236,
    250
  enlargement effects and, 107, 222–244
  euro loss and, 80–82
  exchange rate model and, 74–94
  GDP-debt ratio and, 83–84, 89–91
  gravity equations and, 218
  internal market accession and, 224–229,
    236–243, 245–247, 257
  macro-economic effects and, 232–234,
    236–239
  migration and, 229, 243–244, 248–250
    (see also Migration)
  OCA approach and, 74–94
  PPP, 84
  sectoral effects and, 234–236, 239–243
  trade costs and, 217
  VARs and, 41
  welfare effect and, 79–84
Sinn, Hans-Werner, 113, 130, 132
SITC categories, 280
Slaughter, M., 151
Slovak Republic, 1, 29, 39, 190, 219, 261
Slovenia, 1, 29, 219, 261
Smith, A., 261
Spain, 16
  aggregate effects and, 262
  rotation schemes and, 52

Spain (cont.)
  subsidies and, 23
  WorldScan model and, 219
Stiglitz, J., 138
Subsidies, 22–23
Summers, L., 117, 138
Supply relationships, 268–272
Sweden, 17
  ECB and, 29, 32
  rotation schemes and, 52
  WorldScan model and, 219
Switzerland, 6, 166–167
  Chiswick-Hatton model and, 170
  green cards and, 134
  migration and, 130–131, 140–165
  voter's attitudes in, 148–159

TABS-MFI, 56
Taxes
  customs union and, 222–224, 231–236,
    250
  enlargement effects and, 187–188
  exchange rate model and, 74–94
  inefficient fiscal policies and, 85–88
  inflation and, 85–86
  MFN tariffs, 179
  money supply and, 79
  nontariff barriers and, 227–228, 236, 239–
    242, 245–248
  public sector and, 204
  steady-state, 78
Technology, 8–9, 119n1
  CES, 219–220
  customs union and, 262–263, 272–289
  factor mobility and, 102–106
  incumbent countries and, 262
  safety devices, 269
  sectoral production, 219
  supply relationships and, 268–272
Thisse, J., 272
Trade, 291n2, 297–299. See also Markets
  adjustment costs and, 107–116
  aggregate, 229
  customs union and, 222–224, 231–236,
    250, 262–289
  demand structure and, 272–274
  economic integration and, 99–117
  enlargement effects and, 181–189, 230–
    244
  factor mobility and, 102–106
  gravity equations and, 218
  guest workers and, 135–140

Heckscher-Ohlin, 101, 220
  horizontal, 262–263
  industry barriers and, 185–186, 217
  internal market accession and, 224–229,
    236–243, 245–247, 257
  MFN tariffs and, 179
  mobility factors and, 100–106
  nontariff barriers and, 227–228, 236, 239–
    242, 245–248
  Pareto optimality and, 127
  product restriction and, 262
  protectionism and, 291n4
  PTAs and, 266–267
  real benefits and, 193–196
  sectoral cost variation and, 217
  supply relationships and, 268–272
  vertically differentiated, 263
  WorldScan model and, 219–222, 230–250
Transition economies, 36–39
Treaty of Nice, 3, 14–17
  ECB and, 29
  inadequacies of, 23–24
  vote-weighting and, 43–44
Treaty of Rome, 99
Turkey, 135, 261

Unemployment, 7
  eastern EU enlargement and, 174–175,
    188, 197, 202–203, 207n3
  migration and, 198–201 (see also
    Migration)
United Kingdom, 17
  aggregate effects and, 262
  ECB and, 29, 32, 34
  migration and, 230
  rotation schemes and, 52
  WorldScan model and, 219
United States
  monetary policy of, 32–41
  NAFTA and, 266
  U.S. Civil War, 264
  U.S. Federal Banking system, 17
  Federal Open Market Committee
    (FOMC), 32, 34, 36
  governance of, 33–34
  jurisdiction extension and, 45
  rotation and, 45–55

Vanek, J., 265
Van Ours, J. C., 205
Vector Auto Regressions (VARs), 41
Velasco, A., 85

Vienna Institute for International
  Economic Studies (WIIW), 59–60
Viner, J., 264
von Hagen, J., 85
Voting
  direct-democracy model and, 151
  econometric model and, 151–153
  economic determinants and, 151–153,
    164n28
  equal, 67–70
  migration and, 131–134, 148–159, 161n4,
    169–171
  veto power, 12
  weighting of, 43–44
VOX polls, 150

Wages. *See* Labor
Wallachia, 264
Watson, J., 182
Weiss, A., 132
Welfare effects
  adjustment costs and, 107–108
  enlargement and, 230–244
  euro loss and, 79–84, 95–98
  migration and, 129–132
Wen, Q., 182
Whalley, J., 265–266
Winters, A., 261
WorldScan model, 7–8, 219–221, 253–255
  concordances for, 251–252
  customs union and, 231–236, 250
  enlargement shocks and, 222–244
  internal market accession and, 236–243,
    245–247
  migration and, 243–244, 248–250
  sensitivity analysis and, 245–250
Wyplosz, C., 39

Zimmerman, K. F., 130, 132, 148, 244
Zollverein, 264